Patterns of Child Rearing

Patterns of Child Rearing

BY

Robert R. Sears, *Stanford University*

Eleanor E. Maccoby, *Harvard University*

Harry Levin, *Cornell University*

In collaboration with

Edgar L. Lowell, Pauline S. Sears, and John W. M. Whiting

Illustrations by Jean Berwick

STANFORD UNIVERSITY PRESS

STANFORD, CALIFORNIA

Stanford University Press
Stanford, California
© 1957 by the Board of Trustees of the
Leland Stanford Junior University
First published by Row, Peterson and Company, 1957
Reissued by Stanford University Press in 1976
Printed in the United States of America
Cloth ISBN 0-8047-0916-5   Paper ISBN 0-8047-0915-7
LC 75-44903

Last figure below indicates year of this printing:
85   84   83   82   81   80   79   78   77   76

Foreword

This is a report of how 379 American mothers brought up their children from birth to kindergarten age. We obtained the information by long interviews that allowed the mothers to talk fully and freely about the joys and problems they had had, their feelings before and after their child was born, and the methods they had used for training and for making him—or her—happy. Some of the mothers were strict and others were permissive. Some were anxious and unhappy about their own lives; some were gay and confident. Among them were Catholics, Jews, and Protestants— working-class wives and middle-class wives—the mothers of boys and the mothers of girls—the mothers of "only" children and the mothers of several. They were not a completely representative sample, even of the metropolitan suburbs in which they lived, but they were very diverse in their origins, their manner of life, and in their ways of bringing up their children. We have tried to present what they told us in a way that will permit the reader to sense this diversity for himself, but we have sought to go beyond the uniqueness of each mother's ways and uncover the more general patterns of child rearing that characterized this group of American mothers.

This is a book of facts, not of advice. It tells how mothers *do* bring up their children, not how they *should*. At the same time, we cannot hide the fact that some practices proved more successful than others. From the mothers' own reports we could get estimates of the effects of different methods of discipline and of various other aspects of child rearing. We have presented these findings along with the descriptions of child rearing itself.

The interviews on which this report is based were part of a larger research study undertaken by the staff of the Laboratory of Human Development of the Graduate School of Education of Harvard University. That research was designed to discover what kinds of child-rearing practices are most conducive to the development of children's identification with their parents. Our interviewing had a dual purpose, however; in part we were measuring the child-rearing experiences of each of the 379 children whom we were studying, with a view to relating these experiences to certain aspects of each child's personality. But of equal importance was our aim to secure reliable information about the varieties of experience that many American children have had in their homes—with their parents—by the time they go to school. This is a kind of information that is of extreme value not only to every mother, who must choose which of many ways to rear her own child, but to every teacher, who annually faces a new group of children. It was, and is, our conviction that education can progress only as rapidly as careful scientific study can provide sound evidence concerning the nature of the child who is being educated and of the society in which he is growing up. This book reflects our belief that the surest way to better education for our children is basic research in the behavior sciences. The Laboratory of Human Development is itself a continuing representation of this conception.

Quite evidently we are indebted to many people for encouragement and support in our enterprise. The Laboratory of Human Development owes its existence to the vigorous and far-sighted championing of research on the basic behavior processes by Dean Francis Keppel. The other senior members of the Laboratory staff, whom we have designated as collaborating authors, were intimately involved at many stages of our work. The design and performance of the research were the joint work of the six of us; when the data were all in, we separated into teams for purposes of analysis and report writing. The present task fell to the lot of the three of us first mentioned.

Many other people also were involved in the study. First, and foremost, were the 379 mothers who shared their experiences with us; we have quoted them liberally, but needless to say, all names used in the quotations are pseudonyms. We made our acquaintance with the mothers through the schools, and we owe great appreciation to the many teachers, PTA groups, and administrative officials who helped with planning and programming. Especially we must mention the helpfulness of Harold B. Gores, Superintendent of Schools, and Edward Landy, Director of Counselling Services, of Newton, Massachusetts; and of Francis A. Kelly, Superintendent of Schools, and Thomas F. O'Brien, Assistant Superintendent, of Watertown, Massachusetts.

For years, the research and technical assistants at Palfrey House worked on "the identification project," collecting and analyzing data and preparing working papers. We salute with special gratitude for their contributions to the part of the project here reported: Lucille Bennis and Gertrude Tourtellot (statistical assistants), and George W. Goethals, Willard Hartup, Jr., Christoph M. Heinicke, Gloria Leiderman, Claire Olson, Henrietta Smith, Mary Winslow, and Grace Wyshak (research assistants). We are indebted, too, to G. A. Milton, of Stanford University, for his careful work on the factor analysis of the interview scales.

We wish to express warm thanks to our interviewers. They carried heavy recording equipment through icy streets, made evening calls when the mothers' busy schedules did not permit daytime interviews, and entered with tact and sympathy into a mutual exploration with the mothers of matters that were not always easy to talk about. Our interviewers were: Barbara Burt, June Freeman, Gloria Leiderman, Sarah Mordecai, Charlotte Opler, Lois Paul, Betty Rosenthal, Marjorie Thaxter, and Barbara Weinberg.

Research costs money. The Laboratory of Human Development was established, and maintained through the early stages of this research, by generous grants from the Graduate School of Education and the Rockefeller Foundation. The main support of the final study was provided by grants from the National Institute of Mental Health (M461, M844, and M1096).

Finally, and most warmly, we express our appreciation to Dr. Urie Bronfenbrenner, whose patient questioning and thoughtful reading of our manuscript helped us greatly.

ROBERT R. SEARS

ELEANOR E. MACCOBY

HARRY LEVIN

January 1, 1957

Table of Contents

Patterns of Child Rearing

A Report on Ways of Bringing Up Children

from the Laboratory of Human Development

Graduate School of Education

Harvard University

CHAPTER ONE

A Study of Child Rearing

The process of child rearing, in spite of its proverbial importance as a determinant of adult character, has not been much investigated by scientific procedures. In the history of Western science, the study of man came late. Newtonian physics was a part of history before more than the crudest of scientific observations of normal human social behavior had been made. Although educators and social philosophers had long speculated on the kinds and amount of influence that childhood experience might have on social and intellectual functioning, empirical study of the problem did not begin much before the twentieth century.

Why science remained so long at arm's length from human behavior can be a matter only for speculation. Doubtless the philosophic assumptions underlying Western thought were partly responsible. To many, human behavior has never seemed a proper subject for science, man himself being considered as an essentially lawless event in an otherwise lawful universe. Perhaps, too, in the case of child rearing, the fact that science was a male preoccupation was relevant. Men have always tended to dissociate themselves from female functions. Even today, those scientific and medical specialities pertaining to children attract fewer than their share of male practitioners. In any case, whatever the causes for its late arrival among scientific problems, child rearing

has become in recent years a matter of considerable interest to behavior science.

There are good reasons for this interest. Clinical studies of disturbed children, as well as experimental observations of normal ones, have shown a number of important causal relationships between mothers' child-rearing practices and the behavior of their children. Some personality characteristics of adults, too, appear to be extensions of the effects of early experiences. This is particularly true of those qualities that involve personal relationships such as love, dependency, jealousy, and competition. Since a child's earliest interpersonal experiences are with his family, and particularly with his mother, there is good reason for examining the mother's behavior to see whether there are consistent consequences of different practices.

If personality is partly a product of childhood experiences, then there seems some likelihood, too, that the forms of behavior which characterize a whole society may be partly explicable on the same basis. Recent anthropological studies have shown, for example, that the kinds of folk tales a culture transmits are consistently related to certain aspects of child training in that culture. (See Wright, 1954.) [1] Any process that can help to explain both the development of personality and the transmission of culture is important to the behavior sciences, for these two problems are the focal points for the study of man as a social organism.

This scientific interest, however, is only a weak and recent reflection of a concern that has been felt strongly by the general public for several decades. Indeed, if one looks at the social history of the United States, he must conclude that the demand for scientific study of child rearing arose long before science had methods suitable to the task, or even knew there was a task to be done. We are so accustomed to note the social progress which follows from scientific discovery that we often forget the fact that science itself is partly a product of social needs. The scientific study of child rearing offers a case in point, however, and the research findings to be reported in this book are as much a response to pressures expressed by American parents as they are a necessary step in the development of behavior science.

[1] References to published books and articles are given alphabetically by author on pages 537–540.

FROM "EXPERTS" TO RESEARCHERS

From the beginning of time, no doubt, there have been mothers who were driven to distraction by the problems of controlling and training their children. Such pangs and puzzlement left little imprint in written records, however, until the general literacy of the nineteenth century made women as articulate as men. Then various things happened together that, more than metaphorically, left a baby in the lap of twentieth-century science.

There was the great growth spurt of humanitarian values. The time for shrugging off human misery and indignities had passed. The poor, the ill, the young, the underprivileged became suffering equals who needed help and understanding. Care and protection of those who had not reached their place in the sun became a matter of public morality and private ideal. Humanitarian motives had become values that could be invoked in support of nearly any action.

What actions came to be supported depended on another development. This was the astonishing nineteenth-century success of science and engineering as instruments for improving man's control of his environment. The mid-century application of steam to transportation improved the distribution of material goods and tremendously increased the mobility of enterprising people. The development of electricity as a source of power eliminated the time-barrier in communication. And late in the century the application of scientific methods to the control of disease gave man a sense of mastery over the most tragic of all the forces arrayed against him. Solution of problems by rational means replaced reliance on tradition, personal experience, and the self-arrogated wisdom of those who had decision-making power.

These changes did not all come at once. "Wise men" gave up their power reluctantly. The rational problem-solving of science was accepted grudgingly and only in those material matters where financial rewards or improvement in health gave blunt demonstration of the worthwhileness of scientific methods. But the growing absorption of humane values pressed the battlefield into more and more corners where human welfare could still stand improvement. Divorce, criminality, mental disease, and other behavioral sources of human waste and anguish began to be looked upon as social *ills*. The most vigorous champions of humane values and of rational problem-solving began to demand attack on these problems as well as on the more material ones.

So it came about, near the turn of the century, that some people began to concern themselves with the welfare of mothers and children. Many of the problems that caused waste and misery seemed to stem directly from maternal and child labor conditions, and these matters were given first attention. But one wise and courageous woman in Iowa—Mrs. Cora Bussey Hillis— saw farther into the sources of social troubles. She urged the scientific study of the whole process of child growth and rearing. In 1917, she and her co-workers persuaded the Iowa Legislature to establish the Child Welfare Research Station at the State University of Iowa. Thus was launched the massive scientific attack on problems of child development that has characterized the last four decades.

Science is slow, however, and by and large it is cautious. Through the twenties, researchers picked their ways among questions of method and measurement, charting carefully the behavior of this new object of study—the human child. The greatest advances in knowledge were with respect to physical growth, nutrition, and childhood diseases. In psychological matters, only intelligence was widely explored. Not until the thirties did children's motives and personalities receive much attention, and the intensive study of child-training practices came still later.

But what about the parents? The measured progress of *Science* may be useful to an impersonal *Society,* but mothers of young children need answers in a hurry. Toward the end of the nineteenth century, the women's magazines recognized this need and began to print columns of advice. At first, following the lead of medical research, they emphasized problems of feeding especially, drawing on what bits and pieces of information became available. This was not enough. Gradually the list of topics was expanded, and the popular magazines undertook guidance on every phase of child rearing.

Thus was the "expert" born. Properly speaking, an expert in child development is one who knows a great deal of what is known about the subject and has had wide experience in applying his knowledge. When research data were nonexistent, a few pediatricians, psychiatrists, social workers, and teachers filled this role. The treatment of parents and children in trouble provided the most fruitful experience for these advisers. In clinics, schools, courts, and welfare agencies, the new concern for social ills forced practitioners to search for causes, and to reach decisions as to what practices were helpful in forming better personalities. Tentative theoretical formulations grew from clinical practice and from a few early experiments. The challenging observations of Freud offered the greatest stimulation in this respect, and as we move gradually from the era of expert opinion to that of research findings, psychoanalytic theory remains one of the most vital sources of our hypotheses.

The trouble with expert opinion is that it rests on the private experience of the expert. There is no substantial public evidence to which either a skeptic or a believer can turn to decide whether or not the opinion is correct. One expert is as good as another, and neither of them can prove the validity of what he says or the value of what he recommends.

During the past half century we have had many writers giving advice to mothers. Some have been truly expert, and have relied heavily on the growing body of child development research. Others have followed fads and prejudices and have probably done more harm than good. Even the wisest and most scientifically oriented have shown notable changes of opinion from time to time, as will be reported in the next section. In any case, it is high time for the behavioral sciences to use research methods to replace common sense (or nonsense) fancies with demonstrable facts.

The present report is a step in this direction. It describes the findings of a study that was based on standardized interviews with 379 mothers of five-year-old children. In these recorded interviews, the mothers reported in detail their feelings about motherhood and their families; they described their child-rearing practices from the child's birth until he was five years old; and they gave enough reports about the child's own behavior that we could determine some of the effects of these practices. The chapter headings indicate the general scope of the information obtained.

In presenting these findings, we are building on several decades of the scientific study of children themselves, as will become evident in the discussion. So far as the study of mothers' child-rearing practices is concerned, however, the present investigation supplements five decades of clinical observation and theory and only a very small number of specific researches, most of which are post-World War II in origin. These will be cited where they are helpful, but in the main we will devote our attention to the findings from the present investigation that relate to the three problems discussed in the next section.

THE THREE RESEARCH PROBLEMS

There are three kinds of questions that can be asked about child-rearing practices and values. The *first,* and simplest, wants a purely descriptive answer: How *do* parents rear children? The *second* goes deeper and asks what effects different kinds of training have on children. The *third* relates to the mothers themselves: What leads a mother to use one method rather than another?

In pursuing the *first* of these questions, we discovered there is surprisingly little information about what American parents believe or what they do with their youngsters. Do most mothers breast-feed their babies? Do they spank them for being sassy? Are chores and responsibilities a part of most children's lives? Do very many mothers let their three-year-olds run around naked in the house? How serious do mothers think it is when a child strikes a parent? Do any mothers ever actually encourage children to fight the neighbor children? The answers to these questions, and to many others like them, are needed not only to give a frame of reference within which a particular practice can be viewed, but to permit any one mother to gain perspective on her own practices by comparing or contrasting her characteristic ways of treating her child with those of other mothers.

Curiously enough, anthropologists have secured more complete information about child rearing in at least seventy other cultures than they have about child rearing in the United States (see J. W. M. Whiting and Child, 1953, and Heinicke and B. B. Whiting, 1953). With the exception of a few recent studies, the source of most of our knowledge about American child-rearing behavior is inferential, deriving in the main from the books, pamphlets, and magazine articles that give advice to parents. These sources are scarcely data, in the sense of being reports about actual practices, but in certain instances their popularity suggests that a good many people may have found them attractive and may have followed the advice.

One series of pamphlets has provided a unique opportunity to observe changes in what may be called the "official" child-rearing culture of the United States. These are the ten successive editions of *Infant Care*, published by the U. S. Children's Bureau; the first appeared in 1914 and the latest in 1955. This small book provides a great deal of useful information for the young mother. Much of the material is factual, well geared to American economy and conditions of life. But some has to do with methods of child rearing, and it is in this connection that one can see secular changes in attitudes and values.

Dr. Martha Wolfenstein (1953) has studied these variations in advice through the first nine editions (1914–1951) with respect to the handling of five problems: thumb-sucking, weaning, masturbation, bowel and bladder training. We call these "problems" because each refers to a form of child behavior that is *changeworthy,* that is, a kind of action either to be inhibited as much as possible or to be replaced by new behavior of a more mature kind. Such control and training can be done with different degrees of severity. The mother can be highly punitive and refuse to tolerate any lapses whatever, or she can be gentle in her urging of new actions and ignore accidental reversions to the changeworthy ones. Most observers of young children believe this dimension of *severity of training* has important effects on children's personalities, though there is little direct evidence as to just what the effects may be.

Dr. Wolfenstein's evaluation of the degree of severity of training recommended by the authors of the different editions of *Infant Care* shows that there have been substantial changes over the more than forty years spanned. Interestingly enough, changes have been quite different for the five training problems. In 1914, both masturbation and thumb-sucking were to be treated very severely indeed: masturbation, which would "wreck" a child for life, was to be stopped by tying the child's legs to opposite sides of the crib; and thumb-sucking also was to be treated by mechanical restraint. In subsequent editions there was a fairly continuous decline in the degree of severity recommended, the 1951 edition treating the two changeworthy behaviors as rather petty nuisances that might be ignored. Along with this permissiveness there was a distinct devaluing of the satisfactions a child gets from such stimulation.

The other three training problems had quite different histories. There was a steady increase to 1929 in the severity with which weaning was to be done, and there was no noticeable decrease until 1938. Bowel training had a similar development, although severity began to drop off a little earlier. Bladder training severity also increased at first, but there has been a steady decrease since 1921.

These changing patterns of advice are a part of the child-rearing values of their times. What relation there may have been between the values—the "what ought to be"—and the actual practices of mothers cannot now be discovered. The practices of forty years ago are irretrievably buried in mothers' memories, and their only monuments are the personality structures of children who have grown to middle age themselves.

It would be a mistake, of course, to assume that there is any one pattern of child rearing that can be called "the American pattern." The United States contains a rich variety of subcultures. In spite of thirty-six million distributed copies of *Infant Care*, there is no dread uniformity of child-rearing practices. Differences of religion, of ethnic origin, of socio-economic status, and of family size all contribute to the great variety of values and practices.

As an illustration we may cite some comparative findings from three different communities in which we secured information about child rearing. One, called Homestead, is a small New Mexican village with a population originating mainly in the dust-bowl areas of Texas and Oklahoma. A second, Rimrock, is just a few miles away, but its population is of Old American stock with Mormon traditions. The third is the suburban metropolitan area in New England from which the information for this present book was obtained. Our interviewers secured reports from about twenty mothers in each of the two villages, and from 379 mothers in the New England area.

Three items exemplify the extraordinary differences that can be found within our national borders. The first is the age at which mothers weaned their children. In Homestead, for instance, 50 per cent had completed weaning before the child was eight months old, while in Rimrock none had. In the New England sample, 37 per cent had. A second item relates to who, in the family, had the chief responsibility for deciding on child-rearing policies. In Homestead, 22 per cent of the mothers said the father was the chief policy-maker; in Rimrock, 67 per cent said the father; and in the New England group, only 8 per cent reported the father. Or consider the degree to which physical punishment was used as a frequent and major method of discipline. In Homestead, 39 per cent of the families used it; in Rimrock, only 5 per cent; and in New England, 20 per cent.

In child rearing, as in so many other things, America is the very archetype of diversity. In Chapters Eleven and Twelve we will describe some of the differences that are related to sex of the child being reared, his ordinal position in the family, and the age and education and socio-economic status of his parents. But our task, first, will be to describe the variations—and their commonness or uncommonness—in the whole population of mothers we interviewed. This will give a provisional answer to the question: How *do* mothers rear their children during the first five years?

The *second* type of question leads to an inquiry about the effects of training on the child. Does self-demand feeding make children more dependent? Does punishment for bed-wetting just make the matter worse? Does early insistence on complete modesty make children more curious than ever about sex? Does spanking insure the development of a good strong conscience? Answers to such cause-and-effect questions as these will eventually provide some help to parents in making decisions about how to rear children. If a mother knows the effect of a particular practice, she can decide whether to use it or not. She can base her judgment on a knowledge of what product she will get.

Clinical observations, and theories developed from them, have suggested a number of hypotheses about the relation between certain kinds of child rearing and the personality qualities produced by them. Ideally, to test these notions, the measures of mother and child behavior should be entirely independent of one another. The present study, relying entirely on the mothers' interview reports for measuring both, is not ideal for answering all such cause-and-effect questions. However, there are a few kinds of child behavior that a mother can probably describe about as objectively as could an independent observer. Where we have been able to get such measures from the interviews, we will report their child-rearing antecedents. The most successful examples will be found in the chapters on feeding, toilet training, dependency, aggression, techniques of training, and conscience.

Third, and finally, one can ask what leads a mother to use one method rather than another. Child-rearing beliefs and values and practices do not just appear out of the blue. They are products of the mother's own personality, her values and attitudes. She may feel, for example, that she has reasoned herself quite objectively to an answer as to how she *should* handle her child's quarreling, but the extent to which she *can* tolerate open fighting influences her decision. All reasoning rests on assumptions that, in turn, rest on the values and attitudes the mother has developed throughout her own life. Her own upbringing has influenced these, and of course the nature of the family situation at any one time helps dictate a decision as to how to treat the children. Hence it will not prove surprising to find that there are substantial differences in mothers' values and practices depending on the satisfactoriness of her relations with her husband, on her self-esteem, and on certain of her own pervasive moral values, such as her attitudes toward sex and aggression.

To put the matter most succinctly, child-rearing practices can be viewed as both causes and effects. They are responsible, in some degree, for the personality characteristics of the child, and they are themselves the products of cultural factors operating in the life of the mother. We will not attempt to untangle these reciprocal relationships, but will present our findings with respect to the three main problems outlined above.

WHAT WAS MEASURED—AND WHY

In order to give a description of child rearing, and to compare one mother with another, we must have a set of attributes, or *dimensions,* that are common to all the mothers. A *dimension* is some describable aspect of behavior that can be clearly and accurately differentiated from other aspects, and that is quantifiable as to amount. Just as the action of an automobile can be described by reference to its "speed," "rate of acceleration," "noisiness," and so on, so can child-rearing behavior be described by such dimensions as "warmth," "use of praise," "permissiveness to be aggressive," and a host of others. These descriptive words or phrases may refer to consistent traits in the mother's personality, or they may be simply qualities of action for which there are many unorganized causes. For example, one mother may insist on neatness and orderliness around the house because she has a well-structured personality trait that leads her to deal with all aspects of her life in that way, while for another mother, such behavior is only a necessary requirement imposed by living in a small house. In either case, it is an attitude, or practice, that impinges on the children of the household, and may be expected to govern their actions and their learning.

A carefully selected set of child-rearing dimensions provides a standard language for describing maternal behavior. This language is quantitative, too; it permits a description in terms of amount. One can say, for example, that a certain mother "uses physical punishment" (if this is one of our dimensions) to an extent represented by "point 6" on a seven-point scale. Or we may be able to say she uses it "three times a week, on the average," if we happen to have that kind of information.

When all the mothers in a study are measured with respect to all the dimensions used in the study, two important benefits are gained. First, that group of mothers can be compared with any other group similarly measured. An example of cross-cultural comparison was given earlier, and in Chapters Eleven and Twelve we will use this method with several subsamples from the present group. Second, if one wishes to discover the effect of a given practice on children's behavior, he can examine the relationship in *all* the children and not be limited in his conclusions to a few instances of extreme, or pathological, behavior. For example, one often hears anecdotes that illustrate the alleged beneficial effects of spanking on children's obedience. Is this true for all youngsters? Or do the stories neglect to mention other instances in which the effect was just the reverse? The question can be answered only if we measure *every* mother's use of spanking and compare it with the amount of obedience *every* child in the group shows.

To select the most useful dimensions is not easy, however. Their main function is to provide a common basis for comparing mothers with respect to those attributes of child rearing that are important influences on child behavior. Obviously, we cannot know for certain what is important until we have tested the relations between the mothers' behavior and the children's. Yet, we must have the dimensions before we can make this test. As in any scientific enterprise, therefore, we have had to make some trial guesses. It is not unlikely that some of the dimensions we have chosen will prove to be useless by the ultimate criterion of whether they help to account for children's behavior. However, there is quite a body of clinical observation and psychological theory from which we have drawn hypotheses as to what dimensions might prove important, and we have given particular attention to those defined by other investigators in recent years. We will be able to present evidence that at least some of our dimensions were well chosen.

In making this selection we have been guided by our conception of child development and the child-rearing process. We conceive a child as starting life with a quite small number of ready-made action patterns. These are mainly related to biological drives; they are ways of satisfying biological needs. He can suck and swallow, eliminate waste products, and move his arms and legs somewhat. He can breathe and sleep and vocalize. As he matures physically, these action patterns become more complex, and permit him a greater mobility. Sheer physical maturation does not provide sufficient development, however, and from the very beginning the child is adding to his repertory of actions by learning how to do new things. This is the aspect of his development in which child rearing plays its most significant role.

The maturing action systems of the human child tend to lag behind the requirements society places on him. His early behavior is changeworthy in the sense that it is not of a kind to satisfy the standards of conduct established by the culture. Sucking, for instance, is an efficient way to get milk, but the time comes when a mother wants her child to eat solid foods and she can no longer provide breast milk for him. He must be weaned. The sucking behavior becomes changeworthy, by definition, and a new kind of eating behavior must be learned.

Along with the learning of new actions, there is development of new motives. The original biological drives become modified, and the acquired motives begin to direct behavior. These latter appear to depend on new expectancies that the child forms. In the beginning he showed no signs of expecting milk; he simply made sucking motions after a certain number of hours of deprivation, or perhaps cried. Later he begins to anticipate feedings, not only for the food they bring but for the circumstances surrounding the food—the mother's talking, hugging, smiling, and so on. In the long run, a child seems to develop a "need" for these surrounding things that is quite separate from his "need" for food. They become "rewards" for him, loved and desired objects or situations which he will strive to attain.

In all this learning, the mother plays a central part, for she is the most common element in her child's experience. She it is who decides what behavior is changeworthy, and she it is who does the changing—or tries to. In so doing she must not only establish in her own mind what new behavior is to be added to the child's repertory of acts, but she must devise ways of training him. Not all her interactions with him are purposefully designed to this end, of course. Much that she does, day in and day out, is simply caretaking or enjoyment of him as another human being whom she loves.. Sometimes, too, she reacts to him as an annoying person, and she hurts or frustrates him. The child-rearing process includes all these because all have some influence on his development.

Our selection of dimensions can be understood as an attempt to find measures of those aspects of the mother's behavior that we conceive to be most influential in this training context. One aspect that requires consideration is the way she disciplines the child in her efforts to get rid of changeworthy behavior and establish more mature forms of action. She can use both rewarding and punishing methods. She can provide either tangible or intangible signs of her approval or disapproval. How she does this training should influence not only the rate and effectiveness of the child's learning but also his expectancies. For this reason we included dimensions that measure the degree to which the mother used various *disciplinary techniques*. These are too numerous to mention here, but they will be defined in later chapters.

A second important aspect of the mother's behavior is her

degree of tolerance for changeworthy behavior. She can be very permissive of infantile dependency and aggression, for instance, or she can dislike such actions quite intensely and feel great urgency for getting rid of them. Her attitudes in this respect govern the amount and consistency of control she applies to the child. This in turn should influence how early he adopts mature ways of acting. Hence, we defined a set of dimensions that describe the mother's *permissiveness* for the child's behavior stemming from each of the major drives: hunger, elimination, dependency, sex, and aggression.

A third aspect of child-rearing behavior that is probably important is the *severity* with which the various techniques of training are applied for the purpose of eliminating changeworthy behavior. Again we can separate the treatment according to the basic drives. Severity refers to the vigor of punishment used toward the child, and we mean punishment in its broadest sense rather than the customary narrow reference to physical punishment alone. For example, a warm and affectionate mother who withholds her normal expressions of love may be providing just as severe pain for her child as the mother who gives a good paddling. The place that hurts is different but the quality of anguish need not be. Whiting and Child (1953), in their study of child rearing in primitive cultures, found these severity dimensions to be significant for the development of several kinds of behavior.

A fourth aspect of the mother's behavior that has an important influence, according to our theoretical views, is what might be called her *temperamental qualities*. These include such things as her warmth, her affectionateness, her level of self-esteem and other pervasive feelings and attitudes that display themselves to the child in subtle and intangible ways. Their importance lies in the fact that they define the mother for the child; they describe what she is like. Since the mother is the person whom a young child first learns to love or to fear (or both!), these dimensions represent measures of some of the qualities he comes to expect in other people.

A fifth aspect of the mother's child rearing relates to the *positive inculcation of more mature behavior* to replace that which is changeworthy. What values does she hold up to her child? What restrictions does she place on him? What demands does she make of him? We want to know how high the goals are that she sets for him, and to what degree she limits or expands his freedom of action. The importance of these dimensions stems from the fact that they define the conditions for the child's new learning, specifying the degree of difficulty of the achievements and self-restraints that will be expected of him.

These five classes of dimensions include most of the measures of maternal behavior that we secured from the interviews. Each dimension had to be defined separately and a rating scale constructed that would provide a quantitative measure, or score. The scales are listed in Appendix B.

In addition, we asked each mother to describe certain aspects of her child's behavior. From these descriptions we were able to get measures of a few dimensions of child behavior, but we made no effort to be as complete in this respect as with the child-rearing dimensions. There were two reasons for this. Our main intention in the research was to discover some child-rearing antecedents of certain kinds of childhood fantasies. The interview inquiries about the child's overt behavior in the home were made mainly for comparison with the measures of fantasy that we secured by tests given the children themselves. Therefore, we measured only those dimensions that were relevant to the main problem. Secondly, we were doubtful that mothers could give unbiased and objective reports on very many aspects of their own children's behavior. We will discuss this problem of objectivity in connection with specific measures as these are referred to in later chapters. With the exception of sex behavior, each of the major motivational systems yielded one or more measures.

We can turn now to the interview itself, its construction, administration, and evaluation or scoring. The actual operations of measurement will make our theoretical discussion of child-rearing dimensions more meaningful.

THE MOTHER INTERVIEW

To get a measure of each mother on each of the many dimensions, we had to secure a report, as frank and as complete as possible, of all the mother was able to tell about her child-rearing practices. The interview was recorded with the aid of a microphone and disc recorder, transcribed into typescript, and then rated on a large number of rating scales which provided the actual measures of the dimensions of child rearing with which we were concerned.

Some of the measures were provided by short and simple answers to very factual questions, as, for example, how many children there were in the family. Other measures required the rating of fairly extended discussions, by the mother, of her feel-

ings and behavior. Many mothers spent a full twenty minutes describing their handling of aggressive behavior, for instance; and the scoring of such a scale as that which measured "permissiveness for aggression toward the parents" required the raters' attention to all twenty minutes of that discussion. Still other dimensions were measured on scales that required consideration of everything the mother said during the entire interview; the rating of the mother's self-esteem, for example, was based on the full two hours (more or less) of the interview.

There were a few questions directed toward the father's role in the family. Since it was not feasible to interview the fathers, all the information we gained about their child-rearing attitudes and practices was obtained from the mothers.

Type of interview

The type of interview required seemed to lie somewhere between the flexible, unstandardized, "depth" interview which is characteristic of clinical interviewing, and the completely structured interview with a long list of multiple choice items. Previous experience with interviewing in the area of child-rearing practices suggested that an unstandardized interview (one on which the interviewer was free to devise his own questions and cover topics in any order he chose) would produce a fairly high proportion of cases which could not be rated on all the scale dimensions chosen for analysis. With unstructured interviews, certain items of specific information almost inevitably would be missing from some of the interviews, and the frame of reference in which a topic was discussed would vary so much from one interview to another that the interviews could not be rated on the same scale. Furthermore, it is known that the wording of questions, and the order in which they are presented, can have a significant effect upon the responses which mothers give, and we wanted to maintain as much constancy as possible in order that all mothers' reports would be comparable.

On the other hand, a completely structured interview, involving many very detailed questions, and perhaps a list of answers from which the respondent might choose, had several possible disadvantages. Answers might be suggested to the mother; the interview would not be adaptable to the idiosyncrasies of individual life situations; and worst of all, rapport might suffer if the mother were not allowed to express herself freely and fully. Since reasonably lengthy and free answers were needed for the rating of some rather intangible qualities, such as warmth and permissiveness and self-esteem, rapport was extremely important.

After extensive pretesting, we chose an interview method which fell midway between the two extremes. A schedule was devised (see Appendix A), consisting of a list of open questions (questions without a list of alternative answers from which the respondent was to choose), and the interviewers were trained to use these questions without changes in wording and in the prescribed order. There were 72 main open questions, but following each of them there was a series of suggested probes which the interviewer was free to use or omit, depending upon the fullness of the answer to the original question. For example, here is the question on scheduling of feeding, with its probes:

There has been a lot of talk about whether it is better to have a regular feeding schedule for a baby, or to feed him whenever he is hungry. How do you feel about this?

How did you handle this with (child's name)?

[If schedule] How closely did you stick to that schedule?

This set of questions was designed to yield information which could be used to rate the mother's treatment of the child on a scale which ran from extremely rigid scheduling to complete self-demand. Some mothers answered the first question very fully, giving a description of the way they timed feedings with the particular child on whom the study's attention was focused. In such a case, it would be unnecessary to ask the probes. But sometimes a mother would answer the question more vaguely: "Well, it depends on whether it's your first child. I think you're likely to be more strict with the first one, don't you?" Such an answer would not provide a basis for the desired rating, and further probing would be necessary. The probes were included in the interview schedule as a guide for the interviewer to the specific nature of the information which was needed, and as insurance that the information would be obtained.

Construction of the interview schedule

First, a list of the scales which were to be rated from the interview reports was prepared. Some of these were quite broad (such as the emotional warmth of the mother) and were to be rated on the basis of the entire interview. Others were highly specific and would be rated on the basis of a single question (such as age at the beginning of weaning).

On the basis of the list of desired scales, a preliminary interview schedule was made up. A major problem in the wording of questions was to introduce topics in such a way as to avoid superficial, stereotyped answers based on the mother's feelings about how a good mother *ought* to feel and behave. Mothers naturally want to put themselves in a favorable light, not only to make a good showing for the interviewer, but in order to reassure *themselves*. In most instances, in the present study, rapport was excellent, and the mothers did not appear to be attempting to conceal anything about their child training.

There were some topics, however, on which they could not report accurately if asked directly, because they were not aware of what they were doing. For example, the interview was intended to reveal the nature of the disciplinary techniques which the mother employed. One of these is withdrawal of love. But obviously, an interviewer could not ask "Do you withdraw love from your child when he is naughty?" because most mothers do not realize that they are doing this when they do it, and many would disapprove of it if they realized the implications of their actions. On some topics, therefore, it was necessary to ask about specific instances of behavior which could be used as signs of the underlying characteristic in which we were interested. These examples could then be interpreted and evaluated by the raters.

Following are some of the devices which were employed in wording questions to overcome stereotyping in answers:

1. (*Face saving*) "Do you ever find time to play with Johnny just for your own pleasure?" (instead of "Do you ever play. . . .")

2. (*Assuming the existence of negatively valued behavior*) "*In what ways* do you get on each other's nerves?" (instead of "Do you ever get on each other's nerves?")

3. (*Making a wide range of answers appear socially acceptable*) "Some people feel it's very important for a child to learn not to fight with other children, and other people feel there are times when a child has to learn to fight. How do you feel about this?"

4. (*Pitting two stereotypes—values—against each other*) "Do you keep track of exactly where Johnny is and what he is doing most of the time, or can you let him watch out for himself quite a bit?" (Here the value of being a careful mother, who protects her child from danger, is pitted against the value of training a child to be independent.)

Training interviewers

Ten women did the interviewing. They came from a variety of backgrounds: two were mature graduate students, six were mothers with some background in social science, and two were social workers with predominantly research interests. The first step in training was a thorough discussion of the objectives of the study, and of the variables which the interview was intended to measure. Next came practice interviewing. The trainees first interviewed one another, with group discussion of interviewing technique; then each trainee interviewed a mother in an observation room, while the supervisor and other trainees watched through one-way screens and listened over speakers. If the observation interview was considered adequate, the interviewer began work on the main research sample. The first few interviews taken by each interviewer were played back by the supervisor and problems were discussed. During the initial stages of the main study, the interviewers met as a group periodically for discussions of problems of rapport and technique. At this time, too, the interviewers rated a few of the completed interviews on the scales that were to be used in analysis of the data. This procedure gave them a clearer understanding of the kinds of answers which would meet the objectives of the study, and they learned to recognize answers which would be inadequate without further probing.

Recording

Each interviewer carried a portable Audograph machine to the respondent's house, and the interviewer explained the machine in her introductory remarks about the study in general. Explanations about the machine took the following general form: "I want to be sure to get an accurate record of the things you tell me. I don't take shorthand, and I might not be able to write fast enough if I tried to write it all down. So I have this little recording machine—I wonder where we could plug it in?"

At this point, attention was focused upon the mechanical problems of getting the machine set up for the recording, which became a joint endeavor for the interviewer and the respondent. The mother was asked to say a few sentences for test purposes, and these were played back; if a child was present, the child was allowed to say something into the microphone and hear his voice played back. All this was usually amusing and interesting to the mother, and after a few minutes, any curiosity or anxiety she may have had about recording appeared to be allayed, and the interviewer could turn to the interview itself. Almost all the mothers seemed to forget about the microphone after the second or third question. A few expressed some concern at the beginning of the interview about who would hear the records. The interviewers explained that a typist would transcribe them, and the records then would be stored under a code number, so that they could not be identified except by a few members of the research staff. The main part of the recording apparatus was kept out of sight during the interview on a low chair or on the floor. Only the table microphone remained in view.

Verbatim typed transcripts were later prepared from the Audograph records, and were used for the ratings described below.

Rating the interviews

Each of the dimensions to be measured was represented by a rating scale. There were 188 of these in all. The number of points on the scales varied, depending on how many degrees of a particular quality we found, in preliminary studies, we could discriminate. For example, *rejection of child by father* was only a two-point scale; the best discrimination we could make was simply whether the mother did or did not describe anything about the father that suggested a tendency for him to reject the child. With *extent of use of physical punishment,* however, we found we could discriminate seven different degrees. An analysis schedule was prepared, defining each scale to be rated from the interview, and providing numbered categories for coding onto IBM punch cards.

Parenthetical statements, giving examples of the kinds of instances which would be included in the category, were provided for many of the scales. A number of examples of scales and their defining statements will be given later. For the most difficult scales, excerpts from illustrative cases were prepared to define further the meanings of the various steps along the scales.

The interviews were rated on the 188 scales by ten advanced graduate students who were thoroughly familiar with the plan of the study and with the concepts that were represented by the rating scales. In the initial stages of rating, all the raters rated the same set of interviews, and differences between their judgments were discussed. Some ambiguities in the analysis schedule came to light through these discussions, and some of the scale categories were redefined or amplified for greater clarity. Final rating rules were then agreed upon.

Each interview was rated independently by two different raters; whenever their ratings differed by more than one scale point, the two raters discussed their differences and agreed upon a category. Final scores represented the pooled judgments of two raters in each case.

Periodically during the rating process, the entire group of raters rated and discussed an interview jointly, and the pairs of raters were rotated throughout the rating process, so that no pair of raters would develop a frame of reference which deviated from that of the other raters.

Since there were two ratings on every scale, we can obtain an estimate of inter-rater reliability, i.e., the extent to which the two raters agreed on their ratings. Raw correlations between ratings provide an underestimation of the reliability of the scores actually used in the study, since in every case these represent the pooled judgment of two raters. The uncorrected reliability co-efficients are given with the descriptions of the scales in Appendix B.

WHO THE MOTHERS WERE

The mothers chosen for this study lived in two suburbs of a large metropolitan area of New England. One of the towns is chiefly a residential community. There is a small amount of light industry, but the residents are mainly of middle-class oc-cupational level and the community gives an impression of quiet prosperity. The other town contains quite a lot of heavy industry. It is closer to the metropolitan center, and the population contains a substantially larger proportion of working-class people.

The mothers' co-operation was obtained through the help of the public school officials in both communities. The superin-tendent introduced us successively to the principals, teachers, and PTA officials of the eight schools in which we worked. Six of these schools were in the first town and two in the second. The schools were selected to provide a fairly wide range of apparent socio-economic status of the neighborhoods they served.

In these eight public schools there were 640 children enrolled in kindergarten. How representative of the total population were the 379 mothers we interviewed? The answer cannot be given in any exact terms. In the town from which six schools were chosen, 72 per cent of all five-year-olds were in these kindergartens. No data were available for the other town, but if we assume a somewhat similar proportion, then we were drawing from a little less than three-quarters of the total relevant population. We did not sample mothers who had their children in parochial kindergartens (14.5 per cent), and this may have been a significant loss. However, there were no such kindergartens near some of the schools in which we worked, and Catholic parents in these neighborhoods often sent their children to public kindergartens, planning to transfer the youngsters to parochial schools later.

From the 640 mothers available, there were some further exclusions that were intentional, for reasons that had to do with other research projects associated with this one. We excluded all cases in which either the wife or husband was foreign born, or they were not living together, or they were not both the natural parents of the kindergarten child, or the child was a twin or was handicapped in some way. These exclusions reduced the number of available mothers by 80.

We wanted, also, to obtain a fairly equal representation of mothers of both boys and girls; of mothers of children who were *only, first, middle,* and *youngest* children in the family; and of mothers who represented different levels of socio-economic status. We worked through the schools one at a time, and by the time we had finished the first four schools we found we had a superabundance of middle-class mothers of *first* and *youngest* children; and so, in the later schools where we worked, we excluded 79 cases that fit these criteria. We now had a "target" group of 481 families whom we wanted to include in the study.

Some mothers excluded themselves. Several moved out of town before we reached them. Several simply did not have time (we listened to their reasons and believed them!). Illness, faulty recordings, or other difficulties accounted for a few more. Finally, there were 38 mothers whom we must classify simply as "Refused." They worry us. They are one-tenth as many as our actually obtained sample, and we suspect they may have represented extremes in one way or another. Even if all were low or all were high on most of our scales, they would not have much effect on the numerical distribution of the whole population, but it is uncomfortable to have "ghosts" at large and not know what they are like. (The selection and final composition of the sample are summarized in Appendix C, Tables C:1 and C:2.)

Our mothers, then, were from two suburban towns of a large New England metropolitan area. They all had children registered in public school kindergartens. They were all American born and were living with their American-born husbands. Their husbands were the natural fathers of their kindergarten-age child, and the child was not a twin nor was it handicapped in any way.

Now as to some demographic matters. The median age of the mothers was 33.6 years. Fifty per cent of them were between 30.6 and 37.8 years, and none was less than 24 years of age. Their husbands were about three years older, on the average, and 25 per cent of them were more than 40 years old. So far as education was concerned, 22 per cent of the mothers had finished college, and 14 per cent had not finished high school. However, among their husbands, nearly 36 per cent had completed college, while 16 per cent had not finished high school. There was some tendency, in other words, for the husbands to be a little older than the wives and to be a little better educated. In general, too, the husbands showed a slightly greater social mobility upward than their wives; they had improved their occupational level over that of their own fathers to a greater extent than their wives had improved *theirs,* by marriage, over *their* own fathers.

The ethnic origin of wives and husbands was similar, of course. There was substantial representation of Old American, British, Irish, and southern (Latin) and eastern (Slavic) European stock. Somewhat more husbands (213) than wives (180) had a foreign-born parent. With respect to religion, Protestant, Catholic, and Jewish faiths were all strongly represented.

Occupationally, the husbands ranged from unskilled laborers to top-level professional and managerial men. In terms of Warner's scale of occupational status, the group was quite evenly distributed from 1 (upper-middle class) through 5 (the lower edge of the upper-lower class) with 47 families falling at points 6 and 7 (lower class). Median family income was $7150, and 50 per cent of the families had incomes between $3700 and $8275. These figures suggest a skewed distribution, with a bunching at the upper end. Actually, 23 of the families had incomes over $15,000, and doubtless, as this group of husbands grows older, the bunching will spread out even more, and some of those in professional and managerial positions will move into substantially higher income brackets. It is worth remembering, in this connection, that the median age of the husbands was only 36.5 years at the time of the interviews (December, 1951, through May, 1952).

So, these figures tell who the mothers were. Like most statistics, they hide the very people who comprise them. Accurate enough for describing a population sample, they tell nothing of the warm, vital, striving human beings who were being interviewed. No one of them felt like a statistic; probably few felt they represented any particular category. But the categories do describe at least the external qualities by which it can be known what kind of people the mothers of our study were.

SUMMARY

This book will report a study of child rearing in the United States as one group of 379 mothers was practicing that art at the close of the first half of the twentieth century. We will describe those aspects of the process that can be measured on dimensions that are common to all the mothers. This procedure will offer findings that are relevant to three kinds of questions: (1) What are the customary practices and how much variation is there in a suburban group that ranges widely through lower- and middle-class status? (2) What effects do certain types of child-rearing practices have on some of the personality dimensions of young children? and (3) What kinds of mothers engage in what kinds of child-rearing practices?

We have sought answers to these questions by means of a long interview with each mother. This procedure permitted us to secure a recorded report of the mother's answers to a standarized open-ended interview. From the transcription of the interview, 188 scales were rated for each mother, and these scale measures will be used to make the necessary listings and comparisons required for answering our questions.

CHAPTER TWO

Background for Parenthood

It is not altogether obvious where one should start in describing the rearing of a child. The least ambiguous point might be the moment of birth, or better still, the instant at which the mother first sees her baby. But a great deal has already gone on before this time. The parents have made preparations and developed expectations. They have begun to live a new kind of life, in an anticipatory way. Their reactions to the imminence of parenthood are inevitably influenced by certain qualities of their own individual personalities. And the attitudes they have toward the child at his birth are an important part of his social and emotional environment.

We will start with an examination of these attitudes, recognizing the importance of the mother's own life history as one of their determinants, but without trying to investigate those sources. This is an arbitrary procedure, and it is well to remember, in what follows, that the mother's feelings here reported spring from a lifetime of living. She and her husband were reared in other families, and, not long since, were children themselves, being loved and punished and worried over.

Now, when we interview these mothers—in their roles as mothers—they are adults. They have developed complex person-

alities, and have helped construct a new family that has qualities of its own. They have values, attitudes, ways of adjusting, expectations about the future, plans and policies for their child. They are people in their own right. Childbearing and child rearing comprise only one part of their lives—an important part, to be sure, and by no means uninfluenced by all the other aspects of living.

To the child, all this is environment. He comes into a complex social unit that is itself a product of many experiences from the past. He will exist in a power structure in which husband and wife have certain defined roles of authority. He will live with a mother who has certain qualities of warmth, certain regrets and satisfactions from her marriage, certain feelings about herself and her husband. Perhaps most important of all, she has certain feelings about the child himself, and a certain capacity for loving him. It is these feelings of affection—and the experience and attitudes that influence them—that provide the background of parenthood, the emotional quality that pervades the child-rearing process.

In this chapter we will present our findings with respect to three different measures of this emotional quality. The first has to do with *the mother's feelings when she first realized she was pregnant*. Did she want a baby? Or did the prospect not appeal to her? The period of pregnancy is a time of preparation, emotional and otherwise. Quite aside from the possible influence that such early feelings may have on the mother's later reactions to her baby, the feelings themselves are important. After all, nine months are no insignificant part of any woman's life.

Our second measure is on the dimension we have called *affectionate warmth toward the infant*. Warmth is a pervasive quality. It involves love, acceptance, enthusiasm, an outgoingness of affection. It is not a dimension that a mother can discuss easily, nor is it one on which she can be measured by her answer to a single question. Nevertheless, as will be seen from some of the quotations given in a later section of this chapter, the quality of warmth does stand out in her discussion of other matters.

The third measure is the same as the second, as far as emotional quality is concerned, but it describes the mother's *affectional warmth toward the child in later preschool years*. By the time a child is five years old he has developed very much of a personality of his own; his mother's feelings toward him are based not only on the original attitudes she had toward babies in general, but in part on his qualities as an individual.

The first of these three measures does not refer to maternal behavior that has a direct impact on the child, but the other two do. In later chapters we will examine some of the apparent effects that warmth and coldness have on the child. In this present one, however, we will limit our analysis to matters that properly belong under the first and third questions we raised in Chapter One. We will describe in some detail how the mothers *did* feel about becoming pregnant, and how much warmth and affection they felt (and presumably expressed) toward their child. Then we will examine several possible causes for these feelings and attitudes, to see whether certain objective aspects of the family situation were associated with different amounts of these feelings. We will also examine the relation of certain other attitudes of the mother—her feelings about herself, her husband, and her role in life—to her feelings about her child.

The general scheme of this analysis is best illustrated by the following diagram. In column I are a few factors that have little to do directly with child rearing but that we have thought might be related to the way mothers felt about children. In column II are the dimensions of child rearing and of attitudes or other qualities (e.g., warmth) that impinge on the child directly. In column III are the dimensions of the child's own behavior.

I	II	III
Mother's situation—objective aspects, such as age, work history, and family size Mother's attitudes—feelings about self, husband, work, etc.	Mother's attitudes toward child and child-rearing practices, such as permissiveness toward aggression, warmth, and severity of toilet training	Child's behavior, such as aggression in the house, dependency, and conscience

In the present chapter we will concern ourselves entirely with the first two columns, showing what the relations are between certain column I factors and some column II dimensions that refer to *warmth*. The relations among these column II dimensions will also be reported. In later chapters, we will describe the relations between the column II dimensions and a few of those represented by column III.

ON BECOMING PREGNANT

We can begin our description of child rearing with the time at which the mothers first realized they were to become mothers. We did not ask outright whether the child was "planned," although many mothers discussed this, but we did ask: "I wonder if you'd think back to when you first discovered you were pregnant with Johnny—how did you feel about it?" The mothers' answers are summarized in Table II:1.

TABLE II:1

HOW MOTHER FELT WHEN SHE DISCOVERED SHE WAS PREGNANT

1. Delighted; very happy; had been waiting and hoping for this	50%
2. Pleased, but no evidence of enthusiasm (includes: "This was a planned baby," said matter-of-factly)	18
3. Pleased generally; some reservations	6
4. Mixed feelings; advantages and disadvantages weighed about equally	9
5. Generally displeased, although some bright spots seen	9
6. Displeased; no reservations	7
Not ascertained	1
Total	100%

This table deserves an explanation, for it represents a type that will be used repeatedly in this book. It is designed to show what percentage of the 379 mothers were rated at each of the six points on the rating scale called "How mother felt when she discovered she was pregnant." The numbers at the left show how many separate points there were on the scale, and the descriptive phrases indicate the meaning of each point. The left-hand scale numbers are given only for those descriptive points on the dimension being scaled, of course; no number is given for categories like "Not ascertained" or "Not applicable," because they are not points on the continuum being measured.

The percentage figures at the right show what proportion of the interviews were judged by the raters to exemplify each of the described points. This list of phrases actually serves to define the *dimension* that is given in the table heading. In later chapters, similar scales will be presented, but they will not all have six points. Some will have as few as three and others as many as seven. The number of points used in a scale depended upon how many different degrees of that particular dimension we found we could discriminate with reasonable accuracy. These decisions were made on the basis of pretest interviews before the present study was started.

The category "Not ascertained" refers to those interviews in which the mother did not give enough information to enable us to make a rating on the scale. Perhaps she "couldn't remember," or perhaps she was vague because she wanted to avoid the matter. Occasionally an interviewer failed to probe enough, or felt that too much probing would annoy or upset the mother. Whatever the reasons, on this present scale there were four interviews (one per cent) that could not be rated. The percentage of cases "not ascertained" will vary from scale to scale, of course, *but throughout the book tables like Table II:1 will add to 100% and will always be based on the entire 379 mothers of the sample.*

Now to return to the content of Table II:1 itself, with attention to the percentages and the scale points to which they refer. Most of the children in our sample were "wanted," if we may judge from these later recollections. One mother [1] described her feelings, and those of her husband, as follows:

M. *I was thrilled, delighted, eager.*
I. *How about your husband, how did he feel?*
M. *Pretty much the same way. Well, as an only child, basically he didn't care whether you had children or not. He would have been happy to just go through life with me. But because of my strong desire for children—actually, I think we had them because I wanted them; the second, because he realized the logic of an only child not being as good as more than one. And yet for a man with that attitude to start with it's just amazing the amount of love and attention he has given the children.*
I. *From the standpoint of your financial condition, and so on, did you feel this was a good time to have a baby?*
M. *I would say we didn't even consider that, because financially when the first one is born, that was when we might have hesitated. It was just a question—if you are going to wait until it's easy, it's ridiculous.*

[1] Throughout the book the interviewer's questions will be identified by **I** and the mother's replies will be identified by **M**. In addition, whenever more than one interview is recorded, each case will be signified by **A, B, C,** etc.

I. *Looking back on it now, do you think things would have worked out better for you if you had waited longer to have Sidney?*
M. *No, I don't think anyone should wait. I think the thing to do is to cope with the situation when it comes. Not, of course, to dive in head first. But there is no right time; just go ahead and have them.*

Another mother commented:

M. *I was tickled to death, because, to begin with, I was in my thirties when I got married and I wanted to have a family, and so when I knew I was pregnant, we were both delighted, because naturally we couldn't afford to wait ten years or so to have a child, so we were quite thrilled.*

And still another:

M. *Well, I was glad, very glad, because I had lost two. We were very glad, because my husband loves children.*

A good many of the mothers faced serious obstacles during their childbearing. Some not only suffered serious illness during their pregnancies, but had a number of miscarriages as well. But the desire for a child was strong, and they continued to try. Some faced these difficulties repeatedly in order to have a second or even a third child. A good many, too, decided to have a baby despite unsettled economic or housing conditions. Their general feeling was that there is never a time that is ideal in all respects for having children; one might as well go ahead, and simply adjust to whatever the circumstances are.

However, there were some mothers who, for a variety of reasons, did not welcome the pregnancy. They were a relatively small minority, and for most of them the problem was not that they did not want children at all, but rather that they did not want a child at this particular time. The comments of the following two mothers illustrate these more negative attitudes:

A

M. *I wasn't a bit happy about it at all. That was the fourth one, and I didn't want any more children. I had my hands full then. Not that I wouldn't have liked the baby, because I love babies, but the house was too small and at that time I thought it was hopeless trying to get my husband to buy a larger house. I can see the way he felt. We had the house paid for, and it was a darling little house and economical to run and that was fine, but I was very unhappy there. I was going through an unhappy period of time, anyway. I didn't have any idea of being pregnant—not a bit.*

B

M. Well, I think that unless every pregnancy is a planned one, I think your first reaction is, well—I don't know whether you would call it disappointment—it isn't disappointment, because then nature always makes you glad, but I think your very first reaction sometimes is, if you had your choice, you wouldn't want to be, because there are so many different little things that are involved, but I don't think that anybody—or certainly I know I haven't ever gone very far in pregnancy but what nature seems to take care of that first reaction, and you are always glad.

There is, however, a certain biological naturalness about the bearing of a child that overcomes the seemingly inevitable sense of inconvenience. Whatever may have been the circumstances of their becoming pregnant, most of the mothers appear to have had considerable pride—and no little curiosity—about the baby they produced. If one has a strong feeling of urgency about the continuity of the human race, he may properly hope that this maternal pride stems from some property of the mammalian species to which man belongs. Perhaps the hope is justified— at least it is reassuring—but our evidence suggests that the amount of enthusiasm a mother has for her newborn infant is considerably influenced by a number of things that have only remote connection with biology.

1. Composition of the family

Ordinal position. As might be expected, a mother's desire for a child was related to whether she already had children. Since a first child requires the largest readjustment in the mother's way of life, and involves her facing something unknown, and possibly frightening, one might expect the first child to be least wanted. Indeed, some mothers did express such feelings:

M. I was kinda afraid, because I had never been around babies before and I was wondering how I was going to go about it, how I was going to take care of her, etc., but it came naturally after I had her. I was very happy about it.

If we consider the entire group of mothers, however, there is little evidence of concern over the unfamiliarity of child care. In general, the advent of the first child was greeted with delight; mixed feelings (partly unpleasant) were more common for later children. For example, when the child was the mother's first,

62 per cent of the mothers were judged "delighted" to find themselves pregnant, but when the child was a second or later one, only 34 per cent were so judged. Table II:2 shows the distribution of these ratings.

TABLE II:2

MOTHER'S ATTITUDE TOWARD PREGNANCY: RELATIONSHIP TO WHETHER IT IS HER FIRST CHILD *

Mother's Feeling about Pregnancy	First Children	Later Children
Delighted	62%	34%
Generally pleased	19	32
Mixed feelings or displeased	18	34
Not ascertained	1	—
Total	100%	100%
Number of cases	161	218

$p < .01$ $(t = 5.30)$

* The percentages in this table do not exactly match those in Table II:1. That is, if the reader weights the 62 per cent "delighted" for first children by its number of cases (161) and combines it with the weighted percentage "delighted" for later children (218), he will not get 50 per cent but a number slightly lower. This occurs because of our rating procedures. It will be recalled that each interview was rated twice. When the two raters disagreed by two points or more on the rating scale, they discussed their difference and arrived at a pooled judgment. When they disagreed by only one point, however, the difference was not discussed, but the score was simply recorded as falling midway between their two ratings. For instance, on a five-point scale, if one rater rated an interview "1," and the other "2," the score was recorded as "1.5." For purposes of describing the distribution of the whole sample, as in Table II:1, these mid-point cases have been split evenly, and half of them assigned to each of the two original categories. Thus, on the scale of the mother's attitude toward pregnancy, there were 174 cases (out of 379) rated "delighted" by both raters (category "1"); 49 were rated "pleased but not enthusiastic" (category "2") by both raters; and there were 33 cases in which one rater rated "1," the other, "2." For Table II:1, these latter 33 cases were divided, and 17 of them were assigned to category "1," 16 to category "2." For purposes of cross-tabulating (or correlating) this scale with other variables, however, a score of "1.5" was treated as lying midway between "1" and "2"—that is, the six-point scale was, to all intents and purposes, expanded into an eleven-point scale. This "expanding" procedure has been followed with all the scales, and whenever the ratings have been used for cross-comparison, correlation, or any other statistical manipulation except a simple listing (such as that in Table II:1), the mid-point cases have *not* been divided and assigned to neighboring categories, but have been treated as falling at a true-scale point lying midway between the two categories which the two raters originally chose. It should be further noted that in many tables which show the relationship between two variables, categories are combined, usually on the basis of the number of cases found at different scale points. Sometimes a scale is divided into two major groups, sometimes into three, sometimes more. In this table (II:2), the "delighted" group includes only those cases rated "1" by both raters. That is, the scale has been divided between "1" and "1.5."

The statistic used for testing the significance of relationship will be indicated in parentheses following the *p* value. When *t* is shown for a table reporting percentages, as here, it is to be understood as referring to the significance of the difference between mean rating scores for the two groups.

A word must be said about this table, for it displays one of the main methods we have used for analyzing our findings. Thus in the left-hand column the figures show what percentage of the mothers of *first* children were judged to have felt each of three degrees of pleasure at being pregnant. The right-hand column gives comparable percentages for the mothers of *later* children. (We have compressed the six points of the original scale, as shown in Table II:1, into three, in order to make the table less cumbersome.) There was a clear tendency for more of the mothers of *first* children to be near the upper ("delighted") end of the scale. About equal numbers of mothers of *later* children were rated at each of the three levels. *Relatively* speaking, then, the latter group was rated nearer the lower end ("mixed feelings or displeased"). If one can imagine an "average" mother, one might say she is *more likely* to be delighted by her first child than by a later one. But the table also shows that there were some mothers having a first child who went counter to this trend (18 per cent, in fact); they were "displeased or had mixed feelings." And there were, after all, 34 per cent who were "delighted" even though the child was a later one. Perhaps the best way of summarizing Table II:2 is to say it shows that ordinal position of the child has *some* influence on how pleased the mother is with becoming pregnant. No attitude is ever determined by just one thing, however, and, as will be seen in succeeding sections, the same method of analysis used with ordinal position in Table II:2 has enabled us to discover several other factors that also have *some* influence on how much the mother wants her child.

One further comment is in order for the reader who is unfamiliar with statistical interpretation. Table II:2 shows simply that there is a relationship between the two variables we measured. The difference between the two percentages given in the top line ("delighted") is so large that we have little hesitation in concluding that these two variables, (1) ordinal position and (2) attitude toward pregnancy, are quite closely related to one another. But there will be other instances, later, in which the differences are much smaller, and a cautious reader will not be so confident that there is a "true" relationship between the pair of measures. He will want some criterion by which he can decide whether to give the alleged relationship much credence, or to be rather skeptical and attribute it to chance variation resulting from inadequate ratings or too small a sample of mothers.

There is no absolutely certain way of telling whether one variable is "really" related to another. The best we can do is to estimate, from certain internal characteristics of the data themselves, what *probability* there is that if we were to repeat the research on another group of mothers we would find the same relationship between the two variables. A "true" relationship is nothing more than one that we can estimate statistically to have a *high probability* of occurring again if we repeat the investigation.

There are a number of statistical devices for making these estimates, but they all lead to one end—a statement of such *probability*. This is commonly expressed as a p value; it is an index that states the number of times in a hundred repetitions of the research that a relationship like the one obtained in the actual data would occur *just by chance* rather than because there was a stable and reproducible relation between the two variables. The p value is given in the form of a decimal, as for example .05 or .02 or $<.01$. These figures may be interpreted to mean, respectively, that the obtained relationship would be expected to occur *by chance only,* in another study like this, "five" or "two" or "fewer than one" times in a hundred. The smaller the p value, the more we can rely on the finding. By and large, when p is .05 or smaller, the relationship to which it refers may be considered reasonably well established.

We have used several devices for estimating p, and these will be mentioned where they are relevant to a better understanding of the data. They include simple correlation (r), partial correlation, the significance of differences between means (t) and per cents, chi-square (χ^2), and analysis of variance (F). The statistically untrained reader may safely ignore such references, however, for the p value derived from them is the important thing in deciding how much reliance to place on the findings.

In the case of Table II:2, the p value is shown to be $<.01$, which means that less often than once in a hundred times would sheer chance produce a difference of the size that we have found. This gives us quite high confidence in our conclusion that ordinal position influences the wantedness of the child.

Now let us turn to some of the other possible influences. Since there were 18 per cent of the mothers of *first* children who had mixed feelings or were displeased by becoming pregnant, we can be sure there is plenty of statistical room for quite different factors to influence the attitudes of some of the mothers.

Distance between children. We can consider first the reasons some mothers had for their mental reservations about their pregnancies with later children. In a number of cases, mothers had the feeling that the child was arriving too soon after the last baby. Two mothers described their feelings as follows:

A

M. *Well, when I got married I really didn't have much of an idea of having children. I hadn't thought about it at all. It was sort of a shock. It's nice. The first one. The second one I did mind. The third one I minded most of all. Because they did come so fast. The second one was in 16 months, the third was in 11 months. They were pretty close.*

B

M. *With Joseph I wasn't too keen on the idea, because I had a baby that was just four months old when I became pregnant with Joseph and I was quite young and I was disappointed at first. When he was another boy, I was more than disappointed, but naturally after I had him and took him home, I thought as much of him as I did the first one. In fact, I was quite proud of having two boys just a year apart, after I got over the shock.*

I. *I suppose there are advantages in having two boys.*

M. *Oh, it's wonderful now, yes it has been—as they have been growing up they have been companions to each other, and I can see it really is good; but at the time, of course, I just couldn't see it.*

The representativeness of these attitudes can be judged from Table II:3, which is constructed like Table II:2, and shows the influence, again, of one factor taken at a time. In this case, the influencing variable is *age of the next-older child when this child was born.* If one follows across the top line of figures, which describe the percentage of mothers who expressed themselves as "delighted" at the pregnancy, it becomes clear that the greater the distance between the two children, the greater was the proportion of mothers who were "delighted."

Sex of existing children. The mother's attitude toward pregnancy also seems to be influenced by the sex of the children who were already in the family, although to a lesser degree. There was a tendency for the mother to be happier about a new pregnancy if her existing children were girls only rather than boys only, or both boys and girls. Indeed, she was very likely to be

TABLE II:3

MOTHER'S ATTITUDE TOWARD PREGNANCY: RELATIONSHIP TO THE AGE OF THE
NEXT-OLDER CHILD

MOTHER'S ATTITUDE TOWARD PREGNANCY	AGE OF NEXT-OLDER CHILD WHEN THIS CHILD WAS BORN			
	21 Months or Less	22–31 Months	32–55 Months	55 Months or More
Delighted	9%	28%	42%	52%
Generally pleased	23	39	35	16
Mixed feelings or displeased	68	31	23	32
Not ascertained	—	2	—	—
Total	100%	100%	100%	100%
Number of cases	34	54	92	31

$p < .01$ $(r = -.30)$

least enthusiastic if she already had children of both sexes. Possibly parents are more anxious to have at least one boy than they are to have at least one girl. If they have girls only, parents may plan another child in the hope of having a boy, whereas if they have boys only, they are more likely to be willing to consider their family complete, and a new pregnancy is therefore more likely to be unplanned. Or it may be that girls are easier to take care of in the early years, and thus the mother is more willing to face going through the infant care and training period again.

That a mother's experience with her older children can affect her attitude toward a new child is suggested by the following comment by one mother:

M. *In the first place I was disappointed, because I didn't want any more children, because I had so much trouble with my first one. I had a lot of trouble physically and mentally and everything with Bobby. In fact, I didn't have a good night's sleep for five years with Bobby.*
I. *What was the trouble?*
M. *He really was a problem, and I was so disgusted with him that I really didn't want any more children. So of course I don't know how it happened but I became pregnant with Dorothy; it was never planned or anything, and I was really kinda disappointed and downhearted to begin with, but then after she was born she was such a good baby, I certainly changed my mind.*

On the other hand, difficulties with a first child sometimes motivated parents to have, rather than avoid, another child, in the hope that the companionship of a brother or sister would benefit the older child:

M. *I became pregnant with Steve, because we thought the other one needed a brother or sister, as he was such a devil. I don't think that anyone should have another child thinking it might help the first one—it doesn't.*

Many families had younger children for the sake of the older children. This happened even when the experience with the older child had been entirely satisfactory. Several mothers described the pressure the older children (especially daughters) put on them to have another baby, and some said they decided to have another baby mainly because the older children wanted it so much. (See Appendix Table D:1.)

Mother's age. Another factor that might seem important in determining the mother's attitude is her own age. This has been a difficult factor to examine, because, by and large, the older mothers had had longer distance in time between children, and this was associated with a positive attitude. On the other hand, the older mothers' children who were the reference points for this study were *later* more often than *first* children, and that fact was associated with a negative attitude. These two factors, working in opposite directions, tended to obscure any influence that age of mother might have when we made a simple comparison between all the older and all the younger mothers. However, if we rule out these other factors by selecting small groups of older and younger mothers who were having a "later" child and for whom the time elapsed since the previous child's birth was the same, we find that there was no difference at all in the number of mothers who were "delighted." Age of the mother was not important.

2. Personal adjustment

Feelings toward husband. We have seen that occasionally a mother's difficulties with an older child influences her decision to have, or not have, another child. Probably more important in the decision is another aspect of the interpersonal relationships in the home: the mother's relationship with her husband, and her expectations about how he will behave toward a new child. While most mothers reported that they thought their husbands were pleased over the advent of children, a few felt that the addition of children to the family imposed considerable strain upon their marriages. One mother put it this way:

> **M.** *I think it's wonderful to be a mother. I like being a mother. If my husband were different I think I would have a larger family, but I'd like to stop right now, because we have so many differences about the children. I feel the more children we have, the more it will pull us apart. I really do. It's a very strong thing with me the way I feel.*
>
> **I.** *How about when you were pregnant with Janet, how did you feel about that?*
>
> **M.** *How did I feel when I was pregnant? Many times I wished I wasn't because of the way my husband was with Paul, while I was pregnant. After all Paul was growing up and going into his second year at the time and I often thought—gee, I wish I wasn't going to have another one if this is the way my husband is going to be.*

Possibly when there is a good deal of tension between a husband and wife, the wife is reluctant to have children (or more children) because this ties her more strongly to a marriage which she has begun to feel is a poor one. On the other hand, when the wife feels strong love and respect for her husband, it may be that she is eager to have children because they will resemble him. In any case, we have found clear evidence that, in general, the stronger the wife's esteem and affection for her husband, the happier she was about pregnancy. (This relationship, as well as others described below, is exhibited in a table of intercorrelations, Appendix Table D:3.)

Self-esteem. Of course, in some instances, difficulties between a husband and wife may be a symptom of deeper tensions in the wife herself—conflicts which interfere with her adjustment both to her marriage and to childbearing. There is some evidence in the interviews that her attitude toward pregnancy is related to her self-esteem. On the basis of the entire interview, each mother in the group was rated as to her own evaluation of herself: the extent to which she was self-confident and reasonably well satisfied with her own performance as a person and as a mother. An example of a case rated low on self-esteem is that of the mother who remarked:

> M. *You will notice in most of my answers I know what is right but I do what is wrong . . . I . . . I spend most of my time thinking I am a perfectly lousy mother and I suppose all mothers feel that way. The thing of motherhood brings out my own inefficiencies, my own deficiencies, so terribly, that . . . the outstanding thought in my mind is that I should try to be a better mother each new day.*

Most of the mothers were rated relatively high on self-esteem. But the mothers who did show comparatively lower self-esteem at the time the child was five or six years old tended to be the same mothers who did not want the child in the first place, at least according to their current recollection. Their original reluctance to have the baby may have been, at least in part, a reflection of feelings of inadequacy to cope with a new interpersonal relationship, especially one which involved giving guidance and serving as an example to another individual. More will be said later about the importance of the mother's self-esteem in her emotional relationship with the child as he grew older.

Living arrangements. Naturally, the living situation of a family has some bearing upon a mother's desire for a new child. Most of the children in our study were conceived during the year 1945, the last year of World War II. A number of the fathers were still in uniform. In some families, the wife was living with her parents or her husband's parents or with other relatives, and there was difficulty finding housing which would be adequate for a growing family. Under these circumstances, some young couples would have preferred to wait for children until the husband was out of the armed forces, or at least until they were located in their own house or apartment. The impact of economic circumstances upon the parents' feelings about a new baby is illustrated by one of the rare cases of unemployment in our sample:

M. *Well honestly and truly, when I first discovered I was pregnant with Sally, it didn't make me any too happy. Timmy had just turned fourteen months old when she was born. Between Sally and Timmy, my husband had an accident at work—he was out of work all winter, which didn't make things too pleasant. When I found out I was pregnant, he didn't like it one bit. It wasn't the idea that I didn't want another baby, because I did. I would even love to have another one now. But it was just at that time, things were so bad. I said, "Glory, what is going to happen to us now!" With him out of work in the middle of the winter and everything. But everything is all right now.*

The mother role. An interesting question is whether the mother's feeling about pregnancy reflected any conflict on her part about the role she wanted to assume in life—whether she regretted giving up outside work, for example, or found the role of housewife and mother too confining. Almost all the mothers had worked at some time, so it was possible for them to evaluate their work and home experiences. Possibly, this high incidence of previous employment was related to the wartime situation, with its many opportunities, indeed demands, for women to work. The work history of the group is set forth in Table II:4.

TABLE II:4

WORK HISTORY OF THE 379 MOTHERS

Never worked	7%
Worked before marriage, not after	30
Worked after marriage, but not since this child was born	43
Worked at least part time since this child was born	17
Not ascertained	3
Total	100%

We do not have much information concerning the nature of the work these mothers did. From their discussions we know that some had positions which required considerable training and could properly be called "careers." Others had rather irregular, routine employment at work that did not mean a great deal to the woman concerned; it was primarily a stopgap occupation that permitted her to earn some money until she began having her family. In any case, we can ask whether this work experience in any sense "spoiled" these women for assuming their later roles of wife and mother. We can compare the proportion of nonworkers (of whom there were only 28) with the proportion of workers who were "delighted" over becoming pregnant.

The answer is unequivocal. There was no tendency for the nonworkers to be more pleased over motherhood—quite the opposite, in fact. Among the nonworkers, only 29 per cent were "delighted," while among those who had worked at some time, 48 per cent were; and there was no difference between those who worked only before marriage and those who worked both before and after, or even after this child was born.

There is more to the problem of the mother role, however, than is implied by the simple fact of working. Since the latter part of the nineteenth century there have been progressively greater numbers of young women who have not only worked before and after marriage, but have spent considerable time in formal training for skilled positions. One might hazard the guess that such preparation, together with the independence and pride of accomplishment it offers, have led to a greater enjoyment of working and a greater reluctance to shift careers in midstream. Indeed, some sociologists have queried whether there was not danger that the career of motherhood might become so much a second choice that there would be difficulty in perpetuating our American family structure. This danger is slight, if we may judge from the expressed attitudes of this group of mothers speaking for themselves in the middle of the twentieth century. But, in trying to understand the attitudinal background with which they approach parenthood, it is important to examine some of their problems and feelings about the mother role and its relation to other aspects of their lives.

How much conflict did they actually feel about shifting from a job to motherhood, or about combining the two? We asked about this of those mothers who had had work experience, and their reactions are summarized in Table II:5.

It will surprise no one to learn that the first group, the few who felt giving up work was a great sacrifice, contained very few mothers who were "delighted" at becoming pregnant. These were the mothers who were strongly dedicated to their work. But it is a striking thing to discover that about half the mothers in the second group were "delighted." These were the women who had some zest for work, but also enjoyed the prospect of having a family. The fourth group contained a similarly high proportion of "delighted" mothers. These were the ones who frankly wanted to stop work and have a family. Of the third group of mothers, ones indifferent about work, only a third were "delighted."

TABLE II:5

"How Did You Feel about Giving Up Your Work?"

1. Much sacrifice. Enjoyed work, felt it was important, didn't want to give it up to have children	6%
2. Some sacrifice. Mixed feelings. Glad to have family, but enjoyed some things about work	13
3. No sacrifice. Indifferent, didn't particularly enjoy working, didn't mind giving it up	33
4. The opposite of sacrifice: glad to give up work, more than ready to start having family	28
Never worked	7
Not ascertained (including: gave up work for other reason than marriage)	13
Total	100%

These figures appear to suggest that a woman's enjoyment of a job outside of the home does not necessarily interfere with her acceptance of the maternal role when the time comes for the advent of children. In fact, if a woman shows a certain amount of interest and involvement in her work, whatever it is, the prognosis is better for her interest in (and enjoyment of) motherhood than if she is indifferent to her work. One cannot but wonder whether enjoyment of outside work and motherhood are not both reflections of an underlying "style" of dealing with whatever life situation the individual woman finds herself in.

It should be added that these relationships are largely confined to the upper-middle socio-economic status group. Among the working-class mothers, attitudes toward work made little difference in the acceptance of pregnancy.

Despite the fact that so large a proportion of the women had worked at one time or another, they expressed relatively little conflict about acceptance of the mother role. One should bear in mind that for very many working women, a job is not a "career" in the same sense that it is for a man. It is often regarded as a temporary thing, of interest more for the additional income it provides than for the status it gives or the opportunities for advancement it offers.

There has been a good deal of discussion in recent years of the problems of the woman who must stay home, relatively isolated from the world of affairs, and keep watch over young children. In many cases it is believed she finds herself "tied down" rather completely because of the fact that in our society young couples do not usually live with either set of grandparents, and consequently do not have the help in caring for young children which is common in other societies.

We asked this question: "Some mothers feel that their main job is to stay home and take care of the children. At the same time they sometimes feel that they owe it to themselves to do some outside work or at least have quite a few outside interests. How do you feel about this?"

The women in our sample were almost unanimous in feeling that motherhood was their primary job. While a great many felt that they were better mothers if they could get away from the house occasionally—perhaps one afternoon a week for shopping or a club meeting or party—there was little suggestion of real conflict between the demands of a career and the demands of child rearing. Most of the mothers we interviewed were genuinely, deeply interested in their children, and seemed to feel that they were performing an important function in devoting themselves to child training. We encountered little feeling that a woman who occupies the status of wife and mother is in any way inferior to the woman with a career. In fact, many of these mothers were inclined to pity women who did not, or could not, have children. When asked—"How well do you feel you've been able to solve this problem (of the conflict between outside interests and the demands of the home) in your own case?" and "Have you ever felt you'd rather be doing something else than what you're doing now?"—very few mothers in our sample expressed any real dissatisfaction with their life situation. Only 6 per cent were rated as dissatisfied, and 8 per cent as having mixed feelings; the majority expressed few reservations about their acceptance of the mother role.

A number of mothers made a distinction between their role as mothers and their role as housewives, feeling that they were perfectly justified in turning over cleaning and other household chores to hired help when they could afford it. They saw no reason why they should feel responsibility for doing these tasks personally. But child care was another matter, and most seemed to feel that the mother herself should do this if at all possible.

Furthermore, a number of women made a distinction between outside *interests* and outside *work*. They felt that outside interests were desirable, and even necessary, because the occasional change of scene keeps a woman alert and makes her a better mother when she returns to the home. But, equally, they felt that outside commitments of the sort usually involved in a job are likely to interfere with the primary duties of motherhood. One mother discussed this problem as follows:

I. *Some mothers feel that their main job is to stay home and take care of the children. At the same time they feel sometimes that they owe it to themselves to do some outside work or at least have quite a few outside interests. What is your point of view about this?*
M. *Oh, I think if you possibly can you definitely should have some outside interests, by all means. It makes life pretty dull to just be a housewife and mother, not that being a mother isn't a full-time job; but you can slide in a few little outside activities to keep you alive and up on the world events if nothing else.*
I. *How well do you feel you have been able to solve this problem in your own case?*
M. *Not as much as I would like to. However, I have kept enough contacts outside of just taking care of the children to keep me from being dull, I think, but not as much as I would like to.*
I. *Have you ever felt you would rather be doing something else than what you're doing now?*
M. *Oh, any mother who doesn't feel that way is just not telling the truth. Of course, you have your moments when you wonder why you ever got married, and why you ever had children, life seemed so simple before. When they all three came down with the measles, or one falls and has a bloody nose, or someone else upchucks their dinner— oh, there are moments that are just unbearable—but there are other moments . . .*
I. *Have you ever thought about going back to work?*
M. *No, I don't believe in that whatsoever, not while the children are young. I heartily disapprove of any woman trying to run a business and run a home, and be a proper wife, and I underline proper wife, and also taking care of children—you just can't do it, not without failing somewhere along the line.*

It appears, then, that the problems these mothers had in adapting to their life situation seldom stemmed from conflict between the mother role and the career role (in the sense that they would prefer to be occupying another station in life). Rather, such problems as did exist seemed to be related to cultural isolation. In a highly mobile society like our own, many young mothers find themselves living in neighborhoods where they have no close friends. Some cannot afford to have sitters as often as they would wish, and some live in localities where it is difficult to get sitters, with the result that mothers spend nearly all their time exclusively in the company of young children with whom they cannot talk as they would with an adult friend. Radio and television help to fill the need for adult social contacts, but are a poor substitute for the real thing. Some young mothers begin to feel an almost frantic need to get away from the house for brief periods of respite. This situation was described graphically by one woman whose house was relatively isolated, who did not know her neighbors, and who had had trouble getting sitters:

M. *I think almost anything the children do is going to irritate me. They may not be doing a darned thing and sometimes I think just his presence will irritate me. Here we're so far away from the bus service and I don't have a car at my disposal except to go to my weekly visit to the dentist. I may not leave this house for six or eight weeks at a time, even to go out for a social evening, and I think just being around the children so much irritates me, and for that reason they're irritated and for that reason we all get wound up and nervous. I found that within the last year or so everything about this place is so confining I'm about ready to blow my top. To tell you the truth, I don't like the neighborhood. I think that no one can stay in as much as I do, and unless my mother-in-law will take the children, it's almost impossible to get a baby sitter on this street. My husband, from time to time, is out a great deal at night, because of his work. I see nothing but these walls, day in, day out, week in and week out. Living out here, with the lack of transportation and all, I have no other associations. I don't say I miss it, but I would enjoy it occasionally, talking to another adult, even my mother, just to get away, because I know it does me a world of good. Actually I could have all the freedom in the world, but it's just that I can't get a baby sitter, and of course there's no one in this neighborhood to care. I find it so confining.*

In some instances, however, this sort of dissatisfaction may not be exclusively a function of situational factors (such as the location of the house), but also a symptom of a deeper dissatisfaction with the self, the husband, and the children. This possibility gains a certain amount of plausibility when we note that the mothers who felt most dissatisfied about the restrictions involved in staying home constantly to care for their children tended to be the mothers who did not want the child in the first place. These ratings of satisfaction-dissatisfaction were based on all the mother's comments about the way her life was working out in respect to motherhood and family responsibilities.

However, we must not lose sight of "reality" factors: it will be recalled that the mothers who were displeased over pregnancy were, generally, those who already had another very young child. It is likely that when the new child arrived, these mothers actually were more tied down to child care than the mothers whose other children had grown past the most demanding ages; their dissatisfaction may have been a result of this extra burden rather than of any deeper personality trait. However, when we ruled out this possible reality factor by making the same comparison within subgroups which were homogeneous with respect to the age-gap between children, we found that, regardless of whether the mother had several young children close together or whether the children were fairly widely spaced, the mothers who felt most tied down by their household duties tended to be the ones who were unhappy over pregnancy.

We have the impression that in some instances a woman's conflict over accepting the mother role stemmed from a continuing interest in being "glamorous," rather than from any desire for a career. Some young mothers, especially the unusually pretty ones, look back nostalgically to their dating days, when they were admired and sought after. Dating was their field of conquest. During the first year or two of marriage, it is still possible to keep some elements of these glamorous days alive—the young wife can go dancing with her husband and other young couples; she can shop for pretty clothes and go out often enough to be seen in them. But after the arrival of children, it is more and more difficult to maintain this kind of social life, and a woman to whom it has been especially important finds her new life dull by contrast. Eventually, of course, strong interests in home and children, and perhaps community activities, can emerge to take the place of the old interests, but the transitional years are sometimes rocky.

WARMTH AND AFFECTION

So far we have considered the attitude of the mothers toward their pregnancy. How much did these pre-existing attitudes of pleasure or displeasure carry over after the child was born? A number of mothers said that while they had not been entirely pleased when they first discovered they were pregnant, they changed their minds later on. Indeed, in answer to this question—"Looking back on it now, do you think things would have worked out better for you if you had waited longer to have (child's name)?"—only 4 per cent said they felt it would have been better to wait, although about a fourth had felt doubtful, at the beginning of the pregnancy, whether this was an auspicious time for a new baby. Consciously, at least, very few mothers seem to have carried over their early doubts into the period after the child was born.

We must examine now, however, some of the less tangible feelings reported by the mothers, feelings about the child as a living member of the family, not as merely a potential member. As was mentioned earlier, two judgments were made concerning the warmth of the mother's affectional relationship with her child. One was relative to her warmth when the child was still an infant; the second was relative to her warmth toward the child at the time of the interview, when the child had reached kindergarten age. Each of these judgments was based on a good deal of material in the interview—on the mother's spontaneous comments, as well as upon her answers to specific questions which were designed to reveal information about her warmth. Perhaps the best way of defining these scales is to give illustrations of the kinds of replies rated "warm" and "cold."

Following is an example of a case which was rated warm (during infancy):

> I. *Do you think babies are fun to take care of when they're very little, or do you think they are more interesting when they grow older?*
> M. *I don't know. I love little babies. I love to do with little babies. I love to teach them things. I think it's a feather in your cap to see a little baby be able to do something and know that you taught them that, but at the same time, I think they are interesting when they grow up, too. I found them interesting all the way along. I just love kids.*

In a sense, this mother regarded her dealing with babies as an opportunity to demonstrate her own skill in child training to outside observers; whatever her motivation, the net result was a high level of warm and affectionate interaction. A number of mothers mentioned that their babies seemed like little dolls, little toys, and spoke of their pleasure in dressing them up in dainty clothes

—another example, perhaps, of a feeling for the child that had implications for the mother's self-esteem.

A more child-centered comment is the following:

M. *She was in the crib in the same room with me.*
I. *How did that work out?*
M. *Wonderful. I was right near her, and I could sort of sense her movements at night. I was a very light sleeper and when my children were small—I don't know—every little move they made I wanted to see what it was. I used to pick her up, and I would have a good time with her; I would cuddle her. She was so lovable.*
I. *Do you think that babies are fun to take care of when they're very little, or do you think they're more interesting when they're older?*
M. *Well, to tell the truth, I got a kick out of my children from the minute they were born until today. They do something different every day it seems.*

These cases may be contrasted with that of a mother who was rated near the "cold" end of the scale; she reported:

M. *Well, if I had been well and a little younger, I might have enjoyed him, but I will say frankly that it was just a hard job for me.*

Another mother, given a similar rating, was younger; in describing her experience with her first baby, she said in response to the question:

I. *Would you think back to when he was a baby. Who took care of him mostly then?*
M. *My mother.*
I. *How did that happen?*
M. *We lived with her. I didn't know anything about babies, and he just made me nervous and upset every time he cried.*
I. *Do you think babies are more fun to take care of when they are little, or do you think they are more interesting when they grow older?*
M. *I don't like them too little.*
I. *What was it that bothered you about it?*
M. *I never handled a baby before I had him. Never, not that small.*

Still another mother explicitly described herself as being not responsive emotionally with young infants:

I. *How about when he was younger, did you sing to him and cuddle him and that sort of thing?*
M. *No, I didn't. I'm very lacking in that sort of a thing. I am not an affectionate type of mother. I'd pick him up and read to him but not to sing. I didn't give him that attention where some of the other mothers would.*

I. *Do you think that babies are fun to take care of when they're very little, or do you think they're more interesting when they're older?*
M. *They're more interesting as they get older. Up until they're up to six months old, they're just a routine to take care of them.*

When the child is older, the same contrasts may be found between mothers who are and are not affectionally warm and demonstrative. Following is an example of what we have considered high affectional warmth (during childhood):

I. *I am wondering if you could tell me a little more about how you and Jane get along together—what sort of things do you enjoy with her?*
M. *Well, everything—I think it's because she's so sweet and we seem to get along famously.*
I. *If you were telling somebody about what she's like, what would you say? What do you like about her?*
M. *Everything—how very patient she is, and how understanding. She's very kind. Well, if I'm talking on the phone—sometimes the phone rings continuously here, and especially in the morning when I'm getting her breakfast, she's so good about it, she's so patient; and sometimes I'll tell the people on the phone "I'm getting my daughter's breakfast," and some people seem to ignore the fact that the baby should be taken care of.*
I. *In what ways do you get on each other's nerves?*
M. *We don't.*
I. *Not at all?*
M. *No, I don't think so. I can't think of anything that we do.*
I. *Do you show your affection toward each other quite a bit, or are you fairly reserved people, you and Jane?*
M. *Oh, no, we show our affections—we hug each other, and kiss, and play.*
I. *Do you find time to play with her just for your own pleasure nowadays?*
M. *Yes, I do.*
I. *Tell us about that.*
M. *Well, as soon as my work is done, if she's around, I'll call her and say, "Come on, let's have some fun"; and we'll sit down and she'll sit on my lap, and sometimes I rock her back and forth, and kiss her. She likes to be kissed, she loves it, and I'll cuddle her, and she loves to be cuddled. Or I'll play a game with her.*

Another example of high warmth (during childhood) is seen in the following case:

I. *Could you tell me more about how you and Sally get along together?*
M. *Perfectly, very compatible, much more so than my older child and myself. I like Sally, being with her, she is an awfully nice child, and I*

think maybe it is a little bit because I think she is like her daddy, and I am really head over heels in love with him, and she is so much like him—a little girl, but like him. She looks like him, she acts like him, she even moves like him, and I think that is one reason why we are very compatible, and I am a firm believer in the fact that some mothers and children just—there is nothing wrong with the mother, and there is nothing wrong with the child, but they are not compatible. They just rub each other the wrong way, in some instances; but Sally and I are very happy together.

I. *What sort of things do you enjoy in her?*

M. *Well, I like her sweetness, and the way she speaks, and the way she wants to do something to please, and her interest in things. She is very interested in everything, and of course, very anxious to learn to read, and she will very often get one of her books and read me a story, which is just laughable, but very serious to her, so we listen to it very carefully; and she likes to go and play records for me, and she loves to draw pictures for me, and of course, we make much of that sort of thing— neither one of them can draw worth two cents, but they love to draw. But just as funny as some of these things are, of course, I think they are all wonderful—all of their little accomplishments—and we hang them up on the kitchen wall.*

I. *In what ways do you get on each other's nerves?*

M. *Oh, maybe a day when I don't feel very good, and the things that another day I wouldn't pay attention to become very annoying things on those days. I try to reserve special things for days when I would joyfully sell them to the highest bidder, and I have ironed out a lot of those difficult moments.*

The following two cases present quite a different picture of the emotional relationship between mother and child; both were rated as low in affectional warmth:

A

I. *Have things been easier or pleasanter for you in any way since he's been in school?*
M. *Well, he's away, but the minute he comes home I wish the sessions were longer. While he's in school it's fine, but the minute he steps inside the door, trouble starts. He'll take something his sister is playing with, then the fight starts—oh, an argument starts, or something.*
I. *I'm wondering if you could describe the relationship between you and Bobby—what sort of things do you enjoy in him?*
M. *(Pause) He's naughty an awful lot, but I don't know whether I just take that as part of growing up, but I enjoy him. He talks too much sometimes.*
I. *In what ways do you get on each other's nerves?*
M. *Oh, guns, and the noise in the house get on my nerves most of the time. This constant run, run, run, you know, that shooting business. If I have the baby asleep—she's so finicky, if I do finally get her to sleep during the day—someone starts to cry or something else, and wakes her up, I usually get pretty ruffled. I think he starts to cry for no reason.*
I. *Do you show your affection toward each other quite a bit, or are you fairly reserved?*
M. *No—we—as much as I can. I, as a child, never kissed my parents, but I'll kiss him good night, or kiss him good-bye, something like that, hug him, that's about all. We're not over—not overdo it.*

B

I. *What sort of things do you enjoy in Peter?*
M. *Well, I don't enjoy too many things in him because at the rate he's going, well, he doesn't mind too well; he's got a mind of his own. I don't enjoy too many things. Like sometimes if I want to read or sing to him, he doesn't care to, he doesn't even want to sit down. Sometimes if I want to watch television for a half hour, and rest my brains, he starts annoying me. He doesn't want that, or else he wants me to go to bed with him. So I really don't enjoy too many things that he does because they're not worth enjoying.*
I. *Well, do you show your affection toward each other quite a bit or are you fairly reserved people, you and Peter?*
M. *Well, I don't know whether I show too much affection.*
I. *Do you ever find time to play with Peter just for your own pleasure?*
M. *No, I never do. Once in a blue moon, but he doesn't—he really doesn't care. You know, he'd rather be outside, as I said before, with the other children.*

On the basis of information similar to that quoted here, then, each mother was rated on two separate scales of emotional warmth, one toward the child when he was an infant, and the other toward him as a kindergarten-age child.

We may now turn to a consideration of the kinds of factors which appear to have influenced the mother's warmth toward the child, and particularly to the question raised earlier, concerning how much a mother's attitudes toward becoming pregnant carried over into her feelings for the child after he was born. There was a clear tendency for mothers who were delighted over pregnancy to be warmer to the infant after it was born. The carry-over was somewhat diminished by the time the child was of kindergarten age, however; there was a noticeable relationship between feelings about pregnancy and warmth toward the kindergarten-age child, but it was not highly significant ($p<.02$). Clearly, a good many of the mothers who were doubtful about the desirability of a new child when they first became pregnant talked in the interview as if they had felt a normal amount of maternal warmth toward the child once it was born. And conversely, the mothers who were delighted over pregnancy did not necessarily translate this sentiment into a warm relationship with the child.

We must conclude that, so far as testimony can be gained from these reports and our ratings of them, a mother's attitude toward her pregnancy forecasts slightly—but only slightly—the warmth she will show toward her child after he is born. The forecast is even poorer for her warmth five years later. As to the relation between warmth in the child's infancy and in his later childhood, the forecast is a little better. The correlation between these two scales was .36 ($p<.01$, see Appendix Table D:3).

1. Composition of family

Ordinal position and sex. We have already seen that mothers were more often delighted over their first pregnancy than later ones. This feeling, however, does not seem to have carried over past the child's birth. On the average, mothers were just as warm toward their second or third child (both in infancy and childhood) as they were toward their first child. The sex of the child made a slight difference in the mother's attitude when the child was still a baby—mothers seem to have been a bit more *affec-*

tionately demonstrative with baby girls than with baby boys ($p = .05$), but boys and girls were treated equally warmly by the time they reached kindergarten age.

Distance between children. It was shown earlier that the mother was less likely to be pleased about a new pregnancy if she had another child who was still very young. This attitude seems to have carried over after the new child was born. Mothers were warmest toward a new child when there was a sizable age-gap between this child and the next-older sibling. Moreover, this was true both in the child's infancy ($p = .02$) and when he was kindergarten age ($p = .02$).

Again we are reminded of "reality" factors. A number of mothers commented on the difficulties of caring for two very small babies. It would not be surprising if a mother who still had a quite tiny child was able to devote less time to the new baby than was a mother with run-about children. One can imagine she might also be more generally harassed and hence less affectionate.

However, there is another factor, perhaps less tangible, that may be worth considering, too. There has been much emphasis in the literature on child development on the strength of the child's attachment to the mother during his first two or three years of life; less attention has been paid to the reciprocal of the child's feelings—the mother's strong protective attachment to the young child. This maternal "dependency" on the child must be gradually resolved, just as the child's dependency on the mother must be modified during his later childhood. A two-year-old child obviously has difficulty in adjusting himself to the dilution of the relationship with his mother which is necessarily implied in the birth of a new sibling, but it is also difficult for the mother to make this adjustment to the new child during the period when the nurturant relationship to the older child is still at its height.

Sex of existing children. We saw also, in the earlier section, that a woman's attitude toward a new pregnancy depended somewhat upon whether she already had boys or girls in her family—that mothers who already had girls were more enthusiastic about having another baby than were those who had boys, while mothers who already had both sexes were least pleased of all.

This situation reflected itself in an interesting fashion once the new child was born. When it was a boy, the mother's warmth toward him appeared to depend somewhat on the sex of her existing children. If she already had boys only, she was relatively cold toward the new baby boy ($p<.01$, see Appendix Table D:2). If the new baby was a girl, however, the sex of the older children made little or no difference in the mother's attitude toward it; she was just as warm toward the baby whether she already had boys or girls or both sexes. The same thing was true when the new child had reached kindergarten age ($p<.01$).

These facts are difficult to interpret. They certainly highlight the plight of the little boy who has one or more older brothers, and no older sisters. A sizable proportion of boys in this position appear to have been treated cooly by their mothers, both in infancy and at kindergarten age. We have no information from our interviews that suggests the reason for this, but one cannot help being reminded of the mother-son relationship described by Freud as the Oedipus situation. Freud placed his descriptive emphasis on the boy's attachment to his mother. One might equally well expect, on theoretical grounds, that a mother would develop a particularly strong attachment to her son. If she has an existing tie with the older boy, possibly she finds it difficult to disrupt this relationship for the sake of a new son, while a new daughter demands from her a different kind of relationship, one which does not appear to compete so directly with the existing ties. In any case, whatever the reason, it is evident that, for boys, the existing family structure did influence the warmth of the relationship with the mothers.

Mother's age. The age of the mother at the time the child was born seems to have had little bearing on her warmth, either in infancy or later, *if the child was her first.* However, for *later* children, older mothers were somewhat warmer than younger ones ($p<.05$). This held true regardless of social class, sex of child, or the size of the age-gap between this child and the next-older one.

Perhaps this is not too surprising. A mother who was thirty-two years or younger at the time of the interview would have been twenty-seven or less when this particular child was born. If this was a second or third child, she must have begun her child-bearing relatively early. Possibly, in our society, the advent of two or more children while the mother is so young imposes responsibilities too rapidly, requiring an emotional maturity the young mother does not yet fully possess. Also, when children arrive so early, the parents usually have not been married long, and the young woman is forced to make her adjustments to marriage and motherhood simultaneously. In any case, it is strikingly clear that the older a mother was, the warmer she was toward her child, except when the child was a first one.

2. Personal adjustment

Earlier it was pointed out that the mother's attitude on becoming pregnant was related to her esteem for her husband, to her self-esteem, and to her satisfaction with her life situation. Did these factors carry over into the mother-child relationship once the child was born? In general, yes. The mother's self-esteem was an important correlate of her ability to feel and express warmth toward the child, especially when he had reached kindergarten age.

A similar relationship held true with respect to her esteem for her husband. On the average, those mothers who held their husbands in high esteem were much warmer in their relationships to their children than were those who felt less enthusiasm and respect for their husbands. The relationship was stronger when the child was kindergarten age $(p<.01)$ than when it was an infant $(p<.05)$. Likewise, her warmth was greater when she had a high degree of satisfaction with her current life situation.

These findings, like those reported earlier in connection with the mother's attitude toward becoming pregnant, bring forcibly to mind the possibility that all these variables are simply different facets of a single personality quality in the mother. The intercorrelations among the six rating scales are not high, but they are all positive in the sense that they indicate a relationship between warmth, liking, enthusiasm, and acceptance for the self, the husband, the current situation, the pregnancy, the infant and the child (see Appendix Table D:3).

We have verified this interpretation by a factor analysis of 44 of the main child-rearing scales used in this study. Factor analysis is a statistical device by which one can discover the nature of the larger and more pervasive "traits" that underlie the separate measures obtained from the rating scales. When a so-called "factor" is isolated, the analysis enables one to say which scales contribute to its measurement. In other words, a factor is some quality in the personality that is measured fallibly by several different scales. One can get a notion of what the factor—or trait —is by looking at the scales that measure different aspects of it.

In the present factor analysis, performed by G. A. Milton (1957), seven factors were isolated. We have given names to them as follows:

Factor A: Permissiveness-strictness
Factor B: General family adjustment
Factor C: Warmth of mother-child relationship
Factor D: Responsible child-training orientation
Factor E: Aggressiveness and punitiveness
Factor F: Perception of husband
Factor G: Orientation toward child's physical well-being

The only way in which names can be given to factors is by looking at the rating scales that correlate the highest with each factor. A list of all 44 scales that were factor-analyzed is given in Appendix Table D:4, together with the correlation of each scale with each factor. The reader can judge for himself whether our factor names are well chosen; they were suggested to us by the names of the scales that correlated .30 or higher in each instance. These factors will be discussed at some length in Chapter Thirteen. For the present, it is sufficient to point out that the cluster of scales we have been discussing in the present chapter are largely those which compose Factor B (General family adjustment).

In stating this interpretation, we must raise one caution signal, however. We have assumed that what the mothers told us of their feelings and attitudes was accurate in its essentials, that the dimensions we measured were reasonably stable qualities of the mothers' personalities. Thus, when we found that all the "positive" qualities were associated with one another, we concluded that our six rating scales were measuring different facets of one stable quality.

Another assumption is possible, of course. We might interpret these positive intercorrelations as the reflection of a *response set* that existed only, or mainly, at the time the mother was interviewed. The interview was only two hours long; it occurred entirely within one afternoon or evening; it was done by one interviewer. We do not know what kind of report a mother might have given had the interview been done by someone else on some other day, nor do we know what other facts might have come to light if it had been longer and had been spread over several sessions. We know from experience with psychotherapeutic interviews, for example, that almost any mother has a tendency to defend herself somewhat, both in her own eyes and the eyes of the interviewer. We know, too, that this tendency is strongest in the first few interviews she gives. It is entirely possible that some of the consistency we found among the "positive" qualities was a product of some of these relatively temporary influences.

Too little is presently known about the factors that affect the validity of reports, in this kind of interview, to permit us to choose arbitrarily between the two possible assumptions. Our best judgment is that both are correct in some degree—the interviews do reflect some temporary response set and they do reveal stable personality qualities. However, we will show in a later chapter that there is little correlation among the different types of "complaints" mothers make about their children, which suggests that there was not much momentary response set involving satisfaction or dissatisfaction with the child. Likewise, the changes in the mothers' attitudes from before to after the child's birth, as reported in the present chapter, also seem to reflect a minimal influence of immediate interviewing factors. So we are inclined to place a fairly heavy bet on the validity of our interpretations, which assume the interviews to be reflecting stable qualities with some accuracy.

COMMENT

These various findings provide a little of the home and personality background of the mothers whose specific child-rearing practices we will describe in the other chapters. Some of the facts reported need little comment. No one will have been surprised to learn that the majority of these mothers were glad to find themselves pregnant. Half described themselves as frankly delighted. By the time the child arrived, even those who had had rather mixed feelings were content, and only 4 per cent acknowledged that at that point they still felt the timing was unfortunate.

It is scarcely unexpected, either, that those mothers who had babies crowding rapidly one after another were less happy about becoming pregnant again than were those mothers whose babies were spaced out at a more leisurely pace.

There are three points that do deserve comment, however, for our conclusions with respect to them run counter to some rather widely held beliefs. The first has to do with the problem of women's working and its relation to feelings about motherhood. Except for a very small number of women who were enthusiastically attached to their out-of-home jobs, the prospective advent of a child did not appear to bring about a significant amount of role conflict. Nearly all of the mothers had worked, at least before marriage, and they had experience from which to judge their own relative satisfactions in the two roles of outside worker and of mother. Rather surprisingly, there seemed to be a correspondence between a woman's enjoyment of both; those who were indifferent toward their jobs expressed little delight in the anticipation of motherhood, either.

A similar pattern is suggested by other attitudes that were found to be correlated with pleasure at becoming pregnant and with affectional warmth toward the child both in infancy and later. In the main, high enthusiasm and great warmth were associated with high self-esteem, a high evaluation of the husband, and a general satisfaction with the current family and life situation.

If the conflict between wanting to work and wanting to be a mother does not seem to account for dissatisfaction with motherhood and coldness toward children, what does? There is no way to tell, from the present data, how much of the dissatisfaction felt by some mothers was caused by outside factors and how much by some deep-lying quality of their own personalities. Doubtless both contributed, and to a different degree in different mothers. Quite intolerable living arrangements or a seriously ineffectual husband could destroy the self-esteem and capacity for expressing affection warmly in even the stablest woman. Contrariwise, insecurities arising from long-standing personality difficulties in the woman herself could give her a jaundiced view of all her surroundings, and leave her with little capacity for expressing love to her children.

A second finding that challenges a common notion relates to

the age of the mother. There appears to be a rather common supposition that young mothers have more energy and are more flexible and tolerant and affectionate toward their children. Older mothers are presumed to be more easily fatigued and not able to express love so easily when they have young children. As we have seen, there is no evidence to support this belief, except possibly with respect to *warmth in infancy* toward *first* children only. All the other measures show that, if there is any relationship at all between age and warmth of affection, the older mothers are a little the warmer.

Finally, our data cast doubt on the modern myth of *compensation* among emotional reactions. The doubt stems from the nature of the interaction among the various factors correlated with warmth and personality adjustment. There is no indication of a widespread tendency in this group of mothers to compensate for one unsatisfactory state of affairs by securing high satisfaction in another. Wives with low respect for their husbands did not express high warmth toward their children, nor did low self-esteem find compensation in high evaluation of the husband. There may well have been some few instances in which such a mechanism was operating, but there is no indication that it was the usual or customary way of reacting to a source of dissatisfaction. We must repeat here the caution we have expressed earlier, namely, that some of this appearance of noncompensatory feelings may have resulted from a response set created by the interview itself. Even so, our doubt of the general occurrence of the mechanism seems fully justified.

CHAPTER THREE

Feeding

The human infant has few built-in techniques for adapting to his environment, but he does have the obvious one that links him so distinctively to the rest of the mammals. He gets food by suckling at his mother's breast—or, on occasion, some substitute therefore. While this initial dependence is highly efficient from a biological standpoint, it poses a problem in socialization. Sucking cannot go on forever. Ultimately the child must become independent; he must put liquid food into second place and learn to like solid foods; he must relinquish his sucking technique and gain the skills for eating and drinking in the manner of adults. This change is a tax on both the child and the mother, for the nursing-feeding relationship has social and emotional implications for both of them that go quite beyond the learning or teaching of a new skill to replace an old. The shift from creeping to walking, for example, appears to have none of the emotional hazards of weaning.

The mechanics of infant eating are simple. A baby is endowed with a sucking reflex that is excited by the touch of any blunt object (nipple, finger, thermometer tube) on the cheek or lips. The typical response is turning the head toward the object, opening the lips in a flaring and receptive manner, and starting to suck when the object is thrust deep into the mouth. A newborn baby may take a few minutes to get well started, but once a little milk has trickled into his throat, and the swallowing reflex has

been activated, he quickly gets the hang of it. Practice helps, even with such a reflex as this, and a mother is likely to notice an increasing skill for a few days at least. Even over a longer time she will feel the developing strength of sucking pressure that comes with practice at this hard work. As the baby's control of his neck muscles improves, he becomes more and more efficient at getting into place and finding the nipple for himself. A hungry six-months-old baby nuzzling for the breast looks like a truly skilled performer.

Since the baby has this marvellously efficient reflex, nearly all mothers use it for getting food into him. Whether the food comes from breast or bottle, he is picked up and held fifteen to thirty minutes at a time, several times a day, from the beginning of his life. Each time he sucks and sucks. And each time his activity is rewarded by the filling of his empty, aching stomach. As a result, the sucking response becomes a deeply ingrained habit, and there seems to develop a desire to suck that is somewhat independent of the desire for food. Witness thumb-sucking. More, the child also learns that his mother is an intimate part of this activity. The sight, sound, smell, and feel of her become associated with high gratification. He not only expects her to come when he is hungry, but learns to *need* her in the same sense that he needs the food she brings. In the end, of course, he learns to bring her when he wants her—by crying or calling or rattling his crib.

It is this *wanting* the mother that creates difficulty in the training process. When she tries to change the child's method of getting food, she is not only interfering with a strong habit; she is also upsetting the love relationship that has developed between them. Feeding and being loved are mixed up together from the very beginning, and interference with either is likely to cause difficulty with the other. Mothers have often noted the almost automatic way in which a young child will pop his thumb into his mouth when strangers come at him, or his mother leaves him alone, or another child runs off and leaves him. The sucking looks to be a solace for the lack of love. Likewise common are observations of children's whining and seeking extra love and attention when mothers try to change the feeding schedule or diet. This connection between feeding and the need for affectionate interaction with the mother will be considered further in

the chapter on dependency. It is mentioned here only to emphasize the fact that changing the child's eating habits involves
more serious matters than the mere manipulative techniques by
which he gets food into himself.

There are several issues to be considered. In spite of the ready-
made biology of the mother-child relationship, the first question
a mother has to ask, in Western society, is whether or not to
breast-feed her child. This is no new issue. Among the artifacts
of early Egyptian civilization are a variety of devices for artificial
feeding. They range from objects that look like syringe bulbs to
miniature teapots with a spout. Evidently even that long ago
mothers were already seeking substitutes for themselves, but for
what reason we do not know. Today, in the United States, breast
feeding is so far from automatic that a quite fashionable pro-
breast feeding cult has been formed, as if to resurrect a lost art.

A second question to be answered is when and how often to
feed—what kind of a schedule to follow. Babies begin life with
a built-in cycle of activity that is closely related to their hunger
cycle. The variations among babies are great, however, some having a cycle that reaches a maximum peak of activity as frequently
as every two-and-a-half hours, while others go as long as five hours
between peaks. The length of time between these activity or
hunger peaks is not completely regular for any child, and a baby
who has an average cycle of three hours may have some intervals
as brief as two and as long as four hours. So far as babies are concerned, there is no standard answer to the question of when to
feed.

During the latter part of the nineteenth century, however,
medical science took a turn that led to an answer, albeit a curious
one. Biology and chemistry jointly attacked the problem of
human nutrition and discovered some interesting possibilities in
respect to improving the diet of infants. Artificial feeding had
previously made use of cow's or goat's milk, but now new sub-
stances were found that could be added to milk to make it a more
suitable food. Human mothers could not manufacture these new
formulae, so there was a great increase in bottle feeding.

Someone had to make a decision as to when and how often to
feed the baby. The scientific approach to medical problems had
already won wide esteem for its successes in other areas. It was
natural to seek a scientific answer. At the turn of the century,

however, there was no science of man's behavior, so far as most pediatricians knew, and so a decision had to be made on the basis of a general point of view. The child's innards were looked upon as a fine machine for taking in fuel and converting it to useful purposes. A good machine works best when fuel is introduced at a regular rate. As nearly as one can recapture the spirit of the times, this must have been the beginning of scheduled feeding. Not that there were no controversies; three and four both divide evenly into twenty-four, and so there was argument here and there about the relative merits of the three- and four-hour schedules. But for the next half century a great many American children suffered the peculiar frustration of being fed not when they wanted to be, or when they needed food, but when the alarm clock said it was time.

The realization that scheduling was an unnecessary and often painful procedure has only recently been brought home to mothers by their pediatricians, by popular-priced books, and by other sources of child-rearing advice. The mothers whom we interviewed belonged to a transition generation, in this respect, and they were still making decisions about how rigidly to schedule. Cultural lag doubtless will insure confusion on this matter for many more years.

A third problem is that of weaning. The term *weaning* has been used in two ways, quite indiscriminately, and perhaps this fact serves to illustrate the close connection between early feeding and early loving or nurturing. Weaning sometimes is used to refer to the shift from breast feeding to bottle feeding, as if the nature of the object sucked upon were the crucial factor in the child's experience. Perhaps under some circumstances it is, especially if the initial period is entirely one of breast feeding and the change is to a regime of solely bottle feeding by means of bottle-propping. Such a shift not only changes the object of sucking, but destroys the accompaniment of feeding—being held in the mother's arms. The widespread use of supplementary bottles early in the infant's life, however, and the mother's common practice of holding the baby in her arms while giving him a bottle, have made the process of shift from breast to bottle more a matter of gradually changing proportion than of a sharply defined shift of object. The more common contemporary use of *weaning*, which we will follow hereafter, specifies the time when sucking is relinquished and a new mode of getting food is adopted. This usage seems to describe a more meaningful event in the experience of the child, for the final withdrawal of bottle and breast—of any opportunity to feed by sucking—more clearly denotes the end of a way of life. The old habits must be replaced by the new: loving nurturance is no longer the inevitable accompaniment of eating; the suckling becomes a child.

Weaning involves five main things. The child must learn *not to want* to get his food by sucking. He must learn *to like to drink* the same food he formerly got by sucking. He must learn *to want solid foods*. He must learn the *manipulative skills* required for eating them—biting, chewing, and the use of fingers and utensils, as well as drinking from a cup. He must learn *to do without being held* while he is eating.

There are an inordinate number of ways in which these tasks can be presented to him. One possible variation of the process is with respect to the amount of preparation given for each step. New foods can be thrust on him all at once, or he can begin having a variety of taste experiences almost from birth. He can be forced to learn to chew at the moment the bottle is permanently withheld, or he can have a long period of overlap between the two types of eating. He can be put in a supportive chair for his feeding on the first occasion of getting milk out of a cup, or he can have had long experience with each of these procedures separately beforehand. The degree of frustration in weaning depends on, among other things, the amount of preparation the child has had for his new tasks: the more tastes and skills he has that are applicable to the new requirements of life, the less difficult the transition will be.

Different societies have different customs of weaning. Some are exceedingly severe, providing no advance preparation and using vigorous punishment to stop the old sucking habit. Others are very mild, permitting sucking to continue as long as the child wishes, and offering years of experience with chewing and biting before full reliance is placed on these methods. There is equally great variation in the age at which weaning is begun, and in the period of time allowed for its completion.

Since there has not been adequate information about the child-rearing practices of either American or other civilized societies, we cannot say for certain how they compare with the preliterate societies studied by Whiting and Child (1953). We do know that the modal *advice* given by the most widely read books on child rearing suggests an age for weaning that is earlier than the *actual* age of weaning of all but 4 of Whiting and Child's 75 preliterate societies. We know, also, that the recommended severity of weaning (at least in recent years) is less than the average severity actually occurring in those societies.

The final step in the socialization of eating is the introduction of new foods. A satisfied expectation can be a powerful source of joy; an unfulfilled one can give no end of grief. If new food tastes or textures are introduced at mealtime, when milk is expected, they interfere with expectation. Most children will make a face, roll the new stuff around, and more than likely spit it out. These are not happy first reactions, but there is no way to avoid a few surprises. Eventually a child will learn to expect new foods and will tolerate them as necessary evils. One has only to look at the conservatism of adults, however, to realize that new foods are rarely received with enthusiasm. Immigrants often maintain the food habits and preferences of their native land long after they have adopted their new country's mode of dress, habits of work, and even marriage customs. The young child does not have the option of sticking to his preferred foods, of course, and hence must express his dissatisfaction, if any, by milder and more attenuated means. He may be finicky about a few foods, or adopt a posture of having no appetite, or simply be a food-lawyer—"I'll eat it, if . . . ." or, "You said I wouldn't have to eat two spoonfuls!" or, "Daddy didn't eat his!"

From a mother's standpoint, then, there appear to be four areas of decision and policy-making in connection with the feeding of her child. She must decide whether or not to breast-feed him; she must work out a schedule; she must select a time and method for weaning him; she must introduce him to new foods and new methods of eating.

If we view these rearing problems in the framework of our present study, we can ask first of all what the mothers actually did do. How many breast-fed their babies? How many used a self-demand schedule? When and how did they start the weaning process? We can also examine the reports, in accord with the second type of question raised in Chapter One, to discover what effects different practices appear to have had on the children.

Did one policy produce more feeding problems than another? Was weaning easier on the child when it was started early rather than late? Finally, we can ask the third type of question, that is, what were some of the other maternal personality characteristics that were associated with the mothers' choices of feeding methods. What kinds of mothers chose breast feeding?

We do not have an equal abundance of information on all these questions. The interviews were designed to find out *what the mothers did;* we have substantially less information about the other two kinds of question, which had to do with the effects of these practices on the children, and with the deeper aspects of the mothers' personalities that were correlated with their choices of child-rearing practices. In terms of the schema presented in Chapter Two (page 31), our main concern will be with the feeding practices which belong in column II, and in the relations between these and the behavior of the children (column III). So far as the relations *among* the column II factors are concerned, we will examine only those that seem to have some theoretical or practical significance.

BREAST FEEDING

First and most simply we may ask how many of the mothers decided to breast-feed their children and for how long they did it. The figures are given in Table III:1.

Only about two fifths of the children were breast-fed, the large

TABLE III:1

HOW MANY MOTHERS BREAST-FED THEIR CHILD, AND
for How Long

Breast-fed:		
For less than 1 month	12%	
1 month–2.9 months	12	
3 months–4.9 months	7	
5 months–6.9 months	5	
7 months–8.9 months	2	
9 months or more	1	
	——	39%
Not breast-fed		60
Not ascertained whether breast-fed		1
Total		100%

majority for less than three months. Since feeding a baby at the breast is a very ordinary and normal procedure, biologically speaking, we can only conclude that there must have been some compelling reasons for the use of bottles. We asked what they were, and the mothers gave quite a wide range of answers. The most common reasons are listed in Table III:2, with excerpts from a few interviews to make clearer the mothers' attitudes.

TABLE III:2

REASONS FOR NOT BREAST FEEDING

Mother's Explanation	Mothers Not Breast Feeding	All Mothers
Unable to breast-feed for physical reasons (not enough milk, inverted nipple, etc.)	43%	26%

> **M.** *I had trouble when I was in the hospital. I had an abscessed breast. I started nursing my oldest one, and I was in the hospital for three weeks with complications, so I never did it again.*

Doctor advised against it, not specifically because of physical difficulty	16	10

A

> **M.** *The doctor thought I was a bit nervous and that the formula would be better.*

B

> **M.** *I used the bottle mainly because my doctor thought it would be better for me. He thought where I had the oldest boy, I really wouldn't have time to sit down.*

C

> **M.** *I think I was rushed too much at the hospital. It was the time of the shortage of nurses, and it was very difficult then—they finally decided that I should give up the idea.*
> **I.** *Did your doctor advise that?*
> **M.** *Yes.*

Mother did not want to breast-feed: some indication of emotional barrier	11	7

(continued)

TABLE III:2 (*continued*)

REASONS FOR NOT BREAST FEEDING

A

M. *The doctor asked me about it, and, oh, I don't know, I just decided that I would rather have the bottle for the baby. I don't know why; one of those little things I guess; nothing in particular. It just seemed like a good idea.*

B

I. *How did you decide to use the bottle?*
M. *I don't really know. To tell you the truth, I think I felt a little awkward about the feeding. I knew I knew nothing about it. I was afraid I wouldn't do it right. There were no real reasons but maybe a little fear in the back of my mind. I never really thought about it too much, but I think I had it in the back of my mind that I just didn't want to somehow.*

C

M. *I didn't want to feed him any other way* (than the bottle), *and I felt that breast feeding was done in privacy or within your own home, not in front of anyone, and you could never tell when anyone might walk in unexpectedly. I guess I am pretty modest in that respect, but I didn't want anyone to see me. I could have if I wanted to.*

Mother did not want to breast-feed: did not want to be tied down, too busy, formula more convenient in routine, etc.	12	7

I. *How did you decide to use the bottle?*
M. *I wanted to. I think it's much better.*
I. *What did you feel was better about it?*
M. *You can have your freedom.*

Mother did not want to breast-feed; no reason given	12	7
Baby ill (premature, needed special food, etc.)	4	2
Family pressures against breast feeding	2	1
Total	100%	60%

A few of these reasons refer to factors that were obviously outside the mothers' control, e.g., an ill or premature baby. Others reflect the desire of some mothers to live a less confined life, or perhaps a less child-oriented life, than breast feeding would require. But surprisingly enough, the commonest reason of all was that the mother was *physically unable* to nurse her baby. Twenty-six per cent of the whole group gave this reason. If it were literally true that a quarter of these women were biologically inadequate in respect to nursing, we might well tremble for the future of the human race, or at least for the American part of it. In primitive societies, where bottles and other artificial feeding aids are largely unknown, there are occasional cases of difficulty in which a wet nurse must be found, but ordinarily most mothers are able to nurse.

Why did our American mothers have so much difficulty fulfilling a natural biological function? Possibly the attempt to nurse was given up too soon, in some cases, as when the pressure of hospital routine seemed to discourage breast feeding. In other instances, a supplementary bottle was given by the hospital staff, and since it is easier for a child to get milk from a bottle than from the breast, supplementary bottles at an early stage may have developed sucking responses which were not strong enough for breast feeding.

One other source of difficulty must be considered, however. For some mothers, the alleged "inability" to nurse may have been a reflection of an underlying dislike for doing so. Indeed, 11 per cent of those in the non-breast-feeding group openly expressed emotional reactions against this method of feeding. However, by no means everyone who feels such a dislike can express it as frankly as these 11 per cent did. If the emotion is one that seems a little bit unworthy, or shameful, to the mother, she may not be able to acknowledge it even to herself, much less discuss it with her physician. In such case, her dislike for the action that arouses the emotion may be translated into an "inability" to perform the action. But obviously, if the action is one she feels she *ought* to *want* to perform, she must give herself an acceptable reason for not performing it. Illness or physical inadequacy are commonly accepted as "good" reasons, in American culture. We can ask, then, whether some of the astonishingly large number of mothers who were "unable" to breast-feed their children were thus giving expression to an underlying dislike for nursing a baby.

What kinds of unconscious, or unverbalized, feelings could produce such a dislike? Four have occurred to us. We have tested their possible influence by comparing two subgroups of mothers— those who did breast-feed and those who did not because of physical inability—to determine whether the latter group showed a greater average amount of these feelings.

The first possibility is that the mother had not particularly wanted a child at that time, and when it arrived she felt unconsciously reluctant to devote herself so completely to it. This kind of reaction is occasionally seen by pediatricians and psychotherapists. However, there is no evidence that such "rejection" was a significant factor among the mothers we studied. Just as large a proportion of those who were physically unable to breast-feed were "delighted" at their becoming pregnant as were those who did choose breast feeding.

Another possibility is that those mothers who were judged to be less warm toward the child in infancy might exhibit this quality by avoiding breast feeding. There is no evidence to support this notion, either. The average ratings on warmth in infancy were about the same for the two groups.

Still a third possibility has to do with the mother's feeling of competence to care for the child. We saw in the last chapter that the mothers differed a good deal in the extent to which they felt self-esteem. We know from some of their comments, too, that some of them felt doubtful about their ability to care for the baby properly. However, again we find no general difference between the group of mothers who did breast-feed and the group of mothers who did not breast-feed (because of physical inability).

These negative findings on our first three hypotheses should not be interpreted to mean that feelings of rejection or coldness toward the infant, or lack of self-esteem, never influence the decision about breast feeding. They do, as we know from more detailed studies of some individual mothers. Our figures suggest only that these three factors do not loom large enough in the decision-making of *most* mothers to provide differences in the average performance of a whole group.

The case is quite different with the fourth possibility we tested, however. This relates to the problem of modesty, and the possibly sexual implications of breast feeding. We cited one mother's comments in Table III:2, relating to "emotional barriers," that suggested a feeling of discomfort about displaying herself in this way. We know, too, that in contemporary American society, the breasts have a rather prominent part in sexual symbolism. While feeding a baby at the breast has no intentional sexual meaning, it does involve some degree of exposure. To the mother who has an unusually strong sense of modesty, and is made uncomfortable, or even anxious, by the thought of being exposed, the prospect of breast feeding might seem too upsetting. At the same time, one might expect that such feelings would not be easily discussed, either with the physician or with our interviewer. Hence, the explanation of "physical inability" would be an acceptable and welcome substitute.

TABLE III:3

RELATION OF BREAST FEEDING TO SOME QUALITIES OF CHILD BEHAVIOR

Children Display	Did Not Breast-feed	Breast-fed Less Than Three Months	Breast-fed Three Months or More
"Some," "quite a bit," or "a great deal" of aggression at home	59%	58%	55%
"Considerable" or "high" conscience	24%	24%	27%
"Quite a bit" or "a great deal" of dependency	28%	24%	20%
Moderate to severe feeding problems	40%	34%	41%
Bed-wetting at age five	22%	18%	14%
Strong emotional reaction to toilet training	11%	6%	16%
Number of cases	226	93	56

We had one set of measures of the mother's feelings about sex. These were ratings of the extent to which she was *permissive,* or tolerant, in her control and training of her child with respect to modesty, masturbation, and social sex play. These ratings will be discussed in detail in Chapter Six. It is sufficient for the present question simply to say that by combining these ratings we obtained a measure of what may be called sex permissiveness. A low degree of this quality may be interpreted to mean that the mother had a relatively high feeling of discomfort about sex. Now, when we compare the average rating on this scale assigned to the group of mothers who did breast-feed and the group of mothers who did not breast-feed (because of physical inability), we find that the latter mothers were significantly more anxious (less comfortable) than the former ($p < .02$). We infer from this that breast feeding probably does have some sexual implication for quite a good many mothers, and that those who have a strong sense of modesty, or anxiety about sex in general, may avoid breast feeding.

Effects of breast feeding on the children. In view of the vigorous claims and counterclaims that have been made for breast feeding as an influence on the child's personality, it behooves us to examine the mothers' reports about their children's behavior. It will be recalled that we secured information about a number of child behavior dimensions. Six of these are listed in Table III:3, together with figures that allow a comparison between three kinds of feeding experience: no breast feeding at all, breast feeding for less than three months, and breast feeding for more than three months. A glance at the three figures on each line will show at once that there was no general effect of these early experiences on any of these forms of child behavior. None of the differences between groups is large enough to have statistical significance. Again, we must emphasize, of course, that such group data do not mean that individual youngsters were not influenced, but only that there was no *consistent* effect among *all* the children.

Scheduling vs. Self-demand

A perennial issue in the feeding of infants concerns the regularity with which they should be fed. The alternatives are self-demand feeding, a system in which the child is fed whenever he appears to be hungry, and strict scheduling in which he is fed every three or, more commonly after a few months, every four hours. Under the latter system, if he cries before feeding time, he may be allowed to cry, or may be rocked or otherwise pacified, but is not fed until the clock reaches the appointed hour. Also, when a schedule is strictly adhered to, the baby will be wakened for a feeding if he is still asleep when the time comes. Actually, of course, there are many degrees of scheduling.

Most mothers in the present group used neither the complete self-demand system nor a rigid schedule; they developed a moderately routine way of feeding, and modified the schedule according to the needs of the child. The range of practices is shown in Table III:4.

TABLE III:4

FEEDING SCHEDULE

"There has been a lot of talk about whether it is better to have a regular feeding schedule for a baby, or to feed him whenever he is hungry. How do you feel about this? How did you handle this with Johnny?"	All Mothers
1. Complete self-demand: child always fed when he cried (was hungry). Child permitted to eat as much, and as long, or as little as he wanted at a feeding	12%
2. Schedule set by child himself: fairly regular, but no evidence that mother exerted any pressure to bring this about	17
3. Vague attempts at scheduling, but mother would never wake child for a feeding, and would feed as much as an hour early if it seemed necessary	19
4. Rough schedule, which mother would modify by as much as a half hour if the child seemed hungry	29
5. Fairly rigid schedule, which would not be modified by more than fifteen minutes	14
6. Rigid feeding schedule: child fed by clock, wakened for feedings	8
Not ascertained	1
Total	100%

The following comments illustrate some of the differences in attitudes among the mothers:

A

M. *It is nice to have a schedule if you can keep them on it, but I have never yet had one that stayed on a schedule. It was impossible. In fact, I tried putting B. on a schedule, and I remember very well that I woke him up at ten o'clock one night, and thought, "I will make it every four hours." I tried to wake him up at ten o'clock at night, and it was impossible. You couldn't wake him up, no matter what we did with him; he just slept right on. So we just put him back to bed, and I never tried schedules again. It was just whenever they wanted it, and they worked their own schedules in; so I don't bother with schedules.*

B

M. *I think they should have a feeding schedule, but I do think that if they seem very hungry, you can push it ahead a little; or if he doesn't seem to be, and you're busy, he can wait a little while. I think you should keep to a schedule somewhat.*

I. *How much leeway did you give in the schedule? You say you altered it somewhat.*
M. *Oh, I'd say within a half an hour.*

C

M. *I gave her a bottle at ten o'clock in the morning, and if it was a quarter of two when she cried, I wouldn't give her the bottle until the clock said two o'clock. When the clock would point to two, then she would get the other bottle. Isn't that ridiculous?*

This last mother employed a rigid feeding schedule with that child who is now of kindergarten age, but she no longer advocates this system and has used self-demand with her younger children. Several other mothers reported that while doctors had advised them to use a schedule with their older children, the same doctors had begun to advocate self-demand by the time the younger children were born. This shift is in accord with the general tendency for child-rearing advice to move in the direction of less rigidity and less severity. The excellent section on "Scheduling" in the Tenth Edition of *Infant Care* (1955) is well worth examining in this connection.

We have had only two hypotheses as to the possible personality qualities that might be associated with a mother's decision to use scheduled feeding. It seemed likely that such a choice might go along with a general lack of warmth toward the infant; this proved to be the case ($p < .05$), although the relationship is very slight. More importantly, we suspected that the choice of feeding schedule was more influenced by the pediatrician than by the mother herself. If this were the case, then we also suspected that the mothers with the least confidence in their ability to care for the child correctly would be the ones who would follow pediatric advice most closely. One of our rating scales measured the mothers' child-rearing anxiety, and since a large proportion of the doctors appeared to have been still advising scheduling of feeding in the mid-1940's, we looked for a positive correlation between the *use of scheduling* and the measure of *child-rearing anxiety*. The hypothesis was verified ($p < .01$; $r = .27$).

WEANING

A third area of decision for a mother is when and how to wean her baby. For several weeks after his birth, she will have noticed that he became more and more skillful at sucking. If he was fed at the breast, his strength of sucking increased, and no matter whether he was breast-fed or bottle-fed, his speed increased. At some point, however, his mother began to view this fine performance as changeworthy. She decided to shift him from sucking to drinking.

There are two aspects of this process that can be distinguished for our present purposes. One is the timing of it, the child's age at the beginning of weaning. The other is the severity with which the change is made. We will describe our findings on these matters first, and then discuss their effects on the child's reactions.

Age. Weaning can occur gradually, with frequent reversals, or it can be an all-or-none event. The child can be prepared for it by being given many experiences with a cup or spoon beforehand, or he can be faced with learning completely new skills all at one fell swoop. What we have called the *age at beginning of weaning* is the age of the child when the mother gave evidence of her intention by her first substitution of a cup feeding for a regular bottle feeding.

This maternal intention to wean is all very fine, but more than once in reading these interviews we have been tempted to do a bit of paraphrasing—"Mama proposes, but Baby disposes." Weaning may occur at once—within 24 hours—or it may require quite a number of months. We have defined the *age at completion of weaning* as that time after which the mother never gave the child another opportunity to feed by sucking.

In Table III:5 are shown the percentages of mothers who began weaning at the various ages. These figures must be viewed with some caution, for in many cases, the transition from one mode of feeding to the other was so gradual that the mother herself had difficulty in saying, more than four years later, just when she had first substituted a cup for a regular feeding. Similar caution must be used in judging the figures for the age at completion of weaning, although this point in time seemed to stand out more clearly for some mothers than did the age at the beginning.

TABLE III:5

AGES AT BEGINNING OF AND AT COMPLETION OF
WEANING

Age in Months	At Beginning	At Completion
Under 5	5%	0%
5 to 7.9	30	13
8 to 10.9	30	20
11 to 15.9	23	36
16 to 23.9	5	13
24 or more	1	15
Not ascertained	6	3
Total	100%	100%

Granted that there are definitional ambiguities and errors in recall, however, it is still evident that the mothers varied considerably both as to the time at which they started and the time they took to complete the shift (see Table III:6). About two-thirds of them had started by the time the child was eleven months old. A majority had finished within four months, but there were at least 12 per cent who took a year or more. Since this average duration was brief, in comparison with the wide range of beginning ages, the mothers who began early in the child's life tended to finish early, too. This is shown in line 1 of Table III:7. However, this fact obscures a more important finding. From line 2 of this table, we can see that there was a tendency ($p < .01$; $r = -.18$) for the later starts to be more quickly completed. This suggests that either a child is more "ready" for weaning when he is older, or else mothers exert more pressure on an older child than on a younger one.

The duration of weaning is very dependent on the methods used, however, and these must be considered next.

Methods and severity of weaning. A procedure reported by many mothers was that of introducing a cup in place of a bottle

TABLE III:6

DURATION OF WEANING

Under 24 hours (bottle suddenly taken away, never given again)	12%
1 day–6 days	5
1 week–.9 month	12
1 month–3.9 months	27
4 months–7.9 months	17
8 months–11.9 months	7
12 months–17.9 months	7
18 months–23.9 months	4
24 months or more	1
Not ascertained	8
Total	100%

TABLE III:7

AGE AT BEGINNING OF WEANING: RELATIONSHIP TO TIME OF COMPLETION, TO DURATION OF WEANING, AND TO AMOUNT OF EMOTIONAL UPSET

	AGE AT BEGINNING OF WEANING					
	Under 5 Months	5–7.9 Months	8–10.9 Months	11–15.9 Months	16 Months or Over	p
Mean age at completion of weaning (in months)	9.7	11.9	12.9	16.6	24.9	$< .01$ ($r = .50$)
Mean duration of weaning (in months)	6.3	5.5	3.7	4.3	3.6	$< .01$ ($r = -.18$)
Percentage of children showing some emotional upset at weaning	15%	30%	17%	34%	35%	$< .05$ *
Number of cases	21	112	115	87	21	

* A t-test of the difference between mean ratings for "under 5 months" and "11 months or over" is 2.05.

for the morning, midday, and evening feedings, substituting the cup for only one of these feedings at first, then for two, then for all three meals. But often the child was allowed to have a bottle at bedtime and naptime for some time after the mealtime transition was complete. Many mothers felt this helped the baby to go to sleep easily. Weaning from the last night bottle sometimes occurred when all the bottles were broken—the baby would occasionally throw a bottle out of the crib and break it, until there was only one bottle left. When that was broken, the mother would decide not to buy more, telling the child that the bottles were all gone.

There were many variations, both more and less gentle than this, however. Some children virtually weaned themselves. Some mothers began introducing milk by cup so gradually that the time of starting could hardly be specified. Others, at the opposite extreme, made an arbitrary decision to change to cup feeding on a particular day, and never offered a bottle again.

These various methods can be ranged along a dimension of *severity of weaning*. We classified the interviews according to the gradualness with which the mothers approached the training and the amount of preparation they gave the children. The descriptive categories, which represent six points on a scale ranging from very gentle to very severe, are given in Table III:8, together with some quotations to indicate the attitudes represented.

Frustration and emotional upset

What effects might we expect from these differences in timing and severity? The weaning process, except under the most fortunate circumstances, is bound to be frustrating to the child. He has been accustomed not only to getting his food by sucking, but usually also to being held and cuddled while getting it. He is now forced to use new methods, with all the uncertainty that that implies. Which procedures will cause the least frustration?

Since frustration itself cannot be measured directly, we have had to rely on the child's emotional reactions as an indicator. The mothers described such reactions along with their reports of when and how they had weaned, and we were able to rate 356 of the children on a five-point scale ranging from "1 = no reaction at all" to "5 = severe reaction: cried for extended period and would not drink from cup." Of these 356 children,

TABLE III:8

Severity of Weaning

1. Child weans self; refuses breast or bottle	13%

M. *I had him do it himself. If he wanted a bottle now (age five) I would give it back to him, but he stopped the bottle when he was a-year-and-a-half, and he went on milk himself.*

2. Mother weans gradually; trains in drinking mode before transition; allows child to return to bottle or breast at will	22
3. Mother weans fairly gradually; does not allow child to return to breast or bottle completely at will; applies moderate pressure to get him to change	33

A

M. *The bottle would be filled—I tried pouring a little into a cup, and if she would take it willingly, more was put into it. If she balked at the cup, I tried the bottle again, but I would start off with the cup at each feeding after I decided it was time to begin.*

B

M. *He started to drink from a glass, and pretty soon the bottle disappeared until there was only one night bottle and then no bottle.*

4. Mother weans moderately abruptly; withholds some bottles in spite of protests from the child; may allow one night bottle	14
5. Weans quite abruptly; considerable pressure for transition; allows occasional late bottles	11

M. *I discussed it with the pediatrician—asked him when to start, and he said, "Any time. Don't start doing it gradually, just take the bottle away." I thought that seemed awfully drastic, but I did it his way; only I kind of compromised, and I would give her a bottle once in a while.*

6. Weans very abruptly. Mother does not give in if child wants to suck. No late bottles	5

M. *We started by taking the small glass, and by doing it in one meal. Of course, he objected, but I guess they all do; but I didn't stop. I thought once I went back to the bottle I would be in trouble, so I kept with it. Of course, he didn't drink as much milk at first as he objected to it, but it didn't take very long before he was satisfied, and he was taking the amount of milk he did before. The doctor said to stick to it once you started it and of course I could see the point, too; and we just stuck to it.*

Not ascertained	2
Total	100%

228 were rated at the lowest level of emotional disturbance (1), and only 5 were rated at the highest (5). The remaining 123 children were spread quite evenly among the three middle points on the rating scale. We can use these ratings of *emotional upset* as rough indicators of how severely each child was frustrated by his mother's particular brand of weaning.

According to generally accepted frustration theory, we would expect that the stronger the drive whose responses were frustrated, the stronger the frustration and hence the more vigorous the child's reactions. In the present instance, this principle may be interpreted to mean that the stronger the drive to suck, the more upset the child will be by weaning. If we consider the matter of age, we must ask whether the strength of the sucking drive would differ, in any consistent way, from one age to another. If so, we would expect the amount of upset at weaning to vary in the same way.

This problem of age variations in strength of the oral drive has a history that is well worth examining as a case example of the way in which theories develop. Just after the turn of the century, Sigmund Freud published his *Three Contributions to the Theory of Sex* (1905), in which he described the oral component of the libido. This conception was essentially that of an inborn drive to secure gratification through sucking and other oral stimulation. Freud recognized, though he did not much stress the point, that the strength of the impulse was influenced by the child's experience in sucking at the breast or a bottle. He was writing at a time, however, when students of human behavior were still prepossessed with the nineteenth-century emphasis on the biological sources of behavior. As a result, the inborn and maturational qualities of orality were widely noted while the suggested influence of experience at sucking was ignored. Then, in 1928, David Levy reported his research on thumb-sucking, which he found occurred more frequently in children who had had inadequate opportunities to suck in infancy. This finding, together with others reported by Levy in 1934, seemed to verify the proposition that babies had an inborn oral drive which had to be satisfied, or else it would lead the child to seek artificial gratifications.

A good theory and good data have a curiously mind-locking effect. For two decades, no one appears to have questioned the conclusions implied in the observations and theory of Freud and the experimental studies of Levy. The reasoning seemed straight-forward. If one started with the assumption that there was an oral drive, then the thumb-sucking that followed inadequate food-sucking could be interpreted simply as an alternative technique for getting oral gratification. The further inference was that the longer the oral drive went unsatisfied—that is, the earlier the weaning to cup—the more severe the frustration would be. These interpretations would have led to an expectation, in accordance with frustration theory, that early weaning would produce more emotional upset than late weaning.

Eventually, of course, new theories unlock the barrier imposed by an old theory. Then new data are collected, and old principles can be revised. The new theory that was applied to the problem of the oral drive was that of secondary or learned drives. Freud had long before mentioned that sucking seemed to increase a child's need for oral gratification. Sears and Wise (1950) reasoned that, since sucking in infancy was always followed by primary reward (food), the strength of the drive should increase with more sucking. This would lead to an expectation just contrary to that of the Freud-Levy theory concerning the effects of age on weaning upset. By this new reasoning, the amount of upset would *increase* with the age at which weaning was begun. To test their hypothesis, Sears and Wise secured, from 80 Midwestern mothers, information about age at weaning and child's emotional upset. The latter scale was the same as our present one. They found what they had predicted—the later the weaning, the greater the upset.

To return to our present data: similar results are displayed in line 3 of Table III:7. About twice as many children were rated as having shown "some upset" when weaning was begun after eleven months of age as when it was begun under five months. However, there is a puzzling increase in upset among those children weaned between five and eight months, and then a reduction for those weaned between eight and eleven months.

These results are somewhat similar to those reported by Sears and Wise, who divided their total group into two subgroups, mothers who weaned *before* and those who weaned *after* four months. Reports of emotional upset were much more frequent in the children who were weaned *after* four months (but mainly before eight months). Those two groups correspond roughly to the two earliest-weaned groups described in Table III:7, and the results with respect to emotional upset are similar. In our present data, the reduction of upset among children weaned between eight and eleven months may be an important thing to note, or it may be simply a sampling error. The differences are not large enough to give us great confidence in them.

If we interpret the amount of upset as a measure of strength of frustration, and if we assume that strength of frustration is partly dependent on the strength of the drive frustrated, then one possible interpretation of these findings is that *the oral drive gets stronger with age because sucking is rewarded.*

This conclusion does not conflict with Levy's research findings. All his children had had plenty of opportunity to learn a sucking drive and to strengthen the sucking response. We know that when there is interference with goal-directed activity (sucking for milk, in this case), a child will seek new opportunities to perform the satisfying action (thumb-sucking).

As was mentioned earlier, Whiting (1954) has examined the ethnographic literature with respect to age at weaning. The data presented here show that American mothers are *early weaners,* cross-culturally speaking. Whiting also evaluated the amount of emotional upset shown by children in the other cultures, and came to the conclusion that the relation between age at weaning and amount of upset is curvilinear. The longer weaning is delayed, up to a certain point, the more severe is the upset. He found the most severe reaction occurred in those cultures in which weaning was done between thirteen and eighteen months. But after that time, upset seemed to decrease with age. We could not test this finding with our present data because so few of the mothers in our group waited beyond eighteen months to begin weaning.

It appears, then, that there is some tentative support for our proposition that severity of weaning frustration increases with the age at beginning of weaning. We are presently inclined to interpret this relationship as indicating the effect of longer practice and the development of a stronger oral drive and its accompanying sucking habit. However, we must not overlook the possibility that the relationship may be based on some kind of biological maturation. Conceivably, the drive to suck may increase to about twenty-four months and then decrease, quite without respect to practice. Some children reject the breast or bottle before that age: they wean themselves spontaneously. Perhaps they are early maturers. Whiting's finding of low emotional upset after twenty-four months may reflect a maturational decadence of the sucking drive. On the other hand, among children weaned at an early age, there is no evidence of a continuing desire to suck, and babies who have been fed by cup from birth appear to lose their sucking reflex altogether by the time they are a few months old. We simply do not know what the real reason is for the correlation between age at beginning of weaning and amount of emotional upset.

We can examine next the effects of severity of weaning. Again the theory of learning and action is relevant. Sears and Wise hypothesized that a second factor which should influence the strength of frustration was the extent of preparation a child had for his new experiences and new methods of satisfying his hunger needs. The reasoning was that interference with the old would be less discomforting if the child felt confident of his capacity to perform the new. Sears and Wise obtained reports from their group of 80 mothers concerning the amount of preparation the child had had before actual weaning commenced. Preparation was defined as giving water and orange juice, or even occasional sips of milk, by cup. They found that the greater the preparation, the less the emotional upset.

Our present study yields similar results. The correlation between severity of weaning and amount of upset is .26. It was found that at the most severe end of the scale 48 per cent of the children showed some upset, while only 19 per cent of the children whose mothers were rated at scale-point two (gentle) showed equivalent disturbance. These findings support our hypothesis that the more preparation a child has, and the more gradually his mother makes the shift, the less disturbance he will show. We assume this means that he has suffered less frustration.

It was at this point in the study of our interviews that we discovered a third factor which influenced the amount of upset. Oriented toward learning theory as we were, we should have predicted it in advance. This new factor is the mother's decisiveness in weaning. She can be absolutely adamant about the process, never reversing herself, or she can be very sensitive to the child's expressions of discomfort, and go back to bottles over and over again. These two extremes in training would produce comparable differences in the child's *expectancies*. The former mother would create certainty for the child, while the latter mother would create uncertainty. Her child would be placed in a greater state of conflict about what to expect from her. Since conflict is itself frustrating, we would expect such backing-and-filling by the mother to produce greater upset than a more direct approach to the matter. Likewise, of course, the child whose own fussing produces this maternal indecision would simply learn to fuss more!

This dimension of decisiveness is not to be confused with the preparation and gradualness that provided the bases for the severity ratings, although there is doubtless some relation between them. A very quick weaning, without preparation, would almost have to be "decisive," but a very gradual changeover could be either slow and definite, e.g., one feeding at a time, or involve repeated reversals of feeding policy.

Since we had not anticipated the discovery of this new dimension, the interview contained no direct questions about it, and we had no scale for measuring it. The nearest approach to it in our measures is *duration of weaning*. This correlates —.34 with severity. If duration is a measure of decisiveness, then it seems evident that *there was greater indecisiveness among the most gentle weaners*. We have already seen that gentle weaning was associated with low upset, so this relationship seems initially to cast a doubt on our new hypothesis. However, Table III:9 tells the story. It shows the amount of reported upset in relation to the duration. The relation is curvilinear, with both the "instant: one day" and the "more than four months" groups showing the greatest upset. The effect of duration of weaning was greatest for those children whose weaning began earliest (see Appendix Table D:5).

None of the children who weaned themselves showed any upset. They are not included in the "instant: one day" group, of course, for we are concerned here only with those children whose mothers took the initiative in weaning. We are using the *duration* as an indirect measure of the extent to which the mother prolonged the process, doing so in many instances, perhaps, because of the child's reluctance to make the shift. The relatively high incidence of upset in the one-day weaning group is probably a result of the high severity and lack of preparation that is often implied by such speed. Aside from the one-day group, however, it is the mothers who prolonged weaning the longest whose children were most upset. Again it must be emphasized that this dimension of decisiveness is not the same as abruptness, and for purposes of discussion, there may be some benefit to be gained from referring to the dimension of *indecisiveness*. It is too much of this latter quality that seems to cause upset.

It should be noted that while the age at beginning of weaning, the total duration of weaning, and its severity all seem to have some bearing upon the extent of the child's emotional reaction

TABLE III:9

DURATION OF WEANING: RELATIONSHIP TO CHILD'S EMOTIONAL REACTION

	DURATION OF WEANING				
	Instant (1 day)	2 Days to .9 Month	1–3.9 Months	4–11.9 Months	1 Year or More
Percentage of children showing some emotional upset at weaning	33%	22%	21%	38%	41%
Number of cases	30	60	82	71	41
$p < .01$ $(r = .19)$					

to weaning, these factors do not by any means fully account for weaning difficulties. It appears quite possible that there are inborn differences among babies, having to do with their activity level or the size (or speed of emptying) of their stomachs, which help to determine how well they can adjust to their infant feeding experiences.

According to the mothers' reports, there were some babies who were remarkably "good" from the time they were brought home from the hospital, crying very little, but there were other babies who cried a great deal. In a classical study of newborn infants who were still in the hospital, Aldrich, Sung, and Knop (1945) found that the amount of crying which infants did ranged from 48.2 to 243 minutes of crying in a 24-hour period. The reasons for excessive crying on the part of very young infants may be many, of course, but often the digestive disturbances known as "colic" are responsible. This condition may begin early and appear to be quite independent of the parents' techniques of handling the child.

In the current study, although the mothers were not asked specifically how much their babies cried, most volunteered this information, and it is possible to compare a group of babies who cried a great deal from earliest infancy with a group who seldom or never cried.

We found that mothers whose babies cried a good deal were somewhat gentler in their weaning methods than the mothers of the more placid babies. That is, the mothers of the "crying" babies were given a slightly lower average rating on our "severity of weaning" scale (see Appendix Table D:6), and we have seen that for our sample as a whole, these gentler weaning methods were accompanied by relatively little emotional upset during weaning. But the "fussy" babies, who had cried a great deal from birth, showed a greater-than-average amount of emotional disturbance during weaning, despite the fact that their mothers were especially gentle in weaning them. These facts suggest that some babies are hypersensitive to changes in their feeding patterns, and are likely to be upset during weaning even if their mothers use weaning methods which would produce a smooth and easy transition for other babies.

Summary on weaning

Our findings illustrate the influence of three aspects of a mother's training. If we interpret the child's emotional upset as a measure of how severely frustrated he is by weaning, then we find that longer practice at sucking, more severe methods of forcing the transition, and indecisiveness during the process all lead to frustration. There is evidence also, however, that there are wide individual differences among children in their sensitivity to training.

NEW FOODS AND EATING HABITS

Even before weaning is started, most mothers begin to introduce new foods to the baby. Sometimes these are presented in the form of strained baby food; sometimes the child is allowed to taste part of the parents' meal. By the age of one year, most children have a rather substantial menu, although much of the actual feeding may still be done by the mother. During their second year, children take on more and more of the task of feeding themselves. Many go through a period of weaning their parents! If the mother keeps feeding the child—for the sake of efficiency—he may get thoroughly annoyed and demand his independence.

In this interview, we asked relatively little about these changes, concentrating rather on the restrictions and demands that the mother had expressed in connection with later feeding activities. There is one aspect of the shift to new foods that must be mentioned here, however. Eating new things can be a sign of growing up. Eating what Daddy eats can be an indication of new and higher status, and some youngsters revel in this. But new tastes and new textures are not uniformly attractive to children. If these are presented as substitutes for milk, or other accustomed foods, they may represent a frustration. All through the preschool period, children can show a good deal of variation in their eating reactions, not only to new foods but to those to which they have been accustomed, too. They may go through periods of fussiness about food, rejecting certain things, refusing whole meals, eating slowly and seemingly without appetite.

We inquired about such "feeding problems" in the interview, and found that nearly three fourths of the children had shown some sign of a problem at one time or another. Table III:10 shows the percentages of children rated at each level on the five-point scale.

TABLE III:10

FEEDING PROBLEMS

"Have you had any problems about Johnny's eating enough, or eating the kinds of food he needs?"	All Mothers
1. No feeding problems: child has hearty appetite, eats what is given to him, enjoys food	23%
2. Mild problems: one or two brief incidents. In general, good appetite	32
3. "Finicky" about food. Some loss of appetite, periods not prolonged	28
4. Considerable feeding problems: loss of appetite, many fads in eating	16
5. Severe problems: child would gag or vomit, refuse to eat. Resistance to eating prolonged	1
Not ascertained	0
Total	100%

In the households where the child's eating had become an issue, the mother was often acutely worried lest his health suffer from the absence of certain food elements in his diet. Under the pressure of these worries, she was likely to vacillate in her treatment of the problem. Sometimes she would scold and punish the child for not eating; sometimes she would try to force him to eat; sometimes she would simply take food away and try to wait until he seemed hungry enough to accept food without protest. There were instances of mothers' seeking advice from a whole series of doctors, some of whom advised stern measures while others advised ignoring the problem. A mother may have followed several different methods in turn, but without carrying out any one program consistently or for very long. Here are three examples of the kinds of running battles between mother and child which were reported:

A

M. He likes candy, and cookies, and ice cream, and desserts. He won't touch vegetables. It's terrible trying to get him to eat a vegetable, and he has a habit of taking his food when I'm not looking and putting it in the corner of the chair, so that you don't know it until he's gone, or by accidentally spilling it on the floor. I have cut that out quite a bit. It is down to a minimum now, but there was a time when he would sit there, and he would make all kinds of contortions with his face, and up would come all his food, because he didn't want to eat.

I. What do you do about this now?

M. Nothing. I put it in front of him, and if he doesn't eat it, I take it away. I am cooking, and I am putting it in front of him, and what else can you do?

I. What about if you find this little pile in the chair?

M. I get furious, and he knows I get furious, but it doesn't seem to make much difference to him. There are times when he doesn't eat, and I let him get away without a word, and other times I make him sit there and eat. There are times when he will go a whole week without eating his dinner.

B

M. We still have (problems about eating). We took her down to the doctor's last night about it—she doesn't eat anything. She is a terrible eater. She was good about it until she was about a year-and-a-half and then sort of petered out. The doctor said she would grow out of it, and she did for a while. But now she is back the same way. She is an awful lot of trouble. She won't eat anything. I guess we were doing the wrong thing. If she didn't eat her supper, and let it get cold on her plate, we figured we would give her something to tide her over, and give her more milk and a large dish of ice cream, because she likes ice cream, and we figured it was nourishing and would help her out, but he says no—it is wrong. "If she doesn't eat, don't give her anything until she is hungry." That was last night and now we are giving her a tonic.

C

M. I get after him—I say, "Johnny, eat that," and they say that is the wrong thing to do. They say the more you are after them, the less they want to do it, but of course, I am always afraid that he is not getting enough food, that he is going to get sick, or something like that, but with the milk I never had any trouble. I want to give him too much, and put more on his plate than he can handle, which isn't a good thing either, but I want to be sure that he gets enough, you know. He'll eat what I give him, and if he doesn't—not now so much, but I used to help him—I helped him for a long time. Of course, my husband was upset about it—he said, "Don't do that, because when he is going in the Army, you will have to go along with him and feed him." But I don't believe in that, because I think children are doing some-

thing, and all of a sudden they snap out of it, and they are just on their own—they go right ahead and do things. I help him to finish his food a little, because I feel if I can get the food into him, I don't care how it is, as long as I do.

In most of the families studied, however, eating had not become a subject of as much concern as would be indicated by the above instances. More commonly, the child had gone through periods of mild faddishness or loss of appetite, but the mother had exerted relatively little pressure on him for eating. Here are two examples:

A

M. *After her baby brother was born, she went on a little hunger strike for herself. And she really didn't care whether she ate or not, and I mean she'd take eggnog and soft things, but she wouldn't chew meat or anything like that, which she had been eating. And that lasted for probably about three or four months, but then she gradually went back to eating everything.*
I. *What did you do about it?*
M. *I really didn't do much of anything. I just put the food down for her and if she didn't eat it, I just took it away.*

B

M. *I have had no problems. I think all children have streaks when they eat better than they do at other times. She has always eaten everything in her good time, but of course they all take little streaks when they don't want the salad, and then I say I will let her off with half a portion.*

Why do some children have feeding problems and others not? By a "feeding problem" we mean that the child had shown at least moderate signs of such behavior—fairly prolonged periods of loss of appetite, or worse. Approximately 20 per cent of the children were judged to have shown this much difficulty.

To answer the question, we examined two kinds of child-rearing practices, comparing the frequency of occurrence of problems in subgroups of mothers who reported different degrees of each of the practices (see Appendix Table D:7).

The first set of practices included three that characterized *infant feeding.* Do the methods and conditions of infant feeding have any bearing upon later feeding problems? In general, our answer to this question must be negative. The frequency of occurrence of feeding problems in later childhood was unrelated to:

1. whether the infant was breast-fed,
2. the age of the child when weaning started,
3. whether infant feeding was scheduled or self-demand.

Likewise, there was no relationship to whether the child was emotionally upset over weaning.

But if these feeding problems could not be traced to early weaning and feeding practices, what other factors might have been influential? We searched among the *punishment* scales for two reasons. The first had to do with a physiological matter. Loss of appetite is often associated with such emotional states as fear or anger. So are digestive disturbances. Children who are emotionally upset because of severe punishment, rejection, or severe restrictions often have difficulty eating the kinds and amounts of food their mothers prescribe. This was one reason for examining the possible relation of the punishment measures to the occurrence of feeding problems.

The second reason had to do with another aspect of children's reactions to punishment or rejection. Children are extraordinarily ingenious, at this age, in discovering subtle ways of rebelling against too much domination or punishment. Finickiness about food is a nuisance and an annoyance to mothers, and it would be a dull child who did not know this. Nearly all mothers feel a strong positive value about providing good nourishment for their children. Thus, if a mother is putting a little too much disciplinary pressure on the child, or if she is less loving and affectionate than the child may wish, there is good reason for him to seek methods of expressing his resentment. Because his mother is already being a little touchy about his behavior, he has to be aggressive in ways that are not too obviously so. Otherwise he will simply get into more trouble. If he is already digestively uncomfortable because of his emotional reaction to his mother's attitude, food finickiness or an apparent loss of appetite would be a safe and natural response.

This reasoning makes the child seem very wise, and perhaps a little malevolent. He is not. This interpretation is based on theoretical expectations, not on children's reports of their feelings. But we can discover whether the theory is sound by comparing different groups of children with respect to how many in each group have feeding problems. If the theory is good, we should find more problems in those children who have had more severe toilet training, more severe controls of their aggressive outbursts and their supplications for attention, more physical punishment, and more coldness expressed toward them by their mothers.

When we examined the data from this point of view, we found that feeding problems were *positively related* to:

1. severe toilet training,
2. low permission for expression of aggression toward the parents,
3. negative reaction to dependency (by becoming angry when the child clung or demanded attention unnecessarily),
4. high use of physical punishment,
5. low mother warmth toward the child.

It seems clear that infant-feeding practices have little relationship to later feeding problems, but that coldness, rejection, and a high use of punishment—particularly spanking—do. We had two good reasons for examining these latter factors, but we do not know which—if either—of our theoretical reasons is correct. For the moment we must rest content with the facts of the relationship and hope that some later investigation will clarify the reasons.

A question on method. Before accepting these findings at their face value, we must examine one methodological problem. Since all the measures of both mother and child were derived from the interview, it is possible that either a temporary attitude or a deeper prejudice, on a mother's part, could have produced what is technically known as a "halo effect." This is the tendency to judge another person as all good or all bad. In rating employees, for example, a supervisor may judge an amiable and hard-working man as highly intelligent also, even though objective and independent tests show the man to have mediocre intellectual qualities. A lazy employee may be wrongly rated down in intelligence. In other words, one or two outstanding qualities of the person being rated may influence all the other judgments the rater makes about him. Equally, a critical attitude in the rater may lead him to make generally low evaluations of those around him.

A "halo effect" conceivably could produce the findings presented above. The mothers who were cold toward their children, and punished and restricted them severely, might have had a tendency to define anything their children did as naughty. If so, when a mother was asked whether she had feeding problems with her child, she would have been likely to reply in the affirmative, even though her child's feeding problems were objectively no more severe than those encountered by a more indulgent mother.

We can test this possibility in one way. If the "halo effect" were operating, we might expect that the mothers who said they had severe feeding problems with their children would also have defined other things the child did as "bad." We find no evidence for such a generalized attitude, however. The mothers who said their children had feeding problems did *not* ascribe other unpleasant qualities to them. These children were not described as especially aggressive in the home (quite the contrary, in fact), nor were they described as children who would deny something they had done when charged with it, nor as children who gave their mothers trouble during toilet training. In other words, there was no tendency for these mothers to give their children a generalized "bad" rating. (See Appendix Table D:8.)

It appears, then, that we may have confidence in the reports about feeding problems. Severe training practices during the ages three to five were associated with increased feeding problems at that time and shortly thereafter.

COMMENT

Of the various matters examined in this chapter, breast feeding and self-demand scheduling have received the most interested public discussion in recent years. Militant enthusiasts for both have generated more excitement than facts. They have reasoned, in effect, that the "natural way" is best, and that a deep insecurity is created in infancy by bottle-propping or rigid scheduling or other methods of impersonalizing the feeding experience. They have talked much of *good* and *bad* consequences of various infant care practices without sure evidence that there are any consistent consequences at all. It is worth reviewing what we have discovered about these matters.

Sixty per cent of the mothers in this sample did not breast-feed their children. Their reasons were various, ranging from genuine physical disability to frankly emotional rejection of the nursing function. If we may judge by the experience of other cultures, actual incapacity could have accounted for a very small proportion of these cases. In between the extremes were a host of explanations which may or may not have been the major reasons. The comparison of those who did and did not feed by breast, with reference to a measure of sex anxiety, suggested that refusal to breast-feed occurs more frequently in mothers who are uncomfortable about this other biological function. Whether sex anxiety *causes* mothers to reject breast feeding, or whether mothers who are uncomfortable with one major biological drive tend also to be uncomfortable with another, is an interesting question. From the standpoint of guidance for parents, however, it is a minor issue. What is important to recognize is that rejection of breast feeding may be related to other pervasive qualities in the mother's personality, and that sheer exhortation to perform the particular act of breast feeding is not likely to have a comforting effect on the mother who initially rejects the practice.

But let us add a note of caution. We are reviewing facts. The relation between sex anxiety and refusal to breast-feed is a fact, but like all facts it can be misinterpreted. This one is in danger of being given too much importance. The average difference between the two groups is small. Obviously many mothers who did breast-feed their children had high sex anxiety and many who did not had low sex anxiety. The difference is a difference between averages, not a diagnosis of individual mothers. There are many other factors that contribute to the decision about breast feeding, and our present ignorance of their nature does not mean they do not affect behavior.

Now as to the effects of breast feeding. There have been very few careful studies of the question. None so far has demonstrated any important and consistent relationship between breast feeding and any later quality of the personality. Our own data, reported in this chapter, add nothing new to this negative state of affairs. None of the children's characteristics, as judged by the mothers' descriptions of them, were different for the two groups, the breast-fed and the non-breast-fed. There are many other aspects of personality that no one has yet studied in this connection, however, and possibly some day some acute investigator will uncover an important effect. For the present, the only conclusion we can reach is that *there are as yet no demonstrably consistent effects on later behavior of breast* vs. *bottle feeding in infancy.*

But another word of caution is in order. The most important word in the above statement is *consistent.* It means that the specific technique by which the baby is fed is not regularly related to any specific outcome. It definitely does not mean that early feeding experiences are isolated from all the rest of the child's experience and have no effect on him. Every long-continued activity has some influence on the particular child who performs it. Experience with the breast is incorporated in a child's development in one way or another, perhaps in connection with his love relationship to others, perhaps as a source of support or frustration, or in any of many other possible roles. The same is true of bottle feeding. Whatever experience the child has becomes a determining part of his behavior in one way or another. But the evidence suggests that this way is specific to each child, that the technique of feeding does not have any constant effect for all children.

What have we found out about the self-demand *vs.* rigid scheduling controversy? There is a clear indication in the mothers' reports that rigid scheduling is infrequent. So is complete self-demand, which is not surprising, for most infants develop some kind of schedule for themselves. Even the mother who is most solicitous of the baby's needs has some kind of schedule for her own household activities and probably in subtle ways tends to transfer this to the child. The range on this practice is quite wide in this group of mothers, but it tends clearly toward a child-oriented policy.

The findings with respect to weaning fit well with what was already known and add a few new items. The range of ages at which weaning to the cup was begun by this group of mothers was wide, but the central tendency was to begin early, well under the age of one year. This is very early, compared with the practices of nonliterate cultures. But the amount of emotional disturbance produced was not great, and the earlier the change was made, the less the upset. This accords with previous findings, which have suggested that the strength of the sucking habit, and the need to get food by sucking, are increased by more practice at sucking. The stronger such a drive or need is, the greater the severity of emotional upset when its actions are frustrated.

We have known, also, that upset is least when there is extensive preparation for the new mode of eating before the final step is taken that makes the child totally dependent on it. We can now add a new finding, that once the weaning has started, the emotional disturbance connected with it is most severe if the transition takes a long time.

It is always risky to give advice on the basis of group findings, but mothers have to make decisions on weaning anyway, and it may help to spell out what these facts suggest. If the goal is to have as little emotional disturbance as possible—and this is a big *if*, because there may be other goals that are more important, and would be better reached by doing something else—then it appears wisest to begin weaning before the end of the first year or else wait until the end of the second. If the longer period is used, the child obviously will have long since gone on a solid diet and will be taking many of his liquids by cup anyway. Secondly, there should be all possible preparation for the new mode of eating—orange juice, water, and especially some sips of milk by cup from the very beginning of life. Thus the new mode is not a shock and the skill is available. Giving attention to this preparation is obviously more important if weaning is to be done early. Thirdly, once the decision is made to wean—not just to prepare for it—the transition should be made as expeditiously as possible. There is no kindness in keeping a child on tenterhooks. If serious weaning is not undertaken until after the second year, there is always a good chance the baby will have weaned himself before the mother starts.

Finally, there is the matter of feeding problems in the preschool years. None of the infant-feeding practices we have examined—whether severe or gentle—appear to have been related to the later development of such problems. On the other hand, there was evidence that finickiness and other more severe reactions were related to harsh and restrictive methods of discipline. The relation is not a strong one, but it is consistent among the scales we examined.

CHAPTER FOUR

Toilet Training

In some ways, toilet training is much like weaning. A baby has ready-made responses that rid him of his waste products, just as he has a built-in reflex to make the getting of food convenient. Free use of both these infantile skills eventually becomes changeworthy, and his mother feels impelled to train him to new methods of feeding or to more controlled ways of eliminating. She must decide when to begin these trainings and how to do them. With both, her method can be characterized as lying somewhere on the dimension "gentle-to-severe." The child's reaction, in turn, can be described in terms of how emotionally upset he gets and how long it takes him to make a complete transition to more mature ways of behaving.

There are also some differences between toilet training and weaning, of course. One process involves intake, the other, output. One operates through a single physiological system, the other through a pair that appear to be fairly independent of one another in the beginning. With respect to training, weaning involves a complete renunciation of one method of eating and the learning of another, while toilet training requires only the development of control over the original methods of elimination. As will be seen, too, toilet training usually occurs somewhat later than weaning, in our culture. But the most striking difference has to do with the kind of mother-child relationship involved in the original actions.

Just why toilet training occurs at all is a mystery. Unlike eating, elimination requires no help from the environment. A baby would soon die without someone to bring him food, but he can eliminate his waste products without any help whatever. His skill is as great at birth as it ever will be. All that training can do is interfere with what is otherwise a smoothly operating physiological process. Why does every known human society have some kind of regulation?

What is universal, culturally speaking, is keeping the immediate living quarters free of excrement. To this end, all children are trained against free elimination. They are taught either to inhibit sphincter release until they get to the proper spot, or to clean up and dispose of fecal material. Various other animals do the same. Birds do not foul their nests, large den-living animals go outside to evacuate, and cats carefully cover their refuse.

Because of this similarity between man and some of the lower animals, toilet training has sometimes been considered an instinctive reaction to the "unpleasant" odor of urine and feces. This notion deserves a bit of skepticism, however. Cats, whose toilet habits are not inconspicuous, willingly lick excrement from themselves and their young. Other animals do not hesitate to sniff, or even eat, waste matter. And certainly the dog must be a peculiarly masochistic beast if he finds the odor of urine disgusting. Human babies often delight in playing with feces, until they are taught a more proper nose-wrinkling attitude, and many a mother has been startled to discover her child using his own unique manufacture for finger painting on the wall beside his crib. His unsophisticated enthusiasm for the little yellow stream in his bath belies a native repulsion. Furthermore, in many societies, adult emotional reactions to human waste products are not nearly so strong as among ourselves. Some peoples occasionally eat feces, or use them ceremonially; others wash their hair or their clothing in urine. Indeed, old American whaling vessels conserved the crew's urine for cutting the grease in dungarees. In sum, the evidence is not very strong for a "natural" disgust for these odors.

Nevertheless, keeping the living quarters clean is universal, and another possible explanation is that, among human beings at least, these regulatory customs result from a kind of natural selection. Some diseases are carried in feces, and it may be that the societies which have had the more effective rules and taboos for protecting their members from exposure have had the best chance of survival. On the other hand, many societies do manage to survive for hundreds of years with extremely ineffective sanitation methods, and with large proportions of their populations suffering from hookworm and amoebic dysentery. So it seems doubtful that natural selection is the answer, either.

Perhaps the most plausible explanation relates to comfort-seeking through bodily cleanliness. All known peoples have some form of bathing as part of their culture, possibly because an unclean skin itches, attracts insects, and is susceptible to various kinds of skin ailments. It may be that all societies have long since discovered that to keep the skin clean and free of these abominations, the bed, floor, seating and eating space also must be kept free of contaminants.

In any case, whether the control on free elimination and the avoidance of excrement are native or acquired is not the important issue in the present context. Our concern is with the nature of the toilet training that does exist in our own culture, and the effects it has on children. We must ask not whether there is an instinct, but how much influence variations in experience have.

Toilet training in American culture involves several problems for both mother and child. As with weaning, these derive fundamentally from the necessity of the child's changing from an infantile way of behaving to a way more suitable for adults. He must unlearn as well as learn. At birth, a baby is endowed with two sphincter reflexes for elimination that are as efficient for their purposes as the sucking reflex is for its. When sufficient urine or fecal matter has accumulated in the bladder or bowel, the sphincter muscles relax suddenly and the waste matter is expelled. In the early months of life, a child wets and has bowel movements according to a relatively unimpeded physiological rhythm, the timing being at first somewhat related to his periods of food and liquid intake. This is a highly satisfactory mechanism from the standpoint of the baby's internal economy, though it is not very considerate of the external household economy.

This is no problem to the child, however. He is diapered, and the only discomfort associated with toileting occurs if his skin becomes irritated or he develops a gastro-intestinal upset that produces gas pains. The sphincter releases appear to relieve tension and to provide a pleasurable sort of relaxation. The changing of diapers is often rewarding, too, since the mother gives the child affection and attention while changing him, and his genital area is stimulated in the process of cleaning.

But the next step involves some learning. The child must gain voluntary control over his sphincters. He must learn to recognize the internal signals that warn of an impending movement. Then he must discover how to hold in until he is ready to let go. Voluntary control is partly a matter of inhibition—stopping the action—and partly the positive act of releasing inhibition and even adding some impetus by "pushing" or "trying." The gaining of voluntary control over both holding-in and letting-go is a slow process at best, especially in the child under a year. The capacity to develop control undoubtedly undergoes considerable physiological maturation, too, although the exact nature of the maturational changes *independent of the influence of learning* is not known.

Along with voluntary control, the child must learn to signal his mother. Until he is able to undo his own clothes, she must be available to help. She has to be quick, at first, because his inhibition is not very strong. Gradually he develops a characteristic grunt, or call, and often some special and highly personal wordlike sound to indicate that he needs to go. When he can walk, he must learn to go to the toilet himself, but of course he cannot attend to his own needs fully when walking begins, for he cannot yet unbutton his clothes nor wipe himself properly. These final steps must be learned at a later date.

Toilet training can be considered complete when the child has learned to inhibit elimination at will, over fairly long periods of time. But every mother knows how difficult this is for a child when he is playing some distance from home or is occupied in an engrossing game; even at seven or eight years of age he may overestimate his capacity for delay and not get home in time. Families who have taken young children for long automobile trips know well that a child's capacity for delay is very limited at first, and develops but slowly to the adult levels.

A special instance of society's demands upon the child occurs with respect to nighttime dryness. He must learn not to urinate between the time he goes to bed and the time he awakes in the morning. This feat seems to fit in very naturally with some children's physiological rhythm but less so with other children, and special help from the parents is often required. Without training, some human beings will urinate in their sleep all their lives. Occasional enuretics were discovered in the armed forces, during World War II, who came from homes in which they had never been taught that there was anything wrong with bed-wetting.

Besides these actual controls, there are two important attitudes and manners the child must learn in connection with toilet behavior. One of these is cleanliness. He must keep himself and his clothes from being soiled in the process of elimination. Not only must his waste matter go into the proper place—the potty—but afterwards he must make sure that he himself is wiped clean and that no spots or odors cling to him. For many children, the stress placed on cleanliness in this connection is their first contact with the cleanliness concept. Freud, probably rightly, saw in this experience the foundation pattern on which were laid down many future learnings about the importance of being clean and neat and orderly. It is certainly clear, as many observers have noted, that most children's attitudes of disgust toward the texture, color, and odor of feces develop only after considerable association with a mother who expresses these attitudes herself.

The other attitudinal matter that goes along with toilet training has to do with modesty. Since elimination requires exposure of the genital area, the taboos connected with sex in general, and with modesty in particular, influence the manner in which toileting may be performed. If a high premium is placed on modesty, elimination must be done in strictest privacy. Quite definite rules are often established in this respect, and children must learn just how much public reference may be made to toilet functions and who may be with him when he eliminates. In some families, for example, a child may not run out of the bathroom for help with the buttoning-up if guests or children of the opposite sex are present. The stringency of such rules varies with the age of the child, of course, and with special circumstances, such as illness or the unavailability of private toilet facilities.

In our interviewing, we found it difficult to keep the topics of sex training and toilet training separate. The questions were separate but the mothers' answers were not. When we were discussing modesty standards, mothers would describe their efforts to train their children not to urinate outdoors. Or when we were discussing toilet training, the question of maintaining privacy in the bathroom would come up. This problem had its origin in the mother's desire to teach modesty, but it had implications for toilet training, too. In some societies children learn about the adult manner of elimination by accompanying an adult and watching him. While this practice is not unknown in the United States, it is relatively rare in such urban areas as that in which we made this study. Generally speaking, modesty taboos prevent American children from learning their toilet habits in the way they learn many other prescribed forms of behavior—by imitation.

If we may summarize the process of toilet training briefly, then, it goes like this. The baby has reflexes that enable him to expel waste products whenever there is sufficient accumulation. These reflexes must be brought under voluntary control, so that he can choose an acceptable time and place for eliminating. The act must be performed both cleanly and modestly.

In the present chapter we will report on two significant aspects of the training process. One of these is the age at which training occurred, and the other, the method by which it was accomplished. Aside from this descriptive material, which is relevant to the first of the three child-rearing problems mentioned in Chapter One, we can also report findings concerning the effects of certain practices on the children, and we can say something about the personality characteristics of the mothers who chose various methods of training. In terms of the organization scheme presented at the beginning of Chapter Two, most of these findings involve comparisons among the dimensions listed under columns II (maternal behavior toward child) and III (child behavior).

AGE OF TRAINING

Toilet training begins when the mother first puts the child on a potty with the intention of catching a bowel movement. A generation ago, mothers were rather generally advised to start this process as early as possible. There was a gradual recognition, however, that infants do not easily learn the inhibitory control required, and they do not, in the first few months of life, seem to get the idea of signaling. If, in the absence of understanding what they are supposed to do, they are punished for their failures, the learning process is likely to be thoroughly disrupted, and the family's dispositions along with it. More recent advice to mothers, therefore, has been to wait until the child is old enough to understand what he is supposed to do. Dr. Spock has suggested that seven to nine months is the earliest reasonable time (the baby cannot sit up alone steadily before then), and urges the latter half of the second year as the best period.

Evidently the great majority of the mothers in our group were in a stage of transition between old and new—or maybe the laundry problem was just too much in these maidless days. Whatever the reasons, nearly half of these mothers began bowel training before the child was nine months old.

TABLE IV:1

AGES AT BEGINNING OF AND AT COMPLETION OF BOWEL
TRAINING

Age in Months	At Beginning	At Completion
Under 5	6%	0%
5–9	41	8
10–14	30	25
15–19	10	24
20–24	5	23
25–29	1	4
30–34	1	6
After 34	1	5
Not ascertained	5	5
Total	100%	100%

For the group as a whole (see Table IV:1), the average age at the beginning of training was about eleven months, and at completion, about eighteen months, so that the time required to complete bowel training to the point where accidents were very rare was about seven months. As Table IV:2 shows, however, there were very great differences among families in the time required. For some, according to the mothers, the task was finished within a few weeks, while for others it took as much as a year and a half.

TABLE IV:2

TIME BETWEEN BEGINNING AND COM-
PLETION OF BOWEL TRAINING

1–2 months	15%
3–4 months	12
5–6 months	21
7–8 months	9
9–10 months	8
11–12 months	12
13–14 months	2
15–16 months	2
17 months or more	10
Not ascertained	9
Total	100%

TABLE IV:3

AGE AT BEGINNING OF BOWEL TRAINING: RELATIONSHIP TO THE AGE AT COMPLETION
AND THE TIME TAKEN FOR COMPLETION OF TRAINING, AND TO MOTHER'S SEX
ANXIETY

	AGE AT BEGINNING OF BOWEL TRAINING				
	Under 5 Months	5–9 Months	10–14 Months	15–19 Months	20 Months or More
Average age at completion of bowel training (in months)	13.3	15.3	19.4	23.2	29.8
Average time for completion of bowel training (in months)	9.6	8.2	7.9	6.6	4.7
Percentage of mothers rated "high" in sex anxiety	70%	58%	60%	55%	42%
Number of cases	23	154	113	39	31

Line 1: $p < .01$ ($r = .57$)
Line 2: $p < .01$ ($r = -.21$)
Line 3: $p < .05$*

* t col. 1 vs. cols. 2–5 = 1.74, $p < .05$ one-tail; $r = -.10$, $p < .05$.

As was the case with weaning, the total time required to complete bowel training was less when it was begun late. Table IV:3
shows that when mothers began bowel training before the child
was five months old, nearly ten months were required for training, on the average. But when training was begun very late (at
twenty months or later), only about five months were required.

It is clear, then, that the later toilet training was begun, the quicker the child learned.

It is worth noting that the amount of time required to train did not drop sharply at any age. There is a steady reduction from left to right in line 2 of Table IV:3. This point is of some theoretical importance, for recent observations of certain types of animal behavior have suggested that there are "critical ages" at which the organism matures to a state of "readiness to learn." Some mothers reported their children "suddenly reached an age" at which they seemed to train themselves almost over night, but there were not many of these. The figures do not suggest (nor do we get the impression from any very large number of interviews) that there is any age after which most children can simply be *instructed* to go to the toilet when they need to. If there is such an age, it is evidently later than any of the mothers in this group began their training program.

A reason for beginning early. There are whole hosts of reasons why a mother may decide to start bowel training at any given time. She may have advice from her doctor, or a suggestion from a neighbor; it may be a traditional custom in her family; she may be tired of washing diapers; or she may find she is going to have another baby. Doubtless all these influences play a part in some mothers' decisions. However, there is a possibility, too, that certain deeper personality characteristics may contribute to a mother's feeling that she should start early or later.

Since there are so many entirely external reasons for adopting a choice in the matter, we did not seek extensively for other factors. Two things led us to examine the question of the mother's sex anxiety, however. One was the fact that toilet training and control of sex behavior were so frequently linked in the interviews by the mothers themselves. It seemed possible that, if toileting had a sexual implication to many mothers, the degree of sex anxiety (or strictness of attitude) might influence a choice of time to start training. The other thing that led us to look in this direction was the discovery reported in the preceding chapter, that higher sex anxiety was apparently associated with a decision not to breast-feed the child. To be sure, a mother cannot decide *against* toilet training, as she can against breast feeding, but she can decide to get it over and done with in a hurry if it has unpleasant connotations for her.

This reasoning proved to be correct, as can be seen from the third line of Table IV:3, although the relationship is slight. The mothers who chose to start their training before their children were five months old had the lowest average rating on the sex permissiveness scale. That is to say, in their interviews they expressed somewhat stronger rejection of sex and somewhat stricter attitudes about prohibiting sexual activity or play in their children. We interpret this as a sign of higher sex anxiety, as we did earlier in connection with the rejection of breast feeding. This tendency was stronger among the mothers of girls than among those of boys, but why this should be, we do not know.

One other point is worth noting about this relationship. Although early starts on training tended to require a longer period for completion than late starts, the mothers who started early *and* had high sex anxiety pushed the task through to completion more rapidly than those with low sex anxiety who started later. This difference, also, is statistically reliable.

The evidence seems clear, therefore, that the mother's level of sex anxiety—her strictness of attitude about sex—played some role in her decision to start toilet training at an early age and to complete it as rapidly as possible. This seems entirely reasonable, indeed quite sensible, for if toileting is a constant, unconscious reminder of a matter that has unpleasant connotations, the task had better be got over and done with as soon as convenient. Further support for this view will appear later in the analysis of bed-wetting, where it will be shown that some (not all) of these so-called sex-anxious mothers had particularly early results from their training.

Amount of emotional upset. One measure of the satisfactoriness of any training process is the amount of emotional upset it creates. As we saw in connection with weaning, the change from infantile to more mature ways of behaving represents something of a frustration for a child. This discomfort is sufficient, in some children, to produce a noticeable expression of dislike and rebellion. In the case of toilet training, this may involve a breakdown of partially attained success at inhibiting free elimination. It is often accompanied, too, by irritability and crying when the mother attempts to persuade the child to go to the toilet.

Because of the evident maturation that occurs in children's

physiological functioning during the first two years of life, the question must be raised as to whether there is any special time at which training can begin that will elicit less expression of discomfort than other times. One might suppose that, in general, the more mature a child is, the more easily he could learn the new tasks required of him.

We have found no clear evidence for this supposition, however. In our interview, we did not address a specific question to the

TABLE IV:4

AGE AT BEGINNING OF BOWEL TRAINING: RELATIONSHIP TO AMOUNT OF EMOTIONAL UPSET

	AGE AT BEGINNING OF BOWEL TRAINING				
	Under 5 Months	5–9 Months	10–14 Months	15–19 Months	20 Months or More
Child showed emotional disturbance *	35%	18%	29%	44%	19%
Number of cases	23	154	113	39	31

$$p = .05 \ (F)$$

* The percentages in this table are based upon the entire group of mothers, whether they discussed the amount of the child's upset or not. The figures therefore show the percentage of mothers who volunteered that their children were upset during toilet training, in the absence of a direct question about the matter. Appendix Table D:9 shows the percentages based on a smaller group of cases: those mothers who discussed the amount of the child's upset—in some instances saying that the child showed disturbance, in others stating specifically that he did not.

mothers concerning the extent of the child's upset during toilet training. However, we talked at length with the mothers about toilet training in general, and 181 mothers volunteered enough information about their children's emotional reactions to toilet training that we were able to rate those children on our five-point scale of *amount of emotional upset*. If we use what information we have, we must acknowledge that there is no simple relationship between the age of beginning bowel training and tolerance for training. Table IV:4 shows that upsets were least common when bowel training was begun between five and fourteen months of age; they were somewhat more frequent when training was begun either very early or in the fifteen- to nineteen-month range. Evidently the early-middle period is a more comfortable one for the child.

These percentage differences look large, but the statistical tests applied to the data show that there must have been other factors of much greater importance than age that influenced the amount of upset. Following the parallel case of weaning, we might expect that the severity with which the training process is done would be related. In the next section we will describe the variety of methods the mothers used, judging them in terms of severity, and then examine that dimension as another possible determinant of the quickness of learning and the amount of emotional upset that accompanied it.

METHODS OF TRAINING

A bit of cross-cultural perspective is helpful when one examines methods of toilet training. The American penchant for elaborate bathroom aids and facilities, complex clothing, and regular household schedules provides a setting with a good deal of rigidity so far as child training is concerned. We have a highly specialized environment. It sets fairly narrow limits within which variation in training techniques is possible. There are even limits within which the severity of training may vary. Other cultures provide quite different limits, not only with respect to the strictness of the standards they commonly maintain, but also in the physical and social aspects of the environment in which training occurs.

Differences in the surroundings and manner of life of a people influence toilet activities considerably. A nomadic tribe can simply move to another site if its area becomes too contaminated, but a group with stationary residence must be more careful about its toileting places. The availability of an abundant water supply permits the use of washable diapers, but whether washable or disposable, diapers create their own special problems. So does their lack. If the climate is tropical, and the baby is not diapered, a mother's first concern is to avoid being soiled herself when she is holding the child. She must recognize when he is about to eliminate, and hold him away from her or set him on the ground. Either that, or she must wash herself off.

Ecology does not account for all the differences among societies, however. In some, where diapers are not used, the mother who does not act quickly enough calmly cleans herself and the child without reprisals; in others the child is severely punished (from as early as six months of age on) for soiling the adult caretaker. When the undiapered child begins to walk, the mother's problem is much the same as for a child who is being taught to go without its diapers—she must teach him where he may go for elimination, and clean up after him if he makes mistakes.

Nevertheless, with all the fancy appurtenances of modern America, and all the limitations on training methods they create,

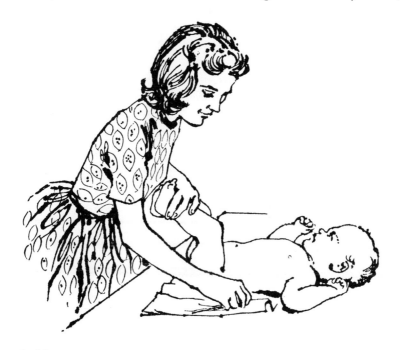

probably no two mothers ever went about the training process in exactly the same way. If we may judge from our interviews, there are differences in belief about the proper age to start, about whether the child should stay on the potty if he does not go immediately, whether he should be talked to while he is waiting, whether he should be punished for accidents, and many other matters.

Underlying these differences there was a basic procedure common to most of the mothers, however. The baby's rhythm of bowel movements was noted, and the mother always tried to get him to the toilet in time for each one. She would use some standard word to describe toileting, and would use it repeatedly as he had his movement. Then she would smile and express approval. As the training continued, she would encourage the child's spontaneous use of this word. Ultimately he would learn to signal his need, and after that would have only very rare accidents. Then the mother would consider her job done.

This skeleton description leaves a lot of leeway for individual differences among the mothers. How often did she take the child to the bathroom? How long did she leave him there if he did not have a movement immediately? How did she handle the situation if he had an accident after he had begun to understand what was expected of him? Some of the alternatives are worth description.

A few mothers did not attempt to teach the child explicitly about bowel control; they allowed him to "train himself." For example:

I. *When did you start bowel training with Jim?*
M. *I didn't. I did it with the other two, and it took a lot out of them and a lot out of me. So I said: "With this one, he'll do whatever he pleases." And it worked out beautifully.*
I. *Just how did it work out?*
M. *There again, by example. He has a sister who is just a year older than he is. I noticed that whenever she went and came out, he would go in, too.*
I. *How old was he when he started this?*
M. *He was completely trained by the time he was two, or slightly over.*
I. *How long would you say it took him to be trained? When did you start?*
M. *I didn't start. He sorta made up his own sound for whatever he wanted to do; what it was, now, I don't remember.*

This mother's procedure was unusual among our group of mothers, however. More commonly, they would put a child on the toilet or a potty at regular intervals, as in the following case:

M. *He was bowel-trained possibly when he was a year old.*
I. *How did you go about it?*
M. *Well, when I found that he used to move his bowels at a certain time every day, generally after breakfast, I would sit him on his toidy at that time. If I remember correctly, he seemed to understand immediately what it was all about. He was pretty good at that.*
I. *How long did it take him until he was pretty well trained?*
M. *Well, as far as really trained is concerned, I would say, possibly, two years. But I feel the fact that he used to move his bowels the same time on the toidy every morning wasn't because he was trained—it was*

because those were his habits, and I don't accept any credit for having trained him.
I. *What did you do about it when he had accidents after he was mostly trained?*
M. *I cleaned him up, and that was all. I didn't make a fuss about it.*

Not all mothers achieved the desired results so easily, of course. Some went through long months of putting the child on the toilet regularly, without establishing dependable habits, and then found he suddenly seemed "ready" to learn:

M. *I started him on the doctor's advice, and he was about seven months old. He was very unhappy, so I spoke to the pediatrician the next time he came, and he told me I was wasting my time, that he was too small, and to wait until he was ten months; and I did, and at ten months it was a totally different reaction. He was fine from that day on, he was no trouble at all after that.*

Another mother said:

M. *I started it when he was about a year old, and I didn't have any success at all. In fact, I didn't have any success with Billy at all until he was three years old. He started by himself when he was ready, and until then it was no use to try to make him. I did have a lot of trouble with him about that.*
I. *How did you go about training him?*
M. *I sat him on the toilet at regular intervals, as far as I could, around the time of day he usually had his bowel movement. It seemed to always be at meal times for some reason, so I just kept after him, and it didn't seem to do much good. There was no use in punishing him, because I tried punishing him, and he didn't seem to be able to do much about it, that's all. He tried, but he just wasn't ready, that was all. I used to keep him on the seat for the longest times, oh, half an hour sometimes, but he couldn't do anything.*
I. *How did he react when you put him on?*
M. *He used to cry and not like it. He used to sit there and cry and whine and talk to himself. When he was over three—I guess about three and a half—he just suddenly decided that it wasn't the thing to do, and he started going to the bathroom by himself. He didn't want anybody to go with him.*

Punishment was another thing on which mothers differed. This last mother said she did not scold or punish her child for toilet "accidents." Some other mothers, however, applied some degree of pressure, usually in an attempt to prevent accidents after training was nearly complete. Here are the replies, made by four mothers, to the question "What did you do about it when he (or she) had accidents after he was mostly trained?"

A

M. *I would reprimand her and scold her, and if that didn't work, I'd give her a few little slaps on her behind.*

B

M. *I would make a big issue of it, and most children don't like to be dirty. He was that way, and it made things easier for me. The minute it happened, and he was all dirty, I would make a big issue of it: "It's an awful thing, look at your clothes; and, oh, what an awful thing for a boy to do! If the other boys knew about it—" and of course, that worked. Sometimes he would be outside playing and he just didn't give himself time to make it. And of course he would really be ashamed when you kept just bringing up the fact that his clothes and everything were all dirty. That really helped him clear the whole situation up.*

C

M. *At the time, I sort of put up with it, until I realized that he realized he shouldn't do it. I'd say he was all of maybe fourteen months or so, and walking, before I really spanked him for having accidents. I mean, there comes a time when they act very shy, and you know that they've done wrong things.*

D

M. *Let me see now, she was about fourteen months when she was fully broken.*
I. *Did it go pretty well then?*
M. *Yes, except lots of times she would do it in her pants. I would just tell her that if she did I would just wipe her face with it. So she decided she was going to go to the bathroom. It was a very good thing to put it under her nose a little bit, and tell her the next time she did it in her pants, she was going to get it in the face; and she didn't like the smell of it, so she learned.*

Whether the mother punished the child for lapses in his toilet training depended in part on how old he was. Many mothers felt that a very young child cannot be held responsible for accidents, but a child of eighteen months (or, depending on the mother, two or three or four years) is old enough to know what he is doing. Accidents at this age were likely to be interpreted as willful disobedience and to be punished as such.

Training for urination control goes more slowly than that for bowel control. Nighttime dryness, in particular, often does not come until much later. Accidents in the daytime occur, in part, because urination occurs more frequently and at less scheduled times than defecation. The child is more likely to be in the yard or the street, less handy to either a toilet or his mother. In our interviews we did not seek special information about daytime urination control, and the mothers volunteered little additional comment beyond what was incorporated in their description of toilet training as a whole. Bed-wetting is a separable problem and will be discussed later.

SEVERITY OF TRAINING

The next question to be considered is the severity with which toilet training was accomplished. As was mentioned earlier, pun-

TABLE IV:5

SEVERITY OF TOILET TRAINING

1. Not at all severe. Child more or less trained himself. Not his fault when he has accidents; they are considered natural. No punishment or scolding	10%
2. Slight pressure. Mild disapproval for some late accidents; mother makes some efforts to show child where, when, and how to go to toilet	42
3. Moderate pressure. Scolding for some late deviations; fairly frequent toileting	29
4. Fairly severe training. Child scolded fairly often; mother clearly shows disapproval. Child may be left on toilet for fairly lengthy periods	16
5. Very severe training. Child punished severely for deviations; mother angry and emotional over them	2
Not ascertained	1
Total	100%

ishment introduced into the training process can be disruptive, not only of the new toilet habits but of the disposition in general. In order to study these effects, we had to have some quantitative measure of severity. To this end a five-point scale was constructed. The scale-point definitions are shown in Table IV:5. The raters took into account everything the mother said about the way she handled toilet training *except* the age at which training was begun and the nature of the child's reaction to it.

Raters were instructed to consider only what the mother did in relation to toilet training.

If we may judge from the number of interviews that were rated at each of the points on the scale, the prevailing mode of training was not very severe. The great majority of mothers used practically no punishment, though there was some scolding for accidents. Only about a fifth of the mothers reported definite punishments or emphatic, repeated scoldings. In spite of the tremendous material emphasis on bathrooms attributed to American culture, there was not a desperate severity in the training of children to use them. Many other cultures, some that even lack outhouses, begin their training earlier and are more severe in their punishment of deviations.

Personality qualities of severe mothers

Before examining the effects of severe toilet training on the children, we may note what other dimensions of the mothers' personalities were correlated with this one. Rarely does any measured quality stand alone. One gets the impression, when looking at the intercorrelations among a number of rated dimensions, that several scales may be measuring different facets of the same thing. What child-rearing dimensions are associated with severity of toilet training?

This scale proved to be related to quite a number of other child-rearing practices. Most of the correlation coefficients are quite small, but the clusters seem meaningful in terms of deeper patterns of personality qualities.

The mothers who were *more severe* also:

1. Placed high demands for conformance to adult standards with respect to—

   a) table manners $(r = .21)$
   b) neatness and orderliness $(r = .19)$
   c) care of house and furniture $(r = .19)$
   d) being quiet $(r = .18)$
   e) doing well in school $(r = .16)$.

2. Used tangible forms of punishment—

   a) physical punishment $(r = .29)$
   b) deprivation of privileges $(r = .13)$
   c) avoided use of reasoning with child $(r = -.23)$.

3. Did not tolerate disobedience or aggression toward themselves—

 a) low permissiveness for aggression toward parents
  $(r = -.27)$
 b) high standards of obedience $(r = .15)$
 c) punished aggression expressed toward parents $(r = .14)$.

4. Were non-permissive about the child's sex behavior—

 a) modesty $(r = -.31)$
 b) masturbation $(r = -.25)$
 c) social sex play $(r = -.25)$.

5. Had high child-rearing anxiety $(r = .20)$ and lacked warmth or esteem toward—

 a) herself $(r = -.16)$
 b) husband $(r = -.15)$
 c) infant $(r = -.12)$
 d) child $(r = -.30)$.

The connection between severe toilet training and low permissiveness with respect to the child's later sex behavior is scarcely surprising, in view of the close connection many mothers made between these two spheres of activity. There may even be some doubt about the independence of the ratings, especially as between the modesty scale and toilet training. There is no doubt about independence of the scales relating to "high standards of conformance," however. These will be treated in more detail in Chapter Eight; for the present, it is sufficient to mention that the only scale belonging in this general group that did not correlate at least slightly with severity of toilet training was strictness of bedtime rules.

In this cluster of scales that correlate with severity of toilet training, we can distinguish two main groups. One of these is the cluster that was mentioned in Chapter Two as forming the *general family adjustment* factor (B). The other is the group that have to do with strictness and high demands for conformance to adult standards (Factor A).

What kind of a "trait" is this? We get the impression of a rather pervasive quality of strictness in the mothers who were most severe in their toilet training. They seem to have been seeking to achieve more mature standards of conduct at a faster pace than the other mothers. They had more tendency to drive rather than to lead their children, and they used a more punitive kind of discipline. They also felt more anxiety about their ability to bring up their children; possibly their strictness was in some sense an attempt to overcome whatever feelings of inadequacy they had. We will discuss this matter further, in Chapter Eight, in connection with Freud's notion of the anal character.

This rather wide range of associated practices and attitudes makes it difficult to separate out the effects of severity of toilet training itself, independently of these other factors. However, in this next section we will examine its apparent influence on the amount of emotional upset the child suffered, as well as on the duration of training required. Then in the final section we will reverse this way of analysis, and ask, rather, what were the practices of mothers whose children had not yet reached regular night-time dryness at age five.

Effects of severity

The mothers who put a good deal of pressure on their children during toilet training (scolding and punishing for deviations, taking them to the toilet frequently, etc.) did not succeed in completing the training any sooner than the mothers who employed more gentle methods. (See Appendix Table D:10.) They did succeed, however, in producing a lot of emotional upset over the matter. As Table IV:6 shows, over half of the most

TABLE IV:6

SEVERITY OF TOILET TRAINING: RELATIONSHIP TO AMOUNT OF EMOTIONAL UPSET

	SEVERITY OF TOILET TRAINING			
	Not at All Severe	Slight Pressure	Moderate Pressure	Quite Severe
Child showed emotional disturbance *	17%	11%	26%	55%
Number of cases	54	117	129	75

$$p < .01 \ (r = .47)$$

* These percentages are based upon the entire group of mothers interviewed, whether or not they discussed the amount of the child's disturbance. The figures show the proportion of mothers who volunteered that their children were upset during toilet training, in the absence of a direct question on the subject. Appendix Table D:11 shows the percentages based on a smaller group of cases: those mothers who discussed the amount of the child's upset—in some instances saying that the child showed disturbance, in others stating specifically that he did not.

severely trained children showed some disturbance, while not more than a sixth of the least severely trained showed it ($p < .01$; $r = .47$).

The relationship of severe training to the child's emotional upset is significant, of course, but other interpretations of the findings must be considered. The children who most commonly showed disturbance during toilet training tended to be the ones whose training was completed relatively late. Since they had late

bowel accidents, and wet their beds after most children had stopped, there were more occasions on which their mothers might be tempted to be angry and punitive. Thus, it might be the child's slowness in training (accompanied by emotional resistance) which brought out severe treatment from the mother, not the other way around.

However, if we examine only those cases in which training was very slow, we find that the general principle holds up just as well as it does with the children who learned more rapidly. So, whatever else may contribute to emotional upset, there is little question but that severity of training is an important source of disturbance.

One word of caution must be added about the actual size of

the differences in Table IV:6, however. When raters rated the severity of toilet training in a given family, they were told not to take into account the child's reactions. This may not always have been possible. There may have been cases in which this type of contamination could not be avoided, instances in which a given training procedure seemed more severe simply by virtue of the fact that it upset the child. These two ratings, therefore, probably have less independence than one might wish.

These various findings present a reasonably clear picture of the effects of the age at which training was begun and of the severity with which it was performed. The later it started, the quicker it was finished. Punishment and scolding did not speed it in the slightest. So far as emotional upset over training was concerned, however, a relatively late start (fifteen to nineteen months) produced as much disturbance as a very early one: the optimum periods appear to have been sometime between the sixth and ninth or tenth months, or after twenty months.

We can turn now to a different kind of question. Did other aspects of the mother's personality, besides the toilet-training methods themselves, influence the child's reaction to that training? There are two main clusters of measures that can be examined.

The first comprises those scales that were related to the mother's affectional relationship to the child. These were the dimensions described as contributing to the measurement of Factor C in the discussion of our factor analysis. This was the *warmth* factor. We reasoned that if the mother's punishment was an expression of an underlying hostility or rejection, we might expect it to be more upsetting to the child than punishment which occurred in a context of emotional security. In a sense, the child punished by a hostile mother was in double jeopardy: there was the physical pain of the punishment, plus the anxiety produced by the loss of love implied in the mother's manner while punishing. To the child of the cold and hostile mother, punishment may have meant "I don't like *you*," while to the child of the warm mother, it may have meant "I don't like *what you did*."

This reasoning led us to expect that severe toilet training would be more anxiety provoking, and hence more upsetting, for the children of cold mothers than for the children of warm mothers. This proved to be true, as Table IV:7 shows. Severe training produced far more upset than mild training in the children of relatively cold mothers, but it had no differential effect whatsoever on the children of warm mothers. This finding requires us to qualify the generalization, made before, that severity of training produced emotional upset. The statement can now be amended and made more precise: *severe toilet training increased the amount of upset in children whose mothers were relatively cold and undemonstrative.*

TABLE IV:7

PERCENTAGE OF CHILDREN WHO SHOWED EMOTIONAL UPSET OVER TOILET TRAINING, IN RELATION TO SEVERITY OF TOILET TRAINING AND WARMTH OF THE MOTHER

Severity of Toilet Training	Mother Warm	Mother Relatively Cold	Horizontal Differences
Mild toilet training	21% (112) *	11% (101)	N.S.
Severe toilet training	23% (48)	48% (98)	$p = .01$
Vertical differences	N.S.	$p = .01$	

* Figures in parentheses are number of cases.

Parenthetically, it is interesting to note here that the mother's coldness *per se* did not serve to upset the child. It had to be manifested overtly, through severe training practice, before it produced disturbance in this particular sphere of behavior.

The second cluster of measures that need consideration as possible sources of upset are those which we described as contributing to Factor A in the factor analysis. These were the scales that had to do with training demands and restrictions placed on the child with respect to several areas of social development. One might suppose that if a child were subjected to a number of frustrations, and not allowed to express his resentment directly, he would express it by showing resistance in the toilet-training process. This hypothesis is not borne out by our findings, however. The child's emotional upset during toilet training was *not* related to the severity of restrictions or achievement demands to which he was subjected. That is, children who were required to be quiet, mannerly, and obedient, and who had a strictly-enforced bedtime were no more likely to show emotional upset during toilet training than children of whom less was expected. Furthermore, emotional reactions to toilet training did not seem to be related to the amount the child was spanked, nor to whether his parents had allowed him to express feelings of anger toward them.

These findings are interesting in two respects. First, they emphasize that single-variable relationships between child-rearing practices and child behavior must be scrutinized with some care before they are accepted as general principles. Simple cause-and-effect relations are probably not common in this area of science. Second, the "factors" derived from factor analysis have proved to be less important as antecedents, at least of the one aspect of child behavior we have called *upset,* than the specific child-rearing practices which we have examined. Neither the *permissiveness-strictness* factor (A) nor the *warmth* factor (C) appears to have been the main determiner of emotional upset during toilet training, if we may judge from the fact that none of the dimensions included in them except *warmth* and *severity of toilet training* was significantly correlated with the child's *emotional upset.*

We do not mean to imply any disrespect, in these two comments, for either the single variable or the underlying traits revealed by factor analysis. Both are of importance, as we are able to demonstrate repeatedly with our present data. But there is still a place for the careful teasing out of relationships that involve interaction between one or two or three operationally defined measures of child rearing.

BED-WETTING

Controlling nighttime urination is in some ways a more difficult task for the child than learning to keep clean and dry during the day. Sleep interferes with, blots out, the none-too-distinct internal signals that he is learning to notice as warnings of sphincter releases. Even daytime inhibitory control is slow in developing in many children; sleep-drugged signaling often leads to night accidents long after day training is complete. In the present group of children, for example, there were no longer any youngsters, at ages five or six, whom their mothers considered untrained for bowel control or daytime urination, but 19 per cent still wet the bed at night, at least occasionally. The percentages of children who achieved night dryness at successive ages are shown in Table IV:8.

Some children seemed to stop wetting their beds at an early age with relatively little training effort on their parents' parts. They simply began to go through the night without wetting, and

TABLE IV:8

"DOES THE CHILD STILL WET THE BED?"

Never now; hasn't since two years old or earlier	44%
Never now; hasn't since three years old	22
Never now; stopped at four or later	6
Never now; age of stopping not ascertained	8
Occasionally wets bed nowadays	10
Fairly often wets bed nowadays	5
Wets almost every night nowadays	4
Not ascertained	1
Total	100%

their mothers began to find them with a dry diaper in the morning. One mother described her experience as follows:

M. *He hasn't done any bed-wetting since he was two. He just stopped. We always picked him up—when we were training we picked him up in the middle of the night, and brought him into the bathroom, but I soon discovered there was no need of that either, not even picking him up, because he just didn't wet then, either. I put him to bed at six o'clock at night, and he would be up at six in the morning, and the bed would be dry, and so would his diaper. He did that himself.*

The most common methods used to train a child about bed-wetting were to get him up in the night and take him to the toilet (often without waking him) and to limit his intake of liquids in the evening. Various kinds of punishments and rewards were also used: sometimes children were required to wash out their pajamas or bedclothes if they wet the bed, or were offered money or other incentives to keep their beds dry. Following are some examples of how mothers reacted to bed-wetting in their five- or six-year-old children:

A

M. *At first I was very strict about it, and I told him I wasn't going to spank him because I knew it wouldn't do any good, but that if he wet* *he wouldn't be able to go out and play after school. I tried that for a week, but I gave up because I knew he had to get some fresh air. I couldn't keep him in every day—it didn't help. Then after the baby was born, another time I was desperate, I put a diaper on him, and he cried and fussed and made himself sick. I just did that one night and I didn't do that again. So I don't know what else. Of course I tried not giving him water after 4:00 o'clock, but I can't refuse him his milk for supper, though. I give him that and I don't know whether that makes him wet, but he wets.*

B

I. *What have you done with Allen about bed-wetting?*
M. *Well, I haven't exactly done anything outside of the fact that I remind him to go to the bathroom every night before going to sleep. I didn't stop giving him liquids before he goes to bed as the milk that he had at night he requires, and if he wets his bed at night, I don't mind terribly. He still does occasionally.*
I. *How do you handle it when you find his bed wet?*
M. *I promptly change his pajamas—this usually happens in the morning. I wouldn't be a bit surprised if it's because he just didn't hop out of bed soon enough to go to the bathroom; he was too sleepy, so I tell him to change his pajamas, and come into my bed or his daddy's bed.*

C

M. *It was very uncomfortable, and she was the type of child who didn't like to stay wet, and in the middle of the night she'd wake up and be all wet and she'd call me to tell me to change the crib. So at first I would do it, but it happened so often after that; so one night I decided I would let her sleep in it, and she didn't like that—so ever since then she stopped it.*

A number of mothers, especially those with younger children, reported considerable irritation when they found their five-year-old's bed wet. They spoke with feeling about the work that was involved in washing and ironing the child's pajamas and bedding.

A

I. *How do you feel about it when she does wet her bed?*

M. *Oh, I am very much upset. I am terribly upset, because at this period her urine is so much stronger, and there is a constant washing, so that it really affects me terribly.*

I. *How do you handle the situation if you find her bed wet?*

M. *"Did you wet your bed this morning, Sally?" is what I'll say, and she'll say "yes" if she did and "no" if she didn't; and like this morning, she didn't, and I said, "Well, that's a good girl. You can stop it if you want to." When she says she has, I say, "Oh, God, now there you go again." But that is as far as it goes.*

I. *Do you say anything else to her?*

M. *No, I don't, I have just given up. I am tired of it all.*

I. *What have you tried to do in the past about it?*

M. *I don't know if it was the smart thing to do—I put fears into her, and told her I would just have to call the doctor and see what he could do about it. And then I'd tell her I would just have to send her back to the hospital and get another little girl that was a clean girl.*

B

I. *How do you feel about it if he wets the bed?*

M. *I don't enjoy it, the washing particularly. I don't really know what to do. We did try getting cross with him about it, and that would be the first thing he'd think of in the morning. "I'm dry," or "I'm wet," and I thought "that's not good," because if it bothered him that much and he knew it he wouldn't do it.*

Despite these examples of mothers' becoming angry over bed-wetting, and letting their children know how they felt, we found relatively few instances in which children were spanked or subjected to extreme disapproval for bed-wetting. Many mothers had a sympathetic attitude toward the child, feeling that this was something he could not control, something which was just as embarrassing and difficult for him as for herself.

A

M. *I don't think they wet their bed on purpose. Who'd want to lay in a wet bed? I wouldn't, would you?*

B

M. *Well, naturally I don't like it, but I just think that perhaps he thought in his sleep that he had gone to the bathroom, or he probably thought about it without getting up to go.*

C

M. *I feel badly, but I don't mention it to him, because I myself wet the bed until I was very old. I think I was around eight years old, and*

I was still wetting the bed, and I can remember my mother never said too much about it. But inside, I can remember I felt very ashamed. And I think that's how he feels, the same way. So I don't say anything about it. I know he will eventually be able to control it. Of course, I have an automatic washing machine. Now if I didn't have one it might be another thing, but I just take everything off and bring it downstairs. I might say, "That's too bad!" When he's waked up dry, he's in seventh heaven. He comes and says, "Guess what, I'm dry." And I say, "Isn't that wonderful!" What else can you say? There's nothing else you can do about it. And I thought I was the only one that had a child wetting the bed at this age, but I'm finding there are more than me. I mean, more mothers are experiencing this than I am. And you know, most people, they think that's such a horrible thing. But of course, being one myself, I can understand.

Some mothers had read enough of the literature on child care that they interpreted the child's bed-wetting as a sign of emotional disturbance. They were anxious and upset about what they feared was evidence of their own failure as mothers.

M. *I was kinda ashamed of the fact that he did it, because I knew it must be my fault. I know from what I've read—oh, I've read a lot about it, too, I've read that usually you're not completely relaxed when they do that. They are emotionally upset or something's bothering them. They say if you press them too hard to make them eat it can disturb them so much that it could make them wet. They have all kinds of reasons for it, so I feel that he mustn't be emotionally secure if he keeps wetting like that.*

Why is it that some children have so much difficulty in this area, others so little? It is likely that there are physiological differences between children which are important, but in the present context we are concerned with the influence of methods of training, and the emotional relationships within the home environment.

The most obvious matter to examine first is the toilet-training method itself. The age at the beginning of training was of no significance ($r = .08$), so we can turn to *severity*. Our ratings on severity of toilet training took into account both bowel training and prevention of bed-wetting. From Table IV:9 it can be seen that the severity of the entire toilet-training process did have some bearing on children's tendencies to be late bed-wetters. When they were scolded and punished in the training process, they were somewhat more likely to be late bed-wetters than if their mothers were milder in their treatment.

TABLE IV:9

BED-WETTING: RELATIONSHIP TO THE SEVERITY OF TOILET TRAINING

	SEVERITY OF TOILET TRAINING			
AGE AT WHICH CHILD STOPPED WETTING BED	Not at All Severe	Slight Pressure	Moderate Pressure	Quite Severe
Before two years old	38%	49%	42%	45%
Between two and three years	30	21	27	11
Between three and five years	4	5	6	9
Before age five; not ascertained just when	11	10	6	4
Still wets bed	17	15	19	31
Total	100%	100%	100%	100%
Number of cases	54	117	129	75

$p < .01 \ (r = .18)$

As was the case with emotional reaction to the training process itself, however, simple severity of training does not tell the whole story. Again we find that the disruptive effects of severe training occurred with some mothers but not with others. As one can see from comparing the top and bottom lines of Table IV:9, severe training apparently had a kind of "kill or cure" effect so far as bed-wetting was concerned. When severely trained, the child either learned to be dry before he was two years old or he tended not to learn before he was five or six. Relatively few of the severely-trained children learned in the middle period.

Which children were "killed" and which "cured?" The answer is a curious one and we cannot pretend to have any theoretical explanation for it. Three things were related to late persistence of bed-wetting. One was the severity of toilet training, and another was the mother's affectional warmth. Both of these, it will be recalled, were also related to the amount of emotional upset during training. But a third factor is new—the mother's sex anxiety. We saw earlier that this quality in the mother was somewhat connected with whether she breast-fed her baby or not, and with whether she started bowel training early. Now we find it positively associated with persistent bed-wetting. The combination of high sex anxiety, a relatively cold and undemonstrative attitude toward the child, and severe toilet training were most efficient for producing prolonged bed-wetting. This is the "kill" prescription. The "cure" combination, that gave unusually high probability of the child's achieving night dryness before he was two years old, also included high sex anxiety, but in this instance it was associated with a warm and affectionate attitude toward the child, and with gentle toilet training. Perhaps an easier way of saying this is that both warmth of affection and gentleness of training were positively related to early night dryness, while their opposites led to night wetting. But both dimensions were much more influential, in their respective ways, in mothers who were rated as having high sex anxiety.

Bed-wetting is a problem, of course, and the connection of severe toilet training with problem behavior has a familiar ring. In the last chapter, we reported that children with feeding problems seemed to have had more severe toilet training, also. This raises the question as to whether children who had feeding problems also tended to be late bed-wetters, or whether problems in the feeding area (loss of appetite, refusal of certain foods) and bed-wetting are two possible *alternative* reactions to severe parental discipline. If the latter is so, the child who had one of these modes of response would not have had the other. There is some evidence that this was the case. Among the severely trained children, a child was less likely to wet the bed if he had feeding problems, and vice versa. Among the severely trained children who had *some* feeding problems, 22 per cent were late bed-wetters, while among the severely trained children who had *no* feeding problems, 47 per cent were late bed-wetters.

For various reasons, we extended our search for correlates of bed-wetting to three other areas of the child's home environment. The first of these was sibling relationships. Our reason was that clinical work with children who are chronic bed-wetters has sometimes suggested that such behavior is the child's response to the frustration, or emotional insecurity, arising from the birth of a younger sibling. We were unable to find any evidence of consistent effects from such sources, however. Although jealousy of a younger sibling may produce this reaction in occasional individuals, late bed-wetting was not more common in our families among children who had younger brothers and sisters than among children who did not. Also, the age of learning nighttime dryness was not related to the age of the child when a new sibling was born.

A second source of frustration that we investigated was the area of infant care. We thought it possible that a general insecurity in the first year of life might have made the child less able to develop control. However, we could discover no evidence for this view. Specifically, bed-wetting was not related to—

1. the severity of weaning,
2. whether infant feeding was scheduled or on self-demand,
3. the mother's responsiveness to the infant's crying.

The third area we searched for possible sources was among the group of measures that contributed to Factor A in our factor

analysis. These were the scales that measured the extent to which the mother imposed high and rigid standards of conformance to adult standards. It will be recalled that severity of toilet training was one of the dimensions in this cluster. However, as was the case with the amount of upset produced by toilet training, these associated dimensions in Factor A do not appear to have been significant determinants of bed-wetting. Bed-wetting at age five was not related to any of the following aspects of the child's home experience:

1. whether he was required to be especially careful not to mark or soil the furniture and walls;
2. whether he was required to stay in his own yard at all times (as compared with being allowed to go to neighboring blocks alone);
3. whether he was expected to obey instantly when asked to do something (or stop doing something);

4. whether he was expected to have good table manners, remain at the table throughout the meal, and refrain from interrupting adults at the table;

5. whether he was subjected to a good deal of pressure from his parents to do well at school.

Summary. What we have discovered about bed-wetting suggests that it may be an alternative reaction to feeding problems. It was found most frequently, in our group, in children who had suffered too severe toilet training by mothers who were cool and undemonstrative in their affectional relations to their children and who had high sex anxiety themselves. Equally high sex anxiety associated with warmth of affectional relationship and gentle training produced very early and successful night dryness. Bed-wetting was not *consistently* related to the general level of infant frustration, to the birth of a sibling, or to the level of restrictions and demands for conformance to adult standards of conduct.

COMMENT

Viewed even from a cross-cultural standpoint, the range of ages at which the mothers began toilet training was wide. An anthropologist might have difficulty in defining just what *the* American custom is. The modal age was between nine and eleven months, but there were quite a number of mothers who started within the child's first half-year and a good many more who waited until well after the first birthday.

Did these variations make any difference? From the mother's standpoint, yes. By and large, the later the training was started, the more quickly it was accomplished. Likewise, from the child's standpoint, training begun after twenty months produced emotional upset in relatively few of the children. These facts sound like arguments for a late beginning, especially when one notes the high proportion of upsets in those cases in which training began in the fifteen- to nineteen-month range.

There are other aspects of the situation to be kept in mind, however. First there is the fact that mothers who began bowel training at the moderately early age of five to nine months found this procedure as successful as a very late start, in the sense that their children accepted the training with few signs of disturbance. Furthermore, we found that the mothers who chose to begin training early were relatively high in sex anxiety. This suggests a problem similar to the one we discussed in connection with breast feeding. If toilet-training activity is an emotionally hazardous part of child care, there is something to be said for the mother's getting the process over speedily, instead of trying to overcome her discomfort and delay her training efforts for the sake of a quicker training period later on. Most normal mothers with relatively high sex anxiety do not recognize this quality in themselves. There seems little point in making a categorical assertion that they *should* overcome their reluctance to delay. Sex anxiety cannot be overcome either by exhortation or by a display of factual arguments.

We have said little about the mechanical details of bowel training. Our interviews, coming as they did three or four years after completion of the process, were not an appropriate method for investigating what might be called "habit training." There are a number of unresolved problems on which we have not sought data. For example, there is a question as to whether children who are "completely trained" during the early months of life have actually attained voluntary control of their sphincters. Some observers have concluded that it is the *mothers* who get trained in these cases. Other observers, basing their reasoning on conditioned reflex principles, have assumed that such early control is bona fide. Another question is whether sphincter inhibition or voluntary sphincter release is learned first. Most writers have assumed that a child learns to hold in before he learns to let go. Both these questions are important in relation to a decision about the optimum age for beginning the training process. Since we have no findings that are relevant to them, however, we are disinclined to add further unverified speculations to a literature already burdened with opinion.

Within the limits of our two measures—duration and upset— we conclude that either of two periods may be chosen for training with an expectation of reasonable comfort. These are the second six months of the child's life and the time after twenty months. The training evidently goes more quickly at the later time and produces little upset. The earlier period is also not immediately upsetting to the child, though the process takes longer. We do not know, of course, whether there are later consequences, in the child's personality, resulting from the choice between these two age periods.

A word is in order about the fifteen- to nineteen-month period. One reason that bowel training in this period may be upsetting to the child is that the *wrong* habits have become deeply ingrained. There has been little or no experience with the *right* responses. In other words, he has been practicing elimination in a diaper, lying down or walking, and in rooms that are not in the future to be appropriate for sphincter release. He has not been practicing in the presence of such correct cues as sitting on the potty, being undressed, hearing his mother talk about toileting, and so on. A further problem is that if training is begun after the child is old enough to run around, he will resist being kept in one place long enough for evacuation to occur and for him to be rewarded. A nine-months-old baby who is not yet walking, and who is still content to be confined to a play pen for reasonable lengths of time, will also sit happily on the potty for five or ten minutes, especially if someone stays with him. If he is at all regular in his bowel movements this is usually enough time for his bowel movement to coincide. His mother can then follow it with rewards and praise. The child of a year-and-a-half, however, finds it confining to be required to sit still, even for five minutes. He is likely to struggle or cry—activity which can in itself prevent sphincter release. Even if it does occur, the child's emotional state is such that his mother has difficulty making the experience rewarding to him, no matter how much she praises and smiles.

In contrast with these various doubts and queries about the most appropriate age for beginning toilet training, there is considerable certainty about the effects of the dimension of severity. The introduction of pressure, impatience, irritability and punishment into toilet training produces resentment, recalcitrance, and emotional upset in the child. It does not serve to speed his learning in the slightest, and may, if the mother is rather cold in her relations with him, serve to initiate a prolonged period of bed-wetting.

Severe training may be an almost inevitable maternal reaction to external conditions, of course. A child gone balky because he has gotten started wrong in his attempts to gain control is difficult to handle gently under the best of circumstances. A siege of illness in either the mother or child at a critical part of the training can prolong the process and be quite frustrating.

Underlying these more or less fortuitous sources of severity, however, is a general quality of the personality that seems to provide a number of correlated measures. These include several indicators of high demand for conformance to adult standards, punitiveness, and an intolerance of counter-aggression from the child. We have no information from which we can hazard a guess as to why these various qualities are associated with one another. None of them seems to have been associated with prolonged bed-wetting, and hence we mention them here not as sources of toilet-training difficulties, but only as correlates of severe toilet training.

Finally, we come back to warmth. As we saw in both the preceding chapters, this dimension has a pervasive influence. So far as prolonged bed-wetting is concerned, warmth is a crucial determinant of whether severe training will create that symptom of disturbance. Severity in a warm mother had little deleterious effect, but in a cold mother it did.

CHAPTER FIVE

Dependency

A newborn baby is not very social. For a brief time after he is born, he is quite unresponsive to most external stimulation. He sucks on appropriate occasions, blinks his eyes to the light, and makes gross muscular reactions to forced changes in posture. But not until he is in his second month does he show much indication of responding to people as people. Then he begins to make rapid strides toward becoming a social being. He learns to turn toward his mother when she approaches, to clutch her, to smile at her. And eventually, when he is three or four months old he begins to "call" her when he is hungry or cold; by six months he has learned to lift his arms toward her when she reaches for him. In a sense, he has passed from the receptive stage to become a social person in his own right, not only responsive to others but actively seeking, controlling, and manipulating them.

Briefly, at least, much of this behavior seems to be instrumental to fulfilling his immediate biological needs. The human child has the longest period of purely physical dependency of any of the mammals. It is doubtful that any child could survive were he entirely abandoned by nurturing older persons before he was four or five years old. But being a quick learner, he also develops early his techniques of co-operating with those who care for him, and of controlling them and ensuring their nurturance. As new wants develop, he utilizes help from others to bring him the new satisfactions.

This physical dependency is not a one-way street, however. Almost as rapidly as the child learns to seek help he also learns to get along without it. Independence becomes an end in itself. Once he has learned to stand steadily and take a few sure steps, a child begins to rebel against the proffered hand. He is eager to walk by himself, and the bold grunting strut of the fifteen-months-old is the very antithesis of his earlier timid clutch for support. Each of the action systems—locomotion, eating, dressing, toileting, construction, etc.—goes through this sequence of development. First the child is passive and has everything done for him. Then he learns to co-operate; then to begin doing it for himself with help; and finally to get along without help.

But somehow, during the first few months of life, children develop an emotional dependency on their mothers that seems not to follow this sequence. At least, not so easily and spontaneously. By the time a child is six months old, he has begun to respond warmly and enthusiastically to his mother. He distinguishes her from other women, and from his father. He turns away from strangers, seeking with his eyes for his mother. Soon he begins to want her, to be lonesome and to cry, when she is absent. He welcomes her talking and laughing, and smiles happily when she picks him up or jabbers at him. When he can walk, he sometimes follows her around, reaching for her and holding to her dress if she does not pick him up. By the end of his second year, his love and affection for her are expressed not only by open displays of adoration—hugging, kissing, clinging—but by a seeming need for her attention and orientation toward him.

Delighted as they often are by these reactions, most mothers nevertheless soon begin to look on this emotional dependency as changeworthy. It has a little the quality of something infantile, of something that must be put away in favor of more mature kinds of expressed affection. The child should love his mother, to be sure, but with a less embarrassing degree of openness. He should want her attention, but not hound her for it or insist on it as a complete gratuity. The ultimate aim of the socialization process, as it relates to dependency, is for the child to be fond of the mother rather than passionately attached to her, to be pleased by her attention and interest but not incessantly to demand it.

Emotional dependency on a mother figure is a normal aspect of human development. Indeed, there is reason to believe that children who grow up under conditions which fail to develop such motivation will have asocial personalities of the kind described as psychopathic. They lack both conscience and the capacity to affiliate with other human beings. Only rare instances of such developmental mishaps have been reported, however, and the virtually universal sequence is for a child to become warmly affectionate and dependent in his early years and then gradually to become less so as the socialization process is invoked.

In a normal young child, the dependency motive appears to be a powerful one. It cannot be eliminated and it cannot be ignored. In fact, the more the child's efforts to satisfy it are frustrated, the more insistent and all-absorbing are his supplications. The socialization task for the mother is one of gradual modification of the form of expression, therefore, rather than one of blunt elimination. She must help the child learn to seek attention and affection from his peers and from other adults, as well as from herself, and she must help him to change from his clinging, engulfing manner of expression to a cooler, perhaps more verbal, one. And withal, she must teach him to "ask" for signs of love and attention and reassurance in a fashion less demanding, more subtle, more in accord with the propriety and dignity of adult behavior.

In offering this description of the growth of dependency and the mother's training problem, we are necessarily oversimplifying the situation. As was mentioned in connection with both weaning and toilet training, the relationship between mother and child is not a simple cause-and-effect one. For research purposes, sometimes we have had to adopt a fiction that what the mother does is independent of her child's behavior toward her. It is as if we were saying that when a mother does so-and-so, her child responds by doing, or learns to do, such-and-such. This is rarely if ever true. What a child does influences his mother, just as what she does influences him. When he hangs onto her skirts or tries to keep in some kind of verbal contact with her, or does something else that we point to as an example of dependent action, he is not just behaving blindly. He has already learned that these are ways of insuring desired maternal responses. He wants his mother to orient toward him, talk to him, be in contact with him. The actions he performs are ones that have become part of his repertory *because, by and large, they have worked.*

A mother and her child are a *dyad*. That is, each has expectancies about how the other should behave. If these are fulfilled, each is happy and comfortable. If expectations are *not* met, however, there is frustration. Both mother and child learn how to control each other, that is, how to produce in the partner those actions which will make for satisfactions. However, during the child's early life, he no sooner learns one way of behaving than his mother's expectancies change. Then he must learn a new way. For example, he learns to hug and kiss her, to express his affection very openly. But then she begins to view such behavior as changeworthy; she wants him to *talk* his love more and *hug* it less. If she begins to be less responsive to his customary ways of seeking her affection and attention, his first reaction will be to redouble his efforts. That is, he will behave "more dependently." Ultimately, if his mother just never responds at all, we would expect these specific forms of supplication to be eliminated (because of non-reward).

There are two types of maternal behavior that can be examined as possible sources of the child's dependent behavior. One is the initial learning situation in infancy. What kinds of treatment create a strong dependency motive? Breast feeding? Warmth and affectionate demonstrativeness? Or do the psychological "distance" of bottle feeding and the lack of intimacy offered by a cool and reserved mother produce insecurity and renewed efforts to gain affection and attention?

The second place to look is in the mother's current handling of the changeworthy behavior. Does punishment reduce it, or just make it flame into desperation? Does a permissive attitude allow the child to retain his more infantile forms of interaction, or does it ease the pressure in some way?

In this chapter, we will describe first the various forms of dependent behavior the children were reported to display toward their mothers and other family members. From the mothers' reports we made an estimate, on a five-point rating scale, of how dependent the child was at the time of the interview. We will examine the relation of this measure to those infant experiences which we have believed, for theoretical reasons, might influence the amount of dependency the child developed. We will then describe the various ways in which mothers reacted to early dependency behavior and attempted to change it into more mature forms. We will note, too, what the mothers' own theories about such training were, and try to determine which of them were correct. Finally, we will indicate what other personality qualities in the mother seem to have been associated with the choice of various methods of handling dependency.

Measuring Dependency

It is important to keep in mind that a mother's own attitudes toward dependency influence her perception of her child's behavior. Affectionate parents who welcome physical contact may be delighted with a child who follows the mother around and wants to be picked up, or at least to be near her. Some mothers, in fact, are not themselves happy unless their children are nearby and in contact with them. They have little desire to push the child into less intimate ways of seeking affection.

Then there are other mothers who, when they have time to respond, do not mind a child's being near and wanting help and attention, but are driven to distraction by such behavior when they are busy. "Mother free, mother busy" is as clear to many children as a "No trespassing" sign posted or down. These mothers are perhaps less oriented to the notion of training, and react to the child more in terms of their own immediate needs and feelings.

At another extreme are those parents who, for various reasons, do not countenance dependent behavior under any circumstances. It is taboo. They want to separate the child from themselves as much as possible. If the child wants attention, he must learn to get it by indirect and ingenious methods, or perhaps by creating so much unpleasantness that the mother gives in simply to restore peace in the household.

The very words that parents use to describe a particular form of behavior give us a clear sign of their attitudes toward it. Some mothers describe dependent acts in such terms as "he's an affectionate child," or "she's such a cuddly baby." Others make comments like "he's so clingy," or "she's always hanging onto me," or "he's whiny."

The following excerpts from interviews exemplify this mixture of behavioral description and the mothers' attitudes toward the behavior. First we have a mother who described her son's rather extreme demands for a *body contact* kind of affection and attention; she indicated clearly her dislike for such actions.

M. *The oldest child appeals to me in a very affectionate manner, and John (the five-year-old) doesn't have quite the same appeal; of the two, John is the one that would like the affection. It might be because I have felt an affection but not demonstrative. You know what I mean. The oldest child isn't either, where John is kind of—well, he could be loved and kissed constantly, and I'm not like that myself as much as probably I could be. A little bit is all right with me, but Johnnie could just sit there. Like if people come in to the house, it embarrasses me; he has to go sit in their lap. He would like to have you hold him constantly. Like looking at television, he wants to sit in your lap, and have you bill and coo and love him, and all this stuff. I don't think in the first place it's healthy, and yet I don't know why he should be that way.*

Later she expressed similar feelings for her son's *seeking of reassurance.*

I. *How do you generally react if he wants attention when you're busy?*
M. *Well, I give it to him. It isn't that so much, that kind of babyish way; it's not that much with him, as—well, like in the morning, when they get ready for school. I do tell them both how wonderful they look, and David is very satisfied with the compliment, but John will say, "Do you like the collar on me, or should I have worn this," until you get ready to scream.*

A second mother reported little dependent behavior by the five-year-old. What he did show, she responded to a little more positively:

I. *How much attention does Peter seem to want from you?*
M. *Very little. He can be left to his own devices for two or three hours at a time except to occasionally show me or ask me something.*
I. *How about following you around and hanging on to your skirts?*
M. *Never.*
I. *Did he ever go through a stage of doing that?*
M. *Nope.*
I. *How do you generally react if he demands attention when you're busy?*
M. *I would say I would have to ask for a definition of your term "busy."*
I. *Well, say if you were rushing to get dinner and he was—*
M. *I'd tell him to wait five minutes. So that was why I asked you what you meant by busy. If I cannot be disturbed, and that occasionally happens, then I'll have to say, "I'm busy," or "I'll be with you in five minutes,"—or if I'm expecting dinner guests and I must be ready on*

time tonight. If he's insisting, I will drop what I'm doing and see what he wanted, but I'm impatient about it. But that doesn't happen very often.

I. *How about if Pete asks you to help him with something you think he can probably do by himself?*

M. *I will sit down with him and act as if I were helping him, and all the time he will do it himself, and then when we are finished, I will say: "You know I never touched that. I just told you to put that block there. I never touched it. Look, Pete, my hands are still folded. I was smoking all the time. You did it yourself." And then he will do it himself the next time and realize that he did.*

An excerpt from a third child's mother describes a good deal of dependent behavior in the form of *talking* as a means of seeking attention, but the mother evidently did not regard this as much of a problem:

I. *How much attention does she seem to want from you?*

M. *Quite a good deal. She's pretty companionable. In fact, I'm going through a spell right now where she wants to be pretty much the center of the stage, and I find that when I have guests she's inclined to want to come right in and take over. I'm not awfully smart at handling that. I don't want to shut her up too much. I want her to feel she is welcome and to join in the conversation, but she's just apt to take over and she's inclined right now to just want my attention terribly. I try to give it to her and also try to explain to her that there are times that you just can't break in like that. Sometimes I actually distract her by getting her something else to do, but I find that she likes to follow me around and talk; she's quite a talker and lots of fun.*

I. *How do you feel about it when she hangs on to you and follows you around?*

M. *I don't mind that; I really enjoy having her. She's fun, and I get a lot of fun out of her. I don't know whether she feels she hasn't been getting enough attention or whether she's just gotten spoiled—her brother and sister think she is spoiled and wants the center of attention all the time because she has been the baby.*

From these verbatim comments it can be seen that the mothers varied immensely with respect to how much and what kinds of dependent behavior they saw in their children, and how they regarded and treated it.

It is these very differences in attitude of the mothers, of course, that give us trouble in any attempt to get an objective and unbiased measure of the child's dependency from the interview. We do not know to what extent a mother's fundamental liking or disliking of such behavior influenced her description of it. Doubtless the effects were different for different mothers. Further, it must be remembered that most mothers do not have wide personal experience with whole groups of five-year-old children. Therefore they lack a frame of reference against which they can view their own child's behavior. What seems like much dependent behavior to one mother may seem like little to another. This lack of standard perspective, coupled with the unknown effects of attitudes toward dependency, requires us to interpret the dependency ratings as a measure of the *mothers' perceptions* rather than as direct

and objective and comparable-from-one-child-to-another measures of children's behavior.

By using standard questions in the interview, it was possible to sample the mothers' observations concerning four common forms of dependent behavior. These are exemplified in the first four tables presented below, which show the percentage of children rated as exhibiting each of the degrees of dependency on each of the four scales. In addition, an over-all rating of "total dependency" was made, on the basis of everything the mother said that had to do with dependency. The distribution of these latter ratings is shown in Appendix Table D:13.

The first question was, "How much attention does (child's name) seem to want from you?" The answers were rated on the five-point scale shown in Table V:1, which gives the percentage of children who were judged to belong at each level of the scale.

Some examples of answers rated as low or high on attention-seeking will perhaps make clearer than the scale descriptions can do just what dimension is measured by the scale, and what de-

TABLE V:1

"How Much Attention Does X Seem to Want from You?"

1. Practically none (only when hurt)	8%
2. A little (occasionally has a mood when wants it, but usually not)	27
3. Some (at certain times of day, goes through periods)	26
4. Quite a bit	27
5. A great deal	10
Not ascertained	2
Total	100%

gree of dependency is implied by each level. The following three mothers' reports were rated *low:*

A

M. *Well, we're kind of a funny family. I mean we don't show too much affection towards one another. I mean affection is there but we just, we're not the very sloppy kind. She comes in from school, she kisses me good-bye in the morning, and of course, I go to the door with her, and I watch her down the street. She's not a child that you would say would fall all over you. She'll kiss you and all that, but I mean she's not a child that you would say was exceptionally affectionate.*

B

M. *She has her sister, and she's quite a bit with her. My oldest daughter has taught her how to write, and when Susan does her homework, Nancy is right with her making numbers and she amuses herself in that way so she doesn't come to me for any certain thing, because Susan reads her stories and that's how the time passes with her.*

C

M. *Oh, very little, he is so grown up it is painful. He loves to have a story at night. . . . He is very affectionate, but he does have a little life all his own, and he enjoys being grown-up. I have been a Den Mother, and he has entered in with the Cubs like he was one of them, and he is a very likable child. All those boys are crazy about him and they never objected to having him around. He is real popular in the neighborhood. He comes out with funny remarks and everybody enjoys having him around. He has quite a social life, and I don't see him too much actually.*

Two examples of answers rated as *high* on attention-seeking were:

A

M. *He wants a lot of attention. He wants all my attention.*
I. *How does he go about this?*
M. *He doesn't let me talk on the telephone—he is climbing all over me, interrupting me, and if I were talking to anyone—even here now —he would resent it terribly. He would have to be climbing all over me and want my attention, and if he can't get it he does something very naughty to get it.*

B

M. *She wants an enormous amount. Janet likes a lot of affection. She is naturally a very affectionate child, more so than the other one. They are both affectionate, but she seems hungry for it, somehow or other. She likes to play with you, and she likes to hug and kiss. She loves to be fondled, and she likes a lot of attention.*

The second question followed immediately in the interview: "How about following you around and hanging onto your skirts?"

TABLE V:2

"How about Following You Around and Hanging onto Your Skirts?"

1. Doesn't cling, follow, or seek to be near	55%
2. Slight tendency to do this	20
3. Some tendency	15
4. Considerable tendency	8
Not ascertained	2
Total	100%

Sometimes the wording varied a little, because of the way the mother had ended her last sentence, but the words "following you around and hanging onto your skirts" always got into the interviewer's query. Table V:2 gives the distribution, in percentages, of children who were estimated to be at each of the four levels the scale defines.

Again it will be helpful to present some excerpts that illustrate the kinds of reported behavior that were rated at different scale points. These first two mothers' answers were rated as *low:*

A

M. *She doesn't do that too much.*

B

M. *No, I don't like that. As a rule, she doesn't. Once in a great while she's tired, and she doesn't like to give in to sleep when she's tired, and she will hang on to me then, but as a rule she doesn't.*

Here are two answers that were rated *medium:*

A

M. *No, not too much, only from boredom really.*
I. *Does he do it occasionally?*
M. *Yes, I'd say in the afternoon when the other children are in school and he's not, and the two smaller ones are sleeping. He just doesn't know what to do with himself, and then he'll tag around until you can get him interested in something, and he'll go off and do that.*

B

M. *If she is with me alone, she likes to be with me, she likes company, but if her sister is home, she won't bother me at all; she will go off with her sister and play with her all day.*

The following examples were rated as *high:*

A

M. *I wouldn't say hanging on to my skirts, but I would say he follows me around, and he likes to be more or less where I am. I mean, in the sense that if I were upstairs in this house, he would prefer most of the time—he may be in another room upstairs, but he would prefer being upstairs at the time. Right now, I think that is the way he does feel. Not that occasionally he wouldn't be downstairs. The majority of the time he would prefer being, well, in the next room, I would say. That is why I didn't say he hangs on to my skirts, but still he would like to be in the next room anyway.*

B

M. *He doesn't play too well alone. He likes to be around me. He used to follow me around in every room—in fact, even now, if I am in the bedroom making beds, he is in the bedroom, too; or if I am in the living room, he is in the living room. He follows me around.*

C

M. *Janet is the type that wants a lot of attention, and she will stay under your feet and get it—she will always be around.*
I. *How about following you around and hanging on to your skirts?*
M. *She doesn't actually hang on to my skirts, but she follows me around to see what I am doing, or what I am going to do—that's one thing about her.*

The third question pushed the matter back to earlier childhood; it was phrased as, "Did he ever go through a stage of doing this (following mother around, hanging onto skirts)?" The answers to this question were rated on a very simple three-point scale, since the mothers were not able to give very detailed reports on this feature of their children's earlier behavior. Indeed, nearly a fifth of the replies could not be evaluated on this scale at all. One cannot help suspecting that the gradualness of the socializing changes that occur, with respect to dependent behavior, tends to blur a mother's memory of the behavior she had observed three or four years before she gave her report to the interviewer. Table V:3 presents the percentage of children who were judged to have shown each of three levels of behavior defined by the scale.

TABLE V:3

"Did X Ever Go Through a Stage of Following You Around and Hanging onto Your Skirts?"

1. Never showed this	29%
2. Some such tendency earlier	27
3. Went through a stage of being very "clingy"	25
Not ascertained	19
Total	100%

The answers that were rated as *low* were nearly always brief and undescriptive. They simply said, "No." Those that were rated as *high* were more detailed and gave some basis for believing that the children had at least been slower in giving up the changeworthy behavior. Following are some examples:

A

M. *Of hanging on to me really? Yes, she did when she was about a year-and-a-half old. She really did. She needed to be right next to me, sitting on my lap, and if I was away for any length of time, a few hours or an afternoon, she would really cling to me when I got back. That whole time between a year-and-a-half and two-and-a-half.*

B

M. *Yes, he definitely was the mama's boy when he was little, and painfully shy when anyone would come. He would hide his head in my lap, which is almost impossible to believe when you see him now, because he is such a complete extrovert—he is so sure of himself, and so extremely grown-up.*

C

M. *Oh, she did. Oh, it was terrible! At one time, if I had to do my shopping, I had to sneak out the back door, and if she ever saw me go, she would just cry until I came back.*

Finally, the fourth scale was designed to evaluate answers to the question, "How does (child's name) react generally when you go out of the house and leave him with someone else?" This question was designed to provide a different approach from that provided by the three previous questions. Whereas the others had inquired simply as to the amount of spontaneous *seeking* of mother's responsiveness, this last question sought a measure in terms of how vigorous the child's *frustration reaction* was when he

TABLE V:4

"How Does X React When You Go Out of the House and Leave Him with Someone Else?"

1. No objection to separation	62%
2. Occasionally objects, in mild manner	19
3. Fairly often objects, sometimes fairly strongly	10
4. Usually objects, usually strongly	3
5. Always objects strongly; has been severe problem, throwing tantrums, etc.	2
6. Problem does not arise; mother does not go out	2
Not ascertained	2
Total	100%

suffered interference with his dependency relationship to his mother. We may assume that the stronger and more emotional the reaction to separation, the stronger was the dependency motivation. Table V:4 presents the percentage of children who were judged to show each of the five levels of reaction defined by the scale-point descriptions.

Again the *low* end was unrevealing; most of the answers rated "1" were simple statements that the child showed little reaction to separation. One mother elaborated a little, as follows:

M. *Well, if she's left with someone else, she doesn't seem to mind it. As a matter of fact, as a general rule now she doesn't want to go with me wherever I go. "You go ahead, Momma. I'll stay here," and "I'll stay with (either one of our neighbors)." There's a woman upstairs next door that she does stay with. But she doesn't want to go anyplace with me now.*

There were relatively few reports of strong reactions, at age five to six, to a brief separation. The following two excerpts are fairly typical of those rated *medium*.

One mother replied:

A

M. *She's getting quite used to it, of course; it is her brother she is left with, so it is all in the family. She doesn't mind it too much, but once in a while, if I go out too often, she is somewhat annoyed.*
I. *How does she show it?*
M. *Well, she says that she wishes that I wouldn't go out, and some-times cries. She hasn't very much lately, but sometimes cries a bit about it. It doesn't make a bit of difference about what you do; you tell her, "I am sorry, but I have made these plans and I'm going," and that is that.*
I. *Then you go?*
M. *Then I go.*

The other said:

B

M. *They don't care for that too much. They like me to be there all the time. Like last night I went out, which they don't like at all. She kind of fussed, and she told me that she likes me to put her to bed and all that. I told her I had to go out once in a while.*

More extreme cases of apparent disturbance were rated *high*. Here are two examples:

A

M. *She doesn't sleep. If she knows we're going out, she lays awake in bed, and she makes a great many trips down; she wants to watch tele-vision, or she needs to go to the bathroom. There is always something, and sometimes when I come in—I always look at them anyway before I go to bed—she will be there wide awake. Sometimes she closes her eyes, but I know she is awake. So then I say to her, "Debbie, you're not asleep," and then she tells me, "I was waiting for you to come in."*

B

M. *That's really a problem. She'll screech her head off. She doesn't like it. They all—as a matter of fact, they'll all cry if I go away and leave them. Even if I go out and leave someone in the house to mind them, they'll want to go with me. "Don't go out, Mommy, stay home with us."*
I. *How do you handle it?*
M. *I don't go out.*
I. *You don't?*
M. *I don't go out unless I can take them along with me.*

There is a point worth noting in these four tables. A quarter or more of the mothers could recall a period, earlier in the child's life, when clinging and following around were distinctly troublesome, or at least noticeable (Table V:3). By the time of the interview, however, this kind of behavior had become much less frequent; more than half of the children were reported as showing none (Table V:2). The same can probably be said for emotional reactions to separation, although we do not have in-

fancy measures for comparison; the majority of children at age five showed no objection to their mother's leaving the house.

In contrast, however, the more verbal forms of seeking attention (Table V:1)—those that did not involve physical contact or strongly expressed emotion—were apparently still common at age five. This suggests that, as the mothers saw and interpreted dependency behavior, the physical-clinging kind decreased before the attention-getting type did. It may be that the seeking of reassurance and approval, the attempt to secure social affiliation, is the more socially acceptable method of satisfying dependency needs, and was tolerated longer by the mothers.

The correlations among these four measures were not large (see Appendix Table D:12), and in order to secure a single estimate of each child's current dependency behavior, a summary rating was made from all the information reported to the above questions (Appendix Table D:13). The preponderance of cases was toward the low end, although only three per cent of the children were characterized as having "none." It must be remembered that we are dealing here with dependency for its own sake, not with that dependency which is dictated by a child's actual need for help. There was no child in the group, of course, who failed to ask his mother for help with tasks for which he was too small, or light in weight, or lacking in actual knowledge.

This summary rating of the children's dependency was a measure of the mothers' perceptions, of course. How closely it corresponds to what an outside observer would have reported we do not know. When we remember the great variations in attitudes toward the training problem, and the differences in the mothers' tolerances for changeworthy behavior, we cannot but be doubtful that the ratings are an exact representation of how hard the child was working, at age five, to secure maternal attention. Furthermore, the number or intensity of dependency episodes a mother reported—even the vigor of the adjectives she used— probably influenced the raters in estimating her child's amount of dependency. We must assume, in other words, that a given mother's report about her child was not entirely independent of her report about her methods of handling his dependency.

Sex and ordinal position of child. Although there is a widely held belief that girls are more dependent on their mothers than boys, we found no sex difference in the summary ratings.

With respect to ordinal position, however, there was one interesting difference. The mothers of *only* children reported more dependent behavior than the mothers of children with siblings. The difference is small, on the summary scale, but fairly substantial ($p < .01$) on the scale measuring how much objection the child made to brief separations from his mother. A good many of the mothers who had two or more children commented that, by age five, the child had come to rely on his brothers or sisters for company. When the mother was away, he would turn to siblings. The *only* child, lacking such alternates in fact, and without as much experience in turning to other children, was more seriously deprived by his mother's leaving. His stronger protest is scarcely surprising.

INFANCY EXPERIENCES

There are two aspects of early infancy experience that might be expected, on theoretical grounds, to influence the strength of dependency motivation a child would develop. One of these is the amount of reinforcement for such actions provided by the mother. If we are correct in our assumption that this motive is created through the caretaking relationship, with its many repetitions of affectionate contact and help that are followed by such primary rewards as food and caresses, the child who had more such experiences should have a stronger drive than the child who had fewer or less intense ones. Psychoanalytic observations and theory have emphasized the role of the early feeding relationship in this connection, and some writers have suggested the possible strengthening of the motive by breast feeding.

Our findings provide no support for this reasoning, however. There is no relationship between the *warmth* of the mother toward the infant and her report of his later dependent behavior. Likewise, the breast-fed children were neither more nor less dependent than the entirely bottle-fed ones, regardless of how long the breast feeding continued. We had thought possibly that a prolonged period of feeding by sucking would be associated with greater dependency, but there proved to be no evidence of such a relation. The age at beginning of weaning, the duration of the process, and the age at completion of weaning were all irrelevant to the dependency measure.

We would hesitate to conclude that the rather wide variations in these dimensions were of *no* importance to the development of the dependency motive. Psychotherapeutic practice has revealed too many instances of "positive fixation" to permit such a generalization. Possibly, either the influence of infant experiences was being masked by later influences, or else our measure of dependency was inappropriate for the test. In any case, we could not detect any effects of these infancy experiences that were strong enough to affect group averages.

The second aspect of infancy experience that might be relevant is the degree of frustration that occurred in connection with the infant's attempts to secure an affectionate and nurturant response from the mother. After all, the experiences most children have with their mothers is quite sufficient to establish a dependency motive. Certainly this was the case with all the children in this study. Given such a motive, the child would then react to any partial deprivation by increasing the strength of his efforts to gain attention and expressions of affection. Our summary measure of dependency, we suspect, was more a measure of these efforts than of any underlying motive. Within the limits of the mothers' perceptions, then, we might expect that dependent behavior at age five would be greater if the child had been frustrated during infancy in his efforts to secure the hoped-for maternal response.

Sadly, we must report that this hypothesis, too, gains little support from our data. We will show later that the general principle is sound—frustration of dependency supplications *does* produce an increase in such behavior at the time the frustration occurs— but we have not been able to discover very much evidence that frustration in infancy has an effect at kindergarten age.

We sought for evidence in three places. One was infant feeding, of course. In an earlier research, at the State University of Iowa (Sears *et al.*, 1953), we had found an apparent relationship between the *severity of weaning* reported by the mothers of 40 three- and four-year-old children and the amount of dependency the children displayed in nursery school. The measure of dependency at home, in the present study, was not so related, however. The Iowa children were about two years closer to the actual weaning experience, of course, and it may well be that later attitudes of the mother or other family members masked the effect of weaning in our present group of kindergarten-age children. In one case, too, the dependency was measured in the school situation, and in the other, in the home. Whatever the reason, we find no general connection between severity of weaning and dependency.

Another aspect of the feeding process that is relevant to the frustration problem is that of *scheduling*. Presumably, a child on a fixed schedule gets about as much reinforcement of his dependency as a child on a self-demand regime. Eventually, too, he adjusts to the schedule, but in the early weeks he goes through a period in which food sometimes is forced on him when he is not hungry, and other times is withheld from him when he is. We reasoned that this kind of experience might lead to more persistent efforts to get the mother's attention. Again, in the Iowa study, there was some support for the hypothesis; the *girls* (but not the boys) who had been fed on a rigid schedule were more dependent in nursery school than those who had been fed at self-demand. In the present study, however, the girls showed no relationship at all, while the *boys* showed just the opposite! Those who had been fed on self-demand were reported to be more dependent than those fed by schedule ($p < .02$; $r = -.17$). These contradictions leave us with some strong impetus to further research, but not much else.

Another aspect of infant frustration that seemed worth examining was the mother's *responsiveness to the baby's crying*. Many mothers reported that they had definite ideas from the very first as to how they should treat the child in order to get the kind of dependency behavior (or lack of it!) they wanted. Some were responsive and affectionate in the hopes of creating a warm and loving, cuddly child—others remained more aloof, refusing to respond to crying or other forms of supplicative behavior because of a belief that to respond would spoil the child and make him too clingy or whiny. These beliefs were often held strongly. especially by some of the younger and less experienced mothers; those who had had several children were a little more likely to express doubt as to whether the matter was as simple as it had seemed when they began their families.

In actual behavior toward their children, retrospectively reported, the mothers had differed greatly. Even in brief excerpts one can see clearly that the methods of handling crying in infancy were usually rationalized in terms of their effectiveness for training. In Table V:5 are shown the percentages of mothers who were rated at each level of a five-point scale designed to evaluate answers to the following question:

> All babies cry, of course. Some mothers feel that if you pick up a baby every time it cries, you will spoil it. Others think you should never let a baby cry for very long. How do you feel about this?

There were very few mothers rated at the extreme of unresponsiveness, but the following exemplifies a *low* rating:

M. *Well, I think along this line—if you pick them up too often that does spoil them and if they cry too long I think something will come of it—so—if they cry too long you should try to pat them or stop them—or something—but I don't believe in picking them up all the time.*

An example of a *medium* rating:

M. *Well, it depends on the age. If they are—when they're small, if they cry you know there's something wrong. I don't think they'd cry for exercise, like psychologists seem to claim. I think they cry when they're uncomfortable and that's the only reason. And it could be from hunger, pain, or any number of reasons like that. Wet diapers,*

TABLE V:5

MOTHERS' RESPONSIVENESS TO BABIES' CRYING

1. Extremely unresponsive. Believed child must not be spoiled; didn't want to "give in" to crying	1%
2. Mother relatively unresponsive. Child generally picked up only when mother believed something was wrong; allowed to cry for extended periods	15
3. "It depends." Picked up if mother thought child was hungry; allowed to cry if mother thought it was simply "fretful." Would allow to cry for a while, but not too long	33
4. Relatively responsive. Usually picked child up, although occasionally allowed it to cry for brief periods	33
5. Highly responsive to infant's crying; always picked it up immediately	15
Not ascertained	3
Total	100%

for instance, and so forth. But after you've checked everything and they still want to cry, I will let them cry. For a while, I mean, not to excess. But we never had any trouble with our children crying. They were very good.

The following two instances were rated *high* on responsiveness to crying:

A

M. *Well, I would pick her up as soon as I could. The first two months were just terrible as she cried almost all of the time, and naturally I was pretty much exhausted; and I'm afraid she got a bad start, but that was not because of our convictions but because of her condition, and after the two months she suddenly became the happiest thing you could imagine, was perfectly contented. She would lie for hours, cooing, and talking quietly to herself, examining her toes and fingers, and then, if she did cry, I fed her or just played with her for a little while, and she immediately stopped.*

I. *How about when she cried in the middle of the night?*
M. *Well, she didn't very much after that two months. I think she had a ten o'clock feeding, or around that time, never a rigid schedule, but around that time, for about three, maybe a little more months, and we would go to her as soon as she cried out at that time, eleven or twelve, and feed her then.*
I. *The crying was for feeding really?*
M. *Yes, and then she would sleep the rest of the night very nicely; and if she cried during the day, I would go to her.*

B

M. *I don't see any reason for letting a baby cry. I always pick them up right away and see what the trouble is, because they don't cry unless there's something the matter with them. So I never let them cry unless I'm tied down hand and foot somewhere else.*

Again, we find no relationship. The correlation between the mother's responsiveness to crying when the child was in his infancy and her report of his dependency at kindergarten age was an insignificant .08. We must conclude that the mothers' theories —as well as ours—gain no support.

Finally, we examined the effect on later dependency of early infant separations from the mother. A number of recent studies, particularly those from the Tavistock Clinic in London, have emphasized the potential damage to the normal development of dependency motivation when children are traumatically, or for long periods, separated from their mothers during the first two years of life.

In our sample, there were no instances of the extreme varieties of maternal deprivation that are found among institutional children, of course. In fact, instances of even very brief separations of child from mother during the early years were rare. We had only seven instances in which the infant (during his first nine months of life) was separated from his mother for more than three weeks; during the nine-month to twenty-four-month age range, only 11 of the children in our sample had been separated from their mothers for a continuous period of three weeks or more; and even after the age of two years, only 27 children had had this experience. The practice of leaving a young child with grandparents for a month or two during the summer was very rare among these families. The most common cause for separations of as much as a week's duration appeared to be the advent of a new baby. For this event, the mother would go to a hospital for a week or so, and the child would find himself at home without his mother for the first time in his life (except for the occasions on which he had been left with a baby sitter for an evening or part of a day).

Since we have so few cases of lengthy separations, we have little basis for drawing any conclusions concerning their effects. When we examined the records of those children who had been separated briefly from their mothers in early childhood, we found no greater dependency at the age of five than in children who had not had this experience. If there was any increase in dependency among these children during the time just after they had been reunited with their mothers, the behavior does not appear to have been lasting. Of course, whether there were effects in areas of behavior other than dependency we do not know.

In sum, we have found little to indicate that there are massive effects of the infant experiences we have examined, so far as later dependency is concerned. There was no evidence that high responsiveness to crying or the expression of warm affection in early infancy influenced our measure of dependency. Neither the variations in amount of reward or frustration associated with infant feeding seemed to have influential later effects. These statements must be taken very literally, however, and must not be overgeneralized. As we saw in Chapter Three, some of these variables were quite influential in other aspects of the child's behavior. Furthermore, our summary measure of dependency is an extremely limited reflector even of the total complex dyadic motive we have called dependency. All we can say is that we have been unable to discover any *consistent* effects of a few infant experiences on one measure of dependent behavior displayed by kindergarten-age children.

The Handling of Dependency

By the age of five, a child has lost much of his tendency to demand close intimacy. He still seeks a good deal of contact with, and attention from, his mother, and at least a few youngsters are still easily upset by their mothers' going out of the house.

One of the major areas of exploration in our interview was the mother's attitude toward the various aspects of behavior that the child was showing currently. Our questions included the following:

How do you feel about it when he hangs on to you and follows you around?

How do you generally react if he demands attention when you are busy?

How about if X asks you to help him with something you think he could probably do himself?

The mothers' discussions of these problems were rated on three different dimensions. The first was *permissiveness* of the mother's attitude toward dependent behavior, that is, how tolerant she was of attention-getting and other dependent actions. The second was the extent to which she *rewarded* dependent be-

TABLE V:6

PERMISSIVENESS TOWARD DEPENDENCY

1. Not at all permissive for dependency	11%
2. Low permissiveness	26
3. Moderate permissiveness	30
4. Quite permissive	19
5. Dependency perfectly O.K.	11
Not ascertained	3
Total	100%

havior by giving attention, or help, when it was sought by the child. The third dimension was her *punitiveness* toward dependency, that is, the amount of irritation she showed at dependent behavior, sometimes in the form of punishment, sometimes only by scolding or pushing the child away angrily. Tables V:6, V:7, and V:8 show the proportion of mothers rated at each point on these scales. We also rated the interviews on a summary scale, called "Mother's treatment of dependency," which ran from positive through neutral to negative. This summary scale is used in other chapters where a less refined breakdown of maternal actions vis-à-vis dependency is needed.

We chose these three dimensions for describing the handling of dependency because they represent significant theoretical variables in connection with the child's learning process. They are by no means independent, of course. Mothers who felt that dependent actions were perfectly acceptable in a child of five generally did not become irritated when their children behaved dependently; and they usually tried to help when the children wanted help, even though the help might not have seemed needed. Likewise, an irritable and punitive attitude toward de-

TABLE V:7

AMOUNT OF REWARD OF CHILD'S DEPENDENCY

1. Never rewards	10%
2. Occasionally rewards	31
3. Sometimes rewards	33
4. Often rewards	19
5. Tries always to reward	4
Not ascertained	3
Total	100%

pendency, a tendency to be non-permissive, and not to reward dependency when it did occur, usually went together. The intercorrelations among the scales are shown in Appendix Table D:14.

There were instances, however, in which a good deal of maternal irritation was coupled with reward. The child would whee-

TABLE V:8

PUNITIVENESS TOWARD DEPENDENCY

1. No irritation or punishment	12%
2. Rarely irritated or punishing	11
3. Some irritation and/or punishment	25
4. Often irritable or punishing	23
5. Considerable irritation and/or punishment	13
Not ascertained	16
Total	100%

dle for help and attention until the mother gave in; she would resent the necessity, and would respond angrily. For example:

I. *How do you feel about it when she hangs on to you and follows you around?*

M. *It depends on what I'm doing. If it's sewing, something that I'm sitting down doing and she can participate in it, too, to some degree, I don't mind. But if I'm trying to get something done—for instance, the hours before dinner, I'm feeding the baby and so forth—I get exasperated and just tell her to get out and let me get this done; (laughs) that she'll have her reading after supper.*

I. *This is part of the next question, which is, how do you generally react if she demands attention when you're busy?*

M. *I realize that I shouldn't react. I try to save myself from reacting antagonistically, but I do. I become peeved and I think she feels that. But at this stage, though, she seems to have become antagonistic herself. At that stage—just the both of us, we both become very antagonistic. And my voice rises and finally I threaten her with having to stay in her room or to—I tell her what to do and usually she goes and does something else. But in the meantime there is quite a bit of hullabaloo. Often, I must say, at this point, if my husband is at home, which if it's after six o'clock, he usually is, he intervenes and straightens things out right away. If I am very angry with her, he will often calm and soothe her, which also soothes me because I'm left free to do what I was going to do, if it's getting a pie out of the oven or whatever it was.*

I. *So when she does want attention when you are busy, you generally ask her to wait or what?*

M. *Yes, I ask her to wait. Or if it's a serious attention, I mean, that she needs something buttoned or something she can't do for herself, ask her to wait. She, however, she is soon impatient about it and doesn't want to wait. She'll ask me every minute until it's done.*

I. *How about if she asks you to help her with something you think she could probably do herself?*

M. *Then I tell her she should be able to do it by herself and if it's a question of conflict of wills, which it often is because I know she can do it by herself, well, it's just that, and finally one or the other of us wins out. Either I do it for her or she does it herself. It often takes ten minutes, fifteen minutes. . . .*

I. *You try to get her to do it by herself?*

M. *I try to and if it just doesn't succeed, I end up by doing it. I know that she can put on her snowsuit by herself even though it's a little hard and she has another pair of pants underneath, but finally I'll come and help her when I've gotten what I'm doing done. If she doesn't get it done by herself in the meantime.*

The mothers showed a wide range of attitudes with respect to their willingness to *reward* dependent behavior and to maintain a *permissive* attitude toward it. One mother who was judged high both in offering reward and being permissive said:

I. *How did you feel about it when she hung on to you and followed you around?*

M. *Well, I didn't think too much about it. I mean I wouldn't say that it was an aggravating situation by any means because, after all, a mother's love is pretty strong. It never bothered me.*

I. *How do you generally react if she demands attention when you're busy?*

M. *Well, if I'm busy I'll just say I'm busy, that's all. When I get through doing what I am, I'll see what she wants or what her demand is. And usually then I'll take care of it.*

I. *How about if she asks you to help her with something you think she probably can do by herself?*

M. *Well, in a case like that, I usually ask her if she can do it by herself; and if she says that she can, but she isn't sure, I'll tell her I'll help her. I usually help them with all their problems, as far as that goes. I mean Helen's homework—I help her with that if there's anything puzzling her. As for catechism and things like that—I usually give her a lift on that. If I don't, my husband does. I mean any problems they ever have, we have always tried to face them together and to help them in any way that we could.*

I. *How about the little things, such as, putting things away, putting things on. . . ?*

M. *Well, we've always waited on them hand and foot—the both of us have. We've always done that, I don't know why. Some people say it's a very bad habit to get into—waiting on your children and having your children depend upon you so much. As for putting on their things, why if they ask me to put on a coat or anything like that, I gladly stop what I'm doing and do it for them.*

An opposite point of view was illustrated by the mother who expected a child of kindergarten age to be quite self-reliant, and had little sympathy for "clingyness" or "attention-seeking" in her child:

I. *How did you feel about it when she wanted to be with you all the time?*

M. *Well, I had to teach her she had to be alone at times and not have me around.*

I. *How do you generally react if she demands attention when you're busy?*

M. *I don't pay attention to her.*

I. *How about if she asks you to help her with something you think she could probably do by herself?*

M. *I tell her she's supposed to do it herself, and I'm not going to help her.*

I. *And then does she do it?*

M. *Oh, yes, if she feels like it.*

I. *Otherwise, what do you do?*

M. *Otherwise, I just let her alone, let her have one of her stubborn streaks, or just take things away, tell her she can't play any more if she's going to be like that.*

The next excerpt illustrates a common problem—how to decide when a request for help is justifiable, in terms of the child's lack of skill, and when it is simply a bid for attention, an attempt to retain a nurtured role. This issue provides a continuous tug-of-war in many families, a kind of low-grade internecine power struggle that goes on and on and on. It is more complex than it seems, often because it represents the mother's effort not only to control "needless" dependency, but to create new skills and independence. The word "needless" well deserves its quotation marks. As we have seen earlier, the securing of such help may not serve a required function physically, but it does represent a reassurance of affection and support that the child began to learn to want from the very beginning of his life. Here is the way one mother described her own behavior:

I. *Well, how do you generally react, if he demands attention when you're busy?*
M. *Well, if it's a legal demand I try to give it to him.*
I. *What do you mean by "legal"?*
M. *Well, if he asks for me to help him with something, to do something that he's doing, that he seems to be struggling with, he can't do himself, I usually try to help him. If he just seems to be hard up for something to do and I'm very busy, I try to suggest things for him to do until I'm free enough to get him started on something else. Ordinarily he has plenty to do. He's very busy unless he's tied in with poor weather or something like that. . . .*
I. *Well, how about if he asks you to help him with something you think he could probably do by himself?*
M. *Then I usually suggest that he try again. I mean oftentimes he'd want me to help him get dressed because he's late. And I'll say, "Well, I have been telling you for the last ten minutes that it's time for you to get dressed, and now it's time for you to hurry." And I usually try to see that he does it himself. If it's something that I think he should do himself. He gets mad once in a while and says, "Oh, you always want me to do things by myself." And I'll say, "Well, there are some things that Mommie should help you with and some things that you should do just as well as Mommie yourself." And those are the things I expect him to do. Sometimes he fusses about it, but usually he does it, even if he fusses.*

We have seen, then, that some mothers used non-reward as part of a well-calculated effort to reduce dependency behavior. A few so heartily disliked seeing a child ask for attention that they reacted with exasperation or even anger, especially if such demands came at an inconvenient time. In contrast, a good many other mothers were frankly pleased by their children's warmth and friendliness, and viewed dependent behavior as something to be encouraged. These mothers' positive reactions were, in some instances, simply a reflection of this pleasure, and in others were at least accompanied, if not initiated, by a desire to reinforce the more mature forms of dependency.

How did the mothers' attitudes toward dependency fit in with their other attitudes and practices? The three aspects we measured—permissiveness, rewarding, and punishment—were by no means independent of one another, of course. (See Appendix Table D:14.) A permissive attitude toward the child's supplications was much more likely to lead a mother to reward such behavior ($r = .57$). It is not surprising to find, therefore, that all three dimensions were related very similarly to other attitudes and practices. Indeed, the similarity was so great that we included only the single summary scale, called *response to dependency*, in our factor analysis.

The mother's reaction to dependency was related to two of the underlying traits uncovered by this analysis. One of these was the *permissiveness* factor (A) and the other was the *warmth* factor (C). Those mothers who had an accepting tolerant attitude toward the child's dependent behavior were also:

1. affectionally warm toward the child ($r = .37$)
2. gentle about toilet training ($r = .30$)
3. low in their use of physical punishment ($r = .27$)
4. high in sex permissiveness ($r = .19$)
5. low in punishment for aggression toward parents ($r = -.23$)
6. high in esteem for both self and husband (r's $= .39, .32$).

The next question is what effect these practices had on the child. We have already seen that the various infancy measures had little relation to the amount of dependency he showed at kindergarten age.

CURRENT SOURCES OF DEPENDENCY

The mothers themselves had a number of theories to account for such behavior. These were of two general kinds. One had to do with the original production of dependency, and the other with the methods of handling it once it had developed. It is difficult to treat these matters separately, because *warmth,* which was a commonly suggested originator of dependency, is somewhat related to the dimensions that refer to methods of handling the already developed dependency.

Warmth and affectionate demonstrativeness. Some mothers expressed the opinion that a great deal of fondling and cuddling would make the child over-dependent *during the period such practices were being followed*. The reasoning was that such experiences directly reinforced the child's efforts to be near the

mother and follow her around, which are the behaviors we have described as "dependent."

To test this idea, we have examined the relation between dependency and the mothers' *current* level of affectionate behavior. There was a slight relationship between a mother's current *affectionate demonstrativeness* and her report of child's current dependent behavior. Of the small group of mothers who were exceptionally demonstrative, 41 per cent had children who could be described as quite dependent, while only 24 per cent of the remaining mothers' children could be so described. This relationship is greater than one would expect by chance ($p < .02$; $r = .13$), but it is small, and one must conclude that the dimension of demonstrativeness contributed only slightly to the amount of dependency the children were described as showing.

It is interesting that the more global dimension described earlier—that of maternal *warmth*—was not related to the child's dependency, even though the mother's demonstrativeness was taken into account in rating warmth. Evidently, it was the overt demonstration of affection rather than the mother's underlying attitude of love that led a child to seek attention and physical contact with her.

Rejection and withholding of love. Another commonly suggested source of dependent behavior was the amount of frustration the child suffered in his efforts to secure the mother's affectionate attention. Many of the mothers interpreted dependent actions as direct attempts to satisfy this want for attention. Since they considered over-dependency undesirable, they viewed it as something to be eliminated by changing their own behavior in the direction of giving the child more affection and security. A recurrent theme is suggested by the following excerpts:

A

M. *After she's done something bad, she's very sorrowful and needs to be reassured that you love her—she'll say many times, "I love you, I love you," and wants obviously to be reassured that you love her, too.*

B

M. *I try to be understanding about it—I realize he needs an awful lot of security. I try to give him as much as I can, but there are limitations—it gets to a point where I just can't do any more than I have already done. He is very much inclined to say, "You don't love me," and of course it kills me, it breaks my heart, but I really don't know quite what to do about it; and yet I feel that I give him more than his share of love and affection. He gets much more than the other children do, and I really feel that I have neglected the baby terribly for him. I have ignored the baby completely for him, but I think that there would be no limit to what he would want from me. I think he would want me to be around whenever he wanted me, so he could sit*

*in my lap and I could tell him a story, or I could play a game with him,
or talk to him.*

C

M. *There was one period when he would go out to play, and he would
suddenly come in the house and throw his arms around me, and he
would ask, "Do you love me?"—and then I would assure him I did
love him, and he would go out again, but he would keep coming in. He
just seemed to feel the need of security, to be assured.*

These mothers traced dependency to the child's insecurity,
to his need for reassurance that his mother loved him. There
is an implication that he had a strong impulsion to receive
nurturance and affection, and that somehow or other the mother
never quite allayed his essential uncertainty.

This inference is not unreasonable. Many mothers reported
that their expressions of love and small attentions reduced these
dependency supplications, at least briefly. But in the more extreme cases, the reduction did not last long. As the third mother
put it: "He would keep coming in (for more)."

Such persistent efforts by a child to get affectionate responses
from his mother have all the earmarks of a strong motivational
system. Indeed, the constant seeking of a goal, and the display
of emotional distress when the seeking fails, are the principal
criteria by which we can recognize the existence of a motivational
system and identify its aim. In the case of dependency behavior,
the goal is an expression of loving acceptance by the mother.
If she is rejecting, the child's wants are unfulfilled and he will
increase his efforts to secure the desired behavior.

There is some support in our data for these propositions.
There were three measures of maternal behavior that seemed
especially relevant, and all three were significantly (although
not strongly) associated with the measure of the child's dependency. (See Appendix Table D:15.)

The first of these measures was that of *rejection of the child,*
a scale which requires comment here, for it has not been mentioned previously. A mother who never felt irritation with her
child, who never for even a moment felt deprived of her freedom
and independence, would be less than human. Children are not
invariably happy and satisfied, nor are all their needs expressed
exactly at the moments when their mothers are most strongly
motivated to fulfill them. The most loving mother gets frustrated,

exasperated or bored sometimes, and she shows it. This is normal and inevitable and has nothing to do with what we mean by rejection.

Quite independent of such quick emotions, there is an attitude that colors all the relations between the mother and child. At one extreme, this dimension is defined as an *acceptance* of the child; at the other, as *rejection*. Acceptance means that the mother gives love without reservation, not necessarily with great demonstration, but without exacting a price of consistently "good" behavior from the child. He is hers and he is part of her. She loves *him* without regard to what he *does*. Rejection, on the other hand, is a pervasive attitude of withholding love, at least a little bit. It may involve a sense of contingency—"I'll love you *if*"—or an attitude of resentment and disappointment.

The measurement of rejection from the interviews was highly inferential in many instances. An attitude of rejection is much disapproved in American culture, and few mothers can acknowledge it, even to themselves. Hence the raters had to watch, through the entire interview, for small clues. These included expressed feelings of not wanting the child, of belief that he was hindering her freedom or career, or that he was spoiling her youth or beauty. Other signs were complaints or derogation based on qualities of the child over which he had no control— obesity, temperament, deformities—and expressions of dissatisfaction with the child as a member of the family. In general, the raters disregarded what they interpreted as "over-strong" protestations of love and affection, and based their judgments on positive evidence of rejection.

There were 58 interviews that could not be evaluated with respect to this dimension, and 220 were judged by both raters to fall in the lowest category, which was defined as: "No rejection. Complete acceptance for what child is. Mother respects child as individual." The remaining 101 interviews were concentrated mainly at the second and third points on the five-point scale, and only 9 cases were rated at the fourth and fifth.

In determining the relation between dependency and rejection, we simply compared the child dependency rating for the 220 mothers who showed *no* rejection with that of the 101 who were judged to show *some*. The latter group of children were slightly, but significantly, more dependent, according to the mothers' reports (biserial $r = .12$).

The other two relevant measures were *use of withdrawal of love as a disciplinary technique* and *severity of punishment for aggression toward parents*. Both were significantly related to amount of child dependency. The former will be discussed at some length in Chapter Nine, and the latter in Chapter Seven.

It is interesting to note that the extent of the mother's total use of *physical punishment* (a reasonably good measure of her "punitiveness") was *not* related to the child's being dependent. It was only when punishment was focused upon a particular kind of action in the child—aggressive acts directed toward the parents—that a relationship between punishment and dependency emerged. We suspect that the reason punishment for aggression proved to be significant here is that the child's aggression toward the parent is in itself an action which threatens the affectional bond between them. Possibly the parent's response has the quality of a response in kind—it may mean "All right, if you don't love me, I don't love you either." Such implications evidently provide a stimulus, as we have seen above, for the child to seek reassurance that his parent does in fact still love him.

The handling of dependency. Some mothers suggested that a too positive and accepting reaction toward the child's dependency by the mother would increase it. They expressed the belief that if such actions were punished sufficiently, they would be eliminated and attention-getting would be reduced. This belief in the efficacy of "strong discipline," or more severe punishment, is common in American society, of course. Public demands for these methods of control are the usual consequence of every publicized increase in juvenile delinquency, truancy, or any other form of child behavior that meets with general disapproval. Indeed, many a minor politician has secured a momentary cathartic applause by urging that the best way, or place, to apply "child psychology" is on the seat of the pants.

In the present case, however, there is no evidence that *punishment* for dependency helped to eliminate dependent behavior in the child. Quite the contrary. Punishment for dependency only made children more dependent than ever. It will be recalled that we rated jointly the mother's irritation with and her punishment for dependency. The reason for this was that we found very few instances where a mother had recourse to overt punishment (spanking, withdrawing privileges, etc.) when the child was too clingy or too insistent on attention. More frequently, her negative reactions were expressed in the form of irritable scolding or impatient pulling away from the child. The more the mother behaved in this negative way when the child was dependent, the more dependent he was likely to be ($p < .01$; $r = .28$).

The inference from this finding is that punishment of dependency increases the very kind of behavior the mother is trying to prevent. There is another possibility, of course: perhaps the mother's negative reactions did not *make* the child more dependent, but were an exasperated response to a kind of behavior in the child that had already developed for other reasons. Once he had become dependent, his dependency made his mother irritable. We faced this same kind of chicken-*vs.*-egg problem in connection with toilet training, and it will arise again in Chapter Seven in connection with the punishment of aggression. Mother and child are always influencing each other. We cannot sort out, from our present information, whose behavior is cause and whose is effect. Probably both. The real question—to which we do not presently have an answer—is whether a reduction of punishment would serve to interrupt this cyclical process.

A second aspect of the handling of dependency is the extent to which such behavior is rewarded. With our present rating scale, this was measured pretty largely in terms of the extent to which a mother responded to dependency by dropping what she was doing and responding at once to the child's demands for attention or help. Neither this *reward* nor our measure of a general *permissiveness* of attitude toward dependent behavior was related to child dependency. As seen and reported by the mother, dependency did not appear to be increased either by a sympathetic attitude toward dependency or by the mother's responding positively to the child's dependency demands.

This conclusion is based on a simple comparison of the reward and permissiveness scales with the dependency measure, without taking anything else into account. However, if we consider reward in relation to punishment, we get a quite different impression, one which has a good deal of theoretical as well as practical importance. The influence of punishment and irritation, as described above, was much greater in those children who had also been most frequently rewarded for their dependency behavior ($r = .39$). (See Appendix Table D:16.) The mothers who showed irritation but who ultimately gave the child the attention or help he was demanding were the mothers who reported the most dependency in their children.

When there was little reward for dependency, the amount of punishment for such behavior did not seem to make much difference in the amount of it that occurred. Only when punishment was superimposed upon a fair amount of reward was there an increase in the child's tendency to show the very behavior he was being punished for. Looked at another way, reward for dependency had a tendency to increase dependency *only* when it was superimposed upon punishment for the same behavior.

We can regard these findings as merely suggestive, because the statistical significance values are not uniformly high and because of the above-mentioned possibility that punishment is an effect rather than a cause of the child's dependency. Nevertheless, it may be worth while to speculate about what the findings could mean. In certain studies of basic psychological processes, it has been postulated that conflict has an energizing effect. That is, when an individual is in conflict about how to behave in a particular situation, whatever behavior eventually results will be more vigorous than it would be if conflict were not present (see Whiting and Child, 1953, p. 294). The situation in which the mother sometimes loses her temper over the child's dependency and sometimes responds sweetly and nurturantly, or in which she becomes irritated but nevertheless turns her attention to the child and gives him what he wants, is one ideally calculated to produce conflict in the child. On the one hand, he anticipates unpleasant consequences to his behavior, and this anticipation produces anxiety. On the other hand, he simultaneously anticipates reward. When he has an impulse to be dependent, the impulse makes him both anxious and hopeful; the fear of the mother's irritation may make him inhibit his impulse temporarily, but the hope of getting the mother's attention through dependent behavior is still there. If eventually the dependent behavior does show itself, it will be of an "overdetermined" sort—exceptionally intense, doubly irritating to the mother, and impossible to ignore. Thus the mother's double response of giving the desired attention in the midst of irritation is made more probable and a vicious circle is established.

We saw earlier that dependency seemed to be, at least in some instances, an expression of the child's fear that he had lost his mother's affection. It represented an effort on his part to reassure himself that her affection could be restored. Now, if his dependent acts are greeted with both reward and punishment, his feelings of insecurity about whether he is loved must certainly be intensified, and this insecurity in turn can lead to a repetition of the very behavior which has aroused it.

COMMENT

Even though we must maintain a cautious attitude toward the validity of our measure of dependency, these findings provide a consistent picture of the sources of dependency. They fit the theoretical expectations which stem from our discussion of the development of such behavior in the introduction to this chapter.

Mothers who repeatedly demonstrate their affection for children are providing many supports for whatever actions the children have performed in order to obtain such demonstrations. These actions often involve following the mother around, touching her, smiling at her and talking, and keeping some kind of contact with her. These are the actions, of course, that we have labeled dependency.

Once the child has developed these habitual ways of acting—and all children develop some—he may be expected to use them as devices for reassuring himself that his mother does love him. That is to say, if she shows signs of rejection, if she uses withdrawal of love to discipline him, and if she is punitive toward his aggression, he may be expected to double his efforts to secure her affection. This will simply increase the frequency and persistence of the acts we have defined as dependent, and hence the mother will describe more of them.

The influence of affectionate demonstrativeness, if we may suggest a theoretical point, is an influence on the *learning* of dependent behavior. The effect of withdrawal of love, punishment of dependency and aggression, and other behaviors that threaten the child's security, is an effect on performance or *action*. Therefore, the actual amount of dependency observed and reported by a mother is a product of both factors. It follows that the most dependent children should be those whose mothers express openly their affection for the child but repeatedly threaten the affectional bond by withholding love as a means of discipline and by being punitive toward his displays of parent‑directed aggression.

These relationships are exactly what we have found, but just which way the cause-and-effect arrows point is impossible to say. We are skeptical that there is any single direction of cause-and-effect relations in the child-rearing process. True, the mother's personality comes first, chronologically, and she starts the sequence of interactive behavior that culminates in the child's personality. But once a child starts to be over-dependent—or is *perceived* as being so by his mother—he becomes a stimulus to the mother and influences her behavior toward him. Perhaps, within the present group of mothers, over-dependency of their children increased the mothers' rejective feelings, made them more angry and hence more punitive for aggression. The whole relationship could be circular. An enormous amount of painstaking research will be required to untangle these phenomena.

CHAPTER SIX

Sex

Sex, like aggression, is an impelling force to action. Its initial forms of expression must go through substantial changes before they become acceptable to adults or effective as a means of procreation. The infant's earliest sexual behavior appears to have little social reference. It develops its social forms of expression as a result of the child's experiences, both within the family and outside it.

A newborn infant is quite responsive to stimulation of the genital area. A gentle touch there, or the soft rubbing of clothes or bed coverings, seems to catch his attention. If he has been active or restless, or if he is having a crying spell, such stimulation tends to quiet and relax him. As he gets into the third or fourth month, it may cause him to smile a little and make a few soft sounds. Both sexes show this responsiveness, and the boy, from birth, is likely to have an erection on such occasions. An adult, watching, finds it difficult to avoid the interpretation that the infant is pleased and gladdened by this experience.

In addition to external sources of stimulation, there are internal ones that can evidently produce a sexual reaction. This is most easily noted in the boy, of course, whose erection provides a sure sign of responsiveness. Strong sucking, a full bladder or a full bowel can set the reflex off. After evacuation, or when the sucking stops, the erection slowly subsides. These reactions, un-

like the ones to external stimulation, are less likely to be accompanied by signs of pleasure and relaxation.

There is no present evidence as to whether genital sensitiveness increases or changes during the early years of childhood. Many children of both sexes learn to stimulate themselves at a quite early age, often before they can walk. When they reach a more sociable age, in the third and fourth year, some of them begin to explore the social aspects of sex. At this point, the biological properties of the sex motive become of less interest than the influence of experience, at least so far as the forms of observed behavior and emotional attachments are concerned.

The young child's impulsion to secure sexual stimulation creates a severe socialization problem for many societies. If the mores require that self-stimulation be prohibited, mothers must find a way to discourage the almost inevitable consequence of the child's discovery of his capacity for self-enjoyment. If social sex play is prohibited, still another kind of control must be instituted. Infantile genital sex behavior is brought under control, in one way or another, by all societies, but the strength of this biologically established drive gives trouble to all of them. The restrictions which American families impose on sex behavior in their young children are more severe than those found in many, if not most, "primitive" societies. (See Ford and Beach, 1951; Murdock, 1949; and Whiting and Child, 1953.) They are no more severe, however—probably even less so—than those which prevail in some of the western European countries. In any case, training about sex in many American homes involves a good deal of emotional intensity and considerable conflict on the part of the parents.

These training problems can be more easily understood if they are placed in a wider social context. Before reporting our detailed findings, we will describe, in the next two sections, the nature of societal problems with the control of sex behavior, and the learning problem as children seem to encounter it.

THE SOCIAL PROBLEM

The context in which an anthropologist sees sex training is succinctly stated by Professor Murdock, of Yale, who has described the social control of sex in the following manner:

The imperious drive of sex is capable of impelling individuals, reckless of consequences while under its spell, toward behavior which may imperil or disrupt the co-operative relationships upon which social life depends. The countless interpersonal bonds out of which human association is forged, complex and often delicately balanced, can ill suffer the strain of the frustrations and aggressions inevitably generated by indiscriminate competition over sexual favors. Society, therefore, cannot remain indifferent to sex but must seek to bring it under control. Possibly in man's long history there have been peoples who have failed to subject the sexual impulse to regulation. If so, none has survived, for the social control of sex is today a cultural universal. . . .

Regulation must not, however, be carried too far. To survive, any society must grant to the individual at least sufficient expression of the sexual impulse to maintain reproduction and prevent population decline. Still further concessions are presumably also necessary. While the sex drive may be more capable than others, such as hunger and thirst, of being diverted into substitutive forms of expression, or sublimations, the clinical evidence strongly suggests that excessive sexual deprivation produces personality maladjustments that are inimical to satisfactory social relationships. A society must therefore permit sufficient sexual gratification to maintain the mental health and efficiency of its members as well as their numbers.

All societies have faced the problem of reconciling the need of controlling sex with that of giving it adequate expression, and all have solved it by some combination of cultural taboos, permissions, and injunctions. Prohibitory regulations curb the socially more disruptive forms of sexual competition. Permissive regulations allow at least the minimum impulse gratification required for individual well-being.[1]

Where does American society stand in this balancing of control and freedom of expression?

Like every other, it prohibits sexual contact between all members of the immediate family group except between husband and wife. While brother-sister marriages have been condoned, or even required, in a few royal families in human history (among the Incas and in Ptolemaic Egypt), incest has been otherwise universally tabooed. Some societies even administer the death penalty for it. We know from the study of crime and neurosis that incest does occur occasionally in our own society, but unlike many other forms of sexual deviation, it is so strongly abhorred that it is rarely the subject for surreptitious humor.

The strength and universality of this taboo probably arise, at least in part, from the nature of human social living. Professor

[1] G. P. Murdock, *Social Structure* (New York: The Macmillan Company, 1949), pp. 260–261. Used by permission of author and publisher.

Murdock suggests, convincingly enough, that incest taboos are necessary to avoid disruption of the family unit. He points out that parent-child sexual contact would disrupt authority patterns within the family, and impose intolerable strain upon the strength of the husband-wife team.

The taboo is evidently not a matter of simple absence of sexual attraction. Repressed incestuous impulses of considerable intensity are often uncovered during the process of psychotherapy, not only in emotionally disturbed individuals, but in those who are undergoing psychoanalysis as a part of their professional training. Further, most mammals (including apes), appear to experience no barriers to copulation with parents or siblings.

Freud's description of the Oedipus complex is the classical statement of the way in which sexual impulses enter into the emotional relationship between parent and child. He observed that the mother's warm and loving care served to arouse sexual love for her, in the child, and that the physical expression of this love was rejected and punished by the parents. We may disregard here the details of the process: the point of importance is that overt sex behavior between family members is strongly inhibited.

This taboo is passed along from one generation to another as part of the process of training the young child. Mothers, in particular, bear the responsibility for establishing it. As will be seen from some of the interview material presented later, they do this in many instances quite without formulating the objectives of their own training efforts.

A second type of control required by the mores of our society is the suppression of sexual self-stimulation. Human children the world over, as well as primates and other animal species, discover that they can derive pleasure by rubbing their genital areas. In some societies, this practice among children is regarded as perfectly natural, part of growing up, and is engaged in publicly without incurring any disapproval from the community. As a matter of fact, among some peoples, mothers rub the genitals of young children to soothe them, and in effect, teach them to masturbate. In our own society, however, masturbation is quite generally discouraged as a matter of policy.

Similarly, before adolescence, all forms of sex play with other children are discouraged. This prohibition is in sharp contrast to the customs prevailing in some nonliterate cultures, where children are allowed to engage freely in sex play and may even, in some few instances, be permitted to watch the sexual activities of adults. There are some societies where nearly all children have practice at complete copulation, with several partners, before they reach puberty. On the other hand, there are also societies that are even more strict in their control of childhood sexuality than is American society.

It is idle to speculate about the origins of these mores. There are other aspects of American culture that provide support for them, however. Our relatively high level of education, which is a prerequisite for such a complex industrial society, requires that young people in their late teens remain in school and become prepared for their careers. They are expected to postpone marriage and childbearing until a later age than would be common in many more primitive societies. Furthermore, our monogamous marriage system requires that young people be trained toward the cultural ideal of confining their sex interest to one partner. They must receive early training in impulse control and must acquire the ability to postpone gratification of sex impulses. Kinsey (1948, 1953) has shown that this cultural ideal is far removed from reality, to be sure, for a very large number of young people do engage in full sexual activity before marriage. But the striving toward the ideal doubtless supports the prohibitory training, which is directed toward restricting the age of beginning, the number of partners, and the frequency of premarital sex activity.

The task of the mother in our society, then, involves training the child to inhibit sex impulses toward family members, avoid erotic play with other children, and avoid sexual self-stimulation. Partly as a means to these ends and partly as an end in itself, efforts are made to inculcate modesty standards. Some modesty training occurs in all societies; none tolerate complete nudity at all times. There is much variability in Western standards, both from group to group and from time to time, as witness taste in adult evening gowns and bathing costumes. But in early childhood, modesty is not connected with ritual display.

The mother's task also involves information control. She attempts to govern how and when the child learns the "facts of life," and maintains a screen of secrecy around the sex activities of herself and her husband. Many modern parents ostensibly accept the doctrine that sex is perfectly natural, and that children should be given complete information about it whenever they appear interested. The implication is that sex is no more to be ignored than other events in the child's world. But such parents very rarely carry this doctrine to its logical conclusion and show the child how to perform the sex act. Whether consciously or not, parents in our society evidently assume that if children knew all the facts of life, they would want to experiment with sexual activities themselves. Information control, then, is one of the methods by which adults attempt to induce the growing child to postpone sex gratification and limit sex activities in the early years.

THE CHILD'S PROBLEM

These mores and their accompanying attitudes set several problems for the young child. He must adapt himself to the standards of conduct of our society. He must learn to do some things and not to do others. Let us look at it from his point of view.

Sometime during his early explorations of his own body, he will discover that it is pleasurable to touch his genitals. He must learn not to bring about repetition of these pleasurable sensations by any acts of his own, despite the fact that in other areas of behavior he is allowed, and even expected, to behave in such a way as to bring about, or maintain, pleasurable states (to eliminate when he has bladder tension, to drink when he is thirsty, etc.).

He must learn that it is permissible to expose some parts of his body in public but not others. He must learn that the rules are different in different circumstances; in some families, for example, he may appear in the nude before family members but not outsiders, or before brothers but not before sisters. He must also learn some related rules about general posture and deportment; he (or more pressingly, *she*) must sit with knees together, not roll on the floor with feet up, and not call attention to his body with gestures.

When he learns to talk, he must master the control of sexual language. He must not use "naughty" words, nor ask certain questions, nor talk to other children nor outsiders about some of the things he learns in the bosom of the family—such things as the differences between boys and girls.

He must inhibit any sexual impulses he has toward other people, both within the family and outside. How difficult this task is for the child depends on the degree to which his sex impulses have been aroused and have been directed toward others. It depends also on how specific an idea he has about how to express these impulses. Clinical investigation suggests that a not inconsiderable number of small children have at least a vague notion of the copulatory act itself. Doubtless many others do not. We know that many an adolescent suffers the pressure of an active sex drive without having identified it and without knowing specifically what the behavior is which will satisfy it. Probably, many young children do not have any concept at all of what adult sex behavior is like. Nevertheless, even the very young child has some opportunity for learning about certain aspects of sex, for he is exposed to the more attenuated forms of sex play that are publicly acknowledged—for example, kissing—as portrayed in the movies or on television. If young children are left to themselves, they will sometimes rub their genitals against other people, attempt to look at or touch the genitals of others, and will sometimes appear to be sexually aroused while making these attempts (as evidenced by giggling, excited voice, quick breathing and sighing, and, in boys, an erection). These are the kinds of activities which young children in our society must learn to inhibit completely.

How severe a task is this for most children? That depends on how impelling and how directed their sex motives are. Unhappily, the best generalization we can make is that children vary greatly in the extent to which they have strong sexual impulses. From a theoretical standpoint, we may suppose that a major consequence of overt sexual experience is to increase the specificity of acts that the child learns to perform in satisfying his sexual needs. There also should be an increase in desire to perform the acts, and a greater degree of frustration when the acts are prevented from occurring. These principles apply to the development of the oral drive, as we saw in Chapter Three, but whether they are also applicable to the sex drive we do not yet know for certain. If they are, then we may presume that, while young children find sexual stimulation desirable and seek to enhance it, the absence of extensive overt sex experience makes them less demanding of specific kinds of gratification than are sex-experienced adults. Obviously, too, the hormonal changes at adolescence increase both the strength and specificity of sex demands.

We can turn now to the interviews. Three aspects of sex training were examined in some detail. These were immodesty, masturbation, and social sex play. Our aims were similar to those displayed in connection with dependency. For each of these types of behavior we wanted to discover the methods by which the training was done, to estimate how *permissive* each mother was of her child's uninhibited expression of the changeworthy behavior, and how much *punishment or pressure* she placed on him to change his behavior.

We did not seek any objective measures, via the mothers' eyes, of the children's actual sex behavior. The replies to our queries about training produced a plenitude of incidental descriptions of the youngsters' sex activities, but the conditions for a mother's observation are so unreliable that we have made no attempt to estimate any quantitative aspects of these behaviors.

In this chapter, therefore, we will limit our discussion largely to the child-rearing variables, those exemplified by column II in the schema presented in Chapter Two. We will describe first what we learned of the mothers' major techniques for handling sex behavior. Then we will consider the special problems connected with each of the three aspects of sex control—modesty, masturbation, and social sex activity—and describe the range of attitudes and practices that characterized this group of mothers. Finally, we will examine the sex permissiveness dimension in its relation to other aspects of the personality. Although we have no column III measures of child *sex* behavior, this permissiveness dimension warrants careful attention, as we saw in connection with breast feeding and toilet training.

METHODS OF CONTROL

The control of sex behavior poses a problem that has no direct parallel in the other spheres of behavior we have discussed. In the case of infantile feeding, toileting, and dependency, there are changeworthy forms of action, to be sure, but there are also well-accepted "mature" forms that can immediately replace them. When the mother begins to prohibit sucking, she offers substitute methods by which hunger can be satisfied. When she disapproves random elimination, she shows the child where and when he may relieve himself with approval. When she starts to control the passionate enthusiasm of his early dependency, she continues nonetheless to give him affection and attention; she does not withhold herself or her nurturance altogether. With sex, however, there are no immediate alternatives to the initial ways of securing satisfaction. For the preadolescent child, there is no form of genital stimulation, no form of sexual love, that is acceptable. When the mother begins the socialization of her child's sex motive, she has recourse only to inhibition.

This problem is clearly reflected in the methods of control that were described by the mothers. Whereas they talked often of their methods of developing new eating habits to replace infantile sucking, they almost never mentioned any positive sexual actions to replace masturbation or social sex play or immodest display. The emphasis was on stopping the changeworthy behavior, not on the starting of some other form of sexual behavior. This led, naturally enough, to the use of techniques that would minimize stimulation and thus prevent sex activity from starting. As a corollary, there was an aura of indirection in the training process.

We have made no attempt to count the frequency or intensity with which different control methods were used. We have tried, in the following paragraphs, to abstract the major trends that seemed to characterize the group as a whole. No mother used all the devices, of course, and this description must be considered as a survey of methods, not a composite picture of a "typical mother."

Preventing stimulation

One way of avoiding sex activity is to keep away all the cues that might suggest it to a child. To this end, the mother often arranged the child's life so that provocative situations simply did not occur. There were several ways of managing this. Boys and girls in the family usually had separate rooms when this was possible. Brothers and sisters might be bathed together when they were very little, but this practice was discontinued if the mother noticed the children showing what she considered to be undue curiosity about each other.

Rules of conduct designed to minimize the opportunities for contact with sex were established early so they would be taken for granted by the child. He must not go into his parents' room, when the door is closed, without knocking. He must "take turns" with other children in using the bathroom; they must not go in together. When outdoors, he must stay out in the open "where Mother can see you," and not go into enclosed places (garages, basements, cars) with another child.

On the assumption that some children develop the habit of handling their genitals because of local irritation, some mothers made a practice of buying their children's underclothes a size too large in order to avoid binding or pressure. They were very careful to keep the child's body clean, applying oil or talcum powder immediately to any rash or chafed spot that did appear.

The mother may have tried to prevent the development of sexual interests from the very beginning of the child's life by controlling and guiding his behavior directly into more desired channels. This was particularly evident with respect to modesty training. When she lifted him out of the bath, she would wrap a towel around him. She kept a diaper on him at all times; when he was old enough to stand alone and walk, she would help him off with his pajamas in the morning and stand ready immediately with his underwear, preventing him from doing anything else until he had put on at least this much clothing. If he escaped this control for a moment, and ran out naked into another room, she would follow him and bring him back to be dressed, perhaps saying: "Let's hurry and get dressed now, so you can play." A mother often did not feel free to do anything else until the dressing routine had been completed; she was always present when the child was nude, exerting pressure for dressing, and creating the unspoken assumption in the child's mind that dressing is the *first* step in any of the behavior sequences he may wish to engage in. What wonder that so many parents reported that their children were "just naturally modest"!

Changing stimulation

Distraction was probably the favorite of all techniques for the control of sex behavior in these families. In other spheres, if the child did something of which she disapproved, the mother would refer to it directly; for example: "Don't hold your cup like that, you're going to spill your milk." But if she saw him touching his genitals, she might just move his hand away without direct comment. This was sometimes followed by taking his hands gently and teaching him to do something else with them, such as play a game of pat-a-cake.

Similarly, when the child was older, if he was playing with another child and the mother detected any signs that things might be getting "out of hand"—excited giggling, certain children's words—she would separate the children, or drastically change the situation in some way. Perhaps she would take them outdoors and start a new game, thus effectively interrupting the undesired behavior. But she was not likely to explain her reasons for this interference. The avoidance of mentioning the sexual aspect of behavior seemed to be part of a general pattern of de-emphasis. Over and over again, mothers said they felt they should not "make an issue of it," nor give the child "food for thought." Rather than get into a discussion with the child about exactly what he was doing wrong, the mother changed both his behavior and the stimulation by handing him a toy or thinking up a game which she knew would interest him.

A typical comment was:

M. *When he was a baby and was sitting on the toilet seat, he used to notice himself, and I would give him a toy. Just hand him the toy and take his hand away. But I would never say "No, no, naughty, don't do that."*

Another mother described her reactions this way:

M. *Well, I think I just probably try at first to take his hand to do something else—hold his hand in my hand and be talking about some-*

*thing, and try to divert his attention to that. Or, if I'm not near him,
I might say "Don't do that" in sort of a quiet voice that nobody else
would hear.*

Borrowed sanctions

There were times, of course, when the mother felt she could
not avoid issuing direct injunctions to the child. Sometimes she
simply told him to stop what he was doing, without explanation,
perhaps adding that what he was doing was "not nice." When
she did explain, however, she was likely to redefine the situation
so that the problem appeared to be related to some other area
than sex. Then she would borrow the rules from that other
area and thus control the sex behavior.

When mothers explained to their children why running
around without clothes was forbidden, they often referred to
the danger of catching cold:

M. *I just tell them they had better keep their clothes on so as not to
catch cold, and they don't think anything about it themselves. If you
bring it up in any other manner, they start thinking things and wondering, and being small, you couldn't explain to them.*

One explanation sometimes given to a child as to why he
should not touch his genitals was that he would hurt himself.
For example, one mother reported that her little girl had once
fallen out of a tree, and had hurt herself in the genital area.
So the child knew what it meant to be hurt there. Thereafter,
the mother had found it very effective to warn the child that she
would hurt herself if she did not leave herself alone. Another
mother told her child: "You know if you pick your eyes they'll
be sore, and if you pick at your nose you'll make it bleed, and
if you pick at yourself there you'll make a sore." Another mother,
when she saw her little boy rubbing his penis, said: "Do you
want me to get a Band-Aid to put on it?" A number of mothers
reported that in similar circumstances they would ask the child
if he was chafed or itchy, and would put oil or talcum powder
on him when he was seen playing with himself.

Another rationale offered to children by some mothers was
that rubbing the genitals is "dirty." Partly, this thought is con-
veyed by the association with toileting. As one mother put it:

"Your eyes are to see with, your mouth is to eat with, and that part of your body is to go to the toilet with." Some mothers explained that the parts of the body which were used for toileting were not clean, and that the child must not touch them or he would get his hands dirty. Other mothers put the matter the other way around: his hands pick up germs from everywhere, and he would infect himself if he touched the private and "sensitive" parts of his body. Another very common device that served to interpret genital interests as related to toileting was that of asking the child, when he was seen holding himself, whether he had to go to the toilet. Actually, of course, this behavior on the part of the child *is* ambiguous, and the mothers chose to interpret it in terms of its non-sex implications.

Avoiding labels

There appeared to be a tendency to avoid labeling in connection with sex training. In fact, one mother said very explicitly, concerning sex play between children:

M. *We try to ignore it. We don't notice it as any such thing, and we don't label it by any names.*

And another mother remarked:

M. *I think it is very important for them to hardly realize any difference between different parts of their body.*

Many families got along without any names for the genital area, using vague terms of reference like "it" or "there," as may be seen in some of the quotations already cited. When communication was necessary between parent and child, one of the babyish toileting terms current in the family was used, as in a child's "Mommy, my wee-wee hurts." Such terms were used, when the child was small, if communication was required in order that the parents might minister to the child's bodily needs. As he grew older, these terms tended to be discarded as part of baby talk. Despite the absence of explicit language, however, mothers and children seemed to be able to communicate with each other fairly effectively about some events in the intellectual shadowland of sex, as was illustrated in the following interchange between mother and son:

The mother saw the boy rubbing his penis. She said:

> "Johnny, what are you doing?"
> "Nothing, Mummy."
> "Well, stop it, then."
> "O.K.," and he stopped.

When the parents refrained from labeling their children's sex behavior they did not always do so simply as a device to divert the child's attention. Sometimes the mother herself preferred to believe a non-sex interpretation. We asked the mothers about sex play between children, and one mother said:

M. *He and his brother get very giggly now when they see each other in the bathtub. Sort of poke each other like two little puppies.*
I. *How do you feel about it when you notice this sort of thing going on?*
M. *Well, I let it go on until it begins to get so silly that I can't handle them, and I just tell them they are too silly. It has nothing to do with sex, really. Just silliness.*

While some parents avoided any sort of labeling in the area of sex, some did provide their children with names for the genital parts of the body. We did not encounter anyone, however, who helped the children to identify the *emotional* states related to sex. Many mothers said to a child something like: "You're angry and upset now. We'll talk about it when you're calmer." But none, as far as we could tell, said: "You're feeling sexy, that's why you're acting like that."

Information control

Considering their general de-emphasis of sex, we might well expect the mothers to have had considerable conflict about answering their children's sex questions. They did, if we may judge from the frequency with which they asked our interviewers how much information should be given. We did not ask explicitly, in the interview, about the mother's policy on this matter, but there were a good many comments about it. Some mothers were clearly antagonistic to what they called the "modern doctrines" that they felt were advocated in some child-training books and newspaper columns. For example, one mother said:

M. *I don't believe in what they write nowadays, that when a child asks about sex you should very openly tell them everything. I don't believe in that. Maybe I'm wrong, maybe I'm not, but I just can't see telling a young child all that business, because as I say, a child that age says things at times that you never know when he's going to say them. All of a sudden when I'm out visiting some relatives of mine, I don't feel like having my son come out with some long sexual term. I don't approve of it, and I can't see it. This article that was in the* Reader's Digest *recently about all this hogwash you should tell your child when he says, "Where did I come from?" And I'm supposed to immediately say, "You came from inside me." And I'm supposed to go on a long term this long. I'd have to get a book and read up, because I don't think I'd know about it myself, and I've had three; and I don't intend to tell him. I might be all wrong, but that's just the way I feel.*

Mothers who felt this way sometimes mentioned their hostility to sex-education programs in the schools.

When a mother was opposed to giving any sex information to children, however, she had to be prepared to give the child some other explanation when a younger sibling was born. One said to her young son: "Gee, I'm getting fat. I guess I'll have to go away for a week or so, and go on a diet." When she came back from the hospital with the new baby, her son said: "You sure dieted all right." Others spoke of "putting in an order for a baby at the hospital."

Most of the mothers were willing to tell their children a little more than that about the reproductive process, however. At least, they described the presence of the new baby inside the mother. Mothers who had tried to be completely free and open in their information-giving usually found, however, that there was a point beyond which they were unwilling to go in answering the child's questions:

M. *I have never made any bones about it at all, and I have answered every question that I felt that I can answer correctly. There are a few that are—at this point—I don't feel he is old enough to take the answers. He is very interested in his organs at this moment, and fascinated by what he can do about them, and he naturally realizes he is very different from little girls and wants to know why. And yet, I haven't really explained to him yet. Because he is one of those guys that will want to go out and try it.*

Some mothers found that, aside from their embarrassment about some of the questions they were asked, they did not know the answers themselves. A few expressed the belief that boys should get their sex information from their fathers, girls from their mothers. This argument was based on the grounds that women do not know enough about the sex physiology of boys to handle the questions properly:

M. *I used to put them in the bathtub together, but lately I haven't been doing that. They really notice too much. They are very noticeable children. For instance, John has been circumcised, but Dave hasn't been, and he notices the difference. I think it's kind of early to tell him, but he wanted to know why he didn't have one like John's. I—half the time I wish my husband was home, because I don't know what to say when they say some of the things they do, and I don't know what to say in regard to a boy. They are asking now why sometimes it bends up and they can't bend it down.*

It is safe to say that not one family in our sample was completely free and open in the discussion of sex with their young children. This is by no means surprising, for the control of sex information is intimately bound up with the control of overt sex behavior itself. Parental efforts to keep children from thinking, talking, or knowing about sex are part of the more general problem of teaching modesty and inhibition of sex impulses.

Modesty Training

In our interview, we asked about three aspects of sex training: (*a*) teaching the child about modesty, (*b*) teaching him not to handle his genitals, and (*c*) teaching him to inhibit sex impulses in his play with other children. With respect to modesty, mothers were asked the following sequence of questions:

Now we want to talk about sex and modesty training. How do you feel about allowing Johnny to run about without his clothes on?

What have you done to teach Johnny about this?

When did you start teaching him about it?

[If not mentioned] How about modesty outdoors?

The mothers' answers to these questions were rated on two scales, one for the mother's *permissiveness* for the child's being

TABLE VI:1

PERMISSIVENESS FOR CHILD'S GOING WITHOUT CLOTHES INDOORS

1. Not at all permissive. Child must be clothed at all times; nudity "not nice"	30%
2. Slightly permissive	14
3. Moderately permissive. Child may go without clothes briefly (on way to and from bathroom)	16
4. Quite permissive. Mother doesn't object to nudity but exercises some restraint	23
5. Entirely permissive. Mother does not value modesty; allows child to be without clothes indoors whenever he wants to	13
Not ascertained	4
Total	100%

without clothes indoors, and the other for the amount of *pressure* the mother had brought to bear upon him to be clothed indoors. The percentages of mothers who were rated at each level on these two scales are shown in Tables VI:1 and VI:2.

TABLE VI:2

SEVERITY OF PRESSURE MOTHER HAS APPLIED TO TRAIN THE CHILD TO BE MODEST INDOORS

1. No pressure. Issue hasn't come up. Child always keeps clothes on without having to be urged	18%
2. No pressure, although child does go without clothes in the house	28
3. Slight pressure—gentle remonstrance or teasing for nudity	15
4. Moderate pressure. Mother may urge child to get clothes on; scold moderately	27
5. Considerable pressure—scolding, some show of irritation; warning of consequences	6
6. Severe pressure, punishment. Mother angry and emotional	1
Not ascertained	5
Total	100%

Following are two examples of answers which were rated toward the *permissive* end of the scale:

A

M. *I don't think it spoils them. In fact, I think that they should see each other with their clothes off. I don't think they make as much of it. They see parents or brothers and sisters and they just accept it "that you're a boy and I'm a girl." I think if you try to get them to hide things and say, "Put your clothes on, you should be ashamed; someone is looking at you"—I don't think that's a good idea at all. We're handicapped here with one bath, and very often one is running in while the other is running out. So they don't—it's no secret with them, and it's nothing that they hide.*

B

M. *Well, I have allowed him to go about without his clothes on. I mean, he's very slow about dressing, and he might be getting undressed, and in the meantime he'll see something he wants, and he goes and gets it, and I don't believe he has any modesty about that.*

Answers which were rated as *not permissive,* on the other hand, are exemplified by the following:

A

M. *Well, again, I guess I am a strict mother, in spite of my large family. We don't have freedom in that respect. In fact, my little boy is wearing nightshirts, and one of the primary reasons they wear nightshirts is that they can put their nightshirts on, and they are covered before they take their underpants off. Or, they can put their underpants on before they take their nightshirts off in the morning, and I try to teach them that that is just a nice way of doing it, that people don't run around without clothing.*

B

M. *I think they should be covered at all times.*
I. *What have you done to teach her this?*
M. *We always tell her to cover up—don't let Daddy see her, things like that.*

C

I. *How do you feel about allowing Sally to run around without her clothes on?*
M. *Well, we don't. We teach them to—the first thing in the morning —to at least put their pants on anyway. I mean get dressed right away. We had a young couple live next door—she had a little boy, eleven or twelve months—and she let him walk around without diapers in the*

swimming pool. Well, we all felt that she shouldn't have done it, because—I don't know why, but—I wouldn't let mine do that outdoors, and they don't do it in the house, either.

As may be seen from Table VI:1, a majority of the families exercised fairly close control over the child's modesty. At the same time, the amount of pressure exerted in this training was relatively mild (Table VI:2). Mothers very seldom actually punish their children for appearing in the nude. Again we note the widely-held preference, described earlier, for not making an issue of these matters, but for correcting and guiding the child calmly and inconspicuously.

Some parents managed the modesty problem in an atmosphere of family humor and teasing. One family had a rule that if anyone saw anyone else in the family without his pants on, he was allowed to give the guilty person a spank. These opportunities were enjoyed by one and all, including the eighteen-months-old baby, who would toddle after his three-year-old sister to give her a "big spank" whenever the situation permitted.

As can be seen from the tables, approximately one fifth of the mothers reported that they had never had to correct their children for breaches of the modesty rules; the child just seemed to understand without being told. Most of the mothers who reported this also said that they very definitely would not have allowed their children to appear without clothes. Their general attitude about modesty appears to have been transmitted implicitly rather than explicitly, either by example or else by subtle forms of pressure which must have been applied when the child was very young.

Some of the teaching by example was definitely explicit, however:

M. *She's very modest about herself. She goes to the bathroom and she closes the door—you can't go in there when she goes to the bathroom. Then she'll call you to wipe her, so that really struck me funny. She doesn't like to be seen when she's getting undressed. Of course, I don't let her in the bathroom when I'm there myself, so I suppose that's the reason why.*
I. *What have you done to teach her about that sort of thing?*
M. *Well, I try to shame her into it by saying, "Nobody wants to see you like that; you don't see your mother running around like that; Mother always has clothes on."*

While the dressing process seems to have been the focus of the modesty problem in the first year or two, it is evident from the remarks quoted above that, at a little later age, the problem of modesty in the home centered around use of the bathroom. The families in our sample varied enormously in their bathroom rules; some insisted on absolute privacy at all times for all family members, even though the family was large and there was only one bathroom. Some permitted small children to use the toilet while other family members were bathing, but otherwise they maintained privacy rules. This procedure occurred especially when the young child was being toilet-trained and the mother feared an accident if he had to wait. Other families apparently had no privacy rules within the family itself, imposing restrictions only when guests were present. Some mothers found that the pressure of circumstances sometimes forced them to relax standards which they would have preferred to maintain; for example, the mother of a two-year-old reported that occasionally she felt she must leave the door open when she was using the bathroom herself, in order to keep the child within earshot in case he got into trouble.

A final point which should be emphasized about training for modesty is that many of the mothers felt they were not "teaching" the child at all. In fact, we found it impossible to rate the age at which modesty training was begun, because the mothers were not conscious of having begun such training deliberately. In general, from the mother's standpoint, the child spontaneously began to be modest when he was old enough to notice that this was the way other people in the family behaved.

MASTURBATION

Another series of questions in the interview had to do with genital self-stimulation by the child. We did not use the word *masturbation,* because so many people interpret this term as referring only to the self-stimulation which occurs after puberty. Some of the mothers in our sample did refer to self-stimulation by younger children as masturbation, but others insisted that such activity in young children was quite different—something which might lead to masturbation later on, but which was not yet the same thing. In the discussion which follows, because for economy we need a single word, we will use the term masturbation to refer to any activity on the part of the child by which he stimulates his own genitals.

The kinds of behavior reported by mothers which would be included under this heading are not only the more usual kinds of manual touching and holding of the genitals, but also the child's rubbing them against furniture or other objects, or sitting on his heel and bouncing. For girls, there were also instances of putting objects in the vagina (including, for one little girl, pieces of wool she picked off the blankets at night).

In the interview, the following questions were asked of each mother:

What have you done about it when you have noticed him playing with himself?

How important do you feel it is to prevent this in a child?

TABLE VI:3
PERMISSIVENESS FOR MASTURBATION

1. Not at all permissive—would always stop if noticed. Consider it wrong, harmful	25%
2. Slightly permissive (might not do anything if it happened once, but wouldn't like it)	24
3. Moderately permissive—don't want to make too much of an issue, but important not to let it become a habit	28
4. Quite permissive—would worry if too frequent, but a certain amount to be expected	13
5. Entirely permissive. It's natural, just curiosity; mother makes no efforts to stop or distract	5
Not ascertained	5
Total	100%

From the answers to these questions, each interview was rated in terms of both the mother's *permissiveness* for masturbation, and the *amount of pressure* which had been applied against masturbation. Tables VI:3 and VI:4 show how the mothers were rated on these scales. A few excerpts will illustrate what is meant by the categories which appear in the tables.

TABLE VI:4

SEVERITY OF PRESSURE WHICH HAS BEEN APPLIED AGAINST MASTURBATION

1. No pressure. Issue hasn't come up. Mother has never noticed it	41%
2. No pressure, although it has occurred	4
3. Slight pressure. May ask if child needs to go to toilet; no forbidding. Mother makes light of it	22
4. Moderate pressure. Mother may scold moderately, warn about slight consequences, with little intensity. Stop the child, but not punish	27
5. Considerable pressure. Forbid with some show of emotion; scold	4
6. Severe pressure—punishment. Mother angry or disgusted—may warn child of extreme consequences	1
Not ascertained	1
Total	100%

The following examples of parental attitudes and treatment of the child were rated as *permissive:*

A

I. *What have you done about it when you have noticed him playing with himself?*
M. *Nothing.*
I. *How important do you think it is to prevent this in a child?*
M. *Well, I think it is important, but I think if you say nothing and ignore it, they will stop; and if you make an issue of it, and a point of it, it is like telling them to stay off the sofa. They won't stay off it; they will go right after it; so I leave him completely alone. There was a time when he was at himself all the time, every time he had his clothes off, but now I haven't seen it for six months anyway.*

B

M. *I have ignored it.*
I. *How important do you think it is to prevent this in a child?*
M. *I don't really feel as though it is important because I think it's a phase a child goes through, and I think the more you bring it to their attention the more they're apt to do it.*

C

M. *I think they get over it. It's something new—they've found themselves. They look you over when you're undressing, and of course they want to see if they have the same things. I think they grow out of it. I mean if you make a big issue of it, they're going to think there is something wrong.*

D

M. *My husband and I have spoken of it often, and we both said that neither one of us were immune to it as children, so why should our children be? It's part of growing up.*

The following examples were rated as *non-permissive:*

A

M. *I don't think there is anything worse to see than a little boy running around doing that.*

I. *How important do you think it is to prevent it?*

M. *I think it's quite important. If they get the habit it's awfully hard to break them of it.*

I. *How would you deal with it?*

M. *I don't know. He is pretty reasonable, and I think you could just reason with him; and if you couldn't, you would just have to take more drastic measures.*

B

M. *I told him not to do that. I didn't have too much trouble with that until he was—well, just before he went to school he started in. And a friend of mine told me she thought his underwear was a little bit too small, so I got new panties, but he was doing it just the same; not too much, though. I didn't have too much trouble with it then, but he started in, and I think it really was a habit then. He didn't realize he was doing it, and I would say, "Jimmy, Jimmy," and I would try to get him to do something else. I would say, "Come over here, and help me do this," or "Hold this for me," and do things like that to distract his attention, rather than call his attention to it too much; but I did say, "You can't do that." And then when he started school I said, "If the other children see you, that isn't nice"; and I said, "Miss Jones wouldn't like that," and he said, "She wasn't looking when I did it."*

It may be seen from Tables VI:3 and VI:4 that the mothers, as a general thing, were not very permissive toward masturbation. They thought it undesirable. When they noticed it, they attempted to stop it. On the other hand, very little punishment was employed in the effort to teach children not to masturbate. As we noted earlier, mothers made a strong effort not to become emotional; they treated the situation lightly, and tried to bring about the desired results with a minimum of pressure upon the child. This de-emphasis of the problem appeared to come, in part, from mothers' reliance on the advice of pediatricians and modern child-training books. Some mothers attempted to follow guidance from these sources even when it ran counter to their own feelings. As one said: "It nearly drove me crazy to see him do it, but my doctor told me to just let it pass, so I did."

The mothers differed considerably in the extent to which they expressed belief that the child actually derived any sort of pleasurable sensation when he stimulated himself. Some denied it explicitly—"It's just curiosity; they want to know what they've got," or "His clothes were too tight—he was itchy and chafed, that's all." Others, however, recognized that something akin to the sexual sensations of adults was involved. One mother was forced to recognize this by the comments of her son:

M. *He did tell me that it made him feel good, because it made him ticklish; and I said I know it did but not to do it again as it wasn't nice.*

Some mothers expressed fear that if a child showed a good deal of interest in his own body, or in sex in general, this might mean that he was over-sexed, and that he might become a "problem child" in adolescence, or even a "sex fiend." More commonly, however, if a mother had any view at all about why she felt masturbation was wrong, she expressed concern about the child's own later adjustment. She feared that if masturbation became a habit, the child would not give it up for more socially acceptable forms of sex behavior when he reached marriageable age. In a few instances, she worried about homosexuality. As one mother put it: "If they (boys) aren't stopped, as they grow older I think they'd be more girl than boy, to tell you the truth."

As far as we could tell, though, most of the mothers had not rationalized their antipathy for masturbation. They simply said it was something they did not like to see; they felt it was not "nice"; and they were embarrassed when their child did it, especially in the presence of outsiders.

When we consider the effect on the child, of course, we must not overlook the possibility that even when a mother carefully refrains from being overtly punitive about her child's sex activity, her feelings of being shocked or ashamed or disgusted will show in subtle ways that will be recognized and reacted to by the child. If this is true, the effective pressure which mothers applied in sex training was probably greater than the mothers themselves realized.

Reports of masturbation. Two fifths of the mothers said they had never noticed their children's doing any of the things we have called masturbation. We can hardly interpret such a report as a valid measure of whether a child had or had not masturbated, however. Mothers differed too much in their opportunities for observation; even under the closest supervision, a child has plenty of time to do what he wants when his mother is not looking. We did find, nevertheless, that those mothers who had *not* seen any such actions were rated substantially higher on how closely they kept track of the child ($p<.01$). Apparently, a mother's tendency to check frequently on her child's whereabouts and his doings kept him from masturbating or led him to be more cautious about where he did it.

There may well have been differences among mothers in their willingness to report, of course. Perhaps those who were relatively anxious and disturbed by a child's sex behavior tended to avoid seeing what made them uncomfortable. Or perhaps they were too embarrassed to acknowledge to the interviewer that they had noticed such behavior. It is interesting to note, however, that there were no differences in masturbation permissiveness between the mothers who did and did not report observations.

SEX PLAY WITH OTHER CHILDREN

The same pressures that lead to self-display and self-stimulation lead children to explore the excitement of sex play with other youngsters. This may be partly due to the forbidden quality of all sex behavior; most children have a strong curiosity to see behind the curtain of parental disapproval. They like to turn on the garden hose, light matches, peek at Christmas presents, and pinch the cat's tail. When there is intrinsic sex pleasure to add strength to this inevitable curiosity, it is not surprising that a good many children experiment a little with one another even by the time they are five years old.

In the interview, we asked a series of questions about the mother's observations of such play and her attitude toward it. These were the questions:

How about sex play with other children—has this come up yet?

[If yes]
What happened? What did you do about it?

What about children wanting to look at each other, or go to the toilet together, or giggling together—how do you feel about it when you notice this sort of thing going on among the children?

[If never noticed it]
    Would you allow this, or do you think you'd step in?

Approximately half the mothers reported some activity on the part of their children which could be identified as sex play.

Some was between brothers and sisters, some with neighbor children; some was with children of the same sex and some with the opposite sex.

The mothers had learned of these episodes in a number of ways: by a child's guilty confession, by his chance remarks that unintentionally revealed what he had done, by reports from other mothers, or, not infrequently, by direct observation. A few mothers reported, rather sheepishly, that they had been concerned about the possibility of sex play between children and on occasion had tiptoed to listen at the door when a pair of children spent too long in the bathroom or hidden in a closet. Usually, these mothers added, the children turned out to be engaged in some other—but more mildly—forbidden activity, such as splashing in the toilet bowl or trying on their parents' shoes.

A few examples of incidents reported by mothers will help indicate the problems of control that were involved. The first one concerns two sisters:

> **M.** I used to give them their baths together, and they were having a gay old time in there, so I give them their baths separately now. I know they used to share the same room, and in the morning they would close the door and play hospital. They were on top of each other—general things. I disapproved—not overly horrified. I just told them to leave their pants up, that they would hurt each other. They can play without doing that.

Another mother reported that her little boy came home from playing at a neighbor boy's house and said that he had been sent home by the other boy's mother. His own mother asked him what he had done, and he reported that he had "sort of rubbed himself against Tommy."

Not uncommonly, sex play occurred among a whole group of children, usually in some place normally unobservable by mothers or other adults. One game among neighbor children was graphically described by another mother:

> **M.** Now Jimmy, two years ago, was three. There are a number of children around here—in fact, there's about fourteen of them, all about the same age—and I used to leave my cellar door open down cellar, and they used to come in there and play hide and seek and everything else. I never thought anything about it until one day I heard—I was up street, and I heard someone say—"Well, that's the lady lives down the end of the street," and, "My little boy came home and tells me they're playing in the cellar, and they're taking their clothes off down there, and changing into costumes, and this and that." I thought, "That's funny."

So I visited a number of my neighbors, and one of my neighbors said, "Do you know that the children are taking off their clothing down in your cellar?" I said, "In my cellar?" She said, "Yes." I said, "Have there been any little girls down there?" "No, all little boys—in fact, my little boy come down and said they were playing 'Shame me.' " I said, " 'Shame me'—well, now we won't say anything"—so I didn't say a word.

I let it go by a day. Then the next afternoon, I left the cellar door open, and I hate spying on children, I really do . . . but I did . . . and I heard my little boy say first to this other little boy, "No, we're not going to play 'Shame me' today, it's too cold out." And this other little boy said, "It isn't cold, it's hot out, Jimmy, and today you've got to take your clothes off." And I let it go, and I thought, "I'll let it go a little while longer." So the little fellow—his name was Timmy—said, "O.K., if you're not going to play 'Shame me,' it's your turn, Joseph." So I thought I'd wait—see, I have two cellar ways, they were at the front—and I come around the back and I watched.

They took off their shirts, calling, "Shame me, shame me, shame me." I thought, if that's all there is to it, that's nothing to talk about.

Well, they took off their shoes and stockings, calling—oh, more "Shame me," and they were dancing and clapping their hands; they thought it was a great joke. Well, when they come to take off their little drawers—mine had two pair—and of course, when he saw the other one stripping, he started too—he went right down until they didn't have a thing on; and all they done was dance around and laugh, so I walked in. You should have seen the expressions. "Mummy, Mummy, I didn't mean it, I'll dress," and all the others scampered. I said, "Don't you go outside, put on your clothes," and "How long has this been going on?"—"Oh, we just started today"—I said, "I'm sorry, I heard from your mother it's been going on a week, and I heard from your mother that you've been playing 'Shame me.' " And my little boy started to laugh: "Shame me, Ma, we've got no clothes on." So I said, "Put them on, that's the last time. I'm going to put a nail in the door," and I did. I nailed the door up.

Then I heard they used to go down to the field, so I said, "Well, it happened in my cellar, and no other mother was interested to come over, and so I'll find out from the other mothers to see if they were down to find out." — They never did; it was always me.

Very commonly, sex play among neighborhood children seemed to take the form of "show it" games. Another example was reported by a mother who found her little boy hiding in the car with a neighbor boy:

M. *I went out to the garage one day, and I couldn't get into the car. It was locked, and I heard giggles, and I looked into the car, and Nick and the little boy next door—who is a year older than Nick—were in there, and they both had their pants down. And it was quite a cold day, and I had them open the door for me; and I told him that they were ridiculous, that it was very cold, and they were liable to catch cold; and that it was a very dangerous thing to be playing in a locked car, danger of carbon monoxide, and so forth. And I said to them, "What were you doing this for anyway?" "We were playing." And I said, "Why?" "We like to look at each other." So I said, "I don't know why you like to look at each other, you both have exactly the same thing." And they said, "We haven't the same thing, one is fat and one is skinny"—something very silly like that—and, of course, I had to laugh.*

Afterward I told him that I didn't think it was a nice thing to do, it was very silly, that he had nothing to gain by doing that. And then a couple of weeks later, I heard a report about something that had gone on at some little girl's house, and I called the little girl's mother on the phone—I happened to be friendly with her—and asked her just what happened . . . and it seemed that he had given the little girl three pennies to pull her pants down, and that—as far as I know— those are the only episodes that have happened.

A related game was the game of "doctor," which involved the children in examining one another and sometimes taking temperatures rectally.

Sometimes "show it" took the form of a group of children urinating together outdoors. One mother reported that she saw two boys giggling excitedly, having a contest to see which one could "wee-wee" the farthest. Mothers had two reasons for discouraging this sort of thing: they considered it unsanitary, and they also recognized its sex-play implications. Strong efforts were made to teach the children to come indoors to go to the toilet. When they were playing too far away from home, they were instructed to go to a neighbor's house and ask to use the bathroom there.

Mothers are not entirely free agents in the matter of controlling such behavior. Any mother who does not enforce this rule for her children is subject to considerable pressure from other mothers, as was illustrated in the following instance:

M. *He did piddle once—and about three neighbors called me and told me he just stood in the middle of the street and just did it; and when he came home I asked him about it, and he said, "I don't know*

why more people don't do it, Mother, it was wonderful." I told him it
wasn't good manners and it would be a terrible thing if everybody
went to the bathroom outdoors.

Sex play among neighbor children is a matter in which a
mother may find herself in conflict with the standards and attitudes of other mothers, of course. In this, as in other aspects of
child training, there is an unwritten rule that one mother must
not punish another mother's child. Most commonly, when a
mother detected a neighbor child in some improper act, she
would send the child home, or tell the other mother. Neighborhood agreements were sometimes worked out:

M. *I explained to them that it was wrong to undress in front of other*
children outside, and the other children in the neighborhood were told
the same thing. If anyone suggested it, that they were to tell the
mother, and the mother would talk with the other mothers. We have
discussed it amongst ourselves, and tried to straighten out the situation,
and I think we have succeeded.

If one child persistently behaved in a manner which the other
mothers disapproved, the other children were told not to play
with him. Knowing that her child would be ostracized if he did
not conform to neighborhood standards, a mother might teach
him that he had to conform to these neighborhood standards
even if his own family disagreed with them:

M. *I explain to him that we have to live in the group, and we have to*
have the respect of the group, and unless he accepts some of those
things—which I always explain are ridiculous to me but we still have to
observe some of the amenities—they will not get along well, and they
will not be happy. That's the way I handled that, and it has occurred
two or three times . . . this voiding outside. It's a great delight when
he finds that he's got a little fly, and it's just more than he can bear.
He does get a little encouragement from the older child he plays with,
but I don't by any means think it's entirely the other child's fault.

As may be seen from Table VI:5, there was a fairly wide
range of attitudes about the permissibility of sex play. Most felt
that such play should not be allowed. Examples of answers which
were rated as *not permissive* are the following:

A

M. *I wouldn't allow it, no, I definitely wouldn't. I think there's plenty*
of time for that later. When they get older, I think you can talk to
them more sensibly about it, but I don't think there's too much in the

TABLE VI:5

PERMISSIVENESS FOR SEX PLAY AMONG CHILDREN

1. Not permissive. Mother always steps in and stops at once. Considers it wrong, harmful	28%
2. Slightly permissive	29
3. Moderately permissive—might let moderate forms go on (such as going to bathroom together); tries not to make too much of an issue, but in general would discourage it	23
4. Quite permissive	14
5. Entirely permissive—sees nothing wrong with it, just a natural form of play; would not attempt to stop	2
Not ascertained	4
Total	100%

way of reasoning that would impress them at their age anyway. Just step in and stop it, is all.

B

M. *I have always told him: "Billy, you know when you do something that isn't right. When you do something that isn't right, you don't feel good inside." So he came in one day and he says, "Mother, I don't know whether to tell you this or not." And I said, "What is it?" And he says, "This little boy told me to take my pants down, and they told me they'd tell you if I didn't do it." But then he [Billy] says, "I'd just as soon tell you myself." And I says, "Well, I'm glad you did tell me." And I said, "Now when they tell you to do it again, you can tell them that your mother already knows. So you don't have to do it." I says, "You might catch cold, darling." It was fall, I think, at the time, and I says, "You might catch cold, honey, that's silly business. Did you*

TABLE VI:6

SEVERITY OF PRESSURE WHICH HAS BEEN APPLIED AGAINST SEX PLAY AMONG CHILDREN

1. No incidents have occurred, so far as mother knows	46%
2. No pressure, although incidents have occurred. Mother has made no attempt to stop	8
3. Slight pressure. Mother tries to distract, but does not scold or make an issue	16
4. Moderate pressure—some scolding, preventing, warning, but not intense	22
5. Considerable pressure—forbidding, scolding; some show of emotion	5
6. Severe pressure—punishment. Mother angry or disgusted; warns of extreme consequences	2
Not ascertained	1
Total	100%

ever see Daddy go and pull his pants down? That's silly, you might catch cold."

C

M. They were showing their bottoms to each other, and as I understand it, they were examining each other quite well. It was a little group of girls—so I explained it—I told them all I could compare them to was animals, and I got a dog and I told Ellen if she wanted to be an animal, that was the way they acted. It seemed to impress her at the time, because I never have had any more of it.

In contrast, some mothers were *permissive* about sex play among children:

A

M. She had this little boy friend, this summer. They used to go out in his tent, and take off their clothes and peek at each other, but the other mother and I talked it over and we didn't make a lot of bones about it. The little boy did it with an awful lot of children, but Betty fortunately limited it to him; and they used to take off their clothes and, I suppose, examine each other.
I. Did you do anything about it?
M. No, it stopped by itself. Oh, I might say to them, "Let's play ball," and they'd quickly get on their clothes backward or something. But they were very easy to divert.

B

M. A lot of them like to go in the bathroom with each other; I don't know why. They did, but this year they don't. They close the door on one another. I think it's not much fun watching each other go to the bathroom. I think it was just something that fascinated them, that's all.
I. What did you do about it when this happened?
M. Oh, nothing. I just let them go to the bathroom, and forget it. They outgrew it, that's all.

C

M. A little girl and Donny used to go in the bathroom together, and giggle and laugh, and we just looked at each other and ignored it, the little girl's mother and I. They are both healthy children, and they are not sneaky. If they were sneaky, I would be very upset.

D

M. I saw two boys showing themselves, going in the bushes, and so forth, but Jimmy didn't care about doing that. He's all boy. He joins with the rest of the children, but yet when it comes to something like that, I don't think he'll do it. Not that I'd mind. He's only a boy, and all boys are boys.

As may be seen in Table VI:6, mothers who did encounter instances of sex play attempted not to make the situation appear too serious. As with other varieties of sex behavior, there were few instances of severe scolding or punishment.

Most mothers of five-year-olds have discovered that sex play occurs as easily between children of the same sex as between children of opposite sexes. We did not tabulate the reported incidents to determine whether they involved mixed-sex or same-sex groups of children more frequently. Many instances of each kind were reported. This fact suggests that children of this age have not yet narrowed down their sexual interests to the particular sex that will be regarded as appropriate when they are older.

Reports of sex play. Nearly half of the mothers had not encountered any instances of sex play in their children by the time the children were five or six years old. Again, as with the reports of masturbation, we must be skeptical of the significance of such reports. Mothers were not with their children all the time, and there is no reason to believe that they actually knew whether their children had engaged in sex play or not. Further, one must question what the occurrence or nonoccurrence of such play would mean from a child's standpoint. There were undoubtedly differences in the opportunities which arose in different children's neighborhoods, e.g., the number and age of other children, and the degree of supervision exercised by the neighboring mothers. However, as was the case with masturbation, those mothers who reported that they did *not* know of any sex-play incidents were rated higher on the *keeping track of child* scale than were the mothers who *did* know of such incidents ($p = .01$).

One other finding is rather interesting, too, although we are uncertain of its implications. Those mothers who *did* report instances of sex play were neither more nor less permissive about sex play itself, but they were somewhat more permissive about the child's being unclothed in the house (higher modesty permissiveness). This may merely have meant that the more permissive mothers were more willing to mention such incidents. They did not report observations of masturbation more frequently, however, so this explanation does not have much to support it.

One possible interpretation of this finding is that social sex play is partly a result of the child's difficulty in discriminating what is permitted from what is not permitted. If he is allowed to be without clothes in the bosom of the family, some of this permissive treatment may carry over into situations where nudity is not appropriate. He would find it more difficult to maintain barriers against any impulses he has to expose himself to other children if he were not required to maintain these barriers in all situations. This is pure speculation, however.

PATTERNS OF SEX ATTITUDES

Since the nineteen twenties, when Freud's theories and observations began to pervade Western thought, there has been a popular tendency to think of the sexual motive as a rather unitary thing. The view is not uncommonly expressed that an individual has *a* sex drive of a certain strength and *a* certain amount of sexual inhibition. Or he shows so-and-so much sex anxiety or sex permissiveness or defensiveness against sex. Perhaps this conception grew out of Freud's vigorous championing of *libido* as a unifying motivational construct. However, clinical experience suggests that there is great diversity in the strength of the various sexual attitudes and attachments that a person has. One kind of expression may be quite free of anxiety (e.g., marital sexuality) while another (e.g., homosexual activity) is provocative of severe feelings of guilt or shame. We may acknowledge some underlying unity in the sexual motive, and equally recognize the variations that can occur among its manifestations in a single individual, but we are still left with an empirical question: how much generality is there in attitudes toward different kinds of sexual behavior?

In the present context, this question can be given a tentative answer with respect to mothers' attitudes of permissiveness toward modesty, masturbation, and sex play in their five-year-old children. Does a given mother have much the same attitude about one sex training problem as another? Or may she be quite restrictive about one while being quite permissive about another?

Consider permissiveness first. We find that the mother's permissiveness in one sphere of sex behavior was fairly closely related to her permissiveness in the others. The intercorrelations range around .60. (See Appendix Table D:17.) This means that if one picked just any mother at random, and looked up her score on permissiveness for the child's going around in the house without clothes, he could make a much better than chance guess about how permissive she would be with respect to masturbation and sex play with other children.

The "pressure" scales show a considerably lower degree of generality. The intercorrelations range around .37. This indicates less consistency than is shown for attitudes of permissiveness, but there is some consistency nevertheless, and one could still improve on a chance guess if one wanted to predict any individual mother's score on one pressure scale from her score on another pressure scale.

One can also ask whether the amount of pressure put on a child for conformity in any area of sex behavior was closely related to the mother's permissiveness in that area. If she strongly disapproved a particular kind of behavior, did she therefore put strong pressure on the child to stop that kind of behavior, by punishing him severely for it? There were mothers, of course, who despite strong disapproval of a particular form of sex behavior tried not to show their feelings openly, and avoided punishing the child for it. But in general, the amount of direct pressure a mother applied was closely related to how she felt about whether the behavior should be allowed to occur. The intercorrelations between permissiveness and pressure for the same variety of sex behavior range around —.75.

It must be kept in mind, in the interpretation of these findings, that all the measures were taken from one section of a single interview. They were not truly independent measures of actual behavior. Each expressed attitude would necessarily be influenced by the same general level of feelings of that particular day. The raters themselves could not help but be somewhat influenced by their *general* impression of a mother's qualities. We suspect, therefore, that these correlations are spuriously high, and that the true consistency of attitude and behavior toward these three areas of sex training was somewhat less than it appears here.

In any case, even were we to accept these indices as accurate, there is clear evidence that mothers do not have *an* attitude toward sex training as a whole, but have perhaps a *range* within which their attitudes fall.

Personality correlates of permissiveness. The best single measure of where this range lies, whether high or low, is the average rating given the mother on the three permissiveness scales. The fact that this range is moderately narrow—that is, there is some consistency in a mother's degree of permissiveness about sex—suggests the possibility that there may be a general trait of permissiveness covering other areas of the child's behavior as well.

There is evidence to support this notion. The correlations between average sex permissiveness and ratings on several scales that measure strictness of control or attitudes in other areas of child training are all in the direction that indicates some slight generality of this aspect of maternal behavior. These correlations are small. They range from .21 to .39. This means that one would find a great many mothers who differed quite radically from one area of control to another. Nevertheless there would be a *slightly* better than chance prediction of a mother's rating on any of the items listed below if one knew her rating on sex permissiveness.

Mothers who are *not permissive* with respect to sex tended to:

1. Permit little aggression from the child toward themselves.
2. Toilet-train their children severely.
3. Check frequently on the child's whereabouts.
4. Use physical punishment fairly often.
5. Be relatively cold emotionally toward their children.
6. Respond negatively to dependency.
7. Be strict about noise, table manners, and care of property in the household.
8. Emphasize that their daughters should be "feminine," their sons "masculine."

An interesting minor point is that the mothers who were non-permissive with respect to masturbation also tended not to allow the child to use his fingers for eating. One cannot help wondering whether part of the emphasis on the proper use of utensils at the table stems from a mother's concern that fingers may be especially "unclean."

All but two of the measures listed above are contributors to

Factor A (*permissiveness*) in our factor analysis (see Appendix Table D:4). The three sex permissiveness measures are the largest contributors, but permissiveness for aggression toward the parents is also a heavy contributor. In general, this factor seems to reflect, at one extreme, a concern to keep the child under rigid control, and to demand of him conformity to more mature standards. The control is punitive and restrictive. At the other extreme, the factor reflects a relaxed attitude toward the child's pleasure-seeking, an awareness of his needs for expressing himself by means of the early changeworthy actions, and a willingness to tolerate, without punishment, the less mature forms of dependency, sex, and aggression. Punitive methods of control are generally rejected.

Sex anxiety, as we used the term in previous chapters, is closely related to the non-permissive end of the three sex measures. It will be recalled that the mothers who explained their decision not to breast-feed their children by reference to some physical disability were high in sex anxiety, on the average. So were the mothers who decided to begin toilet training very early. Sex anxiety apparently contributed in some way to the occurrence of bed-wetting in the child also. It is regrettable that we have no measures of the actual sexual behavior of the children, for it would be interesting to know whether a non-permissive attitude increases or decreases the child's interest and exploration in the sexual sphere of life. The answer to this question will have to await further research.

COMMENT

So far we have discussed the socialization practices of mothers with respect to four areas of behavior: feeding, toileting, dependency, and sex. There were certain similarities and some differences. By comparison with nonliterate societies the average American standard that these mothers set for their children seems to have been fairly demanding. That is, children were pressed to give up changeworthy behavior comparatively early, and they were required to conform to rather restrictive adult standards. For example, both weaning and toilet training occurred unusually early, and the mature standards demanded with

respect to sex behavior were relatively rigorous in their requirement of inhibition and self-control. On the other hand, the typical training methods the mothers used were not especially severe
in any of these four areas. While punishment for toilet accidents
at a late age was by no means uncommon, there was a general
avoidance of a strongly punitive approach in any area.

There was one striking difference, however, between the methods used for controlling sex behavior and those used in the socialization of the other three areas. This was in the matter of
labeling the changeworthy behavior and controlling the stimulation that produced it. Mothers seem to have followed a rather
uniform practice, in connection with feeding, toileting, and dependency, of indicating as clearly as possible to the child what
they did and did not want him to do. They seem to have given
little attention to avoiding the stimulation of changeworthy behavior, although many of their practices with both weaning and
toilet training had this effect, of course. But in the case of sex
behavior, a major method of training and control was the avoidance of stimulation; the avoidance of labels for sexual matters
seems to have been one rather notable method of achieving this
aim.

We do not know just what effects these methods have on the
child's developing attitudes toward sex or his sexual motivation
and behavior. We have already commented on the possibility
that early sexual stimulation *may* tend to strengthen sex drive
and increase the specificity of the acts necessary for its reduction.
If this is the case, then quite likely the nonstimulating and nonlabeling process of control is as effective a method as can be
found for keeping the child's internal demands for sex experience at a minimum during the preadolescent years.

On the other hand, there may be some side-effects of these
methods that many people would consider undesirable. We know
that labeling is an important aid to learning. Something named
is easier to reason about. It can be distinguished from other
things more accurately. And it can become the object of appropriate behavior more readily. The child who has not been
provided with proper labels for certain parts of his body, or
for behavior related to sex, or for sexual feelings, may be somewhat handicapped in developing an understanding of sexual matters and an acceptance of his own sexual feelings without anxiety.

Mislabeling may have still other consequences. If a child is told not to touch his genitals because they are "dirty" from going to the toilet, or if he is sent to the toilet whenever he is seen holding himself, on the assumption that he needs to eliminate, he may attach to sex some of the emotions he feels in connection with toileting: for example, disgust. Or, when sexually stimulated, he may experience anxiety that will be reflected in disturbances in toileting activities. And possibly the common warning to the child that he will "hurt himself" if he touches his genitals may strengthen an association between his sexual feelings and a feeling of impending injury or danger. None of these associated attitudes would be helpful to his sexual adjustment either in childhood or later.

At the same time, it must be recognized that our culture places quite narrow restrictions on parents in their task of socializing the sexual motive of their children. Since no sexual gratification of any kind is publicly permitted before adolescence, parents are constrained to make sure their children conform to what is in fact a fairly severe form of self-control. Instances of self-stimulation or social sex play are often looked upon as mere curiosity or mischief in younger children, but in the later school ages such behavior may be very severely criticized. In our interviews, mothers not infrequently referred to some older child as having been initially responsible for such sex activity as was displayed by the five-year-old. Parents are therefore under strong pressure to eliminate signs of sexual interest or excitability in their children.

Faced with this difficult training task, mothers use what is probably one of the most effective means of accomplishing their ends. They try to prevent sex activity from starting at all by minimizing, in every conceivable way, stimulation that could arouse sexual impulses and thus lead to the strengthening of the drive by experience.

Doubtless this method of socializing sex motivation has some undesirable consequences, at least in some children. The clinical literature is heavy with instances of adolescent and adult anxiety, misunderstandings, and paralyzing ignorance about sex. Retrospectively, not a few of these disturbances seem to have developed through the process of mislabeling sexual acts and feelings in early childhood. Psychotherapy has not shown quite so clearly just what the effects of *nonlabeling* may be. Perhaps this is because traditional psychoanalytic theory has assumed that the child always *does* have labels for his infantile sexual feelings, but that he represses them by the time he reaches adulthood. This may well be the case, but we have no present information on how generally this may be so. Evidently many children must have to do their own private labeling, for their mothers give them little help. This means, in effect, that a child's understanding of his feelings—his conception of what sex behavior means in its social context—is developed without the kind of "correcting by reality" that occurs in the development of most of his other conceptions about himself and others.

We find it hard to believe that this state of affairs is a desirable one from a mental health standpoint. But when we look at the alternatives, we are not encouraged to urge any very radical changes in the methods of training. Certainly *mislabeling* can do nothing but harm, but *nonlabeling* is one effective method of avoiding stimulation. If a society requires that its children display no seeking of sexual gratification, then the removal of stimulation is one important aid to achieving that end.

Some observers of American culture have suggested that we would have less tension about sex if we were less restrictive about its expression both in childhood and in the adolescent years before marriage. There is good evidence that such a relaxing of strictures has been going on during the last sixty years (see Terman, 1938, and Kinsey, 1948, 1953). The frequency of premarital intercourse with the future spouse has been increasing continuously since 1890 at least. Whether there has been a parallel relaxing of restrictions on preadolescent sexual behavior, we do not know.

It must be remembered, however, that our sex mores, and our ways of training children about sex, are intimately bound up with other aspects of American culture. Our monogamous marriage system, our emphasis on prolonged formal education, and various other features of our highly industrialized society are by no means independent of sex customs. It seems unlikely that radical changes in sex training could be introduced without producing repercussions in other areas. Just what these effects might be is difficult to foresee.

It is important to remember, too, that many, if not most, of the current generation of mothers have deep inhibitions and some anxieties about sex themselves. Considering the kinds of sex training they report, we may expect their daughters to be not unlike them. If mothers attempt to adopt a new and more open set of standards for dealing with their children, standards which violate their own deep feelings, the ensuing conflict may have a more damaging impact on children than do the current restrictive sex-training practices.

Societies which suffer sudden changes in important aspects of their culture do not adjust quickly or painlessly. As witness, notice the dislocations produced by the introduction of improved medical care in underdeveloped areas. It may well be that the ultimate mental health of the American people can be improved by more open recognition of childhood sexuality and by the giving of more complete information in early childhood sex training, but, if so, this culture change must be paced at such a rate as to avoid creating new problems in the process of solving old ones.

CHAPTER SEVEN

Aggression

Aggression, as the term is commonly used, means behavior that is intended to hurt or injure someone. Most human adults have quite a repertory of acts that fit this definition. Some of these are bold and violent, others sly and attenuated. Some are accompanied by rage or annoyance; others are done coldly and seemingly, to the perpetrator, without emotion. The complexity and subtlety of adult aggression is the end product of two or three decades of socialization by the individual's parents and peers, however, and bears little resemblance to the primitive quality of the infant's action patterns, from which it developed.

To understand the problem of aggression in child rearing, one does well to remind himself firmly that man is a mammal, and that there are certain kinds of behavior which characterize all mammals. The two that are most relevant to the problem of aggression are *fighting* and the *expression of rage*.

From the lowest quadruped to the highest biped, physical attack is used for defense. Techniques vary, depending on the sharpness of hooves, the strength of jaws, and the presence of specialized weapons like antlers. Man, being the most intelligent and inventive of all, makes use of many of the other species' techniques and adds a host of new ones that, happily, no other animal has ever dreamed of. He can bite like a dog, claw like a cat, kick like a stallion, trade insults like a howling monkey, squeeze like a gorilla; and he constructs his own clubs, blow-pipes, knives, and guns to make up for his lack of antlers and

horns. The evolutionary continuity becomes crystal clear in any TV wrestling match.

In spite of this ingenuity, however, physical fighting is not the commonest form of human aggression. *Injury* is a broad term, and the socialization process develops many motives that can be thwarted. Interference with any of these motives causes pain or anguish, and if this was the intention, the interfering act was truly aggressive.

Defensive fighting is usually accompanied by expressions of rage. The older child or adult, who can report his feelings, may recognize his desire to hurt, and be very aware of his angry emotion. But this quality of aggression is attenuated, too, in the process of socialization, and there are many forms of hurt that an adult inflicts with little emotional arousal.

In a civilized society adults are rarely beaten or knifed or lashed. More often, they are hurt by attacks on their pride or status, their desire for social approval, or their feelings of affection for their families and friends. These kinds of hurt can be far more serious and more prolonged than most physical hurts. The withholding of affection by a loved spouse, for example, can have the meaning of pain that goes far beyond that from broken legs or crushed fingers. Nor do injuries that come through sheer accident, the vagaries of nature, hurt like injuries to self-esteem. Contrast them with the gratuitous insult from an admired and intimate friend, or the malicious gossip that one is "slipping" at his job, or the suggestion by a neighbor that one has been a failure in child rearing, or the rejection of a young girl seeking membership in a college sorority. And it is a strong and seasoned old man who can recall without pain his first failure as a lover—and his mistress's amusement.

Not all injuries are so great as these, of course. There are tongue-lashings that do not hurt—much—and insults that are shrugged off. There are the little obstinacies in one's friends, and the non-co-operative indifferences of one's working associates. There are the irritants of family living—a tired and sassy child, a grumpy and complaining husband, a daughter who dawdles. Since all these cause discomfort, they *can* be forms of aggression. Whether they are in fact, however, depends on whether the discomfort they engender was *designed* by the perpetrator to hurt someone else.

Not all acts that hurt are intended to do so. Even sophisticated and sensitive adults sometimes fail to anticipate the effects of what they do. The unanswered letter can seem a slight; the unasked question can be interpreted as indifference. With children, the problem is especially noticeable in the manipulation of physical forces. A child's innocently swinging stick only too easily turns into a painful club, the experimental bombing into a brother's broken toys.

Since these hurts are obviously unintentional, they do not qualify as *aggression* in the technical sense of the word. There are certain borderline examples, however, that are hard to be sure about. There are acts that sometimes are and sometimes are not aggressive. Most mothers consider obedience of some importance, for they use much verbal guidance in instructing and controlling their children. The children know their mothers want compliance with directions, and hence willful disobedience is widely recognized as a form of aggression. Now if a child has been told to pick up his clothes a dozen times, and if he has remembered to do this the last half-dozen times, his mother may look suspiciously at his motives if he forgets the thirteenth time. Did he just forget? Or was he angry and disobedient? People differ considerably in the degree to which they perceive an aggressive intent in the behavior of others, and what one mother calls carelessness another will call disobedience.

If we disregard borderline cases and accidents, however, there is still a great deal of human behavior that is designed to hurt. Such activity develops early in life and is a disrupting influence on family living. Later it becomes a problem for the peer group, and, universally, societies find necessary the adoption of techniques for curbing aggression among adults. At the same time, certain kinds of aggression are tolerated or even approved and required, as for example fighting in self-defense or in the defense of the cherished values of one's own social group.

DEVELOPMENT OF AGGRESSION

There are two aspects of aggression that can be considered separately. One is the fundamental emotional quality of rage or anger; the other is the desire to hurt, to inflict injury. The former appears to be an instinctive response to certain kinds of restraint and discomfort. The desire to hurt someone in the process, however, is not so clearly instinctive. Nineteenth-century biologists were inclined to attribute a good many characteristics of man's emotional behavior to instinct. Today, with our better understanding of the ruling influence of culture as a source of behavioral universals, we are inclined to suspect that the determination of which stimuli will arouse rage, and the focusing of the emotion into an actual *desire and intent* to hurt others (or the self), are products of learning experiences begun in early infancy.

Rage, or something very like it, occurs soon after birth. For caution's sake, let us emphasize the "something very like it." One can never know what the feelings and perceptions of an infant are, whether he has the true sense of fury or whether he just flails his limbs and screams. And *if* he has the sense of fury, we cannot know whether he has also the feeling of blaming someone for something and wanting to hurt in retaliation. In any case, his behavior sometimes has certain qualities, when he is hungry or colicky or pricked or restrained, that look so like the rage of older children who do report their feelings that we incline to say that this is the early beginning of aggression. There are the flailing limbs, the blasting cry, the scarlet face and hoarse breathing. After such an episode there is likely to be a period during which food does not sit well on the stomach, and the child may even vomit.

Within the first year, a child learns to use his hands somewhat more manipulatively, and he begins to strike at people who are close enough to him to be hit when something arouses this hot behavior. He learns to bite, too, and to kick, as he gains more control over his movements, and to let loose ear-piercing screams.

Gradually he begins to supplement these direct attacks with other techniques that are effective not because they hurt the mother physically, but because they interfere with her efforts at child care. The baby discovers how to cry "miserably," how to turn his head away when his mother wants him to smile, how to remain rigid when she wants to cuddle him. He has discovered the invaluable principle of non-co-operation as a means of control.

By the latter part of their second year, many children have

begun to add still another kind of behavior to the repertory of actions that they use for controlling other people. Throwing, smashing, dropping, spilling, pushing, knocking over—all begin to appear. At first these acts do not necessarily involve what adults interpret as destructiveness, but most children soon seem to learn that to destroy (or threaten to destroy) some valued object has a wholesome influence, on other children and adults, from the child's point of view. It secures compliance or wards off further interference.

It would be a mistake, of course, to assume that destructive or hurtful acts are the only kind of controlling techniques a baby learns. There are other kinds that adults can recognize as being learned for this purpose. Even before his first birthday, a child develops many subtle devices for influencing his mother, ones that do not involve strong emotional reactions at all. These include the various forms of dependency described in an earlier chapter, and all the many ways of persuasion that depend on the child's making himself loved and wanted by his mother. Gradually he learns, too, simply to ask for compliance with his wishes, and he discovers that his mother will often remove discomforts for him when he does no more than point out what is troubling him.

On the other hand, no mother can ever be a perfect slave. She has her needs, too, and one of her most important ones is the successful rearing of her child. Not everything she does in this process is satisfying to him. He is inevitably frustrated, and develops defenses against such occasions.

One thing he discovers during the first couple of years is that when his mother wants his co-operation, he can give it or not as he chooses. If he does not choose, his mother will make continued efforts to ensnare him. Some of her acts are good to have happen: she may pick him up, cajole him with little murmurs and kisses, talk to him lovingly, offer him food or a toy, or tickle him. As he gets older, and proud of his skills, she may urge him to walk a little more or build a little higher or say another word. He learns that he has the power to require that a price be paid for doing what his mother wants. This is extremely important for the development of aggression, for by learning what things he can withhold from his mother, he has learned how to cause pain without using his impotent fists.

The sequence of development, then, seems to go like this. In the beginning, the child can do no more, in response to discomforting situations, than express angry emotion. However, his maturing skill for controlling his own movements soon enables him to learn other ways of reacting, ways that help to get rid of the frustrating state of affairs. Some of these acts are constructive from the mother's point of view, as when the child willingly cooperates with her wishes and thus ends his own frustration by making unnecessary his mother's pressure for compliance. Some of the child's acts are hurtful to her, however, and may be looked on as the earliest forms of aggression in the child's repertory of behavior.

It is difficult for parents to realize, sometimes, how often a young child achieves some relief from an uncomfortable state of affairs via aggressive actions. The mother may not know how tired, or how frustrated, he is until she sees signs of a temper tantrum, at which point she realizes that something must be done and goes into action. Even if she is irritated with him over his show of temper, she will put him to bed, or feed him, or open the sticking door, or somehow change the situation so that the source of trouble has been removed. Thus, even if she scolds the child for being aggressive, she simultaneously solves his problem and hence strengthens his aggressive behavior. Many a child has learned that his busy mother pays little attention to him so long as he is getting along all right, and that it is primarily when he screams or otherwise makes his mother uncomfortable that she will turn her attention to his difficulties and help him solve them. Understandably, a child is especially likely to learn to get attention by aggressive action during the stage of his life when he cannot yet talk clearly, for the more "rational" process of telling his mother specifically what is wrong is not yet possible.

By the end of the child's second year, certain further developments have taken place. One of these is that the child has begun to respond aggressively to a good many frustrations in a purely automatic way. Even though his mother may be absent at the moment and his aggressive act may be quite futile as a means of removing the frustration, he will perform the act nonetheless. It is as if he had learned, in a blind sort of way, that aggressive acts were often followed by the relief of discomfort.

So, without evaluating the probable effectiveness of his behavior, he simply aggresses whenever frustrated.

Children differ a great deal from one another in the extent to which this type of development occurs. Some seem to reach a point in their third and fourth years at which almost every little irritant or interference triggers off an aggressive reaction. Indeed, many situations that have no frustrating quality at all— to an outside observer—are sufficient, too. There may be many expressions of destructiveness or hitting or verbal attack which appear quite spontaneous. Other children, in contrast, have a relatively low tendency to act this way, and perhaps have a greater propensity for reacting with some kind of dependency behavior. Every child, in other words, develops a repertory of actions to be used when he bumps up against frustrations: some children tend to use aggression as their typical reaction; others use some other type of act. In the last section of this chapter, we will examine the mothers' reports to determine what child-rearing practices are associated with these differences.

The other change that becomes evident in the child's second year, and is increasingly notable the older he gets, is in the apparent satisfyingness of some of his aggressive acts. Most of his aggressive behavior continues to be a device for gratifying other needs—but occasional acts now seem to have the quality of gratifications in their own right. We think this comes about for two reasons. First of all, even this early in life, few children have been allowed to show aggression without suffering some reprisals, as will be seen later in this chapter. Thus, aggressive impulses are accompanied by fear of the consequences, and the child is in conflict. The more he wants to hit out, the more afraid he is of doing so, and the tension mounts. When the balance is finally tipped and the aggressive action occurs, the tension generated by the child's attempting to inhibit himself is momentarily relieved. Adults often experience this relief of tension after they have lost their tempers—they speak of "letting off steam," and feel better even though the aggression itself may not have accomplished much in the way of improving the objective situation. Young children, too, can find aggression relieving in this sense.

A second reason why aggressive actions may occur, even when

they do not solve any of the child's immediate problems, is that he has developed what we described in Chapter One as an *acquired motive*. In the process of learning how to gratify their basic needs, children learn also to seek the circumstances which surround gratification. Even in the absence of the primary gratification itself, they will act as if they *wanted* these surroundings, at least for a time. This principle holds equally true for the lower animals; for example, white rats which have been fed by a noisy machine will work to produce the noise of the machine, even when no food is forthcoming. Similarly, children who have repeatedly gotten rid of frustrations through hurting others, and who have seen the signs of pain in the other person at the very moment the frustration was removed, will begin to enjoy, and seek, the signs of pain in others. These signs seem to be sought for their own sake alone.

We doubt that this acquired motivation is the only factor underlying the development of impulses to hurt or injure. The common occurrence of behaviors that represent a kind of sadistic cruelty, during the preschool years, suggests that some other motives may also be involved. The habitual tormenting of animals or younger children not infrequently involves a sexual element, and psychoanalytic theory is very likely correct in assuming some kind of connection between the sexual and aggressive motives. But we do believe that in most normal children there develops, in greater or less degree, the impulse to hurt for the hurting's sake, and that at least one reason for a child's developing this impulse is the repeated experience of seeing the signs of pain in others at moments when the child's own needs are being gratified. This hurting for the sake of hurting is the final developmental stage of human aggression.

SOCIAL CONTROL

Needless to say, this sequence of development does not go unnoticed by parents and peers. Aggressive behavior must be kept under strict control if life is not to become too painful for the victims.

All human societies, even all colony-living subhuman primates, have rules to limit the kinds and direction of aggression that may be expressed. The most fundamental of these is the high degree of prohibition on in-group fighting. The closer together people live, the more interdependent they are, the less they dare be aggressive toward one another. Free fighting and antagonism within the household—whether it be a nomad's hut or a suburbanite's four-bedrooms-and-two-baths—could only lead to wreckage of the family unit. Hence, all societies require that only very attenuated forms of aggression be expressed among family members, and that, within the parent-child relationship, aggression be expressed only downward. One mother described this principle with great clarity:

I. *How do you handle it (if he strikes you)?*
M. *I don't allow it. I slap him and punish him for it, and explained that he was never to raise his hand to anyone older than himself, that he must respect older people—his mother and father especially. Never! But they do attempt it, of course; but I do think it should be checked right away.*
I. *How did you handle this?*
M. *I would just put him right in his room. Just take hold of him right at the moment and put him right in his room, and say "You mustn't do that! You never should hit your mother and father, ever; they're always right." I always make a big issue out of it.*
I. *That your mother and father are always right?*
M. *Always right; "You must never raise your hand to your mother or father."*

Not all mothers felt as strongly as this one did, and different societies have different degrees of tolerance for in-family aggression, but the prohibition exists in some degree in all known societies.

Outside the family, limitations are less severe in most societies. As will be seen later, the mothers in this present study were less concerned—more permissive—about fighting between their own children and neighbor youngsters than about sibling quarreling. There were a number of instances in which mothers felt children must be encouraged to fight, to protect their own interests. Even so, there is still a good deal of necessary restriction on the more severe forms of aggression, no matter toward whom they are directed.

To insure the firm establishment of these rules, many mothers feel they must begin the control of aggression very early in the child's life. A newborn infant is not particularly dangerous, even to himself, but he represents a potential threat nevertheless. The family, indeed the whole society, has a delicate balance; the forces of aggression are being kept in check, and co-operation and love are outweighing non-co-operation and hate. The baby is an alien who does not know all the rules. He lacks knowledge of when to hit and when not to. He has no skill at securing compliance by a *little* hurting. He cannot be counted on to channelize, to displace, or to attenuate his aggressions.

CONTROL *Versus* TRAINING

From the mother's standpoint, this state of affairs poses a special problem. Every action of hers serves as an instigator to some kind of action, or change of action, in the child. If she smiles, or frowns, or speaks, or avoids speaking, the child will respond in some way. Her behavior can be satisfying or frustrating, encouraging or discouraging, goading or relaxing.

Whatever she does, and however the child responds, there are two ways of viewing the interaction. One of these is as the *control* of action and the other as *training*. *Control* means having an influence on the immediate on-going actions of the child. *Training* means influencing his future behavior. Every interaction a mother has with her child has some influence of each kind, although in many instances she may intend only one type. For example, the use of distraction as a device to stop a brother and sister from quarreling may be intended only as a means of clearing the emotional atmosphere, while a spanking is almost certainly intended to "teach" a child something, not just to make him angry or hurt his feelings or set him to crying. The distraction is not designed to have long-term effects, and certainly the spanking is not consciously intended just to create the immediate hullabaloo it usually does create.

Socialization in all areas of child behavior requires both control and training. The distinction was implicit in our earlier discussions of feeding, toileting, dependency, and sex. The methods of weaning and toilet training, for example, were examined as to their effects on both "emotional upset" (a *control* effect) and the future problems of eating-finickiness and bed-wetting (*training* effects). We must make the distinction fully explicit in connection with aggression, however, for in this instance the child's changeworthy behavior has a much higher capacity for arousing counter-aggression in the mother. Her aggressive reaction is likely to involve punishment of the child, and as was evident in earlier chapters, punishment is an extremely influential aspect of the socialization practices of mothers.

Action control involves the handling of such behavior as fighting, quarreling, sassing, disobedience, or non-co-operation at the

time it occurs. As soon as children begin to play with one another, there are opportunities for squabbles and disagreements. Most indoor quarreling, whether between siblings or neighborhood friends, is not dangerous in a physical sense, though some mothers have constantly in mind the possibility of bruises inflicted on younger children, as well as the possibility of broken toys, torn books, and angrily messed up furniture and playthings. But such quarreling does generate noise and angry talk, which are unpleasant to others in the house. Outdoor quarrels are less troublesome for most mothers, so far as noise or the danger of breakage is concerned, but they are generally viewed a little more seriously as possible sources of physical danger. Even three-year-olds can stab with big sticks and can throw rocks; in our interviews, mothers frequently mentioned their worry over injury to eyes. Some expressed fear, too, of what actual injury a child might do to the mother herself if he were not kept under control.

Training is a different matter. It is not sufficient that a child simply be kept from doing damage at a given moment. He must develop standards of conduct that will not require constant policing in order to maintain acceptable kinds of behavior. He must come to possess appropriate internal controls. The kinds of aggression he finally learns to use must be appropriate in form and intensity, and they must be used only under acceptable circumstances.

The necessity for control of both action and learning at the same time leads to some difficulties in training children vis-à-vis aggression, for the consequences of a particular practice may be quite different in its short-term and long-term influences. One can introduce pressures to stop the fussing and whining, but this is only half the problem. Does the child learn to do what his mother wants the next time? What does he learn? How does he behave after the pressure is taken off?

PUNISHMENT AND ANXIETY

The mother's almost automatic aggressive response to her child's aggression creates a special problem in child-rearing tactics that does not seem to arise nearly so seriously in connection with other areas of child behavior. Unless a mother is busy, or annoyed to start with, dependency is likely to elicit nurturance from her, and an expression of affection will evoke its like. But aggression, being a frustration to its object, has a strong tendency to evoke counter-aggression or punishment. After all, the mother was once a child herself and learned the same ways of reacting that her child is now learning.

This built-in relationship between the aggressor and his victim has an important consequence. It means that every child grows up with the experience of being punished in some degree for his aggressive behavior. The extent and severity of such punishment differs greatly from one child to another, of course, depending on the tolerance of his parents and siblings. It is our impression, however, that the average child in our sample received more actual *punishment* (as distinguished from *non-reward*) for aggressive behavior than for any other kind of changeworthy action.

One significant effect of punishment is the production of anxiety. If the punishment is repeated many, many times through early childhood, situations that provoke aggressive feelings gradually come to arouse anxiety, too—anxiety over the danger of being punished for aggression. Eventually, the aggression itself, or the accompanying feeling of being angry, becomes sufficient to arouse anxiety. In such cases the anxiety may properly be called aggression-anxiety.

The formation of such a reaction has two kinds of consequences that are relevant to the socialization process. One is the uneasiness and discomfort that become connected with the arousal of aggressive impulses. By and large, adults in our culture do not tolerate aggression comfortably, neither their own nor that displayed by others. It evokes too much anxiety; this may be reflected in feelings of worry, dislike, avoidance, guilt, or moral disapproval. They cannot feel fully comfortable when they are angry. They are in conflict—ambivalent—about their own impulses. The carrying through of an aggressive act is often followed not simply by the catharsis or satisfaction that one would expect from a successful action (assuming the action accomplished the intended results), but also by feelings that arise from the undercurrent anxiety. These may be shame, embarrassment, guilt, regret, self-deprecation, or even just plain fear of retaliation. A mother's uneasiness and conflict often make difficult a calm use of reason in deciding how to handle a child's aggressive actions.

A second consequence of punishment and its ensuing anxiety is the development, by the child, of techniques for avoiding punishment. The child who is consistently punished for swearing is likely to cease the practice in his parents' presence. This does not necessarily mean he will stop swearing, for punishment seems usually to have a rather localized inhibiting effect. The impulse to be aggressive is not reduced, but only the overt aggressive act that was punished. The total impulse to aggression is made stronger than ever, for the punishment is itself an additional frustration.

One interesting result of inhibiting specific overt aggressions by punishing them is the production of *displaced aggression*. This is aggression that is directed at some other person or object than the one that did the frustrating. The displacement occurs toward a victim who is less likely to retaliate than is the actual frustrator. Thus, the child who is punished for striking the mother may learn to express his aggression more toward siblings or even, as in the following instance, toward household pets.

> **M.** . . . *she seldom turns around and is directly defiant. If she can't get what she wants or if she is angry about something, she'll walk by, and she'll probably fight the first person she comes in contact with. She doesn't usually turn around and defy us or take it out on us. Usually she'll go out and she'll fight with anybody she sees, or she'll turn around and she'll slap the dog on the leg. She seems to go to a certain extent—like she'll say, "No, I won't," or something; and she seems to watch your face, and when she finds she's gone past the limit, she just closes up, and that's the end of it. She seldom turns around and slings anything or does anything to let off steam in front of you. It's usually a walk past the dog, and she'll slap him like this on the way out, or something like that. It—I don't know—it's directed at us, but it's on someone else.*
>
> **I.** *How do you handle that, if she slaps the dog?*
>
> **M.** *Well, if she slaps the dog, I slap her. . . .*

We may expect that eventually this child will stop slapping the dog, too, but then she will find still other objects that can be safely aggressed against.

In addition to producing aggression-anxiety, punishment by parents has one other effect that is important in the child-rearing process. It provides an aggressive *model* for the child to pattern himself after. One mother recognized this and commented as follows:

> **I.** *How do you handle it, when she acts this way?*
>
> **M.** *She's never raised her hand or attempted to kick, but she has shouted. But that is my fault because if I lose my temper, I shout at her. She is copying me. So, I can't scold her for that very well, but I think they should learn to respect the parents in that they should speak kindly to them. At the same time, you can't expect that sort of respect unless you do the same thing. But it is pretty hard at all times.*

One must conclude, in general, then, that punishment is a kind of "natural" method of control for mothers to use in the socialization of the aggression motive. The effects of punishment are complex, however, since it can serve both as an inhibitor and an instigator of aggressive actions, and its effects as an instrument of *control* may differ radically from its effects as a technique of *training*.

We can turn now to the findings from our interviews. In this chapter we will describe first the ways in which the mothers handled aggression, with respect to both permissiveness and punishment. It will be seen that there was some consistency in individual mothers' attitudes, and we will indicate what some of the other personality characteristics were that were commonly associated with gentle or severe handling. Finally, we will examine the relation between these child-rearing practices and the mothers' own reports of their children's aggressiveness to discover what procedures seemed to influence such behavior. Our main concern will be with the kinds of dimensions listed under columns II and III in the introduction to Chapter Two, but we will be able to provide information concerning all three of the kinds of questions we discussed in Chapter One.

THE MOTHERS' PERMISSIVENESS FOR AGGRESSION

In the discussion so far we have talked of aggression as a changeworthy form of behavior, particularly that directed toward the parents. This is a generalization, however, that hides a multitude of individual differences among the mothers. As might easily be predicted from what has been said of aggression-anxiety, parents differ greatly from one another in the amount of aggression they can tolerate. Some set great store by a completely nonaggressive child; others accept the inevitability of a certain amount of aggression even as late as age five; a few believe aggression is such a natural quality of early childhood behavior that they simply ignore all but the most violent episodes. These differences permit us to define a dimension called *permissiveness for aggression*.

Aggression toward parents

The Mosaic injunction to honor thy father and thy mother has left a deep imprint on Western civilization. Its cogency for contemporary family living is equally great whether it be interpreted as a dogmatic law or as an early generalization about the necessary properties of in-group behavior in a successful society. To insure this honor requires training. Training to do what? Like so many other abstracted attributes of human social behavior the word *honor* has a rather imprecise meaning. To some it designates an attitude of respect and admiration. To others it means subservience in word and obedience in deed. Whatever the specific qualities may be, the ultimate role relationship is rather generally conceived to be one in which the child is non-aggressive toward the parents. The question to be answered here is: How non-aggressive did these mothers believe their preschool-age children should be in their behavior toward their parents?

In our interviews, the mothers described the ways in which children got on adult nerves, found ingenious devices for expressing annoyance or getting revenge, and in general created the social and emotional havoc that goes with anger. They also expressed their own attitudes toward their children's aggression, and gave descriptions of how this changeworthy behavior was handled. With respect to aggression of children toward their parents, the mothers were asked:

> Sometimes a child will get angry at his parents and hit them and kick them or shout angry things at them. How much of this sort of thing do you think parents ought to allow in a child of (his, her) age? How do you handle it when (child's name) acts like this?

TABLE VII:1

PERMISSIVENESS FOR AGGRESSION TOWARD PARENTS

1. Not at all permissive. Believes this is something one should not permit under any circumstances. Always attempts to stop child immediately; neither verbal nor physical aggression permitted	38%
2. Slightly permissive	24
3. Moderately permissive. Feels that one must expect a certain amount of this, but that it should be discouraged rather firmly. May permit some "sassing" but no hitting	26
4. Quite permissive	10
5. Completely permissive. Does not attempt to stop child from hitting parent or shouting angrily at him. May express belief that child has right to hit parent if parent has right to hit child	1
Not ascertained	1
Total	100%

The replies were rated on the five-point scale for which the scale points are given in Table VII:1. The percentage of mothers judged to belong at each point is also shown.

Of course, any given case was rated on the basis of everything the mother said about aggression throughout the interview, and we cannot present entire cases here. But following are examples of the kind of statement which led to classifying a mother as *not at all permissive* (1):

A

M. *They never should allow him to hit them back. If he hits them, they should hit him right back. If you let him get away with it once he will always want to get away with it.*

I. *How do you handle it when he acts like this?*

M. *If he hits me I hit him back twice as hard, and if he does it again, I just get my paddle I have, and I give it to him again, and then he stops.*

I. *How do you handle it if he is deliberately disobedient?*

M. *I take off his clothes and he's in for the day and he's not to play with anything—not even his toys or anything that belongs to him— he's not to touch anything—he's to leave things alone and stay in bed.*

B

M. *That is something I will not tolerate—my child has never done it. I mean, they have done it once in a while, both of them, but I would absolutely not tolerate it.*

I. *How did you teach them not to do this?*

M. *I don't know—I guess I just told them once, in no uncertain terms, that it was something that was never done, and I have never had any trouble with it; and if I did, I don't know just how I would cope with it, because I wouldn't stand for it.*

I. *How much of this sort of thing do you think a parent ought to allow?*

M. *I don't think they should allow it at all. I think a child should be allowed to express himself, and all that, but I don't think there is ever an exception for a child to hit his parents.*

C

M. *I don't think you should allow any of it. You should stop it. But they do it.*

I. *Can you give me an example of this with Ginny?*

M. *Well, it might be when I want her to turn off the television and wash up for dinner and she will insist that she won't turn off the television. Well, I will just have to go over and turn the television set off, and she will scream and yell. I have to take her bodily out of the room* *and put her upstairs until she quiets down. And then let her come down after she stops the crying.*

These next two examples illustrate the kind of statements that would lead to a rating of *moderately permissive* (3); although these mothers were disapproving, they apparently accepted a certain amount of aggression as inevitable.

D

M. *I'm afraid I couldn't go it too often. Once in a while he will, but he doesn't do it too often. He will say he doesn't love me any more at times but I can understand how he feels, besides what it is he wants. He is resentful, but that is only something you can expect of a child that old. As far as kicking, I wouldn't tolerate that. I just have given him to understand that they can't do that.*

E

M. *Very little. I think it is pretty hard to stop it until he is older. I think they are quite likely to do it, but I think they should be punished for it.*

The following statements illustrate the most permissive attitudes found in our sample. Compared to 98 per cent of the mothers, these two were *very much more permissive* (5), although our designation of "completely permissive" in the scale description is obviously too strong even in these instances.

F

M. *Well, he has done that a couple of times, and a few times he has said "I don't like you," because I punished him, and I just skipped it. I didn't even pay any attention and went right on with my work. And after he thought it over he realized he didn't feel that way at all, because he loves us very much and he knows that we love him. He gets a lot of attention and knows that we didn't mean anything. He'll tell me himself—I won't tell him he has to say he's sorry—he'll usually tell me himself.*

G

M. *I think there's a certain amount that should be allowed. I think that it's something they have to get out of their system. If I saw that it was a habit, I'd certainly make provisions to prevent it, but in Susan's case every once in a while, she gets so furious with me, that she does strike out, and I sort of overlook it a little bit, because I think it's very natural.*
I. *Even shouting things?*
M. *Yes, I think so.*

It may be seen that our rating of the mother's "permissiveness" for aggression toward herself and her husband took into account the attitudes and values she expressed on the subject, as well as the extent to which she actually, in real-life situations, allowed the child to show such aggression or stopped him from doing so. For our purposes, the mother's attitudes and her behavior are not really separable. Our assumption is that if she believed that children should never be allowed to show aggression toward their parents, this belief would show itself in the way she reacted when the child behaved aggressively.

Some of the ways in which a mother's attitude manifests itself in her overt behavior may be very subtle—she may not be aware of them and may not be able to report them in an interview— but our assumption is that in one way or another the mother's attitude will show itself in her behavior toward the child. These intangible reactions are hard to measure by an interview, but the attitudes that govern them are not.

In the course of adapting themselves to their own impulses and behaviors, human beings objectify their decisions and attitudes into *values*. These values are statements of what is good and what is bad. Usually, and this is particularly true in the Judaeo-Christian ethic, values are set apart from other judgments and are given independent sanctions. Such-and-such a thing is *good per se*—not because it produces satisfaction or joy or some other good thing, but just because it *is* good. Likewise with the *bad*. Since values have become autonomous, there is no need for the individual ever to defend them. Hence, many values never get much discussed by adults, and people have a tendency to assume that all other people (unless they be blackguards or "unbelievers") hold the same values they hold themselves.

Of course, values are not disembodied principles that exist independently of the impulses and behavior of the people who hold them. This becomes very evident in examining mothers' values concerning aggression. Not only is there great variation in the goodness-badness attributed to such behavior in children, but the very statements of values are inextricably mixed with descriptions of the mothers' own behavior toward children's aggressions. Furthermore, not a few mothers gave clear evidence of having changed their values as a result of new experiences.

A mother may or may not have had experience with a particular situation, and she may or may not know what she believes to be "right." Usually she has some idea. Her reaction to the child in any particular instance may not be fully determined by her underlying values. She may feel quite permissive of her child's whining, especially if he is tired or ill or "has had a hard day," but she may have had a hard day herself and react more strongly than her own values prescribe. Conversely, she may have an intense dislike for hitting, but feel that an unusual circumstance has justified the child's fury. When she considers aloud "how she feels" about this sort of aggression, she is referring in part to an abstract principle, but her statement of it is influenced not only by the principle itself but by what she observes herself to have done in response to such behavior. The ratings on this permissiveness scale, then, represent a judgment based on a combination of statements of values and reports of actual behavior.

If we examine the numbers of mothers who were rated at each of the five points on the scale, it becomes apparent that, so far as aggression toward parents is concerned, there was a strong trend among these mothers in the direction of low permissiveness. Nearly two thirds of them were rated in the first two (non-permissive) categories. One might suppose at first glance that this was simply the result of a badly constructed scale, that if more *degrees* of unpermissiveness had been discriminated by the raters, there would have been a more normal distribution, i.e., a few cases at each end of the scale and the majority in the middle. But it would have been difficult to be more discriminative. There was an expression of a quite categorical value in all the 38 per cent of mothers in the least permissive group. They just absolutely would have none of it! They did differ somewhat in the severity with which they enforced their values, but they seemed very, and equally, certain that aggression toward parents is bad.

The fact that the modal value appears to be at the least permissive point on the scale suggests some conformity to an absolute value. But the examples given above represent quite a range of permissible behaviors. If one stops to think what this means in terms of the homogeneity of the culture in which these 379 children are being reared, he is forced to the conclusion that this wide a range provides only a moderate degree of uniformity in the values being held up to the value-wise. This community is by no means homogeneous. It is small wonder that adults find much on which to disagree, not only with respect to child-rearing policies about aggression, but in everything else that involves the expression of aggression toward figures in authority.

Aggression toward siblings and other children

Children find much to quarrel about. This is not surprising, either among siblings or neighborhood friends, for the very young child has neither the skills nor the desires for amicable social intercourse that adults have. Until children learn more effective ways of co-operating in play enterprises, those aspects of their behavior that adults want to change are often as frustrating to the children involved as to the adults. All children are sweetly reasonable at times, but most of them give way occasionally to arbitrariness, egocentricity, and a desire to dominate others and be King of the Castle. Then there are quarrels; the insult hurled is hurled back, and the offered blow returned with interest or fled from with cries of fright and rage.

When parents try to control this aggression, they are up against something quite different from aggression directed toward themselves. Sniping, yelling, threats of destruction, and even physical attacks, between siblings do not have the same quality of painfulness to a mother that a direct attack on her has. She may be frustrated by the noise, or the danger of the children's hurting each other or damaging household goods, but there is not the immediate affront to her sense of propriety, unless she has previously made it clear (which, of course, she sometimes has) that quarreling is forbidden. In this latter case, the mother may properly interpret the aggression as a form of disobedience, and hence really directed toward her.

Sibling quarrels among very young children are rather likely to occur in the house. They are disliked by mothers for several reasons, some of which can only be inferred. Quarrels are noisy, and thus painful. They occasionally result in throwing or other destructive actions. They break up peaceful play periods and bring the children, now in a hostile mood, back into circulation in the family, where they may start a fight with the parents. Because of the similarity to quarrels in which the mother herself has been involved in the past, quarreling excites the mother's own aggressive impulses and perhaps her aggression-anxiety. It represents simultaneous attacks on two (or more) children she loves; and because she feels affection and responsibility for both, this induces a particularly uncomfortable kind of conflict for her. It is no wonder mothers have strong feelings about the matter.

The situation with quarrels involving her own child and other children from the neighborhood is a little different. In the earliest years, many of these conflicts occur in the house, too, but as the child nears school age, an increasing number occur in the yard, the street, or across the way. The imperious quality of angry voices is more distant, and the potential damage to material goods is less. Further, the mother can feel less conflict about who is attacking whom. Only one of the quarreling parties is the immediate responsibility of the mother and has her most basic sympathy. There is less likely to be the discrepancy in size and age of the combatants that usually exists between siblings, and hence less need for protective intervention. At the same time, children outdoors play more with sticks and stones, run harder and indulge in more vigorous types of body contact play, and hence the danger of injury is greater.

When aggression is directed toward the parents or within the family group, the parents have the main stake in the matter. If the occasion for control passes by without any measures being taken, only the parents are responsible; if punishment is severe, only the child voices objection. When neighbor children are involved, however, the community enters—in the form of the other children's mothers. Now the mother is no longer free to settle the issue as she chooses, but must take account of the rights, feelings, and responsibilities of other adults whose interests in the conflict are of similiar origin to, but possibly in opposition to, her own. Thus, in addition to having less pressing call for control, in comparison with sibling squabbles, she has a good reason for treading lightly, for avoiding a direct conflict with other adults.

It is interesting to compare the mothers' values with respect to these two types of aggression. To secure the mothers' reactions to sibling quarrels, these questions were asked:

How do you feel about it when they quarrel?

How bad does it have to get before you do something about it?

How do you handle it?

The mothers who had two or more children were rated on a five-point scale entitled *mother's permissiveness for aggression among siblings*. Table VII:2 shows the percentage of mothers judged to show each of the five degrees of permissiveness.

TABLE VII:2

PERMISSIVENESS FOR AGGRESSION AMONG SIBLINGS

1. Not at all permissive. Parents try to stop quarreling and fighting immediately. Punish severely	4%
2. Slightly permissive	21
3. Moderately permissive. Stop if somebody getting hurt; may allow verbal battles if they don't go on too long. Scolding given but not severe punishment	45
4. Quite permissive	11
5. Entirely permissive. Mother never interferes in children's quarrels; they are allowed to fight it out. Parents do not try to stop or prevent this	1
Children without siblings	13
Not ascertained	5
Total	100%

Some excerpts will illustrate these scale points. The following response comes from an interview which was rated *not at all permissive* (1):

A

I. *How do you feel about it when they quarrel?*
M. *I don't like to see them quarrel. There is no need for it.*
I. *How bad does it have to get before you do something about it?*
M. *I don't let it get too bad. I just reprimand them right away.*
I. *How do you handle it?*
M. *I just scold both of them and tell them I don't like it. That they should love each other. Brother and sister are going to need each other a lot. I explained to Jim that when he goes to high school and you need a girl to take to your prom, you will be very happy to have a sister.*

This next response illustrates the kind of statement which led to a rating of *moderately permissive* (3):

B

I. *How bad does it have to get before you do something about it?*
M. *Not very bad. I am sure they are worse in a multitude of families. What I try to do is separate them. It doesn't happen very frequently, but when it does, and it gets too bad, and I can't seem to turn their minds to something else—which would be my first attempt—then I'd put them in their separate rooms; and that seems to be enough to change the current of their thoughts.*

The following two excerpts are taken from cases which were among the one per cent rated *completely permissive* (5). Again, of course, *complete* obviously does not mean what it usually means in everyday language!

C

I. *How bad does it have to get before you do something about it?*
M. *Oh, if they're making a terrible amount of noise, or if they're going to do bodily harm to each other. And I don't mean slapping—that doesn't bother me. If one of them picks up a shovel or something, then of course, I'd stop it. Otherwise, I have found that if I sit back and watch without their knowing it, they work it out themselves. Two seconds later they're putting their arms around each other and saying, "I love you anyway."*

D

I. *How do you feel about it when they quarrel?*
M. *Well, I feel that Sister—when Bobby is playing at something and he is trying to construct something, I think she should leave him alone, she should not break it, and I am trying to teach her that. But I think*

*when they are playing Bobby should certainly give Sister everything
that she gives to him. They play evenly, though, you know; he doesn't
give her too hard. But still, when she hits him and he comes running
to me, I'll say, "Well, if you hit her, I don't take sides," and I try to
even everything out, as best I can.*
I. *How bad does it have to get before you do something about it?*
M. *Well, until they are almost in tears. I let them play and go at it,
until I see a great injustice being done, and then I'll—right away—I
will speak to them. But as a rule I let them play and fight out the battles, you know.*

Before making any comparison between the mothers' relative
permissiveness for aggression directed toward themselves and
among siblings, let us look at comparable ratings for *permissiveness for aggression toward other children,* as shown in Table
VII:3.

The question asked on this matter was:

How about when (he, she) is playing with one of the other
children in the neighborhood and there is a quarrel or a fight
—how do you handle this?

The following excerpt is from the interview of a mother who
was rated as *not at all permissive* (1):

TABLE VII:3

PERMISSIVENESS FOR AGGRESSION TOWARD OTHER CHILDREN

1. Not at all permissive. Parent always tries to stop or prevent fights. Child severely punished for fighting	5%
2. Slightly permissive	26
3. Moderately permissive. Parent will not interfere unless someone is getting hurt. Child may be scolded for fighting, but not severely punished. Mother will let quite a bit of it go on	36
4. Quite permissive	20
5. Entirely permissive. Mother never interferes, never tells child she does not want him to fight. Considers it natural, part of growing up	4
Not ascertained	9
Total	100%

A

M. *I haven't really had too much trouble as far as Linda and the other
little girl is concerned. The boys will get into arguments quicker than
the girls. If mine have done anything wrong, they come in the house
immediately, and are not allowed out for the rest of the day.*

Here are two replies that led to ratings of *moderate permissiveness* (3):

B

M. I usually say, "Now who started it and why?" And he'll tell me, "Well, he started it first, Mommie, and I hit him back." I'll say, "How did you hit him? Did you hit him with anything?" He'll say, "No, I hit him with a fist." And I'll just tell the other boy, "Listen, you started it; you've got to expect to get hit back." Then I just tell him, "Don't fight, Steve; if you can't get along with him, don't play with him at all." So now . . . he only plays with this little boy next door. He don't go away and play with any of the other children.

C

M. Well, I don't do anything unless it really gets bad and then I try to find out what has happened. Probably, if the children are playing on our property or in this house, I am more inclined to blame Jack than I would the other child. Simply because it is his house and he should more or less control the thing. When it gets bad, I suppose I separate them like I do at home.

The following illustrates the kind of material that was considered *entirely permissive* (5):

D

I. How do you handle it when the children quarrel—give me an example.
M. Well, I leave it up to them to figure it out, and I try never to take any sides, because I think if there are any arguments, it is usually two people that make it, and you get yourself so involved, but I just go in and say, "What's the matter?" And then, of course, they both start in and I say, "Come on, figure this thing out, or stop it right now," and usually they do. Of course, if somebody is definitely off, I think you can almost sense it, but when I say stepping in—these two little girls, Jane and her friend, occasionally will have a little argument, and I have learned with them to stay out of it, it is over in two minutes; and they have found the system of solving it, by simply changing the subject, because I don't think it is very pleasant to either of them. They don't enjoy it, and they both feel very badly as soon as it starts. So I stay out of their arguments, as I find it is over in two minutes by leaving them alone.

One point of interest comes out of the comparison of these three kinds of aggression. The percentage of mothers who were very intolerant of aggression was greatest when the aggression was directed toward the mother herself. The proportion was least when the aggression was expressed between the mother's own child and a neighbor child. This comparison is easier to make when the figures are presented as in Table VII:4, where the percentages are based on the total number of mothers whose interviews could be rated on each of the three scales.

In some degree, these scales are arbitrary, of course, and the frequencies are not based on any common absolute scale. Too much must not be made of them, mathematically, but the reader

TABLE VII:4

PERCENTAGE OF MOTHERS, WHOSE INTERVIEWS WERE RATABLE, WHO
EXPRESSED EACH DEGREE OF PERMISSIVENESS FOR AGGRESSION TOWARD
THREE KINDS OF PEOPLE

	WHEN AGGRESSION IS EXPRESSED AGAINST		
DEGREE OF MOTHER'S PERMISSIVENESS	Parents	Siblings	Other Children
1. Non-permissive	38%	5%	5%
2. Slightly permissive	24	25	29
3. Moderately permissive	27	55	39
4. Quite permissive	10	14	22
5. Very permissive	1	1	5
Total	100%	100%	100%
Number of mothers rated	375	308	346

can judge their comparability for himself by examining the scale-point descriptions and reading the examples. There seems little question that convictions are less absolute and that controlling techniques are less punitive and less readily brought into play when the aggression is not directed toward the parents.

ENCOURAGEMENT OF AGGRESSIVE BEHAVIOR

The discussion of permissiveness has sprung from the problem of control, from the necessity of considering that aspect of aggression which makes it an uncomfortable kind of in-group behavior. There is another aspect of aggression that must not be ignored, however. In the long evolution of man, aggression probably did not persist only as an awkward instinct stemming from prehuman history. Human society has not changed so much that aggressive behavior is entirely lacking in adaptive value. The world is still a somewhat dangerous place; aggression still plays a survivorship role. Since the aim of child rearing is to prepare the child for living in the real world, many mothers—perhaps the majority—conceive of successful aggression against peers as not only useful but essential. There was a quite widespread tendency among the mothers not only to *permit* some fighting, but to *require* it.

To get some estimate of the mothers' feeling about this matter, the interviewers asked the question:

> Some people feel it is very important for a child to learn not to fight with other children; and others feel there are times when a child has to learn to fight. How do you feel about this?

The replies to this question were rated on a five-point scale described as *level of parents' demands for child to be aggressive toward other children in appropriate situations.* The scale-point descriptions, and the percentage of mothers rated at each, are given in Table VII:5.

TABLE VII:5

LEVEL OF PARENTS' DEMANDS FOR CHILD TO BE AGGRESSIVE TOWARD OTHER CHILDREN IN APPROPRIATE SITUATIONS

1. None whatsoever. Parent explicitly says she does not want child to fight with other children—ever. Child encouraged to come home if going gets rough	4%
2. No demands to fight, but no statement that it should always be discouraged	9
3. Slight demands for fighting. If child is really being bullied, he should defend self, but in general should not fight	27
4. Moderate demands for fighting. Should defend self, but never start fights, and not hit back if other child is smaller	51
5. High demands for fighting. Child should never take anything from other children; important to hold up one's own end, not come asking for help	6
Not ascertained	3
Total	100%

An answer illustrating the *no demands* (1) category is as follows:

A

M. *I go out and ask other mothers what happened and when I find out, I say "All right come in the house now." Sooner than go to their mothers and fight with them, I bring her in the house and keep her in for a while and talk it all over with her and tell her where she's wrong or where the other child is wrong and then after a while I let her out* *again and tell her to go—either, she'll end up probably playing with the same child again, anyway—to go play with somebody else.*

Some *slight demands* (3) are exhibited in this one:

B

M. *With our John, due to our experience with his brother, if someone hits him, he is allowed to hit them back. But I have never had that trouble with Susan. If someone takes their toys, I don't think they should hit them for it. I think they should first ask for them in the proper manner and then if they don't get their toys, and the child's mother isn't around, they should try and find out why. I don't believe in grabbing anything away from another child, but if it is theirs, I think they have a right to have them.*

The next reply illustrates *high demands* (5):

C

M. *Well, I believe that a child has to fight and to stick up for his own rights. I hate to see a kid that is always—well—I think if they don't they are whining babies and are always home with their mothers; and we have always taught Bill to hit them right back and to give them one better than what he got. And there are a few children, in this neighborhood, that Bill is afraid of and he will come home and tell me what they have done to him—but the only satisfaction that he has ever got was that, "We have told you if he hits you to hit him back, and until then don't tell me your stories."*

The distribution of ratings on this scale suggests that whatever may have been the mothers' personal values about the desirability of preventing aggression, more than half of them believed a child should defend himself when he was attacked. Not all children did this to their parents' satisfaction, and hence there was a certain amount of training that involved actual encouragement to behave aggressively.

SEVERITY OF PUNISHMENT

The rating of *permissiveness for aggression toward parents* was based on two things: the mother's expressed attitude toward whether such behavior should be allowed, and the extent to which the mother actually did allow it in day-to-day dealings with the child. We made another rating on the amount of punishment which had been employed in dealing with the child's aggressiveness toward his parents. The *punishment* and *permissiveness* scales, while related, are not the same thing. We found a number of families in which aggression was not allowed, but in which the parents stopped it by other means than punishment.

For example, one mother described to us how she caught her son's hand when he tried to hit her, and stopped his action, but without anger on her own part. She talked to him as gently and soothingly as possible, and did not punish him in any way, but at the same time did not allow the aggressive behavior to go on. We also found families in which the parents disapproved heartily of any kind of aggression from children toward parents, but had employed little or no punishment for this kind of behavior because the children had very seldom shown any aggression toward their parents. And surprisingly enough, there were also some parents who were relatively permissive in their attitude toward aggression but had nevertheless on occasion punished rather severely for it.

TABLE VII:6

SEVERITY OF PUNISHMENT FOR AGGRESSION TOWARD PARENTS

1. No punishment has ever been given in any way for this, although he has shown such aggression	1%
2. Mild punishment	8
3. Has had moderate punishment; been scolded, sent to room for short periods. Parents have shown irritation	51
4. Has had considerable punishment. Parents may have slapped or bitten child back, and have been emotional in their reaction	31
5. Severe punishment. Parents very angry or hostile; beatings, severe deprivation of privilege, etc. "Punished him so he wouldn't forget it"	4
Problem has not come up; child has not shown aggression to parents	4
Not ascertained	1
Total	100%

A five-point scale was constructed for rating *severity of punishment*. The scale-point descriptions are shown in Table VII:6, together with the percentage of mothers rated as exhibiting each level of severity. Obviously the ratings on this scale were rated from the same pages in the interview, and the permissiveness scale immediately preceded the punishment scale on the list, so the rater always had his permissiveness rating in mind when he made the other rating. In spite of this lack of independence, the two scales correlate only —.46. That is to say, while non-permissive mothers tended to report more severe punishment than did permissive mothers, the relationship was far from perfect.

The following excerpts from two interviews illustrate the kind of material that led to a rating of using *no punishment* (1):

A

M. *I think he's at the age right now where you're apt to get quite a lot of it. I think as they get a little bit older, you can stop and reason with them, but right now I think that they get pretty angry at times and they do say things. And afterwards they're sorry for it, so I let him say it and it's over with, and afterwards I might say, "You weren't very nice to Mummy," and he'll generally admit it.*

B

I. *In what ways do you get on each other's nerves?*
M. *I think our mutual tempers, as much as anything, as he has one, and so have I. I attempt to control it, so for instance I can understand things that he does. He gets very angry and he goes upstairs and throws things, and I can understand that perfectly. I don't know whether I was ever allowed to or whether I ever did throw things, but I wanted to, so that heaving things into the closet, I can easily understand; so that kind of thing doesn't aggravate me the way it would somebody else, and the same way with getting very angry at me. I never mind that as much, because I also get angry at him, and if I am going to, he has got to be allowed that privilege also.*

These next two mothers were rated as giving *moderate punishment* (3):

C

M. *Well, she'll say, "I don't like you." She seldom says, "I hate you," or "I don't like you anymore," or something like that. I have let her go up to now because I feel she's just getting it out of her system. If it isn't too loud, or if she isn't too angry about it, I just let it go. If it's something that I can't turn my back on, if it's something that she's so angry about that she won't stop, then I speak to her. Otherwise she'll say, "Well, I don't like you." And I say, "Well, that's all right," or something like that. I don't pay too much attention to it because I know that she doesn't actually mean it. She means it because she isn't getting what she wants, and she doesn't mean it actually.*

If she kicked me or if she slapped me, I'd slap her back. I just told her that it doesn't feel good to get slapped. If she didn't want to get slapped herself, not to slap other people. The reaction would be the same in anyone that got slapped—they wouldn't like it.

D

I. *How do you handle it with Jimmy?*
M. *Well, sending him to his room is one of our main punishments, because he is a child who doesn't like it. He stays there until he can apologize, and sometimes it takes him quite a long time to work up to apologizing.*
I. *How long?*
M. *Oh, an hour.*

Two mothers who described their own reactions to a child's aggressive behavior as follows were rated as using *severe punishment* (5):

E

M. *He has done that once or twice, and I'll tell him if he doesn't stop it, he'll just go to bed and stay there; and I'll lock him in another room and let him stay there until he learns how to stop doing that, because I have never done it to my mother, and of course, I don't want it to be done to me.*
I. *Is that the way you usually handle it when he acts like this?*
M. *Oh yes—I usually send him to bed.*
I. *Lock him in his room by himself?*
M. *Yes, and let him stay there.*
I. *How much of a problem have you had with him over shows of temper and angry shouting and that sort of thing in the house?*
M. *Well, not too much. He seems to be very good at listening to me, and doing what you tell him. He seems to be very good.*

F

M. *I don't allow it.*
I. *How do you handle it when Joan acts like this?*
M. *I just take her across my knee and I give her a good licking, and that is one thing she doesn't forget either. The other night she just didn't want to go upstairs to bed, and she stamped her foot, and she started to screech; so I just picked her up and put her across my knee and gave her a couple of wallops, and sent her upstairs to bed, and she hasn't done it since.*

It is apparent that the number of mothers who used relatively severe punishment was substantially greater than the number who used relatively mild punishment.

These examples may suggest that the major kinds of punishment a child can suffer are spanking, isolation, being put to bed, or the deprivation of privileges. Doubtless the mothers' attempts to describe their own behavior led them to emphasize these very concrete kinds of treatment. It would be wrong to assume that there are not more subtle, and perhaps more telling, kinds of control, however. A child's own growing repertory of needs, sympathies, and sensitivities provides a mother with a variety of opportunities to bring home to him the consequences of his acts, and to make him realize the inadvisability of hurting others.

An example has already been given of the use of straight *retaliation,* "an eye for an eye"; this was the instance of slapping the child right back when she slapped. But an even more telling procedure was used by one mother to make the retaliatory experience vivid and painful:

> **M.** *Something happened recently of that nature which upset me a little bit. It was a drawing I had done of her which was—you know— it was pleasing to me, and she had taken a pencil and gone over the mouth. And when I saw it I was horribly angry for a few minutes, really terribly angry. She wasn't about then. If she had been, I'm sure I would have behaved very badly—scolded her, screamed at her, or such things—because it was just pure anger. I just said, "Oh, this is too much! They can't leave anything of yours alone." (Laughs) Well . . . then when she did come in—she was outside—I was . . . by then I had my self-control back again. But I spoke to her very severely about it and told her that was a very wrong thing to do, because we must respect each other's things. And she loves to draw pictures herself, you see.*
>
> *And as it happened, the very next day she and a little boy were playing here. I have a blackboard, because I have music classes on one day—afternoon—a week, which she loves to attend. And on the big blackboard she had drawn a picture and he had drawn a picture. This was after class. And apparently he had scrawled over her picture and she was in tears, and I said, "Well, you can draw another picture." "No, this picture, I loved this picture." So I took the opportunity and at the moment to tell her yes, of course, every picture we do means something to us. If she does something, it means a lot to her and she doesn't like it one bit if anyone else spoils it, because it's hers and, in the same way, of course, I didn't like it when she spoiled my picture. And that was all I had to say because she understood it quite completely. I don't think that will happen again. (Laughs)*

Still another procedure was to appeal to *anticipated shame* as a reason for not being aggressive. The shame in the following example had to do with the child's status, among his friends, with respect to the goodness of his household furniture. This may seem a rather mature type of shame, but pride in material goods develops early in many American children. Even when it does not, a mother's tone of voice can carry the notion of shame, and perhaps experiences like the following help the child to conceptualize such pride.

> **M.** . . . *jumping on the chairs, and I get after him on it. I scold him and ask him if he didn't like our house to be nice. In fact, this morning, I got after him, and I said, "Would you just like us to take all our furniture out, and put boxes in here, so we wouldn't have anything nice at all?" and that seems to—and then I said, "You could invite all your little friends in and all they would see would be boxes to sit on, and wouldn't that be awful," and then he seems to realize that it is really quite destructive to jump on the chairs. That is the way I do it—depending on the mood I'm in. If I'm in a bad mood I might get after him a little more.*

Not all control was done by punishment or shaming or scolding, however. Some mothers were acutely aware of the possible ill effects of inhibiting too much of the child's expression, and they set positive value on his being able to talk out his troubles or explain his problems without fear. For example:

> **M.** *We don't have too much of that, but when it does happen, sometimes she will take a swing at my bottom, you know, give me a slap, as she goes by when she is angry with me. I generally let it go—it depends on what the situation is. I want her to respect her parents, but I don't want respect by fear. I don't want her to be afraid to lose her temper at me for fear I will beat her or spank her. I want her to be able to tell me the way she feels about it. I mean I want her to know she can tell me if something is bothering her. It is a little bit hard for a child of five to realize, but I think that by starting it when they're young, they will tell you, and maybe I'm doing something that's driving her crazy, you know. She isn't afraid that I will give her a spanking, as I say, but I want her to learn to respect me and what I say—to know that I'm going to listen to her, instead of slapping her right then and there.*

Whatever the sanctions, the methods of control or training, two things are clear. There were wide differences among mothers in the extent to which they believed parents should tolerate aggression from their children, and the modal value tended toward nonpermissiveness with vigorously punitive sanctions. The *intent* to secure honor was not lacking. Whether the methods succeeded will be considered in a later section.

PATTERNS OF CONTROL

Attitudes toward aggression, and methods of controlling it, do not occur simply at random among mothers. There are consistent patterns of behavior. Some of these are determined by external factors, such as the sex of the child who is being reared, and some are the reflection of consistent qualities of mothers' personalities.

The sex of the child is of special importance. Observational studies of children in nursery schools and kindergartens have shown that girls characteristically show less overt aggression than boys. Doubtless some of the same biological factors that produce such sex differences in other species also contribute to it in man. But mothers in this group did not rely on biology to insure that the difference would persist in the next generation. By no means all of them felt that boys and girls should behave differently at age five. But in their discussions of the problem, a difference in aggressiveness was perhaps the most commonly mentioned item, the one difference on the desirability of which there would be most general agreement. Some were doubtful that this difference should be expected at age five, but were sure it would come soon after.

Mothers were less permissive toward aggression in girls than in boys. Curiously, this was true only with aggression toward the parents and toward other children outside the family. There was no difference in the way boys and girls were treated with respect to quarreling with their brothers and sisters. Perhaps mothers felt that within the family the frustrations imposed on girls by their siblings were just as severe as those imposed on boys, and that girls had as much right to defend themselves. Or maybe it was the other way around—boys should have no more license to quarrel than girls. Whatever the reasoning, among the children in the family, the sexes were equals. Training for the ladylike role was done in the outside conflicts and in the restriction of aggression toward the parents.

In implementing their values, however, the mothers do not appear to have taken a more punitive approach toward their daughters than toward their sons. There was no difference in the severity of punishment for aggression, as between boys and girls, although girls received very much less encouragement to fight back in their outside quarrels.

A second kind of patterning is to be seen in the different values expressed by the lower and middle socio-economic groups. It will be recalled that the families ranged occupationally from semi-skilled labor to the executive group, with a fairly equal distribution at all the occupational levels in between. If the total group is split in two, the average of each half is approximately that assigned by Lloyd Warner and his associates to what have been called, respectively, the upper-lower and upper-middle socio-economic classes.

These two groups expressed, on the average, rather different values about aggression. The lower-class mothers were more restrictive and punitive. Their interviews were rated as reflecting less permissiveness of aggression both toward the parents and toward other children. They were more severe in their punishment of aggression directed toward themselves. At the same time, they were no more encouraging of aggression toward other children than were the middle-class mothers, nor did the two groups differ in their permissiveness for sibling quarrels.

The differences in rearing accorded the two sexes and the children of different social-class positions both represent patterns in the sense that they provide constellations of values and practices applied to certain children. In the former case, the pattern was determined by the child—girls called out one set of actions in the mothers, and boys another. Every mother *could* behave in the appropriate way for either sex (and many did, with other children in the family), but each tended toward the way appropriate to the sex of her child.

The social-class pattern is of a different type. It is not produced by an external thing such as the sex of the child, but arises either from the values shared among friends and associates or as a result of similar life situations.

These two patterns, based on sex of child and socio-economic status of mother, are independent of one another. The mothers of both classes reacted with the same differential treatment of the sexes; likewise, the same social-class differences were found in the mothers of both the boys and the girls.

In addition to these patterns imposed by sex of child and socio-economic status, there are consistent relationships between the different aspects of aggression control. There is a tendency for the mothers who were most permissive about quarreling with children outside the home to be most permissive about sibling quarrels, too. The correlation is not large, but it is clearly significant ($r = .34$). This consistency does not extend to aggression directed toward the parents, however. There is virtually no correlation between permissiveness for aggression toward them and toward either siblings or other children. It looks as if mothers had one set of values for childhood interactions and another set for the relations of children with adults. The correlations among the various aggression scales are given in Appendix Table D:18.

This latter set of values is perhaps more clearly related to a general trait of permissiveness and non-punitiveness. The same mothers who were permissive with respect to aggression toward parents also showed a tendency to be permissive about sex activity among children $(r = .39)$, and to have relatively low household restrictions such as those having to do with noise, care of property, cleanliness, etc. $(r = -.30)$. In an earlier period of the child's life, they had been less severe in their toilet training $(r = -.26)$, and they tended to use less physical punishment as a technique for discipline $(r = -.21)$. Likewise, of course, they implemented their values with less severe punishment (no matter what kind) for aggression against the parents $(r = -.46)$. While none of these relationships is very high, the cluster does suggest that permissiveness is a quality that runs through the mother's behavior with respect to more aspects of life than simply aggression. It is the same cluster (Factor A) that we described in connection with sex training in Chapter Six.

The permissive mother, however, was not necessarily a *warm and affectionate* one. In fact, the correlation between permissiveness for aggression toward parents and affectional warmth is only .11. This will be important to keep in mind in the next section, which describes the kinds of maternal behavior that seem to have produced, or were at least correlated with, children's aggression in the home.

THE SOURCES OF AGGRESSION IN THE HOME

What makes a child aggressive and quarrelsome? Among these youngsters, there were a few whose mothers could recall almost no angry behavior around home, but this was not the case for most of them. In spite of the general aura of prohibition, the majority of the youngsters had displayed many varieties and combinations of angry emotional response. Some children were more aggressive toward one parent than the other, some quarreled mainly with siblings and were pleasant toward the parents, some expressed themselves openly, and some relied chiefly on non-co-operation for their expression.

Nearly all the mothers gave fairly detailed reports of the typical forms of aggression their children displayed. It was thus possible to make a rating of *amount of aggression exhibited in the home* (excluding that toward siblings). The scale-point descriptions and the percentage of children rated at each level are shown in Table VII:7.

TABLE VII:7

AMOUNT OF AGGRESSION EXHIBITED BY CHILD IN THE HOME, EXCLUDING THAT TOWARD SIBLINGS

1. None. Child has never shown any aggression toward parents, and mother does not mention any other displays of temper	4%
2. Mild. Occasional minor outbursts, but generally even-tempered	29
3. Some	49
4. Quite a bit of aggression	16
5. A great deal. Often screams, hits. "I have had a real problem with tantrums"	1
Not ascertained	1
Total	100%

These ratings can be compared with the mothers' reports of child-rearing practices to discover what characteristics of the latter were associated with high or low degree of reported aggression by the child.

Again, as was the case with dependency, the measures of the mothers' practices and the children's reactions were not independent. Both came from the mother herself. We cannot be certain in any particular case, therefore, that we have secured an unbiased report of the child's actual behavior. It is possible that some quality in a given mother—for instance, a sense of despair about her effectiveness as a child rearer—might lead her to give an exaggerated report about her child's aggressiveness. If we find, as we do, that mothers who felt little confidence in themselves had more (reportedly) aggressive children, we cannot tell whether this finding results from exaggerated reports by these mothers, or whether there was actually something about their behavior toward children that evoked more child aggressiveness. It would not be surprising if both were true, for the same qualities of her personality that influence her perception of the child may also induce a characteristic set of responses in him.

Some possible influences on mothers' perceptions. In this connection, we have examined the relation between the mothers' reports of child aggression and certain long-term characteristics of the mothers' personalities which we have thought might have a bearing on their sensitivity to aggression. If a mother is frustrated and unhappy, particularly in her home life, she can probably tolerate less aggression from her children. Her threshold is lowered; her problems are magnified.

Our information about a mother's own peace of mind came mainly from the end of the interview, where she discussed such factors as her satisfaction with being a mother and her relations with her husband. As we reported in some detail in Chapter Two, we used this information to make judgments about her self-esteem, her apparent esteem for her husband, her anxiety about her capabilities at child rearing, and other similar matters (see Appendix B, most of the scales listed under Card IV). A number of these variables did prove to be related to the actual report of the amount of aggression the child showed at home. The following dimensions were associated with reports of high aggression.

1. *High child-rearing anxiety.* Mothers who worried about whether they were doing a good job—whether they could cope with child-rearing problems—reported that they had more aggressive children than those whose anxiety was low $(p<.01; r = .26)$.

2. *Low self-esteem* $(p<.01; r = -.20)$.

3. *Dissatisfaction with current situation.* Mothers who mentioned other things they would like to do, such as wanting more free time for themselves, reported that their children were more aggressive than mothers who seemed satisfied with their present circumstances $(p<.01; r = .19)$.

4. *Low value for the mother role.* Mothers who valued the mother role and thought their primary responsibility should be to their children had less aggressive children than those who thought that the mother role should be subordinated to other activities $(p = .05; r = .12)$.

5. *Low esteem for husband.* Those mothers who were critical of their husbands reported more aggression in their children than did the mothers who made admiring and commendatory comments about their spouses $(p<.01;\ r=-.19)$.

6. *High disagreement with husband about child-training matters* $(p<.05;\ r=.18)$.

Interestingly enough, the mother's *feelings about her pregnancy* were *not* related to how aggressive the child was at age five, although this scale, it will be remembered from Chapter Two, was correlated with most of the above six dimensions.

These various characteristics present a picture of a mother who was dissatisfied and unhappy for many reasons—the way her life was organized, her relationship to her husband, even her own personality. The picture can be interpreted in two ways, and we have no means of selecting the correct one. Perhaps there is some truth in both. It may be, on one hand, that the mother's unhappiness distorted her perception of all her relationships and made her hypersensitive to her child's hostility. She felt "the world was against her," and the people in it—including her own children— were unkind. On the other hand, it may be that her dissatisfaction made her frustrate the child in many ways, and treat him irritably, and so incited his counter-hostility. Dissatisfied mothers did punish their children more severely for aggression, on the average $(r=.20)$, and such treatment would be associated with increased aggressiveness, as will be seen below. Actually, when the severity of punishment is held constant by appropriate statistical devices, the data show that these discontented mothers still reported more aggression.

Permissiveness and punishment. There is a constant tug of war in a child's behavior between the instigation and the inhibition of aggression. On one hand there are frustrations, threats, or other stimulating situations that tend to evoke aggressive action; on the other, there are warnings that inhibit aggression, and there are instigators to competing responses that the mother finds more desirable than aggression. One of the major research problems in the investigation of the socialization process is the discovery of just what kinds of maternal behavior fall into these classifications. What does the mother do that excites aggression in her child? What does she do that inhibits it?

The two scales of *permissiveness for aggression* and *severity of punishment for aggression* are the most obviously relevant dimensions to examine first. What should we expect of their relation to the reported amount of aggression the child shows in the home? Permissiveness, by definition, is an expression of the mother's willingness to have the child perform such acts. A simple and straightforward prediction is that children with permissive mothers will be more aggressive than children with non-permissive mothers. Similarly with punishment: if we assume that this method of discipline establishes in the child a fear of behaving aggressively, then the more punitive the mother is, the more the child should avoid being aggressive. These two predictions fit together nicely. The scales for *permissiveness* and *punishment* are correlated −.46; that is, to some degree the more permissive mothers tended to be less severe in their punishment.

In point of fact, however, one of the predictions is right and the other is wrong. It is true that high *permissiveness* is associated with high aggression. The correlation is +.23. But *punishment* works just the other way: the more severe the punishment, the more aggression the child showed. The correlation is +.16. Both these correlations are small, but they are significant, and they are artificially reduced by the negative correlation between the permissiveness and punitiveness scales. Their true importance is substantially greater, as will be seen in the next section. (See Appendix Table D:19.)

We interpret these findings in this way. When a mother adopts a permissive point of view about aggression, she is saying to her child, in effect, "Go ahead and express your angry emotions; don't worry about me." She gives few signals in advance that would lead the child to fear to be aggressive. On the contrary, her attitude is one of expectancy that he *will* be, and that such behavior is acceptable. It is scarcely surprising that the child tends to fulfill her expectations. The non-permissive mother, however, does something quite different. She has an attitude that aggression is wrong, that it is not to be tolerated, and an expectancy (often very subtly expressed) that the child will not behave in such undesirable ways. When he is aggressive, she does something to try to stop it—sometimes by punishment, sometimes by other means. He, also, fulfills his mother's expectations. This dimension of permissiveness, then, is a measure of the extent to which the mother prevents or stops aggression, the non-permissive extreme being the most common.

Punishment is apparently a somewhat different matter. It is a kind of maternal behavior that occurs *after* the child's aggression has been displayed. The child has already enjoyed the satisfaction of hurting or of expressing anger—and so has had a reinforcement for aggressive action. But then he gets hurt in turn. He suffers further frustration. This should, and on the average does, incite him to more aggression. If the punishment is very severe, he may gradually learn to fear the consequences of his own actions, and the particular acts that get most repeatedly punished may be inhibited. But the total frustration is increased, and hence the total amount of aggression displayed in the home is higher. The dimension called *severity of punishment for aggression toward parents,* then, is one measure of the amount of painful frustration that is imposed on the child without direct guidance as to what would be a more acceptable form of behavior.

TABLE VII:8

PERCENTAGE OF HIGHLY AGGRESSIVE CHILDREN IN SUBGROUPS DIVIDED ACCORDING TO WHETHER MOTHER WAS IN UPPER OR LOWER HALF OF THE DISTRIBUTION ON PERMISSIVENESS AND SEVERITY OF PUNISHMENT FOR AGGRESSION TOWARD PARENTS

| | HIGHLY AGGRESSIVE * | | | |
| | BOYS | | GIRLS | |
SUBGROUP	Per Cent	N †	Per Cent	N
Low permissiveness and low punishment	3.7	27	13.3	30
Low permissiveness and high punishment	20.4	51	19.1	47
High permissiveness and low punishment	25.3	81	20.6	63
High permissiveness and high punishment	41.7	36	38.1	22

* By "highly aggressive" is meant that the child was rated by one or both raters as being in one of the two highest levels of aggression; these are scale points 4 and 5 in Table VII:7.
† Number of cases.

It is evident from this analysis that the mothers who were most permissive but also most severely punitive would have the most aggressive children; those who were most non-permissive but least punitive would have the least aggressive ones. As may be seen in Table VII:8, this was the case for both sexes. The children of mothers in the other two groups were in between.

These findings are similar to those of an earlier study (Sears *et al.,* 1953) in one respect. In that research, 40 children were observed in nursery school. The amount of aggression they showed there was compared with their mothers' reports of the severity of punishment for aggression that they suffered at home. In that study, too, high aggression was found to be associated with severe punishment, especially in the boys. There was some indication that the *most* severely punished girls had become quite passive and inhibited. They displayed little activity of any kind, including aggression. When activity level was taken into consideration, they tended to be more like the boys, i.e., the more severely punished girls were *relatively* more aggressive than the less severely punished. It is interesting to note the similarity between the present findings and the earlier study, because in that research the measure of child aggression was entirely independent of the measures of child-rearing practices.

A word of caution must be said here about the interpretation of our results. We have shown that the mothers who punished their children most severely for aggression tended to report that their children displayed more than the average amount of aggression toward their parents. We have implied in our discussion that the maternal behavior *caused* the child behavior. It is entirely possible, of course, that the correlation could be explained as a parental response to the child's pre-existing temperament. That is, some children may have been born with a higher level of aggressive impulses than others, and the more aggressive the child naturally was, the more his parents were forced to punish him for aggression. We have chosen to interpret the matter the other way around: that punishment by the mother bred counter-aggression in the child. Our reason is that permissiveness was also associated with aggression, and we cannot see why aggression in the child should elicit permissiveness in the mother.

Our interpretation must be tentative, however, for the other explanation of the results cannot be ruled out without further research. It is quite possible, of course, that a circular process develops: the parent's punishment makes the child aggressive, this aggression leads to further punishment, and so on. Which came first, to set the whole thing in motion, is a problem we cannot solve with our existing information.

We can look now at some of the other possible sources of excitation and inhibition of aggression, for it is clear that permissiveness and severity of punishment are not the only influences.

Physical punishment. There have been a number of studies during the past three decades that have suggested some rather untoward effects of this disciplinary technique. One of the most important is that of the Gluecks (1950), which indicated that the use of severe physical punishment was one of five major factors associated with the development of delinquency in young boys.

In the present study, we have found that those mothers who punished aggression most severely also tended to use physical punishment more ($r = .44$). Not surprisingly, therefore, physical punishment was related to mothers' reports of high aggression in their children ($r = .23$). However, it had an important positive effect only when it occurred in association with quite severe punishment for aggression. That is, if a child was being severely punished for aggression, the high use of *physical* punishment (as distinct from other kinds of punishment) increased his aggression markedly. If his parents did not punish aggression severely, the use of physical punishment for other kinds of misdeeds had no effect on the amount of aggression the child showed.

Our present data do not tell why, but one can speculate a little on the reasons. Physical punishment is itself a form of attack—perhaps often perceived as aggression by the child. If parents serve as models, then it is not surprising that the children adopt similar ways of behaving. Too, physical punishment is like punishing for aggression in general—it is a form of frustration. This is particularly true for the very young child, who is helpless before the physical power of adults and must accept their control whenever it is displayed in physical form. We have no way of telling whether the most physically punished children in this study had learned to avoid certain specific actions that were most often followed by spankings, but it is evident that even if they did, they expressed more aggression in other ways. Whatever the mechanism, we may conclude that strong physical punishment produced high aggression when it was used as a technique on children who were being severely punished for aggression in general.

Affectional warmth of the mother. One serious difficulty in pursuing the search for sources of children's aggressiveness is that the scales for measuring maternal behavior were not independent of one another. Just as the rating of physical punishment was somewhat correlated with severity of punishment for aggression, so the rating of affectional warmth was correlated with both these scales. Mothers who used physical punishment tended to be colder in their affectional interaction with their children ($r = -.26$), and coldness was also associated with severe punishment for aggression ($r = -.22$).

In order to discover the relative amount of influence of each of the four dimensions discussed above, we have used partial correlations (see Appendix Table D:19). These show that permissiveness contributed the most, punishment for aggression next most, and physical punishment and coldness the least. However, all four dimensions were influential in some degree.

Household restrictions. One further dimension is worth examining, though it has proved to be of no significance as a cause of aggression. There has been a rather common belief that placing close restrictions and severe adult demands on a child will lead to aggressive outbursts on his part. There are a number of activities in the home that involve the mother's setting up standards and restrictions for the child. He must learn not to make too much noise, not to eat sloppily or with his fingers, not to interrupt others, not to mark up the walls, not to jump on or mar the furniture, not to leave his clothes or toys lying around, and not to get too dirty. Each of these restrictions has its positive aspect as well, of course; there is a right way to eat, a quiet manner to be assumed, an orderly way to take care of clothes.

The nature of these restrictions and demands will be discussed at length in the next chapter. It is sufficient for our present purpose to point out that much of what the mother tries to teach the child runs counter to his immediate desires (for instance, not interrupting adults) and requires him to inhibit impulses toward vigorous activity. He is also forced by the continuously-being-raised standards to control his movements, to concentrate more on the future effects of his behavior, and to pay more attention to the wishes of others. He must learn to live a more orderly life.

Mothers differ in the level of restrictions and demands they impose on their children, of course, just as they do on all the other dimensions of child rearing. In connection with aggression, it is interesting to note that there was some tendency ($r = .30$) for mothers who had high restrictions to be quite non-permissive about aggression also. In consequence, it is not surprising to find that there was a slight tendency for mothers who had high restrictions to report that their children were low in aggression. When we examine the influence of restrictions independently of permissiveness for aggression, however, we find that the degree of restrictiveness made a negligible contribution to the child's aggressiveness in the home. Our findings constitute one piece of evidence, then, against the notion that any and all kinds of restrictions may be expected to produce aggression in children.

Sex and socio-economic status. Most studies of aggressive behavior in kindergarten children have shown that boys display more frequent and more intense aggression than girls. The difference usually appears to be even greater in fantasy activities, such as doll play, than in the social behavior of a nursery school or kindergarten. One study of home behavior, in which mothers reported by a day-to-day diary, also found this sex difference (Goodenough, 1931).

The present study does not show much sex difference, although what there is is in the same direction. Of the boys, 23 per cent were rated "strongly aggressive," and of the girls, 20 per cent. The difference in average ratings was significant at the .10 level.

This result is rather surprising on two counts. First, careful observations of American children under many other conditions have provided quite formidable indications of stable sex differences. And second, as we have already seen, the child-rearing practices of boys' mothers in the present group were more conducive to aggression than were the practices of girls' mothers. That is, the boys' mothers, on the average, were *more permissive* of aggression, and they used *more physical punishment*. (There was no difference in affectional warmth or in punishment for aggression *per se.*) These factors, as we have seen, were associated with higher aggression in the children. It may be, of course, that the mothers made automatic corrections for the sex of their children, and tended to use adjectives and adverbs that were appropriate to the degree of aggression they expected from a child of a given sex. If there were any considerable tendency for the mothers to do this, the difference between the sexes would be masked, even though within each sex there would still be relatively accurate comparison of one child with another.

There were no differences in reported aggression that were related to socio-economic status.

COMMENT

The control of aggression in the home is obviously not a simple matter. Every mother in our group had had to cope with angry outbursts or quarreling at one time or another, and 95 per cent of them reported instances of strong aggression that had been directed at the parents themselves. It seems evident that the conditions of living are such that all children develop aggressive motivation. It is equally certain that very few parents can tolerate as much hostility in the home as the children are instigated to display.

One can distinguish two important themes in the control of children's aggression. One is what we have called "non-permissiveness"—the tendency for a parent to believe that aggression by a child toward his parents is wrong, and to accompany this belief by action designed to prevent aggressive outbursts or stop them when they occur.

The other theme has to do with the amount of punishment a child receives for being aggressive toward his parents. The two dimensions are obviously not independent, for some parents express their non-permissive attitude primarily through punishment which they administer during or after a child's display of temper. But other parents express their non-permissiveness in such a way as to *prevent* the aggressive outburst's occurring; under such circumstances, punishment is not necessary. Still other parents have non-punitive ways of dealing with the child's aggression once it does occur. Thus, not all non-permissive parents are to be found among the group who do a great deal of punishing for aggression.

Our findings suggest that the way for parents to produce a non-aggressive child is to make abundantly clear that aggression is frowned upon, and to stop aggression when it occurs, but to avoid punishing the child for his aggression. Punishment seems to have complex effects. While undoubtedly it often stops a particular form of aggression, at least momentarily, it appears to generate more hostility in the child and lead to further aggressive outbursts at some other time or place. Furthermore, when the parents punish—particularly when they employ physical punishment—they are providing a living example of the use of aggression at the very moment they are trying to teach the child not to be aggressive. The child, who copies his parents in many ways, is likely to learn as much from this example of successful aggression on his parents' part as he is from the pain of punishment. Thus, the most peaceful home is one in which the mother believes aggression is not desirable and under no circumstances is ever to be expressed toward her, but who relies mainly on nonpunitive forms of control. The homes where the children show angry, aggressive outbursts frequently are likely to be homes in which the mother has a relatively tolerant (or careless!) attitude toward such behavior, or where she administers severe punishment for it, or both.

These conclusions will certainly not astonish anyone who has worked professionally with children and their parents. Social workers, psychologists, teachers, psychiatrists, and probation officers have seen the twin effects of permissiveness and punishment many times in their own experience. What is important in the present report is the demonstration with this group of families. When one works with a few cases, particularly when most of them are quite deviant from the general population, one often has some uncertainty as to whether the relationships he sees would apply to a more normal group. Here is as normal a group of American mothers and their children as one could want for these purposes. The principles hold good.

There is another aspect to the matter worth emphasizing, however. The effects of these two aspects of control may already be known by professionals, but, even with a demonstration of this sort, they will not find ready acceptance by many others. There are two reasons.

First, *punishment is satisfying* to the parent. When a child aggresses toward his mother, he angers her, interferes with what she is doing, with her peace of mind, with her dignity and self-respect. Aggression hurts. It is meant to. And it produces in the mother the appropriate stimulation to retaliate in kind. Combined with her sense of obligation to rear her child properly, this retaliation comes out in a way she thinks of as "punishment" —that is, a form of aggression designed to have a good *training* effect on its recipient. As will be seen in a later chapter, many mothers have developed strong beliefs that punishment is a helpful method of control. (Sometimes it is, too.) These beliefs are essential to the peace of mind of such mothers. Without the conviction that "punishment is *good* for my child," these mothers would be forced to view their own behavior as retaliatory, aggressive, childish—in short, contemptible. This would not long provide a tolerable self-image. It is to be expected, then, that our demonstration of the deleterious effect of severe punishment of aggression will not be an easy finding for many people to swallow.

A second matter has to do with permissiveness. The difficulty grows out of the problem of punishment. During the last three decades there has developed, among the more literate and sensitive part of the American people, an uneasy recognition that punishment sometimes eliminates a few specific responses, but leaves a strongly hostile drive bottled up within the child. There is evidence to support this belief. With this consideration in mind, and an urgent desire to provide better mental hygiene for their children, not a few parents have developed what almost amounts to a cult of being permissive about aggression. Their aim is to avoid repression, to permit the child easier and freer expression of his impulses, and thus to prevent the development of aggression-anxiety, with its accompanying displacements, projections, and sometimes uncontrollable fantasies.

This aim is good, both for the children and the society they will compose, but whether it can be achieved by a high degree of permissiveness for expression of aggression toward the parents is a question. Does a permissive attitude, with the consequent freer expression of aggression, decrease the strength of projective fantasies? There is no indication in our own data that it does. Each of the children in the present study was tested with two 20-minute sessions of doll play. The children of the more non-permissive half of the group of mothers showed little if any more fantasy aggression under these circumstances than the children of the more permissive half. This finding is in sharp contrast to that with respect to punishment; the children of the more severely punishing mothers displayed quite significantly more fantasy aggression than the children of the less severely punishing ones (Levin and Sears, 1956). Permissiveness does not seem to decrease fantasy indications of aggressive impulses.

Permissiveness does increase the amount of aggression in the home, however, and it is worth considering what this does to the child himself. An angry child is not usually a happy child, nor is he one who receives affection and willing companionship from others. He is a source of discomfort to family and peers, and probably receives a certain amount of retaliation. He upsets his siblings, raises the level of frustration imposed on his parents, and inevitably has an increase, to some extent, of his own aggression-anxiety. There seems little advantage in all this, either to the child himself or to his parents.

These comments may seem to encourage a conclusion that parents will find it to their advantage to be somewhat non-permissive of aggression that is directed toward themselves. This can be a dangerous conclusion if the kind of permissiveness we mean is not clearly understood.

Therefore, let us be as clear as possible about the aspect of permissiveness we have in mind. A child is more likely to be non-aggressive if his parents hold the value that aggression is undesirable and should not occur. He is more likely to be non-aggressive if his parents prevent or stop the occurrence of aggressive outbursts instead of passively letting them go on, but prevent them by other means than punishment or threats of retaliation. If the parents' non-permissiveness takes the form of punishing the child (and thus leading the child to *expect* punishment) for aggressive behavior, then non-permissiveness will not have the effect of reducing the child's aggression. On the contrary, the instant that punishment enters, all the consequences of punishment that have been discussed earlier may be anticipated, including that of increasing the child's level of aggression.

One cautionary point: we are not suggesting that parents should band together in omnipotent suppression of every justifiable angry response the child makes. The right to be angry without fear or guilt is as inalienable as any other, and more important than some. But since anger interferes with constructive action in the face of many, if not most, problem situations that the child and his family face, parents are understandably anxious to keep it within reasonable bounds; and our interest has been in showing what parental actions are likely to have the desired effects and what actions are likely to have undesired side-effects.

CHAPTER EIGHT

Restrictions and Demands

There are a lot of *do's* and *don't's* in a child's life. A good many of these are devoted to control or training that has little direct relation to the motives we have discussed in the last five chapters. Rather, they spring from certain desires and responsibilities of the parents, desires that can be met only by developing a mature understanding and sense of responsibility in the child.

First and foremost, parents must guard their child from danger. Within the limits of their knowledge, they must care for his health, keep him from doing things that will end in injury, and train him to do potentially dangerous things in as safe a way as possible. Depending on their beliefs, they must see that he eats the "right" things, gets enough sleep, does not strain his eyes or get overtired or too emotional or "pick up germs." He must be taught to look both ways crossing the street, stay away from fires, and handle knives and scissors carefully. Somehow he must be kept alive and healthy.

Second, parents must protect their own belongings from destruction. American homes are filled with breakables, and these cost money or personal effort—ash trays, books, flower arrangements, lamps, wallpaper, carpets, furniture. By and large, too, houses are neat and clean, and mothers take pride in keeping them that way. They do not want the neighbors to think "the house looks like a pigpen." Children are intensely curious about the objects in their world, however, and the concept of *spoiling*

or *damaging* does not exist for them at first. Until it is learned, mothers must be alert, prepared always to restrict movements and cry a halt to too active play.

Third, children must be taught to be co-operative in the living arrangements of the family. They must learn proper table manners, and come to meals well tidied and on time. They must help with the work of the household. They must be quiet when others are resting, and keep the general noise level within the limits of parental tolerance. They have to curb their enthusiasm and free movements to some degree, and develop the necessary skills and attitudes that will make them agreeable family members.

All these learnings require a good deal of direct instruction by the parents. Much of this is done by verbal direction: do this, but don't do that. The *do's* are demands placed on the child to perform actions the *parents* want. The *don't's* are restrictions placed on actions the *child* wants to perform but which the parents dislike.

Tedious as these instructions may be at the time they occur, they are nevertheless an essential part of child rearing. So far as control for purposes of protection is concerned, their importance is obvious. Their value in training is equally great. As was mentioned earlier, the teaching process involves two major elements. The child must be shown *what* to do—he must be given guidance; and he must be provided with a *why* for doing it—he must be rewarded or non-rewarded or punished. The restrictions and demands described above are part of the *guidance*. In effect, they tell the child which way to turn to secure the rewards of living with his family.

Demands and restrictions are directed toward increasing the maturity of the child's behavior, of course. They are instructions in how to behave more like an adult, or at least more like an older child. They are part of the pressure toward conformity with adult ideals. They represent an effort to speed up the child's learning. Since he is always less mature—one might almost say "less learned"—than his parents' demands and restrictions require him to be, he is always under some degree of pressure. One of the important ways in which mothers differ in their child rearing is the severity or rigor of this pressure. Some push harder than others. Some demand greater obedience, and are more distressed by their child's occasional failures to follow instructions. In the long run, some children work harder at growing up than do others.

There are an extraordinary number of aspects of life to which these demands and restrictions apply. In our American culture, there are special manners and methods of behaving with respect to all five of the motivational systems we have discussed previously, but these are only the beginning. Children have a kind of free-wheeling expressiveness that leads them into activities of many desirable and undesirable kinds. As they grow from infancy into "toddlerism," and from this into real childhood, they develop the ability to tolerate their parents' restrictions, to respond to demands for maturity. Gradually, their curiosity and drive to activity become channelized into socially acceptable ways of living with their elders and their peers.

In this chapter we will describe several of the demands and restrictions that mothers placed on their children. At present, we have little information about the effects on the children of different degrees of pressure, and hence we will be concerned in the main with the variables listed in column II of the schema presented in the second chapter.

From a quantitative standpoint, we will present the variations in strictness, or severity of the conformities required, but in this chapter more than in some of the others we will also try to abstract from the interviews some of the significant qualities of the mothers' attitudes and behaviors. We will give attention to the mothers' problems as well as to their solutions, and content ourselves with giving examples of attitudes rather than precise counts of the frequency with which different problems and solutions were reported.

THE CHILD'S SAFETY

The amount of vigilance required to protect a two- or three-year-old almost must be experienced to be understood. A small child can get into real danger, or damage something irreplaceable, in a few seconds. His mother must be alert to his activities continuously, ready to go into action in an instant if something untoward happens. What wonder that a mother of two young children, when she took a few days' vacation from the children, reported that she felt as though a part of her own body were missing—or, at the very least, as though she were walking downtown without her handbag. She had become so used to responding to the sights and sounds of her children that their absence made her feel as if she were leaning against something which suddenly was not there.

There has been a good deal of discussion in the literature on child training about "overprotective" or "smothering" mothers, mothers who are excessively attentive to dangers, and vigilantly guard their children so closely that the children have difficulty developing self-reliance. Caution can be overdone, of course, but there is a very real necessity for protecting and guarding the young child closely. A few examples of dangerous predicaments reported by the mothers will serve to illustrate the seriousness of the problem.

A four-year-old boy crawled out onto a steeply-sloping roof from an upstairs window, taking his eighteen-month-old brother with him. The children had just started to slip when the mother found them.

A small boy discovered the switch which started his father's power tools. He had started the circular saw, and had begun to play with it, when detected.

A policeman's child was found playing with her father's loaded gun.

A child set fire to the garage, with himself inside.

In addition to these reports, there were a number of the more usual instances of safety hazards—running out into busy streets, falling from high places, and wandering off to the banks of a stream or pool.

These events happened despite nearly constant watching of the children, and despite elaborate precautions taken to prevent dangerous situations from arising. The mothers described many protective devices, such as hiding bottles with poisonous contents on inaccessible shelves, putting a gate across the top of the stairway, putting the screen door latches high enough so the child could not reach them, putting guard bars on second-floor windows, keeping sharp and pointed instruments out of reach, and keeping the back doors of the car locked so the child could not fall out when the car was moving. The emphasis, with two- and three-year-olds particularly, was on controlling the environment.

As the child matured, however, the mother's task was to train him to avoid dangerous situations for himself, without having to be watched. To help in this process, most mothers created rules—some more, some less. Almost universally, children were trained not to throw rocks and not to use sharp sticks in their outdoor play. Many mothers forbade their children to play in or around trucks, since these were a constant source of danger in residential neighborhoods. Delivery trucks are often parked just long enough to allow a child to crawl under them, and are then driven away quickly without further inspection. Another very common rule which mothers had for their kindergarten children was "to come straight home from school." The child was not allowed to stop at another child's house until he had "checked in" and received permission from his mother as to where he might go and how long he might stay.

TABLE VIII:1

MOTHER'S RESTRICTIONS ON THE CHILD'S PHYSICAL MOBILITY

1. No restrictions. Child permitted to go wherever he wishes—across streets, to other children's yards, etc.	1%
2. A few restrictions. Child may go several streets away, visit other children by self, but must let mother know where he is	30
3. Quite a bit of restriction. Child can go to school by self, but otherwise not across street or off street or across boundaries (boundaries in this case larger than own yard)	53
4. Restricted to front of house and own yard, but allowed to go to school alone	11
5. Child restricted to own yard, and not allowed to go to school alone	2
Not ascertained	3
Total	100%

The mothers in our sample differed considerably from one another in the restrictions they placed on the physical mobility of children of this age, however. Some confined the child to his own yard except during school hours, while others allowed him to cross streets alone for the purpose of visiting other children. The range of practices is exhibited in Table VIII:1.

A mother who was rated as *quite restrictive* of her child's movements said:

M. *I don't want him to leave our own little area. I spent a whole summer chasing him and licking him, and putting him to bed, and we have accomplished it. He must come right home from school and play around here; that is one thing I do enforce. I think that is perhaps the most important thing, because I have had the police looking for the children at times, and what I have been through has taught me to do it.*

This mother's motives for restricting her child were revealed by a comment she made later in the interview:

M. *Once in a while he might go to another boy's house. I allow him to because I know I should, but it bothers me. I wonder if the other mother is there. I worry about their getting hurt; I worry about their being unwatched and getting into some foolish sexy thing. Just general worry.*

Another aspect of protective care that varied considerably from one mother to another was the closeness with which they kept track of the child. Some allowed him to be outdoors for considerable lengths of time without checking on his whereabouts, while other mothers were constantly at the window when the child was outdoors, or were repeatedly calling to him, to make sure that all was well. The range of these practices is shown in Table VIII:2.

TABLE VIII:2
CLOSENESS WITH WHICH MOTHER KEEPS TRACK OF THE CHILD

1. Practically never checks. Trusts child to take care of himself; does not worry when he is out of sight or earshot. May have general idea where child is	10%
2. Checks occasionally (if she has not heard voice for an hour); wants to know where child is, but feels he can watch out for himself pretty well	36
3. Checks fairly often (every half hour to every hour)	25
4. Checks frequently, tries to keep track all the time (checks more often than every half hour)	19
5. Whereabouts of child constantly on her mind. Keeps track always; child must be in sight or earshot	8
Not ascertained	2
Total	100%

An example of close control of the child's whereabouts was provided by a mother who said:

M. *I always have my eyes on my children. Even when they're outside, I'm looking out the window or I'll call to them. I always do. Even* *when they're in the house, I'll say: "Sally, where are you and what are you doing?" I always keep tabs on them.*

Quite a different attitude was expressed by another mother:

I. *How often do you check?*
M. *I don't worry until it gets around five o'clock. I do want them in by five, but I think if she were into any trouble, someone would call me. She doesn't go off too much, and is perfectly capable of taking care of herself, and I haven't checked too much. She's in school in the afternoon, and sometimes she doesn't get home here until awfully late, and in the wintertime it does get pretty dark. Sometimes it would be almost five o'clock, and no Betty. I might have gone to the store, and come home, and found that the ten-year-old was home, and the eight-year-old; but Betty, five, was not home. I found that she had gotten off the bus at the bottom of the street and was playing in someone's yard. Well, they all do that. Just lately I taught her to dial our number so she could call me and tell me where she is.*

One mother, who allowed her child considerable freedom to go away from the house unsupervised, reported a certain amount of conflict on this matter with her own mother:

M. *We live very closely together (neighboring houses), and the children are apt to be all here or all there, and it bothers my mother dreadfully. Sometimes she will say to me, "You don't know where she is," and I say, "Oh, she's around someplace," and Mother says, "But you're not sure."*

In the larger families, the mother sometimes entrusted a four- or five-year-old child to the care of an older brother or sister, who was instructed to keep track of the younger child and see that he did not get into trouble.

NEATNESS, ORDERLINESS, AND CARE OF THE HOUSEHOLD

While many of the rules and restrictions imposed upon a young child are devised to protect him from harm, many others are designed to prevent damage to the people or objects around him. Children of four or five can and do hurt younger children and animals—often accidentally, sometimes willfully. They must be trained not to pull hair, poke eyes, close doors on other people's fingers, step on toes, and so forth. The admonition "Careful now, you're hurting the puppy," or "You're hurting Janie," or "You're hurting Mommie" is one of the most familiar refrains of child control.

Damage to property is no less a problem in our society. Parents have certain standards concerning cleanliness, order, and the appearance of houses and yards. Even in the households of the not-so-well-to-do, there are very large numbers of objects that must be replaced (at some expense) if they are broken. Perhaps we can best indicate the nature and seriousness of the problem by listing a few of the damaging things that mothers reported their children had done.

A little girl drank an entire bottle of her mother's best perfume, a bottle which had been a treasured and expensive Christmas gift.

From a shelf in the garage, a small boy spilled a can of paint over the hood of the family's new car. He got up on the car and tried to wipe off the paint, meanwhile getting paint on his sneakers and tracking it all over the car—roof, upholstery, etc. Then, being worried about what he had done, he did not tell his mother for a number of hours—long enough for the paint to dry thoroughly. It never could be gotten off.

A little girl went into a neighbor's yard and pulled up all the tulips (imported bulbs which were the neighbor's pride and joy), and threw rocks in the neighbor's fish pond.

A little boy started a fire in his mother's bureau drawer; the bureau and most of the mother's lingerie were damaged beyond repair.

A brother and sister changed the water for their pet turtle several times, spilling large puddles of water on the floor. The water leaked through to the ceiling of the room below, and the plaster had to be repaired.

A little girl scratched a picture with a pin point on the headboard of her parents' bed.

A little boy took his father's watch apart and lost some of the pieces.

In a fit of anger, a child took a pile of clean clothes his mother had just ironed and threw them on the floor and stamped on them. Another child did the same with a freshly-baked cake.

While such serious, or at least exasperating, damage might be done only once in a lifetime by any one child, the possibility of similar happenings keeps parents on their toes trying to forestall trouble.

The most common problem we encountered in the mothers' reports was that of keeping the walls of the house clean. A very large number of the children went through a period of peeling pieces of wallpaper off the walls, or marking the walls with crayons, pencils, lipstick or anything else available which would make a mark. Also fairly frequent was the problem of the child's poking holes in upholstery with sharp instruments, or making spots and scratches on the furniture with dirty shoes. And of course, there was the problem of breakage—dishes, glassware, lamps, the glass over pictures. Any fragile item may be broken by a child who is excited, angry, clumsy, or in a hurry.

TABLE VIII:3
Restrictions on the Care of House and Furnishings

1. No restrictions. Child may jump on furniture, mark on walls, put feet up, play with other people's things	0%
2. Few restrictions	6
3. Moderate restrictions. May jump on some things, not others. Possibly certain parts of the house set aside for careful treatment	30
4. Considerable restriction. Important for child to be careful of household furnishings	50
5. Many restrictions. Very important for child to be careful about marking and jumping. Must take off shoes before putting feet up. All furniture, all parts of the house to be treated carefully. Not allowed to touch a large number of objects	13
Not ascertained	1
Total	100%

Parents differed widely in the extent to which they believed children should be allowed to manhandle the household effects. As far as we can tell, all parents imposed *some* restrictions (see Table VIII:3). However, those who felt that restrictions should be as few as possible were likely to have durable, washable, non-scratchable furnishings during the period when their children were young, thus avoiding the strain on both themselves and their children that would result from constant efforts at guarding fragile and perishable objects. Other parents took the point of view that children eventually have to learn to avoid damaging household furnishings, and training might as well occur early so that neat, careful behavior would become habitual.

A moderately *permissive* point of view was expressed by one mother as follows:

I. *How important do you think it is for her to be careful about marking on the walls and jumping on the furniture and things like that?*
M. *I think they will do it no matter how much you do. If you don't have it in the bedroom, you will have it somewhere else, because they will pick up a pencil and write, like they did over there (pointing) on the wall, but I think you can just explain to them what is wrong, and as long as they write on the wall, you shouldn't change the wallpaper or improve the room. When they get to Hannah's age—six years old— I notice she is beginning to notice other children's rooms, that they have a new bed or new wallpaper, and she wants it; and we stress that she can't have those things until she knows how to take care of them. I put off buying bedspreads for two or three years, because they would get on the beds with their shoes, and just three weeks ago I felt it was time to buy new bedspreads and I did, and they haven't gotten on the beds since.*

Most parents, however, made more of an effort to control wall-marking and similar behavior when the child was younger, for they felt they could not afford the time and money required for constant redecorating, and they were unwilling to live amidst surroundings which were too untidy. The following comment, in reply to the same question as above, illustrates the *non-permissive* school of thought about wall-marking and jumping on furniture:

M. *I think that's very important. It was hard for me to get the things, and I want them to appreciate them. I don't think there's any reason for marking up walls. They have all the paper they want, and they have their blackboards, and they don't have to mark on the walls. I don't see the necessity of destruction.*
I. *What do you do about it if she does these things?*
M. *If she did it, I think I'd give her a good licking.*

An interesting device for the control of damage employed by some parents was to provide some place in the house, or one or two pieces of old furniture, which the children could treat as roughly as they wanted. A number of mothers told us about an old studio couch, or an old bed or chair, which the children were allowed to jump on. The assumption was that if the child got his mischief "out of his system" this way he would be less likely to yield to the temptation to damage more valuable household objects.

Some of these same mothers told us, however, that even though the children had a place where they could do their jumping "legally," they nevertheless persisted in jumping on the good furniture. In a similar vein, a mother reported that her little girl persisted in picking the neighbor's flowers even though the mother had deliberately planted a large number of flowers, in the family's own yard, for the child to pick. "You'd think she could do her picking at home," her mother commented.

These mothers were sadly—and irritatedly—baffled by the failure of this "permissive" device to serve as a successful preventative. We do not know, of course, just why the children kept on doing the forbidden acts in forbidden places when they could as easily have performed the same acts in other places without any restrictions. We can venture two possible explanations, however. First, conceivably the act as the mother described it (e.g., picking the flowers) had no real interest for the child.

It may have been the *significance* of the act (perhaps as a form of aggression toward the neighbors or even toward the rule-laying-down mother) that was important. If this were the case, picking-*my-own*-flowers would have no substitute value for picking-*their*-flowers.

Secondly, we have an impression that allowing a specific kind of behavior in one part of the house while forbidding it elsewhere produces difficulty in learning the rules. For very young children, at least, blanket rules seem easier to learn than do ones which require a discrimination of *here* and *there*. Our guess is that if children are allowed to jump on any pieces of furniture, or mark on any walls, they will be more likely to do these things in other (forbidden) places.

The assumption about "getting it out of his system" is very important in psychological theory. It has gone under the different names of "catharsis" and "drive reduction" and "goal response" in various theories. As we saw earlier in connection with modesty training, there are some observations of child behavior that seem to be more easily interpretable in terms of a *discrimination* assumption. Our data here are not sufficiently precise to warrant any extended effort to test alternative explanations, but parents of young children may be able to examine the matter for themselves.

Reactions to destructiveness. Among the many factors that seemed to influence a mother's reactions to incidents in which a child damaged household effects, one of the most commonly mentioned was the seriousness of the destruction. Although they might have felt this was not a valid reason, many mothers confessed they could not help reacting more strongly if the thing which had been damaged was expensive or difficult to replace.

M. *She broke a lamp here recently. She was jumping up and down on a chair, and the lamp went over. Well, I had just bought the shade and I couldn't replace it. I went all over town, trying to get a globe for it. We have had the lamp for ten years and they are not making the same shape globe. So of course I did punish her for that.*

The implication was that the child would not have been punished (at least, not so severely) if the lamp had been easier to replace. In the same way, a mother was likely to become more upset if the child spilled food on a good rug than on the kitchen linoleum.

A good many mothers attempted also to take into account the motivation of the child, however. The mother quoted above reported that she felt differently about still another lamp which the child broke, because the accident occurred during the child's efforts to be helpful:

M. *That I don't think was her fault. When I had got the television set, I had changed the furniture around. I was on the phone, and she was trying to put the leaf of the table up. In doing that, the lamp fell over. I didn't feel that was her fault, because she thought that was the way the table should be—we used to keep it that way—so I didn't punish her for that.*

Studies of children, notably those by Piaget, have found that children judge the seriousness of "naughty" behavior partly in terms of the amount of damage which has been done, and partly in terms of the intent of the transgressor. Piaget found, for example, that some children thought it was worse to break 12 cups than 2, regardless of the circumstances surrounding the accident. Others, he found, considered the 12-cup accident less serious if it occurred when a child was trying to be helpful. Piaget thought that these two ways of judging moral values represented two different stages of moral development; he considered that judging on the basis of the transgressor's intent was a later and more mature form of judgment. Our interviews suggest that mothers use both criteria for judging the behavior of a kindergarten-age child, and hence we would expect children to employ both sets of standards simultaneously in evaluating their own behavior and that of others.

Personal property. A principle which mothers attempted to teach, as a way to control damage in the household, was that of the inviolability of personal property. According to this principle, a child is allowed to play with (and perhaps damage) the things which are his own, but he is taught at the same time that there are things which he may not touch because they do not belong to him.

Training children to tell the difference between what is their own and what belongs to others sometimes becomes an especially acute problem when there are a number of brothers and sisters involved. Older children often have toys (chemistry sets, bows and arrows) which would be dangerous for younger children. Disputes over who was to play with a particular toy were perhaps the most commonly reported kind of quarrel between brothers and sisters. Many mothers had learned that one way to handle this problem was to specify clearly who was the official owner of each toy, and then try to train generosity in lending toys to non-owners. For some mothers, this training about ownership and generosity led to conflict:

I. *How about teaching children to respect the things that belong to other members of the family? What have you done about this with Mary?*
M. *I think they should be taught that from the time they are babies. I tried very hard to get them to share always from the time they were little, but perhaps I didn't lean enough on "Well, it's yours, you have a right to it." I think that was one of my mistakes with Janet (the older sister). To keep peace or to have things run smoothly, I think often-times I made her give in when she shouldn't have had to, and I think it shows up now, with a little resentment there. Mary is a much stronger-willed child, and she'd want Janet's doll, she'd want Janet's bike—I don't think they should be allowed to always barge in and take what they want, and with the girls I try to say to Mary, "That's Janet's"; and then on the other hand I will say, "Now, Janet, share it with Mary, show her how to use it if you possibly can." I have tried very hard to make them share, and not ride roughshod over each other's things.*

One mother found that the training about property had worked out well in preventing injury to valuable things:

M. *They know who everything belongs to. I just always said, from the time they could understand, I let them know these things. If something belongs to Dad or if a piece of jewelry or something that belongs to me—I show it all to them, and we feel it and touch it, but if they want to play with it, they have to ask, and I might let them borrow it. But they are never allowed to just come in and take anything, ever. I let them borrow things once in a while, and they respect it very much, and nothing's ever happened to anything that I let them borrow.*

The success of the system of defining ownership and then encouraging borrowing and lending seems to rest on the fact that responsibility for care of the object is clearly allocated. If a child has received permission to borrow something, and then it is damaged, there is no doubt as to who did it; the borrower may expect some form of retribution, such as not being allowed to borrow anything again for a time.

Part of a mother's motivation in preventing damage is her

desire to keep the burdens of housekeeping at a minimum. If something is torn, she must mend it. If a wall or piece of upholstery is soiled, she must clean it; or if the damage is bad enough, she must repaint or reupholster it. If something she needs is misplaced, she must find it before she can go on with her work. Naturally enough, she is anxious to train her child to avoid actions which will mean extra work of this kind for her.

There are also some positive actions a child can learn which will lighten his mother's housekeeping tasks. For example, he can learn to pick up his clothes when he takes them off, and hang them up or fold them neatly, instead of dropping them on the floor wherever he happens to be standing. He can pick up his toys when he has finished playing with them; he can put his bike or scooter in the garage or basement so his mother will not have to keep watch over it to prevent its being stolen, or run over by a car, or rusted from being out in the rain. Many of the mothers in our group reported they had already developed rules to facilitate these actions. Most of them, also, had certain rules which were designed to reduce the amount of laundering: for example, many children were required to change into dungarees or other durable clothing when they came home from school, so they would not soil their school clothes. Often, too, children had been trained to come in the back door when they had been playing outdoors, so they would not track dirt over the carpets and floors of the living room and front entrance hall.

As might be expected, parents differed in how much they believed could be expected of a five- or six-year-old child with respect to neatness, orderliness, and general helpfulness about the house. It may be seen from Table VIII:4 that most of the mothers did not expect their children to be paragons of virtue. Efforts were made to enforce certain minimum standards in the way of picking up clothes and toys, however, although many a mother had found that more time and trouble were required to see that the child did these things than to do them herself. For this reason, she was sometimes reluctant to begin making demands upon the child which she knew would require time and effort on her part for the follow-through.

The problem, as some mothers saw it, was like this. Suppose a child has been told he must pick up his pajamas and hang them up before he may come downstairs for breakfast. If he appears in the kitchen while the mother is cooking breakfast, she must remember to ask, "Did you hang up your pajamas?" and if he says, "No, I forgot," she must insist on his going back upstairs to do it. Or, more of a problem for her, he may say, "I don't remember." If she is to be consistent in enforcing her demands, she then must go upstairs to find out, and stand over the child while he does what is required. All this may occur while she is trying to feed the baby, or get breakfast on the table for the other members of the family. Furthermore, the chances are that the child in question will have dawdled until he is in danger of being late for school; if he has to retrace his steps and carry out his assigned tasks before he can have breakfast, there will just be more trouble.

TABLE VIII:4

LEVEL OF STANDARDS FOR NEATNESS, ORDERLINESS, AND CLEANLINESS

1. Low standards. Mother does not expect any specific acts	2%
2. A few requirements	14
3. Moderate standards—e.g., must wash before meals, hang up coat and hat, pick up toys sometimes	40
4. Relatively high standards	36
5. Very high standards. Many things a child must do: always pick up and put away toys and clothes; put things back in right place after use; keep drawers neat; change to play clothes for play	7
Not ascertained	1
Total	100%

ASSIGNING HOUSEHOLD TASKS

Beyond picking up his own things, a child is usually expected, sometime during the process of growing up, to begin doing things for others in the household. In this category would be the "chores" so familiar to farm boys. In other societies, this kind of participation may begin quite early. Among the Navahos, for example, boys may be seen tending sheep when they are as young as five or six; in still other societies, girls of this age are frequently required to help care for younger children. In our sample of American families, as may be seen from Table VIII:5, it was very rare indeed for children of five or six to be expected to perform any household tasks regularly. And when training of this sort had begun, the tasks required of the child were minimal. Most commonly, they involved emptying ash trays or wastebaskets once a day. Next most common was the requirement that the child systematically pick up toys and clothes in his own room once a day. Relatively few children were required to wash dishes, make their beds, or set the table with any regularity, although many mothers reported that their children volunteered to do these things and were encouraged to do so when they showed interest spontaneously.

TABLE VIII:5

EXTENT OF GIVING THE CHILD REGULAR JOBS TO DO AROUND THE HOUSE

1. Nothing expected of child in the way of performing household tasks; mother feels child is too young for this	12%
2. No regular jobs so far, but mother says she would like to have him do them, and is thinking of beginning these requirements. Mother encourages helping, but does not require regular performance	42
3. One or two small jobs regularly, and with moderate pressure for enforcement	35
4. Several regular jobs (or difficult jobs) fairly strictly enforced	9
5. Many regular, difficult jobs, strictly enforced	1
Not ascertained	1
Total	100%

The reasons mothers gave for not assigning household tasks to children of this age were various. Some had to do with simplifying the mother's housekeeping; others were more child-oriented. Often, the mothers reported, the first stages of teaching a child to help around the house are so troublesome for the mother that she would rather do the jobs herself and let the training go:

I. *Do you think a child of Janet's age should be given any regular jobs to do around the house?*
M. *No. She has offered to dry the dishes, and—but usually the things she wants to do are—well, it's my fault, I'm so busy—but there's so much to do that I think it's easier to do it myself. You know, like now, because if she wanted to do it, then the little one would; and by the time they got through it would be an all-day job, and I don't have too much time to spend like that right now. Every year it's getting better, because they're getting older, but it has been easier to do for them than to try to teach them.*

Another mother, who had already begun training her children to accept responsibility for household chores, mentioned some of the vexations that are involved from the standpoint of efficiency:

M. *It's Susan's job to get the paper—put on a jacket and race out on the porch and get Dad's paper. We leave it out there purposely because that's what—we walk right over it when we come in, you know; fifteen minutes later we ask her to get it. She has some jobs like that all the time to do. And at night, they're told to go and get whatever— I mean I could do it so much faster myself, it drives me mad sometimes—having them get the vegetables out for me. You know, they'll get the potatoes out for baking, and ask just how many, and how big, and so forth. But they have to learn.*

But most mothers preferred to wait until the children were older before they began to train them to help with household tasks. Some mothers took this position out of a feeling of sympathy for the child—a feeling that childhood should be happy and free from burdens:

I. *Do you think a child of Carol's age should be given any regular jobs to do around the house?*
M. *Oh, no. As a matter of fact, I have an older daughter who is almost ten, and I won't compel her to do anything around the house. I figure a woman's job is a lifetime job in the home. Why start them so young? I don't believe in it. Like the old timers will say: Why don't you start training her to start doing this—like washing stairs and things like that, but I don't believe in that. I know from experience— I was always that type to work in the house and it's a long time for a woman, so why start them too young. That's how I feel.*

RESTRICTIONS ON TELEVISION

In 1951–52, when these interviews were obtained, television was still fairly new, but it had gone beyond the stage of being a novelty. Nearly all (92 per cent) of the families in our sample had TV sets, and most of the mothers had developed attitudes toward television, and had formulated rules and regulations for their children's viewing. One could hardly say that TV had been as fully assimilated into family life as automobiles or motion pictures, but it was on the way.

We asked the mothers to estimate how much time their children spent daily with the TV set. The reported average was an hour and a half. From other studies done at about the same time in the same area, we are inclined to think this an underestimate. Researchers who investigated children's own reports of programs which they followed faithfully, or who asked mothers to keep a diary of the children's viewing, estimated an average of three hours daily. Whatever the actual figure may have been, it is clear that TV had become an important part of young children's lives. It evidently had quite strong attraction. In consequence, it had also become an event that mothers had to make rules about.

What rules were made depended partly on the mother's evaluation of TV as an influence on her child. Quite a few had found that viewing served as a soporific. It kept the child quiet and out of mischief. It cut down the amount of quarreling between brothers and sisters during that irritable hour just before dinner. This was doubly rewarding to the mother, for not only were the children better behaved, but they were quietly absorbed elsewhere while she was preparing dinner. Some mothers were particularly happy that this permitted a few quiet moments of talk with their husband when he came home from work.

Not all the mothers emphasized the quieting effect of TV, however. Some reported just the opposite, and they blamed the nature of the programs. Some children became very excited while watching "Westerns," for example, and would jump and shout and pretend to be shooting up the household. This stimulation was looked upon askance by a good many of the mothers, especially the college-educated ones. They feared that too much TV would be harmful. The dangers were thought of as twofold: TV kept the child indoors, and prevented him from doing the active, creative, or more educational things he might otherwise be doing; and second, the TV programs themselves were considered to be too full of fighting, murder, and harrowing interpersonal scenes. One mother described her reactions this way:

M. *As far as TV is concerned, I hate it. I do. I don't think there is a decent program for the children. They stopped reading, they stopped listening to records. I don't like it. Once in a while I get strict and put my foot down and say, "No television. Read a book or play a record." But they rail and they whine. I relent after a while.*

Another mother believed that TV was overstimulating to her son, who was inclined to be excitable:

M. *TV I am kinda a crab on. If it's a good day, I make him go out. When we first got the set he watched cowboy pictures quite a bit, and*

I had to stop it as he was keyed up all the time. That's just his make-up. A lot of children will watch it and think nothing of it. But anything like that, he gets himself all excited and you just can't calm him down. At night when he goes to bed he's just irritable; in every way it's not good for him. So I don't let him watch any more than I have to. Once in a while when he's home if he's sick, or if it's a rainy day, I let him watch.

The restrictions established by most mothers were not particularly severe. They tended to involve an insistence that the child spend at least part of his time, on pleasant days, in more active play outdoors, and that he not stay up beyond his bedtime. This latter rule was often relaxed on week ends, or for special

programs. Illness, or other conditions that required confinement, forced relaxation of the former rule. If a normally active child is ill, the mother's problem is to keep him amused and quiet, and television seems ideally suited to this purpose. If the mother is trying to limit the child's TV-viewing, she must think of some substitute activity. On days when the weather is bad, or if there is no playmate nearby, her own ingenuity is taxed, and she often finds television the easiest solution:

M. *There has been so much rain and bad weather, that she has been in and there really isn't too much for her to do. Outside of crayoning for a few minutes, there isn't much to keep her occupied. So she does like to sit and watch television. Sort of an easy way out, I suppose.*

As can be seen from Table VIII:6, the great majority of mothers were only lightly restrictive. Most of them felt TV did the child little or no harm, and it did help keep him out of mischief. It also had a further virtue in that depriving the child of seeing his favorite program could be an easy and effective form of discipline. Indeed, after reading the mothers' reports of their frequent use of this technique, we are almost driven to wonder how parents ever disciplined their children before TV came along to be taken away!

TABLE VIII:6

RESTRICTIONS ON CHILD'S TELEVISION VIEWING

1. No restrictions. Child may look or listen whenever he wants	17%
2. Slight restrictions	15
3. Moderate restrictions. Child cannot look during meals or after bedtime; certain specific programs disapproved; some leeway with only moderate pressure for enforcement	28
4. Considerable restriction	22
5. Severe restriction. Child may look only during specific times, or at specified programs; no leeway and strong pressure for enforcement	8
Family has no television set	8
Not ascertained	2
Total	100%

We do not mean to suggest that all the mothers found TV an unmixed blessing. It solved some problems, but created others. American mothers seem always to have had difficulty in getting children to come to the table when meals were ready, or to go to bed on time, but television has apparently accentuated these problems markedly in many families. Sometimes a favorite program will be scheduled late, after the child is supposed to be in bed. The child will tease to be allowed to stay up for it "just this once." Older children in the family who are allowed to see it regularly will talk about it in the presence of the younger child, and whet his interest in it. And so the pressure mounts, and the number of occasions on which the child is allowed to stay up generally increases. One mother said:

M. *I like getting her into bed at a certain hour. But the oldest daughter, she stays up a little later because they sleep in the same room and I always like to get one sleeping before the other one goes in. In that way they'll fall asleep with no trouble, but otherwise they'll start giggling and fooling around and they'll be getting a licking before* *they know it. So I manage to put her into bed a little earlier, although now with television it's an awful job—they want to see this and they want to see that—oh, I find it hard with television, I really do.*

BEDTIME RESTRICTIONS

It was very common practice for the parents in our group to establish a certain time at which their children were to go to bed, and to put them to bed at this time whether the children were sleepy or not. Some mothers reported that their children were tired and ready for bed by the time the appointed hour arrived, and went to sleep almost immediately when the lights were put out. Others reported, however, that there was a constant problem of the child's remaining awake after he had been put to bed. Some children apparently lay awake regularly for as much as two hours each evening, after the lights were out.

Why do parents put children to bed before they are sleepy? What would be the consequences if children were allowed to stay up until they felt ready for bed and went to sleep of their own accord? There are societies in which this is the customary practice. Young children may be seen wide awake late on fiesta evenings, watching with shining eyes the gay behavior of their elders, or standing on the side lines imitating dance steps, or, in the end, draped sound asleep over a piece of furniture or cradled in someone's arms while the bedlam goes on. If left to their own devices, will children get enough sleep, and at the proper times?

Man is a daytime animal. With his heavy reliance on vision, he can function much more efficiently in the daylight than at night. Doubtless our paleolithic ancestors retired to their caves at dusk and arose at dawn, sleeping longer hours in the winter than during the shorter nights of the summer. But modern man has invented artificial lights; and just as farmers get more egg production out of chickens by using night lights in the henhouse to fool the chickens into behaving as though it were still day, so man has lengthened his daily period of productive activity markedly by providing light after sundown.

The man who was chiefly responsible for this technical revolution—Thomas A. Edison—was a believer in the notion that man does not require more than four or five hours of sleep for physical well-being; the rest is habit or self-indulgence. He was unquestionably correct in assuming that habit plays an important role in determining the amount of sleep adults seek. Certain it is, too, that sleep can serve other functions than recovery from muscular fatigue. Sometimes it is an escape, as every student knows who has gone to bed because he was falling asleep over his physics textbook but then has found himself fully able to sit up in bed half the night reading a mystery story.

Young infants require very much more sleep than older children and adults. The rate at which the need for sleep declines as the child grows older is a highly variable matter, however. Some children outgrow their afternoon nap before they are three years old, while others continue the nap into the fifth year or even longer. There is little evidence concerning the amount of sleep the average child of five or six needs. If we assume that he needs more than his parents do, we can reasonably ask whether he would get it in adult-dominated households if there were no pressure for him to go to bed at a particular time.

As far as we know, there is no evidence on this point, and we can only speculate. Our guess is that he probably would, or very nearly so, but that the timing might be such as to interfere with what the parents considered. a desirable schedule of activities both for themselves and for the child. It is possible, for example, that a child left to his own devices might well stay up as late as his parents did, and then sleep later in the morning. Or if the parents woke him early in the morning for school, he might fall asleep in school or take a nap in the afternoon. Then he might be wide awake in the evening when interesting things were going on in the family (Daddy at home, exciting TV programs, etc.).

In a society like ours, where adult activities go on for many hours after dark, a young child might have difficulty getting enough sleep unless his parents arranged rules that forced him to get sleep. Children often do not recognize the signs of their own fatigue. They will avoid sleep even when this is what they need most. If a mother tells a child "I think you need a nap," he may protest, but upon being put to bed he may nevertheless fall asleep, and wake up in an hour or so in a relaxed and sunny mood. Sometimes, undoubtedly, the virtue of a nap under such circumstances is not so much its physiological recovery value as its effect at cutting off the stream of stimuli from the environment which are in danger of overwhelming the child temporarily. Many a traveler has noticed that he becomes overpoweringly sleepy during the day, when he has been meeting new people, behaving in new ways, and attempting to speak an unfamiliar language. Similarly, a young child is attempting to learn difficult concepts and techniques, and to adapt himself to situations for which he has not yet worked out habitual modes of response. The barrage of environmental situations often taxes his capacity to respond appropriately. At such times, sleep is a beneficent thing, erasing the sources of conflict long enough for him to recover his emotional equilibrium and start afresh.

The child's welfare is not the only thing that influences mothers to have bedtime rules, however. One mother of a large family emphasized the importance to her of the hours of relaxation she could get after the children were in bed:

> **M.** *Seven o'clock is the time for bed. I feel if they don't get their sleep, they are very cranky in the morning. I usually like to sit down myself at nighttime, knitting or crocheting, and watch the television. The whole lot of them go to bed at seven o'clock, so I can have my evening free.*

Similarly, a number of mothers commented that if they allowed the children to stay up as late as they wished, the parents would never have any privacy. They felt it was especially important for the husband and wife to have some time alone together, free from the pressure engendered by the constant presence of the children.

For a variety of reasons, then, children may be put to bed when they are not sleepy. This leads to difficulties. A child can be forced to do a number of things he is unwilling to do—pick up a toy, turn off the TV, go outdoors—but he cannot be forced to go to sleep. Maybe to bed, but not to sleep. All a parent can do is to arrange surroundings that are conducive to sleep. The primary conditions seem to be (1) reducing the level of all kinds of visual and auditory stimulation, and (2) providing a set of familiar surroundings and objects that are associated with going to sleep. The latter are usually more easily arranged than the former, particularly when there are a number of children in the family. A major problem in establishing and enforcing bedtime arises when the family includes children of only a few years' difference in age, and particularly when these children share the same bedroom. When children are put to bed in the same room at the same time, the older ones are likely to keep the younger ones awake by talking and laughing and "fooling around." If the younger child is put to bed first, he may resent this. Furthermore, he is often awakened when an older child does go to bed. One mother described her younger child's reactions as follows:

M. *He is supposed to go to bed at seven o'clock, but he resents it terribly because Frances is allowed to stay up later than he is. Of course, she would resent it terribly if they went to bed at the same time, so what can you do? I got him to bed last night at seven o'clock, but at eight when she went to bed he was still awake with his eyes open, to make sure she would go to bed at eight on the dot.*

TABLE VIII:7

STRICTNESS ABOUT CHILD'S BEDTIME

1. Not at all strict—no particular rules. Child goes to bed when sleepy, may have lights on and door open if he wishes	2%
2. A few limitations. Parents have bedtime in mind, but allow deviations fairly often; consider child's special needs at time	18
3. Some limitations. Child supposed to be in bed at a certain time, but parents allow some leeway. Mild scolding for not conforming	29
4. Fairly strict. Will not stretch bedtime very much or very often; considerable pressure for conformity	34
5. Very strict—no leeway. Child must be in bed on dot, lights out, door closed; no getting up for company. Punishment for deviation	5
Not ascertained	12
Total	100%

The range of strictness about bedtime behavior is shown in Table VIII:7. While some parents had only a very roughly defined bedtime, others enforced a very specific regime, with complete quiet expected once the lights were out.

Two examples of a quite *permissive* attitude were as follows:

A

M. *His bedtime rules lately have been rather flexible and, well, more or less because they changed his school hours. He did have regular hours, say seven or seven-thirty, but they're kind of flexible. Since we've got the television, and the change in school hours, he stays up a little later than he used to. But, well, next year he won't be able to do it. He'll have to go to bed early, because he's going to be in school all day. They're flexible, though, they're not really too pinned down.*

B

M. *I have an awful hard time getting her to go to bed. I tell her at seven-thirty that it's time for bed, but it don't do me any good. She'll go up and run around and play around and get a doll and fool around, but I just let her go. At seven-thirty I like to keep her upstairs. If she's in bed, she is; if she's not, eventually she'll fall asleep.*

Another mother, however, put her *strict* attitude about bedtime succinctly, as follows:

M. *When it's bedtime, it's bedtime. There is no playing at bedtime . . . just bath, teeth, and bed. Lights out, and that's that.*

As may be seen in Table VIII:8, the time which the mothers considered appropriate for the bedtime of a kindergarten-age child varied from before six o'clock to after eight-thirty. We did not ask specifically what the child's bedtime was, but most of

TABLE VIII:8

HOUR SPECIFIED FOR CHILD'S BEDTIME

6:00 or earlier	2%
6:05–6:30	5
6:35–7:00	24
7:05–7:30	27
7:35–8:00	14
8:05–8:30	3
After 8:30	1
Child has no specific bedtime	7
Not ascertained	17
Total	100%

the mothers volunteered this information. Most commonly, it was six-thirty, seven, or seven-thirty. The time seemed to depend, in part, upon the ages and sexes of the other children in the family. There was a slight, though not significant, tendency for a child with a younger sibling of the same sex to be put to bed earlier, and for a child with an older sibling of the same sex to be put to bed later. There was some suggestion that a child's bedtime was often adjusted to that of the child who shared the same room.

Another factor which helped to determine the child's bedtime was whether the mother worked. There were relatively few working mothers in our sample, but if we group together all the mothers who worked during any of the five years since the child was born, and compare them with the mothers who had not worked, we find that the working mothers put their children to bed later, on the average ($p < .05$). Presumably, for working mothers, the whole family schedule at the end of the day was shifted toward a later hour.

RESTRICTIONS ON NOISE

Very loud or very shrill noise is intrinsically unpleasant, almost painful, as witness the shriek of chalk on a blackboard or the roar of a jet plane at take-off. In the case of children's noise, a shout or scream close by can be similarly hurtful, but the sheer volume of noise made by active children is probably not often the aspect that is most upsetting to a mother. More commonly, when she finds that children's noise is getting on her nerves, she is troubled by the social significance of the racket, and the implications of physical violence. When children are running fast and vigorously, making heavy, rapid footstep noises, they are more likely to bump into something and hurt themselves or break something. When they make loud banging noises, they are usually striking objects, and there is the likelihood that something will be cracked, dented, or broken, or that a finger will be bruised. And when children's voices rise to a high pitch of excitement, mothers know that emotional reactions are developing which can change suddenly from laughter to tears or to temper outbursts. As one mother put it, "When they get loud and excited like that, I know that pretty soon there's going to be a fight." Knowing all these implications of noise, mothers are understandably uncomfortable when they hear very much of it. Loud noise is a signal that things may be getting out of hand and that there will be trouble.

Perhaps without realizing the basis for their feeling, many mothers like to keep household noises at a certain moderate level. They do not want dead silence, to be sure, for this can suggest mischief, too. As one mother commented, "If they are either too quiet or too giggly, something is up. That much I have learned." By listening, a mother can keep in touch with her child's activities even when he is not within her sight, and be reassured that things are going well. Another said, "By the sound, I know exactly where they are, and by the sound I know what they are doing." So too much and too little noise are equally bad. The range of maternal tolerance for noise is illustrated in Table VIII:9, where it may be seen that some mothers kept a very tight rein on noise-making, while others took the attitude that children are essentially noisy creatures and should not be curbed too much in this respect.

TABLE VIII:9

STRICTNESS ABOUT NOISE

1. Not at all strict. Child may yell, run, bang—without reprimand. Rough loud games permitted. "After all, you expect noise from children"	6%
2. A few restrictions on noise	29
3. Moderately strict. Children must not shout, must avoid banging and loudest games, but quite a bit of leeway allowed	35
4. Quite strict about noise	24
5. Very strict. Children may never run in house, shout or yell, or bang doors. Punishment for noise-making	2
Not ascertained	4
Total	100%

Of course, the amount of noise a mother permitted depended in part on the family's living situation—whether there were older people in the household, or young babies whose naptime had to be respected, or whether the family lived in a two-family house where noise might disturb the adjoining household:

M. *I don't allow her to run in the house, because after all we're on the second floor, and people live downstairs, and it would be too noisy. That happens every day, and I have to stop her. 'Course when they start playing hide and seek, I don't allow that—those are outdoor games.*

Another example of a non-permissive attitude about noise was provided by the mother who said:

M. *I don't allow too much noise. Sometimes they're apt to have a ball in their hands, and they bounce the ball and I just take it right away from them. I don't let them play with anything noisy—no noisy toys. I don't believe in noise like that in the home. I figure things like that they should play outside, not in the home.*

One might expect that there would have been greater restriction on noise in families with a larger number of children, but we found no evidence of this in our sample.

The amount of noise a mother can tolerate depends, of course, on whether she happens to feel tired, ill, or upset at the time. She is more likely to become irritated with a child for beating his toy drum in the house when she has a headache than when she feels well and rested. Sounds are something which cannot be completely ignored, unless they are constant background noises like the ticking of the clock. They require some sort of response, and the response must be integrated into the ongoing stream of other activities. The response to the sounds may be partially incompatible with the other activities, as, for example, having to answer a question while trying to concentrate on a delicate and troublesome task like threading a small needle. Integration of responses takes effort, and there is a limit to the stimulus input which any person can integrate. Anyone who has personally experienced a fire, a hurricane, an infantry or tank battle, a bombing or a train wreck is familiar with this general principle. On a smaller scale, the principle applies to everyday social interactions. A mother who is emotionally upset, perhaps because of a quarrel with her husband, cannot adjust herself as efficiently to a great barrage of stimuli as she can if she is feeling calm. It appears that in the home, when a mother is upset, her first impulse is to cut down the confusion by reducing the noise level and generally simplifying the situation to which she must respond.

Requirements for Obedience

Of the great variety of demands and restrictions that mothers impose, some are designed to protect the child and his surroundings from mutual damage, and some to equip him with skills and controls which he will need in later life. Underlying all these is the requirement of obedience. In order to achieve any of her other objectives, the mother must first train her child to listen when she is instructing him, and to do what she asks.

"Why do I have to?" Obedience is not much of a problem during a child's first year, but when he becomes ambulatory, in his second year, it is. At a beach or pool, in the yard, even in the relative safety of the house itself, a few quick steps can lead sometimes to serious danger. Since the very young child often cannot foresee the consequences of his acts, his mother must be on the alert to reach out and stop risky movements. This involves a considerable outlay of energy, however, and is expensive for the mother in the sense that it uses up a lot of her time in just watching. Hence, she is likely to use play pens or other mechanical protectors whenever possible. It is not surprising, either, that she tries to develop *language* control over the child as soon as she can. "No, no!" can be heard from a distance.

The notion of obedience becomes important as soon as control by physical holding is replaced by verbal control. Unless the child obeys commands instantly, without stopping to ask why, a mother may rightly fear that she cannot protect him adequately. For this reason, some parents look upon strict and instant obedience as a matter of great importance. As one mother put it:

M. *If a case comes up and they are in trouble—if they run into the street and they don't see something and they are told to obey and they don't—then it can be bad. Therefore, I think they should obey in the little things as well as the big things.*

Once a mother has gained this kind of control for these serious purposes, she finds its use expedient for other activities as well. We found great variation among the mothers in this respect, however. At one extreme were those who felt that every command should be responded to instantly and without question. These mothers seemed to have generalized the importance of obedient behavior from danger situations to many others. "Run upstairs and get Mommy's sewing basket, there's a good boy," or "Put away your toys, now; it's time for dinner," or "Stop that awful noise," or "Hang up your coat! I've told you a thousand times that you are always supposed to hang it up when you come in." At the other extreme were mothers who used commands less extensively and were much less insistent on immediate response. They seemed to distinguish more carefully between situations in which instant obedience was important for the child's safety and those in which obedience was simply a convenience to the mother herself. The range of attitudes is indicated in Table VIII:10.

A quite *strict* attitude was expressed by these two comments:

A

M. *I think they ought to do it right away, whatever you ask. I stick right there and watch, stand right there and watch if they're going to* *do it. Both my husband and I try never to forget it. You tell them to do something. Don't forget about it once you've said it. If you ever aren't going to follow it through, don't say it at all. That's the way I feel about it.*

B

M. *I myself expect her to obey the moment I speak to her, which I don't approve of myself, really and truly; not that I would ever let her know differently, but I expect her to obey me when I speak to her.*

In contrast, some mothers attached little value to obedience for its own sake:

M. *Usually, with Tommy, you tell him the second or third time, he'll do it.*
I. *Do you expect him to obey right away, when you tell him to do something like that?*
M. *Well, no, because I figure he's only a child, and you can't expect too much until he really gets a little older.*

TABLE VIII:10

OBEDIENCE EXPECTANCY

"Some parents expect their children to obey immediately when they tell them to be quiet or pick something up, and so on. Others don't think it is terribly important for a child to obey right away. How do you feel about this?"	All Mothers
1. Does not expect obedience. May say one should not expect it of a child this young, or that parents can be wrong, too, and do not have the right to expect children to snap to attention	1%
2. Expects some obedience, but will speak several times; tolerant attitude toward non-compliance	21
3. Wants child to obey, but expects some delay. Whether tolerates delay depends on what the situation is. Some scolding or other pressure for not obeying	54
4. Wants and expects obedience. Generally expects child to obey on first or second demand; considerable pressure for conformity	21
5. Expects instant obedience; does not tolerate any delay. Punishment for deviation—very strict	2
Not ascertained	1
Total	100%

Securing compliance. A demand for obedience almost always requires a child to stop what he is doing and do something else. Since he is interested in what he is doing, he does not want to stop. The demand for obedience is therefore almost necessarily frustrating to him. Other things being equal he would prefer not to comply. Furthermore, he can often tell from the objective situation that danger is not involved. He can see no dire consequences for himself, if he does not comply, other than punishment from his mother. Therefore, his compliance may come to depend in large part on his judgment as to whether enforcement measures are likely to be forthcoming from the parent.

Children early develop an astonishing ability to judge from very subtle cues when it is safe to disobey and when it is not. One mother reported that her little girl would look over her shoulder when she went to carry out a task, seeking to read from her mother's expression whether hurry was essential. Mothers themselves sometimes deliberately helped their children to learn to differentiate between demands which had to be heeded instantly and those which could be treated more lightly:

> **M.** *If they're engrossed in something, I don't think it's fair to make them drop it right then. But if it's a matter of their personal safety, I think it's very important. I think the child has to learn to realize when I say, "This time I mean right away," he has to do it. Otherwise, I'll say, "Pick it up when you're finished."*

Another mother relied upon changes in her tone of voice to indicate to the child how seriously her demands were to be taken:

M. *I have tried to make them realize that there are some times when a great deal depends upon their minding immediately and without question, and I tell them they can tell by my tone of voice whether it is important or not. But other times I tell them that if they have a reason, or think they have a reason, not to want to do something, to say, "Why?"*

By no means all the mothers were aware of this distinction, however, or of the necessity for providing the child with cues for deciding whether or not to give instant response. Some mothers recognized clearly that there were times when they wanted instant obedience, and other times when they did not, but they were unable to specify how the child was expected to tell the difference:

A

M. *It depends on the situation. If they're out in the middle of the street and you call them, and there's a car coming, they should move immediately. But on things that don't really matter, I don't think it matters one way or the other.*

B

M. *I find myself saying the same things over and over, two or three times. But if it were a question where I really needed obedience, I expect it.*

The mother's tone of voice is probably a helpful cue for the child in such instances. Or the context in which the command occurs may help. Several mothers reported that they had developed the habit of making a request a given number of times— perhaps three—and that the child had learned the third time "meant business." Each request would be made in a firmer manner, or in a louder and higher-pitched tone, than the one before. This permitted the child to recognize that the mother had reached a point of irritation sufficient to produce punishment. Then the child would comply, often assuming an air of injured innocence: "Mother, I was just *going* to."

Many children had apparently learned that there are extenuating circumstances which make a mother feel that she cannot, in justice, punish for a failure to obey. They become experts in arranging circumstances that permit noncompliance without open defiance. For example, a mother cannot expect a child to comply if he did not hear the request. An extraordinary amount of selective deafness seems to develop in small children. Many a parent has noted with some bitterness that a child can hear the ice-cream man's bell several blocks away, but cannot hear his mother calling him, at the top of her voice, to stop playing and come in for dinner. One mother described the situation as follows:

> **M.** *I usually have to ask him about nineteen times before he does anything, and I usually end up yelling at him, getting hold of him, and making him do it. As a matter of fact, I was just asking my husband last night if he thought we should have his ears checked. He doesn't mind very well.*

According to these reports, then, one of the mother's first concerns when she had directions to give, was to make sure that she had the child's attention. A commonly quoted refrain was "*Listen* to me now. I don't want to have to tell you again." Securing obedience from children would undoubtedly be easier were it not for the fact that their attention span actually is limited in comparison with that of adults. A young child is very easily distracted, too. He may receive directions with every intention of following them, and in fact embark on the first steps, but be distracted in mid-course by some interesting event or object. Such mishaps are not limited to children, as any adult can testify. The number of husbands who have "forgotten" to stop for that loaf of bread, on the way home from work, will scarcely bear thinking on. For a child, the task of resisting competing attractions, even during something as simple as washing his hands, is even more difficult. If a mother is to secure compliance, she must nearly always be ready to remind the child. An obedience demand sometimes requires as much effort from the mother as it does from the child. One mother complained that her husband did not understand this aspect of the problem:

> **M.** *I think it's important if you ask them to do something—either it is going to be done right when you ask them to, and you are going to hold them to it, or you shouldn't have said it in the first place. I know, very often, with my husband, he will be reading and he will know it is their bedtime and he doesn't want to stop reading, and he will say, "Get into your pajamas." Well, the first few times it didn't work at all; they were too young. You have to go in with them and see that they get into them. I would much rather put down the book and go*

in and say "Let's get into the pajamas," do it, and then go back to my work; because it is, I think, better for them to get it done. I don't believe in children dilly-dallying all evening doing some little thing.

The effort required for the follow-through is undoubtedly one of the reasons why disobedience is so irritating to parents. If the child does not comply immediately, the busy mother herself must keep clearly in mind the request she has made, and be ready with a strategy for securing compliance. She must be ready to counter excuses, to deal with anger or sullenness over being required to do an unwelcome task, and possibly ready to bargain a little if necessary: "If you do this for me, I'll play a game of cards with you later on." All this interaction may interfere with other activities on the mother's agenda. No wonder she longs for some blessed occasion on which the child would simply say, in a pleasant voice, "Yes, Mother," and go promptly to do what she has asked.

Once a mother has made a demand, she is concerned not only with getting the task accomplished, but with obedience for its own sake. Through some of our interviews ran the theme of the mother's fear that she might lose control of her child. What would she do if the child simply said "I won't," and could not be made to comply by any punishment the mother could devise? This situation had never yet arisen with the kindergarten-age children we were discussing, of course, since the mother could still use physical force to get what she wanted. But some of the mothers were anticipating the day when the child would be too grown up for this, when they would have to rely upon his *willingness* to follow their directions in order to retain any influence over his actions. They felt, therefore, that they could not tolerate open defiance of their demands.

The mothers differed widely in how often they allowed the naked issue of authority to arise. In haste and distraction, almost any mother will occasionally give a child an ill-advised direction. The child may offer a good reason why it should not be followed, or may simply ask "Why?" and thus cause the mother to realize that she does not have a good reason for what she asked. Some mothers, in this situation, reported saying, "Because I told you to, that's why." They followed through for the sake of maintaining their authority, even though the action was ridiculous to both themselves and the child.

Among our group, an occasional mother had found herself involved in a last-ditch stand with her authority at stake, but most of those who were sensitive to their authority positions had devised elaborate techniques for avoiding such situations. Although their control of the child may have been based on force in the last analysis, they and their children almost always operated short of the last analysis.

Such parents avoided issuing their directions in the form of orders. The famous dictum said to be taught to new army officers—"Never give an order unless you are sure it will be obeyed"—applied here. These parents had learned not to risk disobedience except in crucial situations. Instead, the mother suggested, requested, guided, distracted.

Another common device was the use of preparation. Knowing that the child had difficulty in switching suddenly from an activity in which he was absorbed to something less interesting, the mother would give him warning of the impending change. Thus he could have time to finish at least some aspect of what he was doing and be ready for the new activity:

> **M.** *Well, if it's time for her to come to bed and she's doing something, I tell her to finish up what she's doing, because in a few minutes it will be time to go to sleep. I sort of prepare her for it, because I don't feel that any child—no more than we—likes to be interrupted at something that they're doing, and they can't be right away. It's just impossible. You just can't say, "Now you're coming to bed, and stop what you're doing." So I prepare them always.*

Another reported device for avoiding issues of authority was to make the required task appear attractive either in its own right or as a necessary first step to something attractive. For example: "Let's hurry and get dressed so we can go for a ride."

The ultimate expression of a parent's authority is physical, of course. In extreme instances, socialization may be so inadequate that a father retains control over his son only as long as the father is bigger and stronger and can still give the son a whipping. In such cases, there is likely to be a violent scene sometime during the boy's adolescence; he turns the tables on his father, and proves that he is the stronger of the two. One father, interviewed in another study, who had encountered this situation said, "He needs a strong hand, and I can't give it to him any more. I'm glad he's going in the Army."

This kind of situation is not likely to arise in very many of the present group of families, if we may predict on the basis of the attitudes being expressed by the mothers when the children were five or six years old. Most of them recognized the necessity for the gradual relaxation of their authority and the transfer of control to the child himself. Symptomatic of this was the attitude expressed by a number of mothers that they knew they were not always right, and that they owed the child some explanation of what was expected of him. Furthermore, they felt that if the parents could not give good reasons for obedience to a particular command, and if the child could offer better reasons why things should be done differently, the parent should be willing to yield. The word "we" was used a great deal: "We don't want to do that, do we?" or "Let's get started on our work—you make your bed and I'll make mine." This attitude is partly expressed in the maxim, "If you can't lick 'em, join 'em."

RESTRICTIVENESS AND PERMISSIVENESS

There is a common dimension inherent in all these demands and restrictions. It is the strictness of the mother's standards of what constitutes acceptable conformity to adult behavior. In earlier chapters, we described the child's development in terms of his initial ways of behaving with respect to food-seeking, toileting, dependency, sex, and aggression, and we characterized them as changeworthy. In discussing the mothers' training procedures, we emphasized the dimensions of permissiveness and punishment, i.e., the extent to which mothers tolerated changeworthy behavior or used a punitive method for getting rid of it. However, in the present chapter we have focused more directly on the standards the mothers established for new behavior to replace the initial changeworthy actions. The difference is one of emphasis only, for we are still concerned with the same sequence of maternal control and training of the child.

There is good evidence for making this generalization. It will be recalled that there were moderately strong positive correlations among the permissiveness scales that referred to dependency, sex, and aggression. Furthermore, the first factor (A) we discovered in our factor analysis was one that seemed to describe a general trait of permissiveness-strictness (see Appendix Table D:4). Now we find that all of the restrictiveness scales are positively correlated with one another (see Appendix Table D:20). Also, all but one of them (strictness about bedtime) have a significant contribution to make to the permissiveness-strictness factor derived from the factor analysis. These are simply two ways of saying the same thing, of course.

Our conclusion is that these mothers behaved fairly consistently in respect to the dimension of strictness-permissiveness. If a mother was quite tolerant of her child's aggressive behavior, she was likely to be tolerant of his sexual behavior, too. And if she was permissive in those respects, the chances are she was not very strict about table manners, or noise, or neatness around the house. Likewise, she probably did not insist on rigid obedience to her every command.

In drawing this conclusion, we are inevitably risking some misunderstanding. The correlations among the various strictness scales are not large. Indeed, there is really very little relation between restrictiveness on the child's physical mobility—his freedom to run around the neighborhood—and most of the other restrictions. There is plenty of room, statistically speaking, for a mother to be quite permissive about obedience, for example, and yet be quite strict about noise in the house. There is no question that a vast number of specific aspects of the mothers' personalities and their living arrangements influenced their behavior on this dimension. A generally permissive mother living in a thin-walled duplex could hardly afford to allow the noise level she might permit if she lived on a farm. It would be a mistake, certainly, to assume that mothers were so consistent that they could be characterized as showing some specified degree of permissiveness with respect to *all* their child-rearing activities. At the same time, the findings do show unequivocally that there is a dimension of this kind and that it is exemplified in a wide range of maternal activities.

The anal character. The importance of some of these restrictions has not gone unsung in past attempts to understand the forces that create personality. Sigmund Freud (1908) gave detailed consideration to orderliness as one of the triad of qualities that formed the anal character. He concluded from his clinical observations that severe toilet training produced a rather complex sequence of reaction formations, sublimations, and symbolizations which created an adult character exemplifying a high degree of orderliness, stinginess, and obstinacy. It is therefore of more than passing interest to note that severity of toilet training was one of the dimensions of maternal behavior that contributed to the strictness-permissiveness factor, along with the dimension of strictness of the mother's demands for her child to be neat and orderly.

In Freud's formulation, the mother's handling of toilet training was conceived as the source of the child's (later) orderliness. In the present data we see that there was a tendency for the mothers who were severe in toilet training to be demanding also with respect to orderliness ($p < .01$; $r = .21$). (See Appendix Table D:21.) Indeed, they were demanding about all the matters we have discussed in this chapter; the correlation between severity of toilet training and a score constructed by summing all the restrictiveness ratings is .27.

These interlocking relationships present some difficulty for the theory of the anal character. While adult orderliness may well be heavily influenced by early experiences with severe toilet training, we must recognize another possible mechanism. Since there was apparently some tendency for the severe toilet-trainers to be severely demanding about orderliness, too, the so-called anal character could be a product of direct training. Our data are not of a character to permit a choice between the two interpretations.

COMMENT

We have not discussed the influence of demands and restrictions on the children's behavior because we had few measures of the latter that seemed particularly relevant. The influences of specific kinds of permissiveness on eating, toileting, dependent and aggressive behavior have already been analyzed in earlier chapters. To discover the effects of the *general trait* of permissiveness-strictness will require further research.

The one general conclusion we can draw from the findings reported here is that there *is* an underlying general trait of permissiveness-strictness. The intercorrelations among the various restrictiveness scales are all relatively small, but they are all positive. They point clearly to a quality of child rearing that has, for one extreme, an attitude of tolerance of changeworthy behavior and a low level of pressure for conformity to adult standards. At the other extreme it has a suppressive and unaccepting attitude toward early childhood impulses, and a high insistence on the adoption of more mature forms of behavior.

This is not a surprising discovery, but the facts it describes deserve careful attention. This dimension has been for fifty years —and still is—the battle line of a major struggle in American society. Historically, our public values and moral standards have been toward the strictness end of the dimension. Aggression toward parents, sexual exploration, and attention-getting behavior have long been decried. Children in the last century were to be seen and not heard; they had to show respect to their elders; their virtue was judged by their cleanliness. High value was placed on early independence, as in the Horatio Alger stories; the child was viewed as a miniature—and somewhat savage— adult; punishment was given great credit as a source of character-building. "Spare the rod and spoil the child" was a favorite dictum.

It is perhaps worth noting that a good deal of the responsibility for the stating of public values and dogma in the nineteenth century was in the hands of men. These attitudes reflect a somewhat aggressive point of view toward children and an abundance of ignorance about them, particularly about the very young child. This is scarcely surprising, for in all Western societies the toddler has been the peculiar province of the mother. Effective policies of child rearing suitable for the adolescent may well have been within the competence of some men, but when these values and policies were projected downward in the age scale, they became rigid, inflexible, and ineffective. Nevertheless, these were the public values, and the "old way" was non-permissive and demanding of early conformity.

With the development of wider educational opportunities for girls, and with the gradually increasing participation of women in political and other public affairs, there has been a change in values. Women knew a good deal about younger children. They were strongly motivated to improve their child rearing, too. As they became more confident in their role of participators in public enterprises, they began to demand corrections in public values. Quite practically, they sought to correct obvious ineffectualities in educational methods, and they began to express their opinions more fully with respect to the methods of discipline used in the home. Their way was the "new way." It gave recognition to the child's nature as a child; it was tolerant of childhood and did not demand early conformity or instant obedience. We do not mean to imply, of course, that there were no men who had a signal influence on the new views about dealing with children. There were, as witness Sigmund Freud and John Dewey.

The formation of battle lines was inevitable. The last half century has been a time of rapid cultural change for many reasons. It has created insecurity and uncertainty about values among even the strongest of our people. In the face of uncertainty, the "old way" often has had a sense of safe rightness. One could count on it. It worked in the past, and if the future looked dangerous, safety could be achieved by going backwards. Furthermore, the "new way" is feminine. It says, in effect, that men do not know everything, and especially that they often do not know best about children. So the battle line was drawn. Between men and women. Between the old and the new.

There have been many repercussions of the conflict. One of the most serious has involved the schools. The progressive movement which became widely publicized in the twenties and thirties was, in part, an attempt to take into account the motivation of young children. It was directed toward making the educative process fit the characteristics of the child. It was a revolt against the discipline-oriented restrictiveness of earlier educational methods. Acceptance of the new methods was slow, and their general philosophy met with a good deal of confused resentment both in and out of educational circles. When progressive education finally got mixed up with certain left-wing political views, its critics were able to find a rational basis for its rejection. But the impulse to reject had been aroused long before. It is still with us, most commonly displayed nowadays as an appeal to "get back to fundamentals."

Another area of social action in which the old and new have come in conflict is in the handling of juvenile delinquency. We mentioned in the first chapter that this was one of the first areas to be examined by students of the social process in America. The shift to contemporary methods of treating such disorders has been continuous, but it has been accompanied by agonized resistance from those who are still prepossessed with "strong discipline" as a panacea for all misdoing. Typical of this attitude was the recent statement of a municipal court judge in dismissing charges of brutality against the father of a fourteen-year-old boy: "I believe in the old-fashioned way"!

When two points of view clash, a few protagonists of each are likely to take exaggerated positions. So it has been with this present issue. In the hands of a few, the "new way" became distorted into a philosophy of *laissez faire* in which the parent abdicated all responsibility for controlling and guiding the child. There are parents who have been afraid to try to stop their children's destructive actions or painful attacks upon others, because they thought modern doctrine dictated that one should never frustrate or inhibit a child. The consequences of this practice were displayed in connection with the handling of aggression; the highly permissive mothers reported that their children were more aggressive in the home.

Similar extreme attitudes have occasionally invaded educational theory. We have seen a recent example in the case of a young school teacher who was just completing his teacher training. He could not be heard in class because his students talked so much; but he felt it would be "old fashioned" or "authoritarian" to ask them not to talk while he was trying to explain something to them!

Such an example is extreme, of course, and scarcely represents the position which has developed, during the last half century, as a revolt against the unthinking strictness of an earlier set of values. There are always corrections against too wide swings in any controversy, and it is interesting to note the trend toward "more standards" in much of the recent popular literature on child training. One gets the impression that the spokesmen for the "new way" went a little too far toward a permissive regimen, in their advice, and are now drawing back somewhat. Perhaps they have begun to note the kind of effect we discovered in connection with aggression.

We have been concerned, in this chapter, mainly with matters of guidance, not with the techniques of discipline. These latter are the subject for the next chapter. So far, what we have reported is evidence for the existence of a permissiveness-strictness dimension in respect to standards set up for the child's guidance. We turn next to the sanctions mothers have used for the enforcement of these standards.

CHAPTER NINE

Techniques of Training

As was emphasized in the last chapter, a distinction can be made between two aspects of the training process. One is the substantive—*what* is a child taught; the other is methodological—*how* is he taught. In our five chapters describing the major motivational systems, and mothers' treatments of them, we made no effort to distinguish these two aspects. In Chapter Eight, however, we limited our description largely to the substantive problem, and showed the importance of the descriptive dimension of strictness-permissiveness. In the present chapter we will consider the procedures by which the mothers attempted to teach whatever it was they wanted to teach.

Looked at across the first five or six years of his life, a child's development seems to be a fairly orderly process. He gives up modes of behavior that are no longer suitable, and acquires new actions appropriate for his age and his life conditions. Of course, children differ in their rates of development. Some infants crawl by the time they are six months old, others not until a year. Some children talk at eighteen months, while others take thirty. The range in the pace of normal development is wide. Yet a certain consistency of the sequence may be seen in nearly all children, and it seems as though some stages of development occur inevitably, with the parents doing very little to influence their unfolding.

Among some lower animals, infantile behavior disappears and

mature behavior appears without any direct training of the young organism. As part of their biological heritage, such animals automatically acquire the actions necessary for the next stage of life. There are species of insects, for example, in which each new generation goes through the same elaborate nest-building ritual without having had any opportunity to learn the skills involved. As the species of animal becomes more and more complex, and as it has to live with other animals in a social context, increasing control of its life is assumed by environmental happenings, including training by the parent generation. Tadpoles swim at a given stage in their life cycle without help from frogs. Mother birds, on the other hand, help to teach their offspring to fly; bears teach cubs to climb. Human mothers help their youngsters to walk.

At the level of utilizing large muscles, children's learning is not too complicated. Given physical and mental normality, most children learn to crawl, walk, smile, climb, run, talk, and grasp objects without much difficulty. On cursory analysis, it may appear that the child "just grows" into doing these things; and in truth, when children have reached appropriate physical and perceptual maturity, environmental conditions usually are right for these achievements to occur. But even in these relatively simple acquisitions, parents play a large part. They hold the baby's hands while he walks and maneuver him into putting one foot in front of the other. When he babbles, they single out a few sounds to babble back. And when one of these random sounds is even remotely suggestive of "Ma-Ma," the parent's effusive appreciation doubtless has its effects on the child.

Yet for most of the thousands of acts a preschool child has to learn, there is not even as much biological "steering" as there is for learning to walk or to make speech sounds. He must eat with a spoon and fork and even hold them in an unnatural way; at the same time, he must not spill his food. He must not hit his parents, make too much noise in the house, or fight with his brothers and sisters. He must dress himself, help with chores, and go to school.

The biological needs of human beings do not require any of these. A child would survive as well scooping up the food in his fingers, or shouting in the house, or leaving his clothes on the floor. The required actions are social dictates. Their acquisition obviously cannot be left to any inborn "unfolding" process. Parents are the conveyor belts of society—they transmit the culture and help make the child a sufficiently acceptable member of his social group that he may survive socially as well as biologically.

THE DIMENSIONS OF TRAINING

Whether she realizes it or not—and often she may not—a mother is working within a framework of four kinds of alternatives whenever she does something to influence her child's behavior. Three of these were discussed in a more general way in earlier chapters, but here we must bring them into focus in terms of just what kinds of choices mothers make in their child training. The fourth has to do with a quality of discipline that is especially important in the development of self-control.

1. *Action* vs. *learning.* This distinction was discussed in Chapter Seven, but we will reiterate the main point here. Much of a mother's time, especially when a child is very young, is spent in controlling him and caring for his immediate needs. She keeps him from danger, she protects the furniture, she gets the meal over with, she stops a fight. This is the control of *action;* it does not involve the future, but only the present. The alternative problem does involve the future. The mother must train the child; she must do things with him that change his potentialities for later actions. She tries to increase his independence, or decrease his antagonism toward his sister, or get him accustomed to going to the toilet before he has an accident. She is influencing the child's *learning.*

2. *Impelling* vs. *directing.* No matter whether she is dealing with action or learning, the mother must concern herself with two other matters. These are not alternatives, but two aspects of any behavior sequence. The child must have some impulsion to do whatever the mother wants him to do. He must have a *why* for any action. Perhaps he is hungry and can expect to be fed; or he may want greater autonomy, or independence, and see a chance to get it. Whatever the motive, action occurs only when some prospective sanction—positive or negative—exists. There must be an impelling stimulus.

At the same time, the mother must provide direction. The

child must know *what* she wants him to do. She may show him by example, or point out a model—a good one or a bad one—or she may reason with him. Somehow she must enable him to know what it is she is pressing him to do.

3. *Positive* vs. *negative controls*. So far as the control of ongoing action is concerned, a mother's aim is simply to start or to stop some kind of behavior by the child. On the positive side, she may offer rewards, or incentives; or she may try to put him in a good mood so he will ally himself with her and do things she wants him to do. On the negative side, she may try to stop what he is doing by the threat, or actual use, of punishment of various kinds—isolation, or ridicule, or spanking, or deprivation of privilege. Or she may simply attempt to distract him.

The permanent elimination of changeworthy behavior, and its replacement by more desirable and mature forms, i.e., the control of learning, offers a different problem. To effect elimination of a response requires that it no longer be rewarded, i.e., that it not be followed by a satisfying state of affairs. The strengthening of desirable behavior can occur only when a satisfying state of affairs does follow. It has been found that the introduction of punishment into the *learning* process (as distinct from action control) creates some difficulty, for punishment *after* an undesirable performance breaks up the child's activity but does not give direction toward any specific new behavior, and may produce an emotional state that interferes with the learning of the desired substitute behavior. Usually, punishment provides a fairly inefficient means of non-rewarding the changeworthy actions, and offers a strong sanction that tends to impel some new (but not specified) kind of action, perhaps mainly an avoidance of the punisher.

4. *Love-orientation* vs. *object-orientation*. Two general classes of threats or incentives can be distinguished. One has to do with material objects and the other with the mother's love and affection. On the positive or rewarding side, a mother can offer praise and the promise of maintaining a loving relationship with the child, or she can give more tangible rewards, such as candy, gold stars, money, toys, or permission to play with a prized object. On the negative or punishing (or non-rewarding) side, she can behave in similarly contrasting ways: she can isolate the child from her or withdraw her affection; or she can deprive him of

material objects (dessert, TV, going outdoors), or spank him.

These alternatives are only relative, of course, for it is doubtful that physical punishment or any other kind of discipline can be given a normal child without implying a loss of love, a temporary breaking of the affectional relationship. But as will be seen from some of the mothers' reports, there can be a choice of quite different positions with respect to how much of the object-oriented discipline is introduced into the training process.

In this present chapter, we will describe first the various *sanctioning* methods the mothers used, together with some conclusions they themselves reached as to the effectiveness of spanking, and then describe those training procedures which had as their main purpose the *directing* of children's behavior. These latter were the techniques for providing the guidance discussed in Chapter Eight. In other words, this chapter will describe those maternal behaviors that had to do with the direct control and teaching of the child. In the long run, of course, a child must develop his own internal controls of his actions—he must develop a conscience. The next chapter will deal with that problem.

THE POSITIVE SANCTIONS

There were two techniques reported that had the function of providing a satisfying state of affairs, i.e., a reward. One was *praise,* which is a symbolic reward, implying approval or affection. The other was the offering or promising of a material or *tangible reward,* like money or candy. Technically, both types of reward serve as reinforcers of preceding behavior. They are characterized by coming after the behavior, and marking it as acceptable, good. Mothers also used the anticipation of reward or praise as a training technique: "If you set the table, you can have an extra dessert." At the same time, after rewards and praise have become traditional through habitual usage, the threat of their withdrawal may become a form of threatened punishment. This will be discussed below under "deprivation of privileges."

Our information about mothers' use of techniques is of two kinds. We asked specific questions about each mother's use of a number of techniques. In addition, there were opportunities for mothers to discuss techniques at other points in the interview, when they were asked how they handled various child-training problems and incidents. Some mothers specifically disclaimed any use of rewards, saying that they thought it was too much like bribing the child for something he should do without incentive. Others had very elaborate systems of rewards. Following is an illustration of a mother who was rated somewhat below average in her use of rewards:

I. *Do you have any system of rewarding him for good behavior?*
M. *Why, yes—he gets our approval, but I don't pay him or give him a physical reward for being good. Now this morning, for instance, he was doing the dishes. He was perfectly willing, so I told him I was busy this morning, I had to go to the store for things, you know, would he like to do the dishes—yes, he would like to do dishes, and he did, because he doesn't have a child to play outdoors with as he should have; so he did the dishes. I was putting away the cookies and things, and whereas he almost never gets anything sweet in the middle of the morning, the fact that I gave him these few cookies was really quite a prize, because he's never given them between meals. I said, "Bobby, when you get those things done, here's a cookie," but it was in no way a bribe—he was already doing it.*
I. *Do you have any ways in which he can earn money?*
M. *Yes—no, I don't—we sometimes—well, we tried giving him an allowance you see, and I have found that it is not important to him. When it is important, we'll see that he has a small allowance and pay him for what he does. We don't pay them for everything they do. We think that they can contribute something, and the older ones, each one of them has had an allowance given as a trial, and when they've lost complete interest in it, I think it's just not time, so instead of keeping the money piling up, I just let it go. Bobby is in that stage as far as the allowance is concerned, and he does get paid for some things. But he does not get paid for emptying wastebaskets.*

In contrast, here is a mother who reported extensive use of rewards:

I. *Do you have any system of rewarding him for good behavior?*
M. *Yes, we have a check-out system, a little list of the things that they're supposed to do every morning—teeth, wash their face, dishes, beds, and room, and then they are checked off. And if they're done well, they get a star, and if it's just done, then it's just a check; and then the one that gets the largest number of stars every month, they get a fifty-cent reward, and it seems to work.*
I. *Do you have any ways that he can earn money besides that?*
M. *Yes, Jim gets an allowance of fifteen cents every week, but other than that, if I put him out to mind the baby, or any chores around the*

yard, I will give him an extra nickel or an extra ten cents there. But then for things that they want, they are supposed to save their allowance, or whatever money they have earned, to buy them with. We don't buy the little things they decide they want.

As may be seen in Table IX:1, mothers differed greatly in their use of tangible rewards. Some said they practically never employed them, while others used rewards as their major technique of training.

TABLE IX:1

EXTENT OF USE OF TANGIBLE REWARDS

1. Mother never uses rewards	12%
2. Rarely uses rewards	18
3. Sometimes uses rewards	21
4. Fairly often uses rewards	22
5. Frequently uses rewards	19
6. Regularly gives rewards for "good" behavior; elaborate system for earning money or points; believes rewards are effective; evidence that this is a major technique for the mother	6
Not ascertained	2
Total	100%

A recurrent theme in the mothers' comments was the notion that there is something bad or manipulative in giving children material rewards for their good behavior. This attitude is illustrated by the comments of these mothers:

A

M. *Well, I don't think we think of it in terms of rewards and punishment—we live and work together for the best interests of everybody concerned.*

B

M. *I haven't done any of that so-called bribing business, or any of that. I don't believe in it. If she has done something that she should, I thank her and tell her it was very nice and so forth, but I never could see that bribing business. I mean, I've seen too many cases of it where they just spoil the child till they wouldn't do a thing unless they were bribed.*

C

M. *What I do mostly is to try to teach him that good behavior is his own best reward. I don't ever want it to get to a point where a child feels he's good just to get something. There again, it's the same as school, not being given a nickel or a dime or pennies. I have tried the star system.*

I. *How did that work out?*

M. *He liked it. If I ask him how he feels he stands, up to date, some-times he'll say, "I don't think I'll get my gold star today," but guesses he should have a silver star or maybe a blue one. He's rather fair about that. On special occasions I have a surprise for him, not just for good behavior, but if I'm going out. I try to give him approval and make him feel the importance of being good rather than place it on a mercenary or lollipop basis, because in the long run that is what counts.*

If we may judge from these comments, a number of mothers felt that the use of rewards interfered with teaching the child to behave spontaneously as he was expected to behave, and kept him from learning to be good simply for the sake of being good.

An opposite view was expressed in the following comment, however; this mother felt that rewarding children increased the general attractiveness of good behavior:

I. *Do you have any system of rewarding her for good behavior?*

M. *Yes, I,—that's why I have done these things—that's why I am so liberal with them, because—to show them that life can be very lovely when you're nice and you don't make mother angry.*

We do not have detailed information on any changes the mothers may have made in the use of tangible rewards as the children grew older, though a number of mothers did comment that the use of specific rewards diminished. More general signs of parental approval took their place. In any case, the use of approving statements rather than, or in addition to, tangible rewards was already quite common when the children were of kindergarten age (see Table IX:2).

TABLE IX:2
EXTENT OF USE OF PRAISE

1. No use of praise	1%
2. Mother seldom praises	6
3. Occasionally praises, but very moderately	20
4. Moderate use of praise	28
5. Praises fairly often	29
6. Praises frequently, sometimes extravagantly, for many behaviors	12
7. Mother regularly praises, admires, shows affection for good behavior. Praises extravagantly, or for very wide range of behavior	3
Not ascertained	1
Total	100%

Typical of the mothers who used praise rarely was the mother who said:

M. *Oh, we don't praise him—I mean—we just assume that's the way it should be.*

The following comments illustrate the moderate use of praise by mothers who believed that praise can be helpful but that it has its dangers:

A

M. *Well, I feel more or less in the middle about it. I believe they should have some praise, not too much, but some to encourage them to go on and be good. I think they do need some praise because most adults do, too. Not to overdo it, though, because you can't tell what would come from it if you overdid it, how they'd act. Maybe they'd think they were better than other children, or something, if they got too much praise. But I think they should have some.*

B

M. *Well, I think there should be a middle way there. I don't think that you should praise them all the time. I think that you should expect a certain amount of good behavior from them. But if they do something that is real nice, that you didn't expect them to do—something that you really don't expect them to do and they do it—that's the time for them to be complimented. But there are a certain amount of things they should do anyway. She knows, for instance, what time she is to go to bed. If I might have to remind her once, she will go out and get ready for bed—that's expected. But supposing she decided to get to bed a little earlier—or started a little earlier so it wouldn't be so confusing or something like that—I will say, "That's nice, Sue. You started a little earlier, and now you're all done." Or if she is quiet in the morning, especially on a week end—they are inclined to be noisy, on the whole—and again because there are three of them, I think—and if they are extra quiet I will usually comment on that.*

A mother rated relatively high in her use of praise said:

M. *I think it is rather nice. I think everybody likes to get a little boost once in a while. I think Betty gets a fair amount of it in just a conversational way. I mean her father will come in and say, "You're the best girl today," and so forth; and then the boys will give her a bit of encouragement and praise over things that she's done. It is done conversationally and the way you feel. We have never done it with any purpose in making her feel that she is out of this world, but just like you would like anyone to say to you when you have done a wonderful job. I think everybody loves it.*

Why did some mothers use reward and praise so much, others so little? Possibly they had had different experiences with the effects of these methods. Some believed that too much reward and praise "spoiled" their children, and only made them self-centered and avid for more. Others felt that these methods, by enhancing a child's self-esteem and self-confidence, made him anxious to live up to the standards of behavior that were expected of him, and helped him to set high standards for himself.

In general, the mothers who chose to make a high use of either praise or tangible rewards were also above average in:

1. Warmth of affection they showed to their children.
2. Their satisfaction with being wives and mothers.
3. The esteem they felt for their husbands.
4. Their permissiveness for their children's sexual behavior.

These relationships suggest that the use of praise and tangible rewards are facets of some more pervasive characteristics of the mother's personality—symptoms of a generally satisfactory adjustment to her life situation.

At the same time, it is important to note some differences between the mothers who preferred one or the other of these rewarding techniques. There was virtually no correlation between the high use of praise and the high use of tangible rewards. (See Appendix Table D:22.) Mothers who used one method were no more likely to use the other than were mothers who did not.

Furthermore, the high use of *praise* was significantly (although not strongly) associated with the high use of *isolation* and the low use of *physical punishment* as methods of punishment, and with frequent use of *reasoning* and *pointing to good models* as methods of showing the child what behavior the mother wanted. In contrast, mothers who used *tangible rewards* a great deal also tended toward a high use of *physical punishment* and the *deprivation of privileges* as means of punishing the child.

These findings suggest a certain consistency in the choice of love-oriented *vs.* object-oriented methods of discipline. Mothers who gave material rewards for good behavior also took away material things and inflicted distinctively material pain for wrong-doing. Likewise, the mothers who praised and were affectionate for the child's good behavior used isolation for the bad. The importance of these relationships for the development of one type of behavior that illustrates self-control will be shown in the next chapter.

THE NEGATIVE SANCTIONS

Physical punishment

Punishment means creating an unpleasant situation for the child after he has done something he is not supposed to do. When the unpleasantness is in the form of actual pain, the experience is likely to prove memorable. In some ways, physical punishment is the prototype of all punishment, from the standpoint both of parents and of children. Children who have been spanked only a few times in their lives may nevertheless depict frequent spankings in their doll play, as though physical punishment were the most common device by which their anti-social impulses were held in check. Spankings are dramatic, and it is possible that once the ultimate sanction of physical force has been invoked by a parent, even mild pressures carry the potential threat of its further invocation.

There were enormous differences among the parents, according to the mothers' reports, in the frequency and severity with which physical punishment was used. A few said that they had never administered a bona fide spanking in the child's entire lifetime, although usually even these mothers admitted to a slap or two when their patience was sorely tried. For example, one mother who was much below average in her use of physical punishment said:

M. *I don't spank my children. I can't recall really spanking them. I have had occasion where, when I have wanted—felt the urge—to strike, and oh, sometimes when I've seen her temper and Jill is stamping around, and I'll say, "All right, upstairs you go." And she doesn't go right away, I'll just give her a little motion on her rear and that's about all. But you wouldn't call that a spanking. That's, well, it kind of lets my steam off a bit; it doesn't hurt, but she knows I mean business. And she doesn't recognize it through the pat on her bottom; she recognizes it in my tone.*

At the other extreme were families who used physical punishment as the primary technique of controlling the child:

A

I. *How often have you spanked Edward?*

M. *Pretty often—it might be every time I turn around. Over the week end he's the worst—I don't know if it's the fact he's not in school or what, but over the week end he gets unbearable. So maybe Sunday he will have the living daylights whaled out of him and snap him out of it for a week, and then next week end he just goes through the same process. Seems like every week he's got to get a good hard whaling . . . I'm not saying he's an angel for the week—you have to crack him all during the week, but not really have to turn him over and give him really a hard spanking.*

B

I. *About how often would you say he has been spanked in the last two weeks?*

M. *Twice, today and yesterday. There is one thing they have a great fear of—you don't have to spank them—all you have to do is handle it—and that is a switch. Any kind of a stick, any size, if you just hold it up. When I lived at my other house, there was a tree in back and I broke switches off, and I would just knock that switch against the side of the bed and he would get under the covers and he would behave. I found his bedroom littered with switches—every switch he could get his hand on, he broke into tiny pieces.*

C

I. *How often do you spank Janet?*

M. *I don't know how often, but I spank her when she needs it. As a rule it's not too often, but yet it's often enough that when she needs it.*

I. *Would you say how often—every week? Every month?*

M. *Oh, no, she gets spanked oftener than that. Some days she gets spanked two or three times in one day and another day or time she'll go two or three days without getting one. It all depends, but I couldn't really knuckle down to—well, say, it may be on the average of once a day.*

Our fieldworkers reported one or two instances of children's coming to kindergarten covered with welts and bruises from beatings they had received at home. This kind of thing was very, very rare, however, among the families we studied. More typical are the following reports:

A

I. *How often would you spank Helen?*

M. *I wouldn't consider a slap and a spanking the same.*

I. *What is the difference the way it happens?*

M. *A spanking is something that is for when she does something really terribly wrong—one Sunday she did kick up quite badly and she did* *get a spanking from her father and she has never gotten over it and I don't think he has either, but it was more of a good fit of temper at the time, and I think that was the only spanking she ever received; she has had her hands slapped.*

I. *You mean she has only had one real spanking?*

M. *One real spanking from her father. I have never really spanked her —I slap her hands—and I have slapped them harder than at other times.*

I. *Have you slapped her on the face or her legs?*

M. *I have slapped her on the legs. In fact, I have a stick and all I have to do is hold it up and they run.*

B

I. *How often do you spank Jim?*

M. *He used to get slapped very frequently and finally it was taking more out of me than it was out of him so I just stopped—he was deprived of the television set occasionally or sent to his bedroom. He's had two spankings now within the last month. I really got mad and I turned him over and spanked him with my hand on his bare bottom; that's the only punishment he's ever had.*

I. *How about your husband? How often does he spank him?*

M. *He still does like I used to, just reach out and wallop him, but he is really impatient with them. At the drop of a pin, he's just apt to slap Jimmy for saying something dumb which can't be helped with children. Jim is at a very silly age in some ways and I just tell him to stop being silly, that if he wants to speak to me to stop and think about it first, what he is going to say. But you have to be tolerant around children. He (her husband) loves them very much, and when he's in the mood he'll give them loads of time and attention and he's very sweet and understanding—the next minute he's just apt to be a bear but then he's the same way with me, and naturally, I'm older and I don't pay any attention to him.*

I. *How often has Jim been spanked in the last two weeks? You mentioned that you spanked him twice within the last month.*

M. *Both times came this week. Of course, I can't speak for my husband. I don't think he's slapped him too often but I know he hasn't spanked him, as I would have known about that. I can't say how often he might have slapped him.*

C

I. *How often have you spanked Bobby?*

M. *Oh, I don't know. I'd say he gets spanked good, I'd say about twice a week anyway. He may get scolded in between times more than that. But I spank him about twice. I've found with him punishing seems to be a lot better than spanking him. When I do spank him it's usually when I get too nervous myself, and I don't take time out to punish him and I'll just go ahead and spank him.*

As may be seen from Table IX:3, it was a rare child who had never been spanked at all, although the tendency for the majority was in the direction of infrequent spankings and not very severe physical punishment.

In making the ratings for Table IX:3 we took into consideration not only actual spankings but the parents' use of threats of physical punishment. There were a number of families who kept a switch or stick in view, and brandished it frequently to get compliance; they found they did not have to put it to actual use very often. Such families would be rated fairly high on the use of physical punishment nonetheless. Also, we asked how often the child had been spanked when he was younger—at two or three years of age. Therefore, the ratings in Table IX:3 took

TABLE IX:3

EXTENT OF USE OF PHYSICAL PUNISHMENT

1. Never uses physical punishment	1%
2. Has occasionally slapped hands—only one or two real spankings in child's lifetime	12
3. Spanked rarely (two or three times a year); occasional slaps	35
4. Fairly often slaps; occasional spankings	29
5. Fairly often spanks; some spankings severe	15
6. Frequent and severe spankings; major technique of controlling child	7
Not ascertained	1
Total	100%

into account earlier as well as current physical punishment. The extent of use at the two age periods was similar for the extreme cases: Parents who spanked very rarely when the child was younger were also infrequent spankers when the child was five years old, and those who spanked almost every day in the earlier period did the same currently.

In general, mothers reported that they themselves spanked the children more frequently than their husbands did. The practice of saving up a spanking for fathers to administer "when he comes home" was rare, at least for children of kindergarten age. Mothers did the spanking because they were on the scene. And often a spanking was the result of the mother's momentary anger and desperation rather than a calculated technique chosen because she felt it would do the most good. As a matter of fact, some mothers recognized that they spanked more as an outlet for their own feelings than for any other reason. When they were tired or irritable, they could be provoked into a spanking by behavior that would ordinarily call for much less drastic measures. To the question about frequency, three mothers said:

A

M. *Not very often, but I have spanked him, and I do so on occasion, and I must admit that the times when I spank him are the times when I'm worn out. For whatever reason—sometimes it's a good reason, and sometimes it's a bad one, and I suppose I shouldn't spank him when I'm cross, but occasionally I have spanked him when I was cross, and he knew it.*

B

M. *Every three hours—no, oh, I don't know. I don't particularly approve of it . . . when I haven't had enough sleep, I spank him. I don't use it as a punishment. I use it as a relief for me . . . I don't think it is particularly going to affect him, because he is a happy enough child so that I don't think he will be awfully affected by it.*

C

M. *Well, I wouldn't say there is a limit on it—I still maintain it's the feelings of the parents when something goes wrong. If it is an optimistic day for the parent, it . . . I don't think you can just go ahead and spank a child if you are calm, cool, and collected; that is really more or less being cruel. I think the only way you do it a little is if you are angry about something, and that is the way you give vent to your feelings.*

The effectiveness of spanking. Perhaps one of the most long-standing controversies in the field of child training has been over whether it is desirable to use physical punishment with children. While the "spare the rod and spoil the child" maxim no longer has the following it apparently had a half century ago, there are many parents who believe that the judicious application of the hand to a child's bottom will work wonders when other efforts fail. It may be seen from Table IX:4 that there were great differences of opinion on this subject among the mothers of our study.

The interviewers asked the question: "How much good does it do to spank?" Following are some representative comments:

A

M. *Personally, I don't think it does any good. Because, as I said before, if you take away a privilege, it seems to have more effect on her than* *a spanking would. Five minutes after a spanking is over with, it's forgotten about.*

B

M. *Well, the few times that we have tried everything else . . . talking to him and punishing him by taking things away from him, or putting him up in his room—I finally resort to a spanking, and a spanking helps.*

C

M. *I don't think it does a bit of good. I think you can reason with a normal intelligent child. I don't feel that spanking does any good at all. I mean, I haven't had occasion to use it in the last year.*

D

M. *Oh, it worked, it worked . . . my impression is that children need something . . . to know that this is something to make them mind. I think you need something like that in order to train children.*

E

M. *Well, to be truthful with you, I don't think it does any good. When I revert to spanking, I often feel that I let down on my own end. And I don't really feel that it does the child any good, but I have found that if I could talk to him or deprive him of other things, it goes a lot farther.*

TABLE IX:4

"How Much Good Does It Do to Spank?"

1. Does good, no reservations	26%
2. Does good, some reservations	21
3. Good in some ways, bad in others	8
4. Does no good, with reservations	18
5. Does no good	22
Never spanks or not ascertained	5
Total	100%

The meaning of "How much good does it do?" These excerpts illustrate the diversity of ways in which the mothers interpreted the phrase about how much good it does to spank. Some thought of the immediate effects; they were oriented toward what we have called the control of action. Others considered the strength of the sanction that spanking imposed; they were impressed by the longer term effects it gave, and the implication of final authority that it carried. Still others evaluated it as to what kind of new behavior it produced in the child, whether desirable or undesirable.

In many of the replies to this question, however, there was some consideration given to the problem of aggression. Spanking was often recognized as a form of parental aggression toward the child, a blowing off of steam; one of the criteria mothers seemed to use in judging whether the procedure was effective or not was the extent to which it elicited counter-aggression from the child. If the child responded to spanking by feeling *hurt* rather than *angry,* the mother was a little more likely to consider that spanking had a good effect. In other words, if she saw her child as re-acting non-aggressively, and as showing signs of guilt and of grief about her punitiveness, she concluded that spanking was worth while.

In the interview we asked the question: "How does he act when you spank him—does it seem to hurt his feelings, or make him angry, or what?" About two thirds of the mothers described only one characteristic response. If we consider this two thirds as a reasonably "pure" sample, and work with it alone, we find that 72 per cent of the children displayed "hurt feelings," and 19 per cent were "made angry or cross." To return now to the question of how much good it does to spank: of the former group (those who felt hurt), 54 per cent of the mothers felt spanking did some good, while from the latter (angry) group, only 43 per cent thought so. The difference is too small to have much signif-icance, but it does suggest that a "hurt" reaction was considered more satisfactory by mothers than an "angry" reaction.

As might be expected, the parents who reported that physical punishment did the child good tended to be the ones who used it a lot. Perhaps this was just a matter of rational consistency: "if you use it, you think it is good"—or vice versa. There are some other facts worth noting, however, and, provisionally, we can use this evaluation of effectiveness, given by the mothers themselves, to discover what the conditions were that made physical punish-ment useful as a disciplinary technique—or at least *seemed* to in the eyes of the mother.

Spanking with reasoning. In terms of the learning process, we would expect that physical punishment would work best if it is coupled with techniques which clearly label for the child (*a*) *what the undesired action is* the mother is punishing him for, and (*b*) *what she wants him to do* instead. The most effective punishment, in other words, should combine the two elements of stopping undesirable actions and starting new ones. Thus we should expect to find that the mothers who reported that spanking did their children good were the ones who used *reasoning* in combination with the physical punishment. We will describe the technique of reasoning in a later section of this chapter, but here we must make brief anticipatory use of the scale for comparison with physical punishment.

Mothers who used reasoning extensively tended not to use physical punishment very much ($r = -.34$), but there was a large enough group of parents who used both these techniques more than the average amount to permit the appropriate comparison. Table IX:5 shows that our deduction is borne out: frequent physical punishment was reported more effective by those mothers who combined it with extensive use of reasoning than by those who did not.

TABLE IX:5

EFFECTIVENESS OF PHYSICAL PUNISHMENT WHEN COMBINED WITH REASONING

Technique	Percentage of Mothers Who Reported That Spanking Did Their Children Good	Number of Cases
When physical punishment was frequent:		
High use of reasoning	57%*	68
Low use of reasoning	38%	57
When physical punishment was infrequent:		
High use of reasoning	40%	125
Low use of reasoning	39%	33

* The difference between this figure and each of the other three is significant: $p < .05$. The relationship between the use of reasoning and the effectiveness of frequent punishment is curvilinear. There was a small group of mothers who relied especially heavily upon reasoning but who reported that spankings were relatively *ineffective*. This group is too small to influence the size of the above percentages very much, but there is probably some factor hidden here that we have not been able to isolate from the data we have available.

If we can re-create what happens in these homes, it may go like this: Jimmy is writing on the wall. His mother sees him and spanks him. He stops his crayoning; as a matter of fact, he stops everything to cry. Then the mother tells him why he was punished, that writing on walls is forbidden. Now he knows clearly what it is that he cannot do. There is little chance for him to misinterpret the spanking and to think he got it for taking his sister's crayons, or for standing on the chair to reach up on the wall. He knows now that it was *the writing on the wall* that was wrong for him to do.

This labeling seems to gain its importance from the fact that language provides a relatively quick way for a child to make a backward connection between the two events—from the spanking backward to his own action. In general, research on lower animals has shown that this kind of backward learning is very inefficient. A white rat that is punished after making a wrong

turn in a maze does not quickly learn to avoid that turn unless there is a reward for making some other turn. But a rat does not have language with which to bridge the gap in time between the act and its consequences. When a child is told in words what the "error" he made was, he appears to learn backward more quickly. We suspect that this is why a somewhat larger number of mothers who used reasoning with spanking found the punishment technique more effective than did mothers who did not use reasoning.

Warmth and physical punishment. It is worth considering what there is about physical punishment that produces disciplinary effects that mothers like. It hurts, certainly. But few parents actually beat their children so intensely that the physical pain is unbearable. What seems to hurt more is the blow to the child's self-esteem and the interruption of the free flow of his parents' love and affection. He has done something of which the parents disapprove, and at least for some children this disapproval is very difficult to bear.

If the child's parents are normally cold and unaffectionate, explicit evidence of this fact by punishment is nothing new to him. But if he is accustomed to warmth and affection, punishment that jeopardizes the usually pleasant relationship is harder to tolerate. Punishment signifies to the child that his mother at the moment does not love him. The thought can be more painful than a dozen blows. In a sense, then, spanking by a usually warm parent is more severe punishment to the child than spanking by a cold parent. At least, the child has more to lose by it.

If the punishment is more severe, will it be more effective? Possibly so, although probably it is not the severity *per se* which makes the difference. The child who usually has a warm relationship with his parents is motivated not only to avoid pain but to conform to what they want him to do in order to get back their good will. This suggests the possibility that physical punishment by a warm, affectionate parent would be more effective than that by a cold, hostile parent. There is evidence to support this notion, as may be seen in Table IX:6. Frequent physical punishment did the child most good, according to the mothers' reports, when it occurred in the context of affectional warmth.

A graphic description of the situation was given by one mother, who said in answer to the interviewer's question:

I. *How does he act when you spank him—does it seem to hurt his feelings or make him angry, or what?*
M. *It hurts his feelings. I think Billy feels you don't love him then— that's how it affects him. He'll come back to you and say, "I love you, Mummy."*
I. *How do you react to this?*
M. *Oh, I give him a hug; I love him, too. I've told him and Jean if I get very cross and spank and say something cross to them that, "Even though I'm very cross, I still love you." I tell them to remember that when I am cross.*

Another fact about the influence of warmth has to do with who did the spanking. Each family was characterized according to whether the father or the mother was the usual disciplinarian, or whether both were equally likely to punish, depending on which saw the misdemeanor first or was nearest at the moment. One point must be kept in mind in connection with this scale: mothers are usually home all day to do the disciplining, while fathers, as disciplinarians, probably provide, in most cases, only a small proportion of the over-all punishment. (The father's warmth was rated from the interview, also; since the rating was based on information given by his wife, the measure is obviously more indirect than the measure of the mother's warmth.)

TABLE IX:6

EFFECTIVENESS OF PHYSICAL PUNISHMENT IN RELATION TO THE AFFECTIONAL
WARMTH OF THE MOTHER

Technique	Percentage of Mothers Who Reported That Spanking Did Their Children Good	Number of Cases
When physical punishment was frequent:		
Mother relatively warm	66% *	65
Mother relatively cold	43%	111
When physical punishment was infrequent:		
Mother relatively warm	42%	101
Mother relatively cold	41%	98

* The difference between this figure and each of the other three is significant: $p < .01$.

In families in which the father was warmer toward the children than the mother, spanking slightly more often "did good" if the father, rather than the mother, did the disciplining. Conversely, if the mother was warmer than the father, spanking tended to be more effective if the mother did it. (See Appendix Table D:23.) If both parents were relatively cold, it did not make much difference who did the punishing. But if both parents were warm, spankings in households where the father was the disciplinarian seemed to be more effective than those in households where the mother was usually responsible. Why should this be? We can only speculate that, because fathers are less often home than their wives, their spanking is novel; the child has less opportunity to develop a tolerance for it. Mothers often complained that because they were with the child so much, they had little influence on him, whereas the father's novelty worked in his favor.

Whatever the reason, one conclusion seems clear: the effectiveness of physical punishment in making the child conform to expected standards of behavior depended on the warmth of the child's emotional relationship to the chief punisher. When the chief punisher was a usually warm person, the punishment was more effective, in the sense that the mother observed that it seemed to "do good."

The rejecting or unhappy mother. These various comparisons have been made by examining some correlated characteristics of the mothers' reports as to whether spanking seemed to be a good method of discipline. There is one other question to be considered. By and large, mothers who spanked frequently said that the method was effective; hence they continued their use of it. However, it must be pointed out that there was a sizable group of mothers who hit and slapped their children very often, yet did not think that this punishment was effective. Of the 379 mothers in the study, 66 were frequent spankers who nevertheless deplored the technique.

Why did these mothers resort to a method which, by their own report, did no good? We have already seen a clue to their behavior: the fact that some mothers spanked more as an outlet for their own feelings than because of a belief in the training value of what they were doing. Perhaps the source of at least *some* of these mothers' impulses to punish lay in some aspect of their lives other than the particular action of the child that called for punishment. There is support for this from two additional findings. First, mothers who spanked frequently, even though they thought it ineffective, were rated as having less *self-esteem* than mothers who punished equally often but thought it did some good ($p < .01$). They held themselves in lower esteem as wives, as women, and as mothers. They tended to deprecate themselves in many spheres of behavior and to lack self-confidence. Specifically, they worried more about whether they were doing a good job of bringing up their children ($p < .05$).

Second, these mothers showed more evidence of *rejecting* their children. Among the relatively small group of mothers whose interviews showed some elements of rejection, there were more mothers who used physical punishment extensively even though they felt it did no good (28 per cent) than there were among the mothers who fully accepted their children (13 per cent).

Deprivation of privileges

One of the commonest ways of producing an unpleasant experience for a child is to take away something he values. This can be an important sanction on his behavior, especially if the object is withheld until the desired changes in his behavior have taken place.

Deprivation was widely used by these mothers. A few levied fines against a child's allowance. Others deprived him of dessert at dinnertime. Others refused to take him with them on some interesting expedition. Quite commonly, children were deprived, for disciplinary reasons, of the pleasure of watching a favorite television program. Or the parent might make the child come indoors and stay away from his playmates—a punishment that more frequently followed a quarrel among the neighborhood children. As may be seen from Table IX:7, there was considerable variation among the families in the frequency of their use of deprivation as a technique for controlling their children.

Examples of *infrequent use of deprivation* are seen in the following comments:

A

M. *A couple of times they've gone too far on their bicycles and they've gone to bed when they came home. It's only happened about two times. With my children, depriving never was a hardship. It's a waste of time, because it won't bother them. From the few times I've ever done it they've never asked for the things back.*

B

I. *Do you ever deprive him of something as a way of disciplining him?*
M. *No, I don't think I have ever done that—although sometimes that is a very good thing. I don't think I have ever done that with Bruce. I have with my older boy, after giving him repeated warnings, and he still continued in his conduct. I have kept him home even from a school party, and all the neighbors told me I was the meanest woman in the neighborhood. They said, "You mean to tell us that when it comes to Halloween night, you're not going to let him go to the Halloween party?" and I said, "That's exactly what I mean."— "You're not going to give in at the last minute?" and I said, "Well,*

TABLE IX:7

EXTENT OF USE OF DEPRIVATION OF PRIVILEGES

1. Never uses deprivation	4%
2. Rarely uses, perhaps once or twice in child's life	11
3. Occasionally uses, but not a popular technique	23
4. Sometimes deprives privileges; may be used a few times for extended period, or fairly often briefly or only threatened	28
5. Fairly often uses deprivation, sometimes for extended periods	20
6. Frequent use. Deprives child of something he wants very much; preferred technique	10
7. Very frequent use. Deprives of dearly prized things for relatively long periods of time	2
Not ascertained	2
Total	100%

that is the worst thing I could possibly do, would be to hold it and then give in and then the correction would mean nothing at all."
I. *How did it happen you have given it up?*
M. *I haven't given it up yet, but I haven't found an instance where it would apply with Bruce. I don't think he has been really repetitious in his offenses.*

The following mothers used about the *average amount of deprivation:*

A

I. *Do you ever deprive Hank of something he wants as a way of disciplining him?*
M. *Yes, I take television away from him, but not actually going anywhere or doing anything, because he doesn't go anywhere. Like some children, if they go to the movies, their parents will say, "You can't go to the movies," and that's the way they punish them, but see I haven't reached that as far as going anywhere. If we go away in the summer, we take him with us, and I don't feel that I should stay home just to punish him, as I don't go enough. If I were on the go all the time that would be different.*
I. *How often do you do this—deprive him of something he wants as a way of punishing him?*
M. *Well, not all the time, but if he does it a little while, keeps it up, and I see that he is not going to obey me, then I'll go right in and shut the television off, and I'll say, "Now you let that stay shut off," and then he comes to me in a little while and asks if he can have it, and I say, "Are you going to repeat what you did?" and I do give him a chance very often.*

B

M. *Oh, if he went out, I would deprive him of the privilege of going out to play, if I asked him not to leave the yard, or not to go a certain* *place, if he went, and then I had to go and chase him; then the next time he wanted to go out I would say, "No, you can't go out, Ted, for the simple reason that I haven't the time or the strength to chase you, and I have to have my meals ready, and if I'm looking for you, I can't get the meals." I try to explain why. Neither of my children have been such hearty eaters that depriving them of food was much of a punishment for them—it would be to some children I know, but it would never be to John or Ted, I don't think.*

The following mothers were *above average* in their tendency to take something away from the child as a form of punishment:

A

I. *What are the things you would deprive Susan of as a way of disciplining her?*
M. *We don't let her watch her programs and she misses her ice cream, as she likes ice cream, and we tell her she is not going to get it.*
I. *How often would you do this?*
M. *We do it quite often. I think that is our main way of disciplining her. It comes up once a day anyway because we have that problem of eating and we have to use something almost every day.*

B

I. *About how often do you do this?*
M. *Well, for instance, today, she wanted ice cream in the worst way, and I said, no, she couldn't have it. Well that bothered her very much, so she didn't eat her meal. I had a good reason of why I was depriving her of it. And then she forgot about it. And tonight before going to bed, she wanted a piece of her Easter candy; she wasn't allowed to have it. I said she wasn't allowed to have it because she didn't eat her supper, but her father did turn around and he told her if she selected which hand he had a candy in, she could have it. That was going against me.*

C

I. *Do you ever deprive Linda of something she wants as a way of disciplining her? Can you give me an example?*
M. *Yes, we always do. If there has been some disobedience or a fresh remark or answer that they give you sometimes, we will take something away from her—we'll deprive her of a visit someplace or playing outdoors with the children for a while or something like that.*

It is interesting to note what privileges were denied. It is a sign of the times, no doubt, that nearly half of the mothers (45 per cent) said they used television as a tool to get good behavior, withholding it as a punishment or threat of punishment. The following remarks are typical:

M. *He is very fond of television and if it is something real bad we will take the television away from him, but that is the last resort because he is so fond of TV. It is like eating to him.*

Another mother said, in answer to the question of how much good it did to deprive the child of TV:

M. *Lots of good.*
I. *How often do you do that?*
M. *Well, I'll take it away probably for a couple of days, and then he's good for 3 or 4 weeks; and then if he's done it again, I'll take it away longer.*

Denying desserts follows deprivation of TV as a not very close second (19 per cent), followed by toys (11 per cent) and play-mates (7 per cent).

An argument against the use of deprivation of privileges was given by one mother, who thought that the punishment should be related to the crime, and that withheld privileges are often extrinsic to the misdemeanor being punished.

M. *Perhaps if she is playing with something, I would take it away and she might want it. I try always to have the punishment related to what is happening rather than say, "I will take this away if you do something." It isn't in any way related, and then she doesn't know what I am going to take away from her next.*

The following excerpt indicates another argument against deprivation of privileges—that the follow-through may be harder on the mother than on the child.

M. *I never deprive him of anything that's going to make a hardship on me. Just because if you say, "You can't do this," and it's going to inflict a hardship on the mother to do it, I don't think that's right, and if you can't carry it through; I think whatever you should deprive him of—if you're going to deprive him of something—that should be carried through. So that it would be a hardship on the child but not on the parent.*

If the mother shuts off the television set, for instance, or refuses to let the child play with his playmates, he is likely to cry, or follow her around asking what he can do to amuse himself. The mother must then drop what she is doing to deal with him; in the end, she may be the more punished of the two. An example in point: a mother took away the child's dessert because of something he had done earlier in the day. But when he knew he would not get his dessert, he was not interested in eating the rest of his dinner, and refused to do so. So his mother had to worry about the consequences of his poor appetite. A similar problem was mentioned in an earlier chapter, the case of a mother who was trying to cure her child of bed-wetting. She kept him in the house away from his playmates for a week as punishment for wetting his bed. But then she decided that he was getting pale and listless from lack of exercise and fresh air. A good many mothers had learned to be very judicious in their use of deprivation as a means of controlling and training their children, lest the punishment have unintended consequences that were worse—for them—than the original misdemeanor.

Withdrawal of love

The subtlest of all the varieties of punishment we attempted to measure was punishment by the withdrawal of love. Information about the explicit use of this technique was difficult to obtain in the interview. For one thing, it is an intangible kind of behavior, quite different from the active and definite imposition of deprivation or physical punishment. Often it seems to be expressed more by a *lack* of responsiveness to the child than by any direct or positive action. Furthermore, mothers seemed to have considerable reluctance to acknowledge the use of such a weapon. Most of them could not see themselves telling a child that they did not love him, or did not want him around, or wished he would go away. Saying such things openly to one's child was strongly disapproved by most of the mothers. Even when they spanked their children, many of them made a special point of saying that the spanking did not mean that "Mommy doesn't love you." Nevertheless, certain attenuated forms of withdrawal of love were often employed, and because of its potential importance for the development of conscience, it warrants discussion even though our measures of its usage proved quite unsatisfactory. Indeed, only about half the interviews could be rated on the extent to which the mothers used this method. Table IX:8 shows the results of this rating.

Such withdrawal or withholding of love takes a variety of forms. The mother may simply look coldly at the child; she may turn her back, or refuse to listen to what he is saying; she may tell him she does not want to look at him until his face is smiling and pleasant. Or she may put him in a separate room, with the implication that he cannot be accepted in the family circle until he has stopped being "naughty." She may use a threat of separation from her, such as that she might have to go away and leave him unless he behaves better, or that she might have to send him away. She may tell him that he is making his mother unhappy, or is hurting her feelings, or is making her want to cry, with the implication that only by being good can he restore the happy loving relationship between them. All these actions, on the mother's part, we regard as manifestations of one underlying process: the mother is indicating to the child that her warmth and affection toward him are conditional on his good behavior.

TABLE IX:8

EXTENT OF USE OF WITHDRAWAL OF LOVE

1. Never uses. Mother denies explicitly, and no instances reported	3%
2. Slight use. One or two instances given, but positive evidence that it is not frequent	23
3. Moderate use. Several instances given, but no indication of special emphasis	14
4. Considerable use. Several instances with emphasis	8
5. Much use. Usual technique of control—special emphasis	2
Not ascertained	50
Total	100%

The following excerpts illustrate some of the differences in degree and kinds of withdrawal of love. The first is from the interview of a mother who explicitly disclaimed scolding her child in any way that would imply withdrawal of love:

M. *I definitely disapprove of "You can't be my child" or "I will have to send you away!" That is absolutely horrible. I'd never say that, no matter how much I was vexed at the time.*

And these examples are from the interviews of mothers who did withdraw love from their children, some consciously and some unconsciously, as part of the process of discipline.

A

M. *He'll cry. The minute you speak to him, he'll cry. Like, now that you've brought that up, the day before yesterday, I was over next door talking to the woman; and I came back and my son Stephen was crying. The little boy next door said, "I was standing near the door and Steve put a piece of paper on top of the gas stove and turned the gas on and the paper all burned up on the stove." I said, "Did you, Steve?" He always has a bad habit of putting his hand to his mouth. I says,*

"Steve, when you talk to me, put your hand down. I don't want to hear you talking mumbling. Take your hand away from your face. It isn't nice."

He stood there and I says, "Now don't deliberately lie to me. What did you do?" I saw the paper—little, tiny ashes up on top of the sill. He says, "I put that paper on the gas and I burned it." I says, "You go upstairs and I don't want to see you anymore today. I just don't want to see you. If you're going to be bad, I don't want you around me at all."

I found that if I scold him too much, he'll sulk; and if after I've scolded him and I see he's trying to act a little better, I will take him in my arms, and I'll say, "Now, Steve, you know that's wrong. You shouldn't do it. Mommie has talked and talked and talked. You want me to get a sore throat and go to the hospital and not be around here anymore?" He says, "No." I said, "Well, don't have me talking so much."

B

I. *Would you imagine now that you are scolding Tommy for something he has done that you don't want him to do. What would you say to him?*
M. *Most of the time I say to him, Tommy, now stop it. You're a bad boy when you do something like that. And Mommy doesn't like bad boys." And he'll turn around and ask me if I love him. I'll say, "Yes, I love you, but I don't like you." He tries to figure that one out, but he can't.*

C

I. *What do you do when he acts like that?*
M. *Well, I'd probably yell good and loud and just simply open the door to his room and throw him in bodily and leave him there. I'd tell him he was terrible, just a mean boy and I'm not proud of him. I might say I hate him the way he is acting.*

D

I. *When you are scolding her, what else might you say?*
M. *It's hard to think.*
I. *Do you warn her about what you might do if she doesn't behave?*
M. *Yes, in fact I've used an awful threat with her at times, not recently but when she'd say that she didn't like me, I wasn't a nice mommy, she wished she could live with Gertrude or something like that. I'd say: "Yes, you go ahead, I don't have to keep you either, Carol; I'm going to bring you back to Dr. Phillips and he can find another mommy for you." She almost got hysterical then; she really believed that I was going to take her back to the hospital and she would be sent to some other mommy.*

I. *She would be upset by it?*
M. *Oh, yes, she would scream: "Don't take me back, don't take me back!"*

E

I. *What do you say to her when you are scolding her?*
M. *Well, I usually ask, "Why?" and "Didn't I tell you not to do so-and-so?" We usually start with "Why," and "Why don't you remember," and, "All right that'll be all there'll be to it. You just go up to your room and stay there and I'll talk with you later about it." Or, "I don't want to talk to you; I just don't want to have anything to do with you, that's all."*

F

I. *Do you ever say: "I'll have to send you away?"*
M. *No, I don't say that because that brings on a terrific—well, I might have said, "I'll send you away with Nanna." That is, go to Fall River to our other home. Which wouldn't be outside the family, but would be away from me. But not to send them away with another child. I don't use that either. Because I know it'll bring on a terrific rain of tears. I have said "away," but they know I mean Fall River, you see. "You'll have to go away with Nanna, because I just can't have you around if you're going to act that way."*

It will be recalled, from the chapter on dependency, that one effect of using withdrawal of love appeared to be an increased emotional dependency in the child. The last excerpt above gives a graphic expression of this outcome.

Isolation

Closely related to withdrawal of love is the practice of sending a child to his room when he has been naughty. When the mother does this with the statement that she does not want him or does not want to see him, the implication is that isolation is a means of denying love to the child. If the child is sent to his room so that he cannot go out to play with his friends, the punishment has the connotation of depriving him of a privilege. Isolation must be distinguished from restraint, i.e., the procedure whereby the mother permits the child to be with people, but makes him stand in a corner or sit on a chair. The criterion for isolation is sending the child away from people; his being alone is the punishment.

No specific questions were asked in the interview concerning the frequency of use of isolation as a technique. About five sixths of the mothers mentioned it spontaneously, however, and the extent of its usage is indicated in Table IX:9.

TABLE IX:9

EXTENT OF USE OF ISOLATION

1. None. Mother says explicitly she does not use isolation	0%
2. Slight use of isolation	20
3. Moderate use. No indication that it is an effective or frequent technique	29
4. Considerable use	24
5. Much use, and mother considers it effective	12
Not ascertained. No instances of use reported; no evidence that mother does *not* use it	15
Total	100%

Some examples of the conditions under which a child was likely to be sent to his room for misbehavior are given below:

A

I. *What do you say to her when you are scolding her?*
M. *Ah* (laughs)—*differently with the different offense. If she is just— just pert, I would say, "That isn't very nice; I am sure you didn't mean it"—and if she was very fresh she would have to be sent to her room. Or if she was fresh to her grandparents—THAT to me, I think, is worse than to be fresh to someone outside the family.*

B

M. *For instance, the other day she came in and wanted to know if she could go over to Jane's house—they had been playing together all afternoon and this was about quarter to five—and I said no, it was too late. She went out into the back hall and then came in and said, "You old stupid thing, I am going," and I said, "No, Judy, you can't go." She slammed the door—and really slammed it. I called her back and she said, "No, I won't." I said, "You come back here this minute"— her little friend was here all the time—I said, "Judy, you take your clothes off and you go up to your room and don't come down until you are a nice girl and apologize to Mummy."*

She wasn't going to do that and I told Jane to go home. Finally she did get her things off—slammed upstairs and slammed around up there for a while—and about half an hour later and everything was kind and peaceful. She didn't apologize and I didn't insist. Usually the way I do cope with it is to send her to her room and she usually calms down. I think it is just being exposed to children, since she went to kindergarten, and seeing their actions and trying out things they do.

C

M. *Well, for either of those things, she would be punished either by going to her room or giving up something that she wanted to do. I probably would talk to her, and if she immediately showed signs of being very sorry for it, she wouldn't be punished so much. But if she were defiant, I think I would keep her in her room for quite a while.*

D

M. *Well, my punishment has been isolation for most things. I just tell him if he can't be nice around people, that we'll have to put him off by himself. I think spanking very often only irritates him and only makes him naughtier. I have spanked him. There have been times when I've given him a sharp rap when he did something that I thought was rather naughty. In fact, two mornings ago at the table, the first thing I did was to give him a little rap when he kept doing this kicking. He had a new pair of shoes and he had very heavy heels and the person across got kicked on their shins. And I gave him a sharp little rap, but that didn't seem to work. It did bring him up short and he stopped it for the moment, but he did it again. Then we took him out of the room.*

These examples suggest that isolation was rather commonly used when the child was "fresh" or "saucy," or was guilty of other forms of interpersonal aggression. Often it seems to have been the final disciplinary act in a sequence of troubles between the mother and child. We saw earlier that the parent's efforts to control one unacceptable action on the part of the child sometimes led to a sequence of new problems. For instance, the mother finds a crayon mark on the wall. She begins to scold the child for it, and he says he didn't do it. Now she is faced with two problems: the original wall-marking, and the child's telling an untruth. Or another example: she may take away a television program as punishment for the child's failure to carry out some assigned task. The child becomes angry and defiant over this restriction, and calls his mother a "mean old stupid Mommy." She may regard this defiance as worse than his original misdemeanor, and feel she has to punish for this new lapse as well.

It was in the later stages of these discipline sequences that the mother was most likely to isolate the child. This procedure served to prevent the sequence from developing any further; it removed the child from his target for retaliatory aggression. It also saved the mother from having to deal with some of the later stages of the sequence; if the child, in the privacy of his own room, kicked at something, or muttered angry things about his mother, she was not there to see or hear it, and was not required to take action.

THE DIRECTING OF BEHAVIOR

The discussion so far has been with respect to the sanctioning aspect of discipline; that is, the mother's methods of providing the *impelling* kind of stimulation to action. These are of two main kinds. One involves the offering of attractive incentives to start the action, and the arranging of satisfying consequences to reinforce it once it has occurred. The examples of this positive approach that we have discussed were the use of tangible rewards and praise. The other kind of impelling stimulation involves punishment of "bad" behavior, provided for the purpose of changing the child's actions or extinguishing his tendency to behave in that way. We can turn now to two examples of the other aspect of training, namely, the ways in which the mother directs the child's behavior, showing him what she does or does not want him to do.

Modeling

In positive modeling, the mother points to an example of the kind of behavior she wants the child to acquire. There is negative modeling, too, of course—pointing out examples of how *not* to act. In positive modeling, the mother usually tries to take advantage of the child's tendency to copy people he especially admires and wants to be like. The model may be an older brother or sister, an outstanding child in the neighborhood or school, a fictional hero, or the parents themselves.

During the interview, we asked specifically about the use of this technique. Some excerpts will illustrate the ways in which mothers reported its use.

A

I. *Do you use it in table manners or anything like that?*
M. *Yes, that's what it was. Like sitting at the table and eating nicely. I have often said to her, "You don't see Mummy and Daddy using their hands to eat their food," and such remarks. If she were going to*

do something she shouldn't, like jumping on the bed, I have often said that.

I. *Who else do you hold up as an example—her older brother, other relatives, grandparents, playmates?*

M. *I hold a little cousin of hers up, a little girl. She is older than Catherine, and she is a little lady, and all I have to do is say, "You don't see Betty act like that"—"You don't see Betty do this." She really looks up to Betty, herself, because she is such a little lady.*

B

I. *In training Jimmy do you ever say, "Your mummy and daddy do it this way?"*

M. *Sometimes, but I am more inclined to say, "Bill," because the respect and worship of the older brother, I find, is more a model for him—maybe it is because it is closer to his size. I think that he responds better when Bill is given for an example than when we are, although I sometimes find occasion to say, "That's the way we do it, and even though you are just a child, that is what you're aiming for; you want to learn to do it the same way, because you're growing up, too."*

I. *Under what circumstances would you use that?*

M. *If it is something that is more typical of the future, of an adult—I can't think of an example right now—but if the situation warranted it, and he had seen us do it.*

I. *Who else do you hold up as an example besides his older brother?*

M. *Just ourselves, but mainly the older brother, and if the occasion would warrant, then I would casually mention other children—not specifically, but in general—that we like to within reason follow the things that we should do; and therefore, I might say, if it is something that might happen in school, and I'd say, "Naturally you don't want to be entirely different from the other children; if you are supposed to do thus and so, naturally you want to do it, too. You can do things that you think yourself, you have a chance to do that when you're alone, but when you are with other people, you have to do pretty much what the group has to do."*

Some mothers felt strongly that referring to models is a poor technique. They did not want the child to feel that he can learn what is right and wrong by watching what other people do; rather, they wanted him to learn to do what is right *regardless* of what other people do. In addition, some parents felt that there is an element of bragging in a parent's telling a child to do as his elders do; they did not want the child to develop the notion that his parents were infallible, and then be disillusioned later. Some of these sentiments are illustrated in the following comments:

A

I. *In training Burt, do you explain to him that "Your mommy and daddy do it this way?"*
M. *No, we usually don't. I don't think we are terribly good examples, but if we are not (good examples) we try and show how it hurt us, and wish we had been better.*

B

I. *In training Ann do you ever say, "Your mother and daddy do it this way?"*
M. *No, I don't think so, because I don't think you can compare six- and eight-year-old children to grownups. Their manners aren't expected to be completely grown-up.*
I. *Who do you hold up as an example—grandparents, other relatives?*
M. *I don't think I hold up an example. They understand there is a right and a wrong way, and you just don't do it this way. For instance: "It is just as easy to pick your nightie up and put it in the drawer as it is to throw it on the floor or leave it there; and certainly you don't want to cause more work for mother; you can be such a help—wouldn't you like to be a help?" Usually they do—"Don't you like a pretty, neat, clean room, a tidy room? Don't you like to have sweet-smelling, pretty hands, instead of dirty, grubby, black hands?" —that sort of thing.*

C

I. *Who might you hold up as an example?*
M. *I loathe holding things up as an example. I think it is a horrible thing to do.*

Table IX:10 shows the percentage of mothers who held these different points of view about modeling.

Using negative models has some of the characteristics of punishment. It implies that the child has actually done something or is likely to do something which is undesirable. Like other kinds of punishment, this device shows the child how *not* to behave, but does not give him guidance as to what the mother wants. Mothers appeared to be even more reluctant to use children or adults whom the child knew as bad models than to use them as good ones. When mothers did report the use of negative models, their sheepishness about doing this was often apparent. For one thing, they wanted to teach the child not to be overly critical of other people's weaknesses. And for another, there was always the worry that the child might repeat some of the critical comments he had heard at home, and do so in situations where

TABLE IX:10

EXTENT OF USE OF POSITIVE MODELS

1. Never uses positive models—may say it is undesirable to do so	14%
2. Does use models, but very rarely	15
3. Refers to models occasionally	39
4. Refers to models fairly often	28
Refers to models; frequency not ascertained	4
Total	100%

it would be embarrassing to the mothers. A variety of attitudes toward the use of negative models may be seen in the following quotations.

A

I. *Is there anyone you mention as an example of what not to do? For instance—"You're acting just like so-and-so—you wouldn't want to be like him, would you?"*
M. *No, not too much so, because I don't think it's fair to the other child, and it can be very embarrassing if they started to repeat all the things they don't like about the child.*
I. *Have you ever done that with anybody?*
M. *No, I don't think it is a very good idea, not at all, why should you have to—why can't you just make them understand that there is a right and a wrong way to do it, and let's try to be right, as much as we possibly can—why set any third individual into it? Sometimes, I do say, "Now, look at Shirley's plate, she has eaten her dinner up so quickly, and her plate is shining; let's see if you can do it just as quickly as Shirley did." When it is possible, I hold her sister up, but not especially to get Jill to eat, but to compliment Shirley for having finished her dinner. There is a double thought; it works both ways.*

B

M. *No, I never really hold up anybody as an example, one way or another. I think that can incur dislike.*
I. *Would you mention anyone as an example of what not to do?*
M. *No, no, no. Children who are bad, Harry and I know are ill, or someone hasn't had the time to tell them, and they just need help.*

C

M. *Yes, I do do that, I am afraid. When he does something, especially on this sex business, I sort of hold up one of the children in the neighborhood as an example of what not to be, I don't put it—*
I. *What would you say to him?*
M. *Let me see how did it come up—I guess he was talking about how Teddy was trying to undress one of the girls and taking off her snow*

suit, etc., and was trying to take off her pants, so I told him that was a bad example and that he should not follow it, and that was about the only occasion I had to use that with him.

D

M. *These kids across the street that I told you about—one little girl— at first I thought I was just hard on them, but they had a birthday party last week, and even the other people that were there said you can see the difference in a group of children when one child stands out like a sore thumb; and very often I point to that child, and say, "You don't want to be like so-and-so."*

Table IX:11 shows the frequency of use of negative modeling in our sample.

TABLE IX:11

EXTENT OF USE OF NEGATIVE MODELS

1. Does not use negative models; tries to avoid it; believes it undesirable	19%
2. Does not use negative models, but no statement that it is considered undesirable	31
3. Refers to negative models occasionally	42
4. Fairly often uses negative models	5
Not ascertained	3
Total	100%

Reasoning

Reasoning, as we are using the term here, refers to a *labeling* process by which a mother explains to a child exactly what it is she does and does not want him to do. It often includes some reference as to *why* she wants what she wants, but its main purpose is *directing* behavior rather than *sanctioning* it.

Not all discussion with children which mothers themselves call "reasoning" falls under that heading as we are using the term. For example, a mother who threatened to spank her child when he misbehaved, and showed him that her hand was bigger than his, so that she could hit harder than he could, said: "You can reason with him; he's an easy kid to reason with. I guess you call it judgment, because he can judge from his hand to my hand that he would get a worse beating out of it than I would." Such admonitions by a mother to her child are more properly classifiable as threats of physical punishment than as reasoning.

Reasoning involves not only the mother's labeling of the

child's actions and their consequences, but also her drawing of generalizations for the child from things that have happened to him, so that he will be better able to anticipate probable outcomes of various courses of action when similar situations arise in the future. Usually reasoning occurs after a deviation, but sometimes it involves pointing out to the child, in advance, dangers or rewarding situations in his environment of which he would otherwise be unaware. This latter aspect of the method properly belongs in the class of "impelling" stimulation, of course.

The researches of Professor Piaget have shown how strange (to an adult) some of a child's notions of cause-and-effect can be. If a youngster slips and falls, he may not know that it happened because (according to his mother's more sophisticated interpretation) he came indoors on the smooth floor with rubber soles that were still muddy and slippery. It may seem just as likely to him that he slipped because the clock struck five at that moment. Through "reasoning," his mother can help single out the salient features of events, and he can learn more efficiently than if he has to rely on repeated trials and errors.

For example, one mother made very clear to her son the possible consequences of playing with the gas stove:

M. *Like at the gas stove. I told him that "You're going to get burned" . . . I put some hot water in a pan and I told him, "Touch the pan, go ahead." He said, "No." I said, "Well, you touch it, go ahead. You won't get burned, but just touch it." He touches it and I says, "That's hot." Then I said, "Well, that's what's going to happen, only this time you're going to get burned." And he'll say to me, "Well, shall I turn the gas off or should I turn it back on?" I says, "You shouldn't touch the gas. You shouldn't touch anything like that."
—If he has a knife or anything, he knows enough now not to touch knives. He'll never go in the kitchen drawer. He knows that I don't want him in there because there are sharp knives there. Anything like that I always tell him, just point out what the danger is—each item. And he'll usually listen to me and know what's happening.*

Explaining in detail to a child all the reasons which lie behind the parents' edicts is of course a time-consuming process, one which demands enormous patience. If a mother is in a hurry, or in an irritable mood, she is likely to explain only briefly, or not at all. She may tell the child to do something "because I say so," and tell him not to keep asking so many questions. The parents who take the time and trouble to explain fully do so, at least in part, because they feel that it will save them effort in the long run, since full explanations should make it easier for the child to deal with the situation another time by himself, without having to rely on the parents' "yes" or "no."

Even the best-intentioned parents sometimes find themselves without any reason to offer for what they are asking the child to do, or at least not any reason which they think the child can understand. And when he complains, "But Mummy, *why* can't I wee-wee in the lake?" or *"Why* can't I use my fingers to eat this chop—it's so much easier," the mother may be forced into a weak explanation that "It just isn't done" or "Other people will think you don't know the right way to act." Such reasons have little force for a five-year-old.

It is evident that when the mother reasons with the child, she runs the risk that explanation will turn into argument, for the child may question her logic if he happens to be a quick-witted or talkative child. Even at the age of five, a child can sometimes prove a mother wrong. A recently-overheard family conversation illustrates the dilemma:

Child: "Mother, why can't I go out and play? Jane and Linda are out."

Mother: "It's raining, dear, and I don't want you to catch cold."

Child (*looks out the window*): "But it *isn't* raining, Mummy. It just stopped."

Father (*overhearing the interchange*): "Young lady, if your mother says it's raining, it's raining."

The father evidently interpreted the child's counter-reasoning as a challenge to authority.

Some parents may avoid reasoning with their children just to avoid this challenge. They do not want to be outmaneuvered and forced to change their minds. One might suspect that a mother's willingness to use reasoning with a young child would be related to the extent of her tolerance of aggression from him. There is a bit of evidence to support this notion. In our data, we find a negative correlation of $-.22$ ($p<.01$) between extent of use of reasoning and the scale measuring severity of punishment for aggression toward the parents. In other words, those mothers who used reasoning a good deal were less inclined to punish a child for showing aggression toward them than were the parents who avoided reasoning with their children.

The interview did not contain specific questions about how often the mother reasoned with her child. Yet mention of the method came out spontaneously often enough for a rating to be made on three fourths of the cases. The scores on reasoning are for the most part by-products of the discussion of other disciplinary techniques, as in the comment, "He doesn't need to be punished. He is old enough now so that he understands when I explain things to him." Table IX:12 shows the proportion of families rated at each scale point.

TABLE IX:12

EXTENT OF USE OF REASONING

1. Never uses reasoning. Explicit evidence that it is not used	2%
2. Rare use of reasoning	18
3. Some use of reasoning	36
4. Considerable use. Evidence that the technique is emphasized, that the mother finds it effective, or that she uses it frequently	19
Not ascertained	25
Total	100%

We have mentioned that the parents who were above average in their use of reasoning also tended to be more tolerant about the child's expression of aggression toward them. The "reasoning" parents were also a little more permissive of their children's sexual behavior, and tended to use a little less physical punishment.

These correlations do not mean, however, that parents who relied more upon reasoning were indulgent or undemanding. They were just as strict with their children as were the rest of the parents when it came to requirements for the children to be obedient, quiet, neat and orderly, and helpful around the house. And as a matter of fact, parents who favored reasoning as a technique were *more* likely than other parents to follow through on threats of punishment once such threats were made. In this sense, at least, they were fairly strict.

CONSISTENCY

There is another dimension of disciplinary technique that is important, over and beyond the nature of the technique itself: namely, the consistency with which discipline is applied.

Mothers are constantly advised by the popular literature on child training that they must be consistent above all else. There is some plausibility to this admonition. Consistent behavior by parents no doubt makes the child's world more constant and predictable. If he knows what his mother is going to do under certain conditions, he is less at a loss to know how to respond. If his parents are capricious, he does not know what is coming or which of his own repertory of actions is appropriate.

Inconsistency may take many forms. Behaviors permitted at one time may be taboo at another. Rewards and praise, or punishment, may depend more on the mother's mood than on what the child is doing. Or the mother may tell the child she is going to do something, and then fail to follow through on her threats or promises. In our present discussion, we will concentrate on this latter phase of consistency: the extent to which the mothers followed through on their threats of punishment.

Mothers were asked, "How often do you tell (child's name) that you're going to have to punish him and then for some reason you don't follow through? What kinds of things might keep you from following through?" Of course, many mothers expressed a strong value toward following through whenever a threat of punishment had been made, and we suspect there may be some tendency for mothers to have reported themselves as being more consistent than they actually were. A mother would be a paragon indeed who had never forgotten what she had threatened, or had never been diverted by interruptions or intervening family crises. Therefore, when we see that 13 per cent of the mothers said they never failed to follow through on threats of punishment, we must amend this in our own minds to read "almost never," and take the answer as an indication that the mother believed it is very important to follow through if humanly possible.

As may be seen in Table IX:13, most mothers made an effort to follow through, but a fourth of them admitted that they quite often failed, for one reason or another. For example, two mothers said:

A

M. *With me it is just a threat; I very rarely carry it through. I tell her an awful lot that I am going to spank her, and then I hardly ever do. It is getting more or less to mean nothing to her.*

B

M. *Well, not really punishing—but more or less threats—I think it's a very big fault with me. I'll say, "Now, if you don't stop that, you're going to get an awful whack, or you're going to get this or that," and I think I say it mostly every day and then nothing happens.*
I. *What kinds of things might keep you from following through?*
M. *Oh, either the baby, or something cooking, or you know, just ordinary household things.*

TABLE IX:13

How Often Mother Says Will Punish and Does
Not Follow Through

1. Never. Always follows through	13%
2. Seldom. Makes effort to follow through	38
3. Sometimes	18
4. Quite often	20
5. Quite often; practically every day	7
Issue has not arisen	2
Not ascertained	2
Total	100%

In contrast, the following two mothers followed through, at considerable inconvenience, and, in one case, even when it had become evident that the threat was hasty and ill-considered.

A

M. *I doubt very much that I would ever not follow through, because to me, even if you say something and you don't mean it, you have got to follow through on it. I mean, oftentimes if you're tired . . . and you perhaps would say, "Now, if you make another sound, you will have to go to your room," and if they do, they have to go to their rooms. You shouldn't have said it in the first place, and it was wrong, but yet you have to do it.*

B

M. *I think I always follow through once I've told him. I've sort of made a point to follow through. I think you should if you have made the statement; you should abide by it, and I try to follow that.*
I. *What kinds of things might keep you from following through?*
M. *I don't know of anything that would keep me. Once I've said it and made my mind up to it, I can't imagine what would happen so*

that I wouldn't follow through on it. Unless something or somebody diverted my attention, that I couldn't follow through, for some reason of that sort. Other than that, if we were just here, and I said something, I would see that it was carried out.

It is interesting to note what kinds of things did keep mothers from following through. As Table IX:14 shows, they were mainly fortuitous occurrences, like being interrupted (often by a telephone call), or too busy, or finding that the disciplinary action was inconvenient at the moment. The next most common reason was the mother's re-evaluation of the impasse—she realized that she was wrong and should not have made the threat.

What picture do we get of the inconsistent mother? Two alternative stereotypes present themselves. She may be a warm, loving mother who in the heat of the moment threatens her child with punishment, yet cannot bear to hurt him. So the threat is not carried out. On the other hand, she may be a disorganized woman who lays about her with threats, but does not go to the trouble to carry them out. She makes a show of control by threatening her child, but the threats may be so unrealistic or so frequent that she cannot possibly make good on all of them. One can see her throwing up her hands in despair—she "can't do a thing with the children. They don't listen to me."

In general, the second characterization more nearly fits the evidence from the present study if we take into account only whether the mother reported a high or low degree of consistency. Consistent mothers, i.e., those who made a cardinal principle of following through, were a little above average in affectional warmth toward their children ($r = .12$). They had higher self-esteem ($r = .21$), and thought more highly of their husbands ($r = .23$). Also, they indicated higher acceptance of their children by having wanted them and having been delighted over the pregnancy ($r = .14$).

The converse of this pattern is to be seen among the mothers who found themselves unable to maintain consistent discipline. They appeared to be somewhat unhappy, frustrated, and irritable. The use of threats appeared to be a reflection of their irritability. But follow-through required coming to grips with the situation, and the inconsistent mothers did not do this easily.

However, if we search a little farther, and take into consideration what reasons mothers gave for failing to follow through, we get a different impression, and a different facet of the problem is revealed. The reasons were of two kinds, one "child-oriented" and the other "mother-oriented." The former had to do with the mother's feelings about the child or something the child did: for example, the mother would not act on her threat because she could not stand to hurt the child; or she realized she was wrong and the child right; or the child had already atoned for his misdemeanor. The mother-oriented reasons had to do with some problem of the mother herself—she forgot, or she was too busy, or the situation was too public and she was embarrassed to be seen punishing the child.

TABLE IX:14

REASONS FOR NOT FOLLOWING THROUGH ON THREATS OF PUNISHMENT

Mother just forgets	7%
Mother is interrupted; is too busy; punishment is inconvenient	34
Can't stand to hurt the child	5
Realizes she is wrong; should not have made threat	16
The situation is too public	5
Mother feels tired or sick	2
Child is tired or sick	1
Child apologizes, atones, behaves better	8
Nothing mentioned which might prevent follow-through	22
Total	100%

We can compare two groups of mothers, those who gave child-oriented and those who gave mother-oriented reasons for their failures to follow through. This comparison disregards the actual degree of consistency, and is focused entirely on the reasons for whatever inconsistency did occur. As Table IX:15 shows, the child-oriented inconsistent women were more frequently happy over their pregnancy, and were currently being warmer to their children. So far as their choice of disciplinary techniques was concerned, they tended to refrain from depriving their children of privileges and from using physical punishment. In other words, the mothers who did not follow through for *child-oriented reasons* were very much like the *consistent* mothers who were described above. Those who did not follow through for *mother-oriented reasons* were like the *inconsistent* mothers.

It is clear, then, that to characterize a mother as consistent or inconsistent is suggestive of some of her other possible personality attributes, but her reasons for her inconsistency must be taken into account as well.

COMMENT

This discussion of training methods has been focused mainly on the kinds of methods that mothers themselves distinguished and recognized. It is evident that the atmosphere of warmth and affection in the home, and parental attitudes of acceptance or rejection, play a major part in determining what effects the different techniques have. In this chapter, however, we have concerned ourselves with but one indicator of the "effectiveness" of a disciplinary method—the mother's estimate of how much good it did to spank the child. One major conclusion we reached was that spanking had more salutary effects, in the main, when it was associated with a good deal of reasoning. This finding brings up a more general point about punishment.

TABLE IX:15

CHARACTERISTICS OF MOTHERS WHO GAVE CHILD-ORIENTED AND MOTHER-ORIENTED REASONS FOR NOT FOLLOWING THROUGH ON THREATS

Mothers in Each Group	Gave Mother-oriented Reasons	Gave Child-oriented Reasons
Were unusually warm	30%	40%
Used little or no physical punishment	37%	48%
Used little or no deprivation of privileges	28%	46%
Had mixed feelings about pregnancy	38%	24%
Number of cases	183	112

One characteristic all forms of punishment have in common is that they often leave the child in a quandary: he learns from them what *not* to do, but not what *to* do. Unless punishment is accompanied by signs that suggest what behavior is acceptable, the child has difficulty substituting new behavior for the old, and will be in danger of reverting to the undesired behavior when the momentary effects of the punishment have worn off.

In current psychological thinking there is a good deal of doubt whether punished behavior actually drops out of the child's repertory. What happens more likely is that the actions which follow punishment are incompatible with the disapproved behavior and serve to suppress it, at least for the time being. The youngster who is punished for jumping on the furniture cannot cry or be hurt or go to his room and at the same time continue to jump. After an episode of punishment, he performs many new actions. If punishment is to be effective as a *training* device, it must be accompanied by techniques which actually reinforce the behavior that the mother would like to have persist; otherwise the new behavior will not be learned and will not take the place of the old. And the new behavior will be substituted most readily if it can occur in the same setting that originally produced the misdemeanor.

The learning task for the child is to make associations between certain of his actions and their consequences. Clearly, for maximum effectiveness, the actions that the mother rewards or punishes should be distinct and specific. Consider the child faced with this dictum: "Go to your room; you have been getting on my nerves all day!" What is he being punished for? What should he not do? He probably did dozens of things during the day. The most likely association he will make is between this punishment and his own actions that just preceded the expression of disapproval. If these actions happened to be ones that his mother usually approves, such as his starting to leave the house, the child is put in a quandary and the mother has defeated her own purpose. On the other hand, a child faced with "Go to your room for hitting the baby" has an easier job. The association is made for him clearly. Thus, the chances are that when he next has an impulse to hit the baby, there will also be counter-forces against his misbehavior.

The positive techniques of praise and tangible reward operate under the same conditions. If the mother specifically labels the actions she approves, the child forms the associations more easily. "You were very nice today" no doubt pleases him. But "today" is made up of many experiences, and it is unlikely that he can recall all of them, or repeat the whole day, for future approval. A simpler learning task is posed by "You are eating supper very nicely," or even by "I like the way you hold your fork." As the action is made more and more specific, the likelihood of its perpetuation by reward is greater.

Another factor to be considered in the operation of rewards

and punishments is the interval of time which elapses between the child's actions and the beginning of the disciplining act. Particularly vulnerable to this condition are material rewards and deprivation of privileges. For example: "If you hurry and dress for school, you can have an extra dessert for supper." "You have been so good today that you can go to the movies Saturday." "Unless you take your nap, you can't go out to play." "Your daddy will spank you when he comes home." What the mother is asking the child to do is to anticipate consequences over what may be, for a young child, a long period of time. As children become older, and their language skills mature, they become better able to anticipate these delayed experiences and to make associations between present and future events. For the young child, this is difficult. It is likely that many of the long-range rewards and punishments are lost on him. So many things can happen between today and Saturday.

Of course, what the mother hopes for ultimately is that as her child grows older he will cease to be dependent upon specific rewards and punishments administered by his parents, and will conform to the standards of right and wrong spontaneously. She wants him to learn to behave properly without external pressure. This development of internal controls—the creation of an effective conscience that is neither too lax nor too restricting—is the final stage in the socialization process of early childhood. It is to this matter that we turn in the next chapter, and we will postpone comment on the love-oriented *vs.* object-oriented dimension of discipline until then.

CHAPTER TEN

The Development of Conscience

At the beginning of a child's life, nearly all the control of his changeworthy actions comes from the parents. They watch what he does and decide whether they like it. In a sense, they are required to play constantly the role of policeman.

This direct control is essential at first, of course, for the child has had no opportunity to discover what is wanted of him. He is ignorant of adult standards; he has not yet learned how to do the "right" things. But this would be an intolerable state of affairs if it continued very long. Mothers cannot spend all their time watching and guarding. The child must learn to control himself. He must develop his own standards of conduct. He must apply sanctions to his own behavior. He must, in other words, develop a conscience.

One can distinguish three kinds of control. First, there is the external type that requires constant surveillance and direct intervention. The child does as he wishes until someone stops him. The year-and-a-half-old baby crawls toward the fireplace and his mother picks him up and puts him elsewhere. The children quarrel and the mother says, "Stop that fighting with your brother!"

Second, there is the child's self-control that is based on fear of punishment or hope of reward. This is simply an extension of

external control. It is dependent on the immediate (or near future) presence of someone who can punish or reward. When a youngster is punished often enough for a misdeed, he may learn not to do it any more. At least, he may if punishment is fairly certain and the mischief is self-announcing, like marking the wallpaper with crayons. Control by fear has certain disadvantages, obviously, for there are many kinds of misconduct that involve little risk of being caught. Children learn, inevitably, to appraise the realistic probabilities that they can get away with such matters as filching cookies, pinching the baby, masturbating in bed, or jumping on the sofa when mother is in the back yard. Furthermore, to be at all effective, punishment must be fairly frequent or very severe; and we saw, in the chapters on dependency and aggression, some of the unattractive consequences of such methods of training.

Third, there is the child's inner control that appears to come from a genuine acceptance of the parents' standards of conduct as his own. Deviation from these carries its own punishment from within the child himself; going counter to his self-instruction makes him feel guilty, ashamed, or self-derogating. The term *conscience* is applied to this kind of internal control.

Control by fear and control by conscience are both learned, of course, and every normal child develops some of each. For certain kinds of behavior he may have no internalized standards but only a fear of getting caught. For other kinds, the standards of his parents may be fully accepted as his own, and he acts in accord with them, whether or not there is risk of punishment.

It is difficult to judge what would be an ideal balance between these two for children in our society. Too heavy a reliance on fear tends to make a child opportunistic and unpredictable, while a too severe conscience tends to inhibit him beyond the requirements of social living. A lack of either kind leaves him with changeworthy behavior that is unacceptable to his peers in childhood, and is viewed as infantile and irresponsible in adulthood. It is clear that without *some* conscience, the individual could not live with others.

As with any other learned behavior, the development of internal control is a gradual process. The year-old baby seems to have little of it. What he wants to do, he does. As he gets more skill at locomotion, he must be watched fairly continuously, for he shows little sign of realizing that ash trays and magazines and figurines are not for touching. In spite of continuous instruction, he goes about his exploration and manipulation with an expression of intent concern and an utter disregard of all threats or pleadings. "Nothing in the house is safe if he can reach it!"

Like the two-o'clock feeding, however, this stage will pass. In the middle of their second year, most children begin to show a few signs of restraint. Ash trays and trinkets are not yet inviolate, but on rare occasions a child may be seen to reach for something—hesitate—and withdraw. At first glance, this self-control may seem a simple matter, no more than a kind of primitive self-protection from expected criticism or restraint. No doubt some of his compliance with adult wishes is exactly this and no more (and always will be), but on occasion a parent may be lucky enough to overhear and note the muted birth-cry of conscience itself. Here is an example:

Martha's parents brought her along one Sunday afternoon when they came for a visit. She was seventeen months old, full of curiosity and mischief. While we had coffee and cookies, she thirstily drank down a glass of milk, ate half a cookie, and began an eager exploration of her surroundings. Toddling most of the time, crawling occasionally, she left trails of crumbs and tipped-over cups wherever she went. One of the floor lamps fascinated her especially. It was tall and straight, made of a single glossy round of wood just the right size for Martha to get a good grip on. When she stood up against it, clutching happily, the lamp teetered and swayed in what was obviously an entrancing fashion for Martha.

Twice her father had to put down his cup and leap across the room to prevent a crash. Twice he said clearly and distinctly, "Now, Martha, *don't touch!*" Each time he took her by the hand and led her over to some toys. These distracted her only briefly.

After the second interruption, Martha began a general exploration of the room again. Now she went a little slower, and several times glanced at her father. As she came closer to the lamp, however, she stopped looking his way and her movements were all oriented toward the lamp. Deliberately she stepped toward it, came within a couple of feet of it, and lifted her arm partly, a little jerkily, and then said sharply, commandingly, *"Don't touch!"*

There was an instant of struggling silence. Then she turned and stumbled across the room, flopped down on the floor, and started laughing excitedly. Her father, laughing with her, and obviously adoring, reached out and hugged and snuggled her for several minutes.

Why was this a beginning of conscience? Why not assume, more simply, that Martha was afraid her father would punish her if she touched the lamp again? The difference between fear and conscience lies in the *self-instruction* and the incorporation, in the child herself, of the values expressed by the parents. Martha was playing the parental role when she said sternly to herself, "Don't touch!" Had she continued to look furtively at her father as she got close to the lamp—had she oscillated back and forth in her approach—had she been whimpery or silent and withdrawn after the moment of decision—we would have said she was responding to the dangers of the situation by simple avoidance. But at the crucial moment, she did not have to look at her father; she looked to herself for guidance, and the behest she followed was her own.

This episode gave no real opportunity to observe the two most significant characteristics by which conscience control can be recognized. One is the maintenance of control, in the face of temptation, when there is no one present to insist, and when there is little danger of being caught. The other is the occurrence of guilt-feelings on those occasions when temptation is not overcome, when the child does deviate from his own standards of what is right or wrong. Guilt is difficult to observe, in any case, and occurs only when conscience control fails, or the temptation is strong enough to make the child recognize his wish to perform the forbidden act.

These criteria of conscience control become more and more frequently evident as children grow through their preschool and early school years. The three-year-old becomes trustworthy with respect to handling delicate objects—most of the time. The four-year-old can be left alone with the baby safely, even when the baby is a provocative nuisance—most of the time. Mothers gradually find themselves giving fewer admonitions, making fewer threats of direct control. They hear more frequently a sobbing and spontaneous confession of mischief, and they discover the doubtful satisfaction of being able to tell when a misdeed has occurred by the child's typical hangdog expressions of shame and guilt. Mothers learn, too, that such episodes produce pain and insecurity for a child. He may revert briefly to an earlier stage of dependency, sidling up to her, thumb in mouth, seeking reassurance and expressions of love. Or his self-inflicted pain may be so great that he actively seeks punishment; the spanking may be a better alternative than guilt and remorse. As one mother put it:

> **M.** *I spanked her, and I think it did her good. This idea . . . if you feel guilty, you feel better if you're punished for it. If you're not punished, you feel that you've missed something. . . . Until you have paid retribution, you are upset.*

Conscience, then, does not develop all in one piece. The word itself refers not to a "thing" but to a process—the internal control of impulses that would lead to parentally disapproved action. From the second year, more and more impulses come under such control; more and more of the parents' qualities of behavior and standards of conduct are incorporated in the child's own repertory of actions. Even into adulthood, there is a continuing crystallization of beliefs and values, and the discovery of new areas of action that can be subjected to ethical interpretation.

This growing *scope*, or inclusiveness, of conscience control only partially corresponds to the *process* of conscience development, however. So far as we can tell, there is a learning of internal control that goes on mainly in the years before puberty, perhaps even chiefly in the first six to ten years of life, which establishes the extent to which conscience will operate throughout all the rest of life. As the child matures, and as he develops an understanding of more and more complex forms of social behavior, he appears to subsume new aspects of his own behavior (e.g., religious, political, economic, familial) under the categories of childhood behavior that he has already brought under internal control. Thus the adolescent may work out—often not consciously—an ethical belief that aggressive competition is evil; he may control firmly all his own impulses toward such behavior, even to the extent of refusing to join in competitive sports. It seems likely, however, that these later judgments of right and wrong are the direct successors to his early-childhood incorporation of parental strictures against aggression in the family. The *content* of the new values (i.e., avoiding competitive sport) is determined by the new experiences of maturity, but the *process* of internal controlling of impulses was learned long since. Even the *general category* (aggression control) probably was established as a category subject to such control in the first four or five years of life.

By their sixth year, children are well into the process of developing internalized control, although there are great differences among them in the rate at which this development takes place. Some children, especially some girls, appear to incorporate maternal values very early and to behave like "model" children long before they reach school age. Others have more of a struggle with such learning, and still show considerable evidence of depending on direct external control well after the age of six. What produces these differences? What child-rearing practices are associated with the rapid development of conscience?

We can approach this question best through the theory of *identification*, a process that has been hypothesized by psychoanalytic observers to account for the development not only of conscience but of several other aspects of behavior as well. The theory will help suggest which practices to examine as possible sources of conscience development. In succeeding sections we will then describe the measure of conscience we have been able to cull from the interviews and what child-rearing practices seem to have been associated with the more rapid and intense development of such behavior.

IDENTIFICATION

Long ago, psychoanalytic therapists discovered that many qualities in their adult patients' personalities seemed to be direct imitations of the same qualities in the patients' parents. Persistent probing of the feelings connected with these similarities brought out recollections of powerful emotions—love, anxiety, hatred—that seemed to stem from the earliest years of life and to be connected with both the love and disciplinary relationships the child had had with his parents. Many of the similarities, particularly those having to do with moral standards and values, apparently had developed in a context that made them seem almost like the products of direct parental demands. There was ample evidence that the process of absorbing parental values and adopting some forms of parental behavior was not a passive one. On the contrary, it was associated with very vigorous motives and emotions, and the qualities thus learned were so strongly established that the normal experiences of adult life could influence them but little.

Direct observation of young children, however, has suggested that much of this "learning" occurs without any specific "teaching" from the parents. A child, from his second year, begins to display interests and attitudes similar to theirs; he develops their values, and places their demands on both himself and others. Fantasy, too, shows this. The child acts out the adult role in his play with dolls, making mothers spank babies or require children to eat their cereal or hang up their clothes. He tries out adult-role behavior in his play with other children, trying on parents' clothes, pretending to have their occupations and responsibilities.

Perhaps the most pervasive of these patterns is that of sex-typing, i.e., the development of social behavior appropriate to the child's own sex. The great bulk of boyish behavior displayed by a boy, we suspect, is absorbed in the absence of any direct tuition whatever. Somehow he learns what occupations are male ones; he selects those occupations in his play and in his dream-plans for the future. When a mixed-sex group of three-year-olds is playing house, there may occasionally be a crossing of sex roles —a boy may be "nurse" or even "grandmother"—but this very rarely happens at kindergarten age. Boys are males by then, and girls are females. And they both know how to act appropriately. How did they learn if the parents did not teach them?

We can distinguish three main kinds of learning which occur in connection with social and emotional behavior of the complex level we are considering here. One of these is *trial and error*. Another is learning by *direct tuition*, what we called guidance in the last chapter. The third is *role practice*, the discovery and learning of new actions by observing what others do, and then practicing it by pretending to *be* the other person. The word "pretending" gives us an important clue to the character of role practice as it occurs in childhood: most of this practice occurs as fantasy, and much of it is covert. That is, it occurs in daydreams as well as in active play. We call the third method role practice rather than simple imitation partly because it may not manifest itself in overt, but only imagined, imitative behavior at the time it occurs. But beyond this, it involves the child's adopting the other person's role and then trying to act *altogether* like the other person acts in that role. He does not imitate just single aspects of his model's behavior; he takes on the role itself, at least momentarily, with all the feelings, attitudes, values, and actions that he attributes to the person who actually occupies the role.

All three kinds of learning require the same basic conditions. First there must be motivation. The child must want something. Second, he must perform some action. And third, that action must be reinforced; it must bring about a rewarding state of affairs. The difference between learning by direct guidance and by role practice is that in the latter the child's selection of what actions to perform stems from his own observation of what the role requires rather than from the instructions of his parents (or others). Role practice is more complex than simple trial and error because it requires the child to perceive and imagine himself in the place of a model. We are inclined to doubt that much learning of social behavior or values ever occurs by simple trial and error. We are concerned here, rather, with the distinction between learning by direct tuition and learning by role practice, i.e., learning without direct tuition.

Identification is the name we choose to give to whatever process occurs when the child adopts the method of role practice, i.e., acts as though he were occupying another person's role. Our chief problems in analyzing the process will be the discovery of what motives lead the child to role playing, and what satisfactions he gets from it. Within the framework of our present study, discovering the motives means discovering the kinds of learning experiences—maternal child-rearing practices—that are associated with a tendency to engage in such role practice.

We surmise that an important motive leading to role practice is the child's desire *to reproduce pleasant experiences*. Just as we rehearse in our own minds the compliments people have paid us, to savor once again the pleasure they gave us, so the child will enjoy playing the parental role in fantasy if parental actions have been nurturant, supportive, accepting. A related

motive may be the child's *worry about whether he has his parents'
affection and approval.* He can reassure himself by play-acting
supportive behavior on his parents' part. These considerations
lead us to examine especially the dependency relation between
child and mother, to see if it has any bearing upon what we
have called identification.

As has been discussed in Chapter Five, the normal physical
dependency of the infant provides the conditions for development of a dependency motive. The constant association of the
mother with the rewarding experiences of infancy also establishes
a strong love for her. By the time a child is a year old, he has

become related to his mother in such a way that not only do
many of his satisfying actions require her presence and co-operation, but her very orientation toward him—indeed, her simple
existence near him—is a source of pleasure. He *loves* his mother;
he is emotionally dependent on her.

The nature of a mother's responsibilities is such, however,
that she must gradually withdraw her attention. Perhaps she
has another baby, or she must go to work, care for the house,
devote herself more to her husband. She must return to her
customary role as an individual in her own right. This gradual
withdrawal of attention and support interferes with the child's
satisfactions. He becomes *deprived,* in the technical sense of the
word, even though his own growth of independence and desire
for mastery of his world offer something of a substitution. Quite
naturally, as with any frustration, he seeks methods of recovering

what he has lost, and of overcoming the barriers that have been in his way.

One obvious method of doing this is to perform acts that delight and please the mother, especially those that she herself specifies. Any device that helps the child select and learn such acts will ultimately be rewarded. During the latter part of their first year and the beginning of their second, children start to imitate the behavior of their parents. The rewards for imitation are not hard to discover; the infant being subjected to socialization pressures can use parental behavior as a model and thus can learn more readily the rewarded ways of behaving.

This kind of modeling is still, in a sense, learning by direct tuition. That is, the mother rewards the child, perhaps not for specific actions but for generally patterning himself upon his parents. But there are other satisfactions in practicing parental roles, beyond the satisfaction of winning direct approval for it. Indeed, much role practice goes on when the parents are not present and cannot reward it—when the child is alone playing with dolls, when he is talking to himself in his crib, and when he is playing outdoors with playmates.

Our hypothesis is that a child will be most likely to practice his parents' roles extensively (even in those situations where his behavior is not directly rewarded) if his dependency motivation is strong. He wants to make sure that his mother loves him, and in an effort to do so, he may even perform some of the acts, himself, that his mother ordinarily performs. He can babble and talk, snuggle against his own arms, or offer himself a thumb to suck. He wants his mother near him, and when she is not there, he brings her closer by imagining her soothing words and actions.

If the strength of the child's identification is related to his level of dependency, we must consider again what child-rearing practices produce a strong motive of this kind. In Chapter Five we reported that the mother's warmth and her affectionate demonstrativeness were very slightly related to the amount of dependency the child showed (r's $= .08$ and $.13$). We expect, then, that these same aspects of maternal behavior will be related to the child's tendency to practice parental roles.

Second, we might examine the influence of the mother's method of discipline. If she used *love-oriented* techniques, we would expect that the child's efforts to rehearse love-expressions from her would be more vigorous than if she used techniques such as physical punishment or the deprivation of privileges, which could be adapted to by flight or hiding or by independent activity designed to recover the withheld objects or privileges.

In these comments, we have talked of the mother as the identificand. But whom does the child use as a model? With whom does he identify? The conditions described above suggest that the main *caretaker* will be the identificand. In American culture, this is almost always a woman, and usually it is the mother. Both boys and girls, according to this theory, form their first identification with a female. This is quite acceptable for a girl, for she will do well to possess feminine personality characteristics throughout her life. For the boy, however, it poses a problem. He must shift to a masculine identification, sometime in his early years, if he is to develop a normally masculine personality.

There are several possible reasons why he makes such a shift. The first is that he receives direct rewards from both his parents and his peers for behaving in the way his parents expect, that is, acting like a young male.

A second factor that seems to help boys to shift from a feminine to a masculine identificand is the defensive process described by Anna Freud (1937) as *identification with the aggressor*. During the latter part of the preschool period, boys rather commonly develop some degree of hostility toward their fathers, who may be viewed as rivals for their mothers' affection. This hostility creates an expectation of counter-hostility and a fear of retaliation. As a defense against this fear, the boy may adopt the "father role." There may be several things that conduce to this choice. For one, playing the father role may place the boy in what he perceives to be a more favored competitive position for the mother's attention. For another, he gains some fantasy control over the dangerous father, control in the sense that he now can "make the father do what he wants." He *is* the father. Still another factor is the power advantage that characterizes the father role. Quite aside from the competitive advantage for the mother's affection, the boy gains greater disciplinary and manipulative power within the family when he plays the father's role. This may not be a factor that would *initiate* the boy's more than the girl's identification with the father, but it is a reward that may often serve to maintain such identification when once the other factors have started it.

Still another factor in a boy's sex-typing, we suspect, is the greater number of opportunities he has to behave in a masculine way than in a feminine one. Also, he is more often rewarded for it. People around him *expect* a boy to be masculine; they gear their own activities to this expectation, and hence he is led into appropriate masculinity quite involuntarily. Then—because he does what is expected of him—the other people are satisfied and tend to provide him with the satisfactions he wants. This means, simply, that a boy probably gets more rewarded practice for his masculine identification than for his feminine one. Moreover, not all the contents of others' roles that we practice in fantasy see the light of day in our real-life actions. Many of us know how to take the oath of office for President of the United States, having watched inaugurations, but few of us will be called upon to put our stored-up knowledge into effect. Similarly, we believe that there is a great deal of potential behavior which a boy learns through identification with his mother which he never has an opportunity to employ. A boy can and does employ the learning that involves his mother's values, of course, but not such strictly feminine bits of behavior as putting on lipstick. The items a boy has rehearsed when practicing his *father's* role, however, are much more likely to be appropriate to the expectations others have of his behavior, and therefore are more likely to find their way into overt expression.

These views about identification can be recapitulated quite simply. We suggest that role practice develops in response to a number of motives, a major one being dependency—the child's need to assure himself of the continuance of the affection and nurturance to which he has become accustomed in early infancy. He chooses as his initial identificand the person—usually the mother—who has been his chief source of reward in these respects. He practices especially those aspects of the maternal role that bring important evidences of approval. The moral values and strictures, the attitudes and behaviors that are offered him as replacements for his changeworthy behavior, are the attributes of the adult role which prove particularly useful to him in this process. These include what we characterized earlier as *internal control* and *conscience*.

Along with the adoption of these specific learnings, the process of identification leads to the practice of many other aspects of the role of the identificand. Included are the appropriate sex-typed behaviors and attitudes. These begin to appear by age three in most children, because there is not only immediate reward for adopting the correct role, but there are also ample opportunities for practicing it in interaction with other people who have expectancies for the child to behave appropriately. Certain other behaviors that are part of the identificand's role—such as behaving maternally toward smaller children—may develop more slowly and may not be fully displayed until the child reaches adulthood himself. The reason for this lies in the lack of appropriate qualities in the environment; nobody expects him to behave in parental fashion or provides him the opportunity to be a fully responsible caretaker. Nevertheless these behaviors are practiced in some degree, even in very early childhood (primarily in fantasy), and are ready for evocation when the appropriate changes occur in the environment.

Obviously, we are assuming that the child-rearing practices of mothers are significant determinants of these various developments in the child. Equally obviously, we mean to suggest that differences among mothers' behaviors toward children will produce differences in the rapidity and intensity with which role practice will develop. Our next problem is the measurement of the differences in the extent to which identification has occurred. We will be concerned, in what follows, with one of the major consequences of this process, what we have called conscience. Extensive practice of parental roles enhances conscience, we believe, because in the course of such role play the child practices the value statements of his parents and thus makes them his own.

Conscience, as was mentioned in connection with the example of Martha, is demonstrated in behavior by two characteristics: the success with which temptation is resisted when no "policeman" is present; and the expression of confession and guilt after temptation has not been resisted. Our interviews provided no adequate information concerning the children's resistance to temptation, and reluctantly but necessarily we leave this behavior quality to later research. We have been able to secure a measure of the extent to which the children showed signs of guilt and confession, however. This aspect of behavior is but a limited representation of the effects of the identification process, and indeed is even a limited representation of conscience itself. As will be seen in the next section, our measure of this quality was based on the mothers' reports of how their children acted—whether with guilt signs and confession or with flight and denial—after having broken a rule or having committed some other misdeed. We might well suppose that those mothers whose children had the strongest capacity for resisting temptation would have the least evidence to contribute for our confession measure!

This fact, coupled with the usual problem of non-independence of our measures of the child's behavior and the mother's child-rearing practices, requires us to be particularly cautious in interpreting the findings we will present here. In addition, we must recognize that there are other possible factors besides those we have discussed in connection with the identification process that may determine the extent to which a child will confess his misdeeds—and perhaps seek absolution. These will be discussed in connection with the description of our measure of conscience.

Signs of Conscience

By and large, the mothers had little to suggest as to the best conditions for conscience development; they did not appear to think of this aspect of behavior in terms of their own responsibility for its training. They were nonetheless acutely aware of conscientious behavior. Nearly all were able to describe clearly what they had observed with respect to their children's confessions and guilt reactions to deviation.

What are the symptoms by which we can recognize the growth of internal controls in a child? One, of course, is that he more and more often resists temptation, even when he is not being closely watched by a potential punisher. As we indicated above, we were not able to measure this quality from the interviews. A second indication of his having accepted his parents' standards as his own is his effort to teach these standards to his friends and siblings, i.e., *to act the parental role*. For example:

M. *And I've taught him never to touch a medicine cabinet. I showed my little boy the bottles—medicine bottles—and I've told him. He was sick, oh, about a year ago, in the hospital, and he's never forgotten*

*it, and I don't think he ever will. He's told his brothers about it plenty
of times. And I told him, "If you took your medicine bottle, you're
going to get sick like you did then." He won't go near that medicine
cabinet. And if he sees one of his brothers going to touch it, he'll tell
him, "You'll go to the hospital, and you'll stay in the hospital for a
long, long time; and you won't see Mommy or Daddy. And you won't
have no toys to play with—just lay in bed all the time and get
needles." And now none of them will go up there. I think he's really
the one that broke them of going to the medicine cabinet.*

This child was taking a parental role in real-life interaction
with his brothers. Such role playing is even more common in
play situations. Every mother has heard little girls, when playing
with their dolls, adopt their mothers' tones of voice and phrases,
sometimes with embarrassing precision. This play acting, this
pretending that one *is* one's father or mother, appears to be
one of the major ways in which children come to understand
what their parents' values are and to learn to accept them as
their own. Since we did not inquire directly about the mothers'
observations of this kind of behavior, we had only scattered examples reported and so were unable to use them for measurement.

A third indicator of conscience is the way a child acts *after*
he has done something wrong. Some children, those who are
primarily concerned with the avoidance of external punishment,
will try to get out of their parents' sight, hide the evidence of
the misdeed, and deny the act when asked directly about it.
The child with a well-developed conscience cannot escape so
easily, for he is troubled by self-blame as well as by the fear of
punishment. He applies his parents' disapproving evaluation of
his behavior to himself. He can feel better only after he has
made up for his misdeed in some way, and been forgiven. He
acts guilty and sheepish. He may hang around his mother, acting
in such a way that she will know something is wrong. Sometimes
he will arrange things so she is sure to find out what he has
done, even though he does not actually confess. Or he may simply
come to her and tell her about it openly. Following is an example
of a child who showed *confession* as a sign of conscience:

I. *We'd like to get some idea of how Sid acts when he's naughty.
When he deliberately does something he knows you don't want him to
do when your back is turned, how does he act?*
M. *Very seldom does that. But a few times that he has done something
that he shouldn't do, that I don't know anything about, if I'm in the*

*other room, he just can't hold it in very long. And finally he comes in
to me and he says, "Mother,"—and I'll say, "What?"—"I did something I shouldn't have done." Instead of leaving it and getting away
with it, he usually comes over and tells me what he's done. He usually
comes, I mean, and it's not very long after he's done it. He can hardly
hold it in to himself, you see.*

I. *Are there any situations in which he doesn't do this? In other
words . . .*

M. *Never come across one that he didn't. Even when he does something outside that he shouldn't do, and I don't even know about it, he
could very easily not say a word to me. Instead he comes and he says,
"You know what I did?" And if something goes wrong in school he'll
say, "Something happened today. My teacher had to speak to me."
And he doesn't have to tell me, but he does; he comes right over and
tells me. I don't know why. I should think if I were a child I'd keep it
to myself but he doesn't; he comes and tells me and I would never know
about it. I mean it—you know the old saying, "What you don't know
won't hurt you." He evidently doesn't know it yet.*

I. *When you ask him about something he's done that he knows he's
not supposed to do, does he usually admit it, or deny it?*

M. *He always admits it. I can always tell, of course, with Sid. I can
always tell when he's trying to fabricate something. I mean if I say,
"Did you do this?" And he says, "No." Well, I mean, it's just natural
for a child to say "no." Remember that when a child is accused, even
a grownup accused of something, if you said, "Did you do this?" Immediately the first answer that comes is "no." You say, well, that person's a liar. It's not that at all, it's just an immediate reaction to say
"no." That's the first reaction any person has, and it's not only for a
child; a grownup will do the same thing. But I can always tell when he
says "no" and doesn't mean it because—but he can't tell—I don't
know whether he'll accomplish it later—but he cannot tell a story. He
can't fabricate at all. Or prevaricate. He just gets this silly grin on his
face and I know that he's telling it and I'll say—and he'll just sheepishly put his eyes down and grin; he can't help it, he just can't tell a
lie. Some people can and some people can't. He just can't.*

I. *What have you done about it, if he denies something that you're
pretty sure he's done?*

M. *No, not too many things have happened, but when they have, it's
been almost a puppy-dog fashion in that he's been very quiet and has
led me to it.*

Another child with a highly developed conscience confessed
and took a spanking rather than risk his mother's continued
disapproval:

M. *He knows he has incurred our displeasure, and he says that he's
sorry, he apologizes. Right away when he incurs this displeasure, he gets*

discouraged, because right away he puts his arms around you and says, "I love you so much, I love you, and I won't do it again." And I say, "You've said that now, and if you do it again, that time you're going to have to be punished." And that's what happened. I've forgotten what it was, but it was something that I figured was not safe, so he did do it again, and he came and told me, and I said, "Now, what's going to happen?" and he said, "I guess I have to be spanked." I said, "That's right. Because it's too much to expect you to remember; and it would be dangerous for me to go along on that assumption, because I would be the one that would be sorry if you were hurt. I would never forgive myself, because I slipped up in not teaching you the danger. It's a sorrowful thing to me to have to teach you through pain."

At the other extreme, however, there were children of the same age who went to great lengths to avoid having their misdeeds found out.

A

I. *We'd like to get some idea of how Billy acts when he's naughty. When he has deliberately done something he knows you don't want him to do, when your back is turned, how does he act?*
M. *Well, right now he is lying. If he is caught, he will lie his way out, which is very disturbing to me. If there is anything I can't stand it's lying. I just want him to face the fact he's been naughty, and I will be much kinder with him; but sometimes if he's very bad, I just put him up in his room, which has a terrible effect on him. Sometimes I just give him a good scolding, and sometimes I fall back on the old dodge of telling him when his father gets home he will deal with him, which I know is wrong, but I just don't know how to handle him. I'll admit he is a problem.*
I. *What about if he does something when your back is turned, how does he act then?*
M. *And I find out afterwards? Well, that is usually the story, and it will come to my attention that he has broken something, and I will call him and try to get him to tell me why he did it; and I will admit I don't get very far. I don't know how to handle Billy.*
I. *Does he ever come and tell you about it without your having to ask him?*
M. *No, he would never admit that he has done something. It is only when Dick tells me or I just discover it.*
I. *When you ask him about something he has done that he knows he's not supposed to do, does he usually admit it or deny it?*
M. *He denies it. He will do anything to get out of admitting it.*

B

M. *Jack is inclined to be a little sneaky. Now that's another problem I don't like about him. For example, the things that annoy you, he will* *do more the minute your back is turned, and of course I don't like that at all. In other words, he thinks he is outsmarting you—kind of cute and not aboveboard.*

I. *If he does do something, will he usually come and tell you about it?*
M. *Oh, he wouldn't tell you unless he was caught. He really wouldn't.*
I. *When you ask him about it, will he admit it or deny it?*
M. *Oh—well—for example, just two days ago, there was a lot of scribbling all over the window sill in his room, which hadn't taken place for about two years, and there was an awful lot of it, and I saw it and I immediately asked who did it—so Lee spoke right up and said, "Well, I didn't." And Jackie said, "Well, I didn't!" I found out later he did do it. He'll admit it if you tell him you're going to take away his television if he doesn't, but as far as getting right up and saying, "I did it," he's no George Washington.*

Confession, of course, is not always a sign of conscience. It may indicate a greater fear of the consequences for *not confessing* than of the actual punishment for the misdeed. For example:

I. *What do you do about it if she denies something you are pretty sure she has done?*
M. *She may deny it at first, but she'll usually tell me. She's deathly afraid of being punished—not by me—but we've always told her that any little girl who tells a lie, God always does something terrible to them, and she's deathly afraid of that. Like, for instance, up the street a little boy was hit by an automobile, and Cathy was quite sure it was because he did something wrong at some time and God punished him. Maybe it's not the right thing, but we let her believe it.*

In general, however, a child's ability to admit that he was in the wrong, and to apologize or to make restitution, is an important step along the road to the development of internal controls. It means that he is willing to risk external punishment in order to recover his self-esteem and the esteem of his parents.

On the basis of the mothers' descriptions, a judgment was made for each child as to the "extent of development of his conscience." The ratings are reported in Table X:1.

In interpreting Table X:1, one should keep in mind that almost all the children in the study were in their sixth year, i.e., between five and six. Psychoanalytic theory, which is derived from intensive observations in psychotherapeutic interviews, suggests that this is a critical year for conscience development. Having a conscience is not an all-or-none affair at any age; but especially at this age, some elements of it are likely to be present and others absent. Most of the children in the present group appear to have been on the way to the internal control stage of their development at the time of the interview. As Table X:1 shows, however, the development was by no means complete, nor was it the same for all. Quite possibly, if we had studied older children, the signs we looked for as symptoms of internal control would have been shown by a larger proportion.

SOURCES OF CONSCIENCE

In our search for child-rearing dimensions that are associated with the rapid and strong development of conscience, we are interested, of course, in the larger question of identification. Our previous discussion seems tacitly to have assumed that

TABLE X:1

EVIDENCE OF THE DEVELOPMENT OF CONSCIENCE

1. No evidence. Child hides, denies, does not seem unhappy when naughty	13%
2. Little evidence of conscience	28
3. Moderate conscience development. May not confess directly, but looks sheepish; seldom denies	38
4. Considerable conscience	17
5. Strong conscience: child feels miserable when naughty; always confesses; never denies; strong need for forgiveness	3
Not ascertained	1
Total	100%

there is one single process which produces the tendency to practice roles in early childhood. Such an assumption is not warranted, although it is temporarily convenient for purposes of exposition of the theory. Before examining the findings relevant to our present theory of identification, we must mention one other combination of circumstances that could have the same effects on behavior. This is the *direct reward and reinforcement* of role practicing.

It will be recalled that the final sentence of our description of Martha's episode with the lamp was: "Her father, laughing with her, and obviously adoring, reached out and hugged and snuggled her for several minutes." This was reward of a powerful sort. But what actions did it reinforce? In theory, at least, every action

Martha had performed immediately before that should have been more firmly established. What had she done? Among other things, she had *instructed herself,* she had *not touched* the lamp, she had *run away* from a temptation, she had *acted like her father,* she had *inhibited touching motions.* If all these actions were reinforced, there is little doubt that role practice received reward. In addition, the performance of internal control was *directly* rewarded, and quite independently of role practice.

A theory stands or falls by its effectiveness in ordering empirical observations, however, so without further *a priori* worrying about the possible errors in our present notions, we will examine the relations between our measure of conscience and certain child-rearing dimensions that we have expected to be associated with it.

Warmth and dependency

The first thing suggested by the theory is that conscience will develop more rapidly, and will be more complete at kindergarten age, in those children who were given the greatest love and affection in early childhood. This reasoning rests on the supposition that warm and affectionate behavior increases the strength of the child's dependency on the mother (see Chapter Five), and that the more dependent the child is, the more motivation he will have for practicing the maternal role. We find a little support for this reasoning, but it is precious little. The correlation between *warmth* and *amount of conscience* is only .10 ($p = .05$).

There is one other child-rearing scale worth examination, however. In Chapter Five we saw that *mother's rejection of the child* was somewhat related to his dependency, also. The mothers who were most rejecting reported their children as a little more dependent than did the mothers who were fully accepting. According to our identification theory, then, we should expect the 99 "rejected" children to show more conscience (because they were more dependent) than the 218 "accepted" children. But no, just the contrary is the case; only 18 per cent of the rejected children were judged to have high conscience (points 4 and 5 on the scale described in Table X:1), while 31 per cent of the accepted children were so rated. This difference is not large, but it is directly contrary to the expectations we would have from our identification theory.

Taken at its face value, this finding would force us to reject the theory of identification. But there is one curious complication that makes us withhold judgment. The theory suggests that children who developed a high degree of dependency in their early life would show a more rapid and extensive development of conscience. But in Chapter Five, it was shown that *acceptance* had a slight tendency to *decrease* dependency. In other words, dependency and conscience should go together, but acceptance seems to decrease the former and increase the latter. The sizes of the relationships are so small, however, that there is plenty

TABLE X:2

HIGH CONSCIENCE: RELATIONSHIP TO CHILD DEPENDENCY AND
MATERNAL ACCEPTANCE-REJECTION

ACCEPTANCE-REJECTION OF CHILD	PERCENTAGE OF CHILDREN RATED AS HAVING HIGH CONSCIENCE	
	Less Dependent	More Dependent
Boys:		
Rejected	10% (30) *	15% (26)
Accepted	21% (58)	33% (55)
Girls:		
Rejected	18% (17)	31% (27)
Accepted	36% (60)	37% (46)

* Figures in parentheses are number of cases.

of statistical room for both effects to exist in the data. So far as the relationship between dependency and conscience development is concerned, only the boys show any; divided into two equal groups—the more and the less dependent—26 per cent of the more dependent boys were judged to have high conscience, while only 16 per cent of the less dependent ones were so rated. The boys support the theory.

Now if we separate the effects of these two antagonistic influences, acceptance-rejection and dependency, we can see exactly how each is related to conscience. Table X:2 shows the percentage of "high conscience" children in each of the four possible groups, i.e., more and less dependent children who were either accepted or rejected by their mothers. The relations of both factors, to conscience, are now much clearer. In every comparison, for both sexes, rejected children include fewer "high consciences." Furthermore, we now see that the "more dependent" children more frequently have high conscience than the "less dependent" children in every comparison except that of "accepted" girls.

None of the percentage differences shown in Table X:2 is of very high significance, and we must draw conclusions from them with considerable caution. However, every difference is in the direction that the theory requires, and our conclusion is that, although there are doubtless many other factors that influence the rapidity of conscience development, there is some likelihood that the mother's *warmth* and *acceptance* are positive influences. We must also add that the evidence for this statement is considerably stronger for the boys than for the girls.

Sex differences

This failure of the girls to conform to the theoretical prediction is a reminder that the identification theory calls for certain differences between the sexes in the development of conscience. The girl retains her initial identification with the mother, while the boy must under most circumstances shift his to the father. Although both these identifications are with adults, we are inclined to believe that the boy's shift retards the smooth development of the process. His gradual adoption of a new model is doubtless somewhat frustrating to him, and puts him in a state of conflict as to whom he should act like. Thus, we might expect not only that boys in their sixth year would be less fully identified with their fathers than girls are with their mothers, but that they would have a less complete identification with the adult role in general than girls would have. Also, this means they would show less indication of high conscience, as well as of other signs of identification, than girls.

This prediction is confirmed by our data. Only 20 per cent of the boys were judged to have "high conscience," as we defined it above, while 29 per cent of the girls were so rated. The difference between the mean ratings for the two sexes is reliable at the level of $p < .03$.

Another kind of evidence that supports this finding comes from experiments on doll play. It will be recalled that each of the children in this research was given two 20-minute sessions of permissive doll play at about the same time the mother was interviewed. The test equipment consisted of a five-room, open-topped house, with miniature furniture, and a family of five dolls. Each child was asked to tell a story about the family and show all the things they did. The experimenter recorded the number of times the child used each of the dolls as the agent of some thematic action and also whether the action was an aggressive one or not. Our reasoning was that in this fantasy situation a child would be free to choose whichever doll he wished, and that the stronger his identification with a father or mother role, the more frequently he would use the father or mother doll as the agent of actions in the play.

We would expect, therefore, that if the theory about sex differences is correct, the girls would use the mother doll more often than the father doll, and the boys would use the father more often than the mother. This proved to be true, and the difference is large and statistically reliable. We would also expect that the difference in how much the two dolls were used would be bigger for the girls than for the boys. That is, boys are presumed to have identified first with the mother and then to have had a good deal of pressure to shift to the father, while the girls are presumed to have had much less, or no, pressure to shift away from the mother. Hence the boys would be more nearly equal in their two identifications and they would show a smaller difference in frequency of use of the father and mother dolls. This prediction was also fulfilled (P. S. Sears, 1953).

One other study of children's doll play is worth mentioning in this connection. Dr. Elizabeth Z. Johnson compared boys and girls at both five years of age and at eight years. In her study, however, she made a very detailed record of exactly what kinds of aggressive actions the children performed, and she found she could classify these actions according to whether the aggression was pro-social or anti-social. The former class included mainly disciplinary actions—spankings, threats, warnings, and adult-like punishings of various kinds. The anti-social aggressions were more childlike, and included such acts as hiding, jumping on the furniture, disobedience, and hitting.

If our notion about identification is correct, we would expect the girls to show relatively more pro-social (adult-like) aggression than the boys; further, we would expect both sexes to increase in this form of behavior from five to eight years of age. Dr. Johnson found both these predictions to be true (Johnson, 1951).

Now let us return to the interview ratings of conscience. If the father becomes the principal person with whom the boy identifies, we should expect that the boy would find it difficult to make the shift if the father rejects him. Rejection by the father should have little effect on the girl, however, because the mother remains the main identification figure. In the interview, the mothers were asked to discuss their husbands' relations with the children. In 47 of the interviews (28 boys' mothers and 19 girls') there was some indication that the father was somewhat rejecting of the child. If we compare the conscience ratings of children rejected by their fathers with ratings of those for whom there was no evidence of father-rejection, we find what the theory predicts. Only 11 per cent of the father-rejected boys had a "high conscience," while 22 per cent of the non-rejected ones were so rated. The comparable figures for the girls are 26 and 29 per cent—purely chance variation. The boys' difference is reliable at about the .05 level.

In general, then, the findings about the effects of warmth, rejection, and dependency, and the differences observed between boys and girls, lend support to the theory of identification we

TABLE X:3

HIGH CONSCIENCE: RELATIONSHIP TO TECHNIQUES OF DISCIPLINE EMPLOYED BY THE PARENTS

Parents		Percentage of Children Rated High on Conscience	Number of Cases
High in their use of praise	$r = .18$	32%	181
Low in their use of praise		17%	192
High in their use of isolation	$r = .00$	29%	152
Low in their use of isolation		17%	167
High in use of withdrawal of love	$r = .09$	27%	81
Low in use of withdrawal of love		24%	107
High in their use of reasoning	$r = .18$	30%	192
Low in their use of reasoning		16%	91
High in use of tangible rewards	$r = -.04$	20%	188
Low in use of tangible rewards		28%	181
High in use of deprivation of privileges	$r = -.07$	18%	213
Low in use of deprivation of privileges		33%	156
High in use of physical punishment	$r = -.20$	15%	175
Low in use of physical punishment		32%	197

have described. Of course, these qualities, both those of the parents (warmth, rejection) and the child (sex, dependency), are ones over which parents have little or no control, and the findings are of interest mainly because they do fit the theoretical predictions. We can now turn to some aspects of parental behavior that are potentially a little more modifiable.

Techniques of training

In the previous chapter we described the various methods of discipline the mothers reported. We can now look at the effects of some of these same techniques with respect to whether or not they were associated with the development of high conscience.

According to the theory of identification, the child imitates the mother, and adopts her standards and values as his own, in order to assure himself of her love. This suggests that a high conscience would develop most readily if the mother relied largely on those disciplinary techniques that involved *giving or withholding love* as a means of rewarding or punishing child behavior. Conversely, we would expect that the children of mothers who used such materialistic methods as deprivation of privileges, physical punishment, and tangible rewards, would develop conscience control more slowly. Children do learn to adapt themselves somewhat to the prevailing climate of the family environment. If love is used as a reward, a child learns to do what will bring him love. If his mother withholds love, he will even learn to give himself love, and he will do as she does to avoid the pain of having her separate herself from him. On the other hand, if the mother uses physical punishment, a child is understandably reluctant to confess his misdeeds or to admit, when asked, that he has done wrong. He may use hiding or flight or counter-aggression as devices to avoid punishment.

In Table X:3, we have compared the six dimensions which describe these two classes of disciplinary techniques. The first three—praise, isolation, and withdrawal of love—are ones that make use of love-oriented behavior by the mother. We have added "reasoning" to the table, too, because it was associated with these love-oriented techniques. In each instance, the high use of such methods is accompanied by a greater number of "high conscience" children than the lesser use. The second group of three—tangible rewards, deprivation, and physical punishment—is more materialistic, and in each case the more frequent use is accompanied by a smaller number of "high conscience" children. Again, as with our previous analyses, the statistical reliabilities of the relationships are meagre. Indeed, in four of the seven cases, the correlation coefficients which express the size of the relationships are approximately zero. However, six of the seven are in the theoretically expected direction.[1] And in every case the percentage of extreme cases ("high conscience") shows a rather substantial difference between high and low groups. The consistency of these findings, rather than the amount of influence of each separate dimension, gives us some confidence in the significance of the final results.

These findings all support the theory that love-oriented techniques aid in the development of conscience. Guilt and confession of wrongdoing can be interpreted as the child's expression of fear that he has offended his parents and that they will no longer love him. Coming to the parents for atonement is an attempt to assure the continuation of love.

We can go a little farther with this analysis, however. Withdrawing love where little exists is meaningless. If the mother is relatively cold to begin with, then using withdrawal of love should have little effect on conscience development. The pattern most calculated to produce "high conscience" should be that of mothers who are usually warm and loving and then, as a method of control, threaten this affectionate relationship.

Table X:4 shows that this is indeed the case. The children

TABLE X:4

HIGH CONSCIENCE: RELATIONSHIP TO THE MOTHER'S WARMTH AND HER USE OF WITHDRAWAL OF LOVE

	Percentage of Children Rated High on Conscience
Mother relatively cold, and:	
Uses withdrawal of love fairly often	18%
Uses little or no withdrawal of love	25%
Mother relatively warm, and:	
Uses withdrawal of love fairly often	42%
Uses little or no withdrawal of love	24%

[1] These seven tests are, of course, not independent, since a number of the antecedent scales are intercorrelated.

most prone to behave in the ways we have considered indicative of having a well-developed conscience were those whose mothers were relatively warm toward them but who made their love contingent on the child's good behavior. These were the children who truly were risking the loss of love when they misbehaved.

So we come back full circle on our data. *Warmth* alone did not seem to have more than a minimal relation to our measure of conscience. Neither did *withdrawal of love*. But putting the two together, we find a quite clear influence on this one sign of the identification process.

COMMENT

In general, our findings support our theory of identification. They provide a little more information on the way in which parents' child-rearing practices influence the child's character. We can say with some degree of conviction that mothers who love and accept their children, and who use love-oriented techniques of discipline rather than material or physical techniques, produce relatively more children with high conscience. We can say, too, that girls develop this inner control, and adopt their appropriate sex-role qualities, earlier and faster than boys.

In some ways these are discomforting discoveries. They mix up our adult values a little. Ordinarily, we think of *acceptance* as a good thing; a rejecting mother is thought of as unfair and unkind. The words *love-oriented techniques of discipline* have a good sound, too, especially when they are put in contrast with physical punishment—at least, as we saw in the previous chapter, this is true for a good many mothers. But when we examine these love-oriented techniques more closely, and find that they include *withdrawal of love* as a means of control or punishment, we realize that we are dealing with a form of maternal behavior that is as much derogated as is rejection. Yet both *acceptance* and *withdrawal of love* appear to produce a strong conscience. Is this a good outcome or a bad outcome of child training?

Some degree of inner control of sex, aggression, and other powerful impulses is clearly necessary if a society is to survive. On the other hand, these impulses do exist in every child and in every adult. Too severe inner control can prevent any direct expression of them and can produce a quite unnecessary degree of guilt and anxiety. Too much conscience can destroy the happiness and productivity of the individual, just as too little can destroy the peace and stability of society.

The problem can be approached in a different way, however. We have discussed here only the *strength* of conscience, saying nothing of its *content*. In our interviews we asked about the signs of conscience, not what kinds of behavior the child prevented himself from doing, or felt guilty about after doing. The *content* of conscience appears to be the important thing, both from the individual's standpoint and from society's. A strong inner control of impulses to kill other people, or to make indiscriminate sexual advances to many potential partners, is not severely limiting to the individual's initiative. But if these inhibitions extend to *all* aggressive or sexual actions, the person may be crippled in his efforts to live a normal and productive life. American society is competitive and the American culture tolerates, indeed demands, a good deal of interpersonal aggression. In the sexual sphere, both males and females—in their respective fashions—must take initiative in seeking a marriage partner, and marriage can be misery for those whose inhibitions prevent them from yielding fully to the physical expression of love.

In emphasizing the significance of conscience content, however, we cannot ignore conscience strength. During the early years of life, there is so much changeworthy behavior to be controlled and modified that any training that produces inner control is likely to produce inhibition of a very wide range of behaviors. In the close family circle, there is difficulty in limiting the control of aggression only to the most violent forms. Aggressive impulses *in general* become subject to inner control. Too, if we are correct in the general outlines of our identification theory, the child tends to absorb all the parental values he can perceive. Since most parents have fairly widespread inner controls of their own— conscience content that extends to many items of behavior other than those that are minimally essential for social living—the child is in risk of absorbing more than he needs. If his identification is especially strong, even the parents' mildest and most temporary strictures may become a matter of conscience for him. Role practice means the adoption of *everything* in the parents' behavior that the child perceives as appropriate to the parental role.

There is no answer to the question of what is the optimal strength and encompassment of conscience. We have no units by which we can measure these things objectively. We can make comparative ratings of children, as we have done here, but this does not tell us how strong these children's consciences were on any absolute scale. Could we perhaps assume that the average strength of conscience in this group of 379 youngsters is optimal? We have no way of knowing. Some observers of the American scene think our people are becoming more and more neurotic and guilt-ridden; others see signs of too little inner control, too much reckless violence that requires too many policemen on too many corners. We simply do not know, and the question is far too important to permit the hazards of uninformed guessing.

Uncertain as we may be about the optimal average, however, we can say something about the extremes of conscience and its lack. The child with too strong a conscience is guilt-ridden. His own impulses constantly excite him to confession and to a too instant admission of wrongdoing. He is prevented from experimentation with new impulses; he dares not risk the danger of self-punishment. New ideas and new experiences, even new people, are dangerous to him. He becomes rigid and inflexible in his judgments of others, a purveyor of sanctimony and propriety. His repressed hostilities are brought into the service of his moral judgments. In childhood he is a prig, a teacher's pet; in adulthood he can become cruel and vicious in his expression of moral indignation. Worst of all, perhaps, he can have no fun in life, for fun itself is subject to inner control.

At the other extreme is the child with a weak conscience. What he lacks in guilt he makes up in fear. His actions are bounded only by the possibility of his being caught and punished for his wrongdoings. His moral judgments are based on expediency. He cannot be trusted out of sight and supervision. His infantile impulses remain strong, and in the absence of a punitive disciplinarian he has no reluctance to express them. He may bully younger or weaker children, steal and lie if he thinks he can get away with it, and flee to hide when anything happens that may conceivably be viewed amiss by adults. In childhood he is aggressive and mean, a troublemaker at home and at school. In adulthood, he may be a conscienceless rogue in his social and business relationships, an undisciplinable bum, or a criminal.

Neither of these extremes presents an attractive picture in its pure form. Of course, unhappily, there is a little of the guilt-child and a little of the fear-child in nearly everyone. Conscience is not an all-or-none matter, either as to strength or as to content. The process of identification places certain automatic limits on what the child's conscience can contain—the limit is the behavior and the value systems of the adults with whom the child identifies. We found, for example, that in doll play the strongly identified girls were very aggressive if their mothers were aggressive (i.e., used much physical punishment), but were non-aggressive if their mothers were non-aggressive. With the less strongly identified girls, the degree of aggressiveness expressed by the mother had no influence on the daughter's fantasy aggression (Levin and Sears, 1956). The mother provided the model, and identification helped to transmit her behavior to the next generation.

In the long run, then, if our theory of identification is correct, the process itself places limits on the range within which human morals and values can fall. If there must be *some* parental warmth in order for a child to identify with his parents, then the very same warmth will be an identified-with quality and will become a property in the personality of the child. The same will hold true of the choice of withdrawal of love as a means of discipline. Thus, mainly within the range of parental qualities required to insure identification in the child will there be a continuation of the social and personality qualities that constitute those parents. And equally, the more identification there is in any one generation, the greater will be the absorption of those qualities-that-induce-identification in the next.

If one wants to speculate quite beyond the bounds of any testable hypotheses, one can imagine that the human capacity for identification may be one of the major factors accounting for the extraordinary pre-eminence of our species. No more than a few thousand years ago, man was but a superior kind of ape. Now he is the intellectual master of his universe. The years are too few for biological evolution to have accounted for the change. Of course, the accretion of culture is in part responsible, but human culture is now so complex that each new generation could not possibly learn it all if each tiny element had to be taught through laboriously arranged rewards and punishments. The child's spontaneous tendency to "try on" the roles he observes around him, and thus learn the actions implied in these roles, makes for enormous efficiency in this learning.

The development of man has not been a random matter. His physical stamina and the effectiveness of his bodily structure have not progressed in even a dozen thousand years. It is in the growing use of reasoning and thinking about his problems—and hence solving at least some of them—that man gives the appearance of having capacities that place him almost off the scale of comparison with other animals. What has produced this change?

We call attention to the role of *reasoning with the child* as an influence on our measure of conscience. If reasoning conduces to identification, then the use of reasoning—explanation, guidance, verbal assistance to the young in the arduous process of growing up—becomes a major quality of the parents that, simply because it exists in the parents, will be absorbed by the children. The greater the use of reasoning, the greater will be the probability that reasoning as a form of human behavior will be passed from generation to generation. And it is in the very use of reasoning that man has been developing so rapidly.

If these speculations are true, we can but hope that there will somehow develop a limitation on some of the other consequences of identification—the growth of powerfully inhibiting internal control and the copying of all the qualities of the past. It would be ironic indeed if one and the same psychological process were to bring man at once to the highest point of skill in intellection and then, for all eternity, stereotype him with the elaborate habits of a gigantic ant.

CHAPTER ELEVEN

Sex and Birth Order of the Child

Sex-typing, as we dicussed it in the last chapter, refers to the child's development of those interests, attitudes, and other personality qualities that are appropriate to his or her own sex. Just what is appropriate may differ somewhat from one culture to another, but there is no culture that does not make some distinction. One kind of behavior is expected of men, another of women.

In America, these different expectations involve far more than simple manners. Whatever the talents of some individual women, the feminine role in business is ordinarily that of execution rather than making of policies; and within the framework of group execution, the subordinate rather than the superordinate role. Contrariwise, in the home women have the primary authority for management of the group enterprise and for child rearing during children's early years. At a more individualized level of behavior, women are expected to be less physically aggressive than men, more interested in reading, more sympathetic to people in trouble. If the many differences in these expectations of appropriate role behavior are not to make uncomfortable the individuals who must conform to them, the two sexes obviously must develop somewhat different personalities.

They do. As early as the third and fourth years, there are

average differences between groups of boys and girls. In nursery school, dependent behavior toward women teachers is much greater in girls; aggressive play is greater in boys. There are even subtle differences in the style and quality of the two sexes' doll play. Later in the school years, many other differences in taste and interest develop. Girls become better and more intent readers; boys turn their interests more to arithmetical and mechanical matters.

Doubtless, as we have suggested before, there are constitutional biological differences between the sexes that account in part for these personality differences. In recent years, however, the influence of possible differences in child rearing has been widely discussed. We say *possible* advisedly, for there has been little information available as to whether or not there actually are distinguishable patterns of child rearing for boys and girls.

In our earlier discussions of patterns, we used the term to refer to the combinations of child-rearing dimensions that occurred in the mothers. We sought underlying traits, by way of factor analysis or by other methods of examining intercorrelations among our measures. Now we come to another kind of pattern, one that depends on the stimulus value of the child himself. There are any number of ways, of course, in which one may categorize children as stimuli to their mothers. Sex is an obvious one, and so is ordinal position, that is, whether the child is an *only, first, middle* or *youngest* one in the family. The present chapter will be devoted to these two ways, although one could use a similar approach for comparisons of blondes *vs.* brunettes, blind *vs.* seeing children, big-for-their-age *vs.* little-for-their-age children, or highly active *vs.* very inactive ones, and so on.

INTENTIONAL SEX-TYPING

Role practice, as we discussed it in connection with identification theory in Chapter Ten, is one way in which sex-typing can occur. Another method involves the direct teaching of sex-appropriate behavior. This procedure would require that the mother have different expectations for boys and girls, that she make a differentiation between the two sex roles. Our first step in searching for evidence concerning intentional role training was to discover the extent to which mothers made such differentiation for children of kindergarten age.

In the interview, we asked the following questions:

How important do you think it is for a boy of X's age to act like a real boy (or, for a girl of X's age to be ladylike)?

[For boys] How about playing with dolls and that sort of thing?

[For girls] How about playing rough games and that sort of thing?

Do you feel there is any difference in the way boys and girls ought to act at X's age?

[If X is a boy] What have you taught him about how you want him to treat little girls?

TABLE XI:1
SEX-ROLE DIFFERENTIATION

1. Low. Mother believes little or no difference exists between boys and girls and doesn't value "masculine" or "feminine" behavior at this age	5%
2.	9
3.	22
4.	20
5.	26
6.	13
7. High. Mother stresses and trains for wide differentiation in a variety of areas. Dress, games, toys, manners must all be appropriate to child's sex. References throughout interview to what is manly, boyish, etc.	4
Not ascertained	1
Total	100%

The answers to these questions, as well as spontaneous comments made elsewhere in the interview, revealed a wide divergence of opinion. We were able to rate the mothers on a seven-point scale that ranged from a very low expectation of any sex differences in young children's behavior to a strong conviction that boys and girls should be influenced from the very beginning to act manly or ladylike. The distribution of these attitudes is shown in Table XI:1.

Very few of the mothers felt that boys and girls were exactly alike at this age or that they should be treated alike. Some mothers expressed themselves quite directly about the qualities that they would consider masculine or feminine. The following excerpts are from interviews that were rated *high* on *sex-role differentiation:*

A

I. *Now we want to talk about whether you think there are any differences in bringing up boys and bringing up girls. How important do you think it is for a boy of David's age to act like a real boy?*
M. *I think it is very important. I think he should act like a real boy—and then again I think it is up to the father to help him become a real boy. I don't think a mother can help a boy to become a real boy, especially when they get older. With a father, they will sit down and discuss football and baseball. And especially in my case, I have a husband who is interested in all those things, and who likes sports, and I think he will be very much disappointed if David doesn't go along with him.*

B

M. *I would want him to be a real boy. I don't get alarmed when he comes home and does the things that a boy should do. Last week he came home and climbed a fence and ripped a brand new pair of grey flannel pants. His father was very proud of him. He at last had become a boy. I hope my children are normal children. I want them to do the things that a child that age does. I wouldn't want him to be destructive purposely. But he climbs. I get very nervous. I see him on garage roofs, but I don't think he should be stopped from going along normally. I wouldn't want him to stand on the sidewalk while the other boys did things.*
I. *How about playing with dolls and that sort of thing?*
M. *He has a little bunny who is very dirty and very decrepit, and he talks to it and takes it to bed, and he practically lives with his bunny. He is a live person as far as Fred is concerned. We have never done anything about trying to get him away. He has never liked dolls. We did buy him a "Howdy Doody" doll once, but his bunny is his only doll.*
I. *Do you feel there is any difference in the ways boys and girls ought to act at Fred's age?*
M. *Oh, yes. I think little girls at his age are very soft and feminine. I think they are social. I don't think little boys at that age have social graces at all.*
I. *Are there any other ways in which they are different?*
M. *Their interests are different. Fred is interested in animals and bugs, outdoor life, cowboys. I don't think little girls are. Little girls at that age are usually pushing doll carriages, dressing dolls.*
I. *What have you taught him about how you want him to treat little girls?*

M. *We have tried to teach him manners about helping ladies with their coats, not to hit little girls, and to be a little more considerate of girls because they are a little more delicate than boys. You beat up little boys but you don't beat up little girls.*

In contrast, the following mothers placed very little stress on sex-appropriate behavior:

A

M. *I don't think it's important, because she is only a little girl.*
I. *Do you feel there is any difference in the way boys and girls ought to act at Susan's age?*
M. *No, except that I think both boys and girls should behave when they go anywhere.*
I. *Well, do you think as far as boyishness, girlishness, ladylikeness is concerned—you have had young boys—that they ought to act any differently because they're boys, or because they're girls, or just the same because they're young children?*
M. *No, they're only children. I came to the conclusion myself that they outgrow it, and they do. At least in my family they did—my second child, he used to like to play with dolls—well, it was about a month or two that I noticed he didn't play with them any more.*
I. *How about her playing rough games and that sort of thing?*
M. *I believe in letting her play—it isn't that important to me.*

B

M. *Oh, I don't think it makes too much difference at his age. I mean, I think that boys and girls have many similar likes and dislikes in play. He has a little cousin that's some younger than he, but they enjoy playing together very much. And oftentimes he plays house with her, and she often plays cowboys with him. And I don't think there's too much difference in what boys and girls play with at that age. And just to be a regular boy, because he is a boy, I don't think is at all important.*
I. *Well, what have you taught him about how you want him to treat little girls?*
M. *Nothing specific, except that I've tried to impress upon him that anyone that is younger than he should be more or less looked after or helped, if they need help. And just because they're little girls, I haven't impressed upon him that they should be given any different treatment than any little boy the same age, except that you should try to be kind and do the right thing with all kids. I mean I think it's just as important that he shouldn't strike at a little boy as at a little girl.*

We mentioned, in an earlier chapter, our difficulties in phrasing questions that would be suitable for getting information about the mothers' use of *withdrawal of love* as a disciplinary technique. Mothers did not easily recognize their own use of such a method, and most of them seemed strongly to disapprove it anyway. We had similar difficulties in securing information about sex-role differentiation. Many of the mothers disliked the notion of "doing things differently." They interpreted any comparison of the sexes as somehow invidious. It represented an implied derogation of one or the other, or at least seemed to arouse a feeling that *comparison* implied *evaluation*—a better-than-worse-than attitude. Some said it would be "unfair" to treat boys and girls differently, apparently viewing such possible differences mainly in the light of privileges offered to one sex but not the other. This idea troubled many mothers. Egalitarianism overrode objectivity of report.

Furthermore, many mothers did not recognize any efforts they might be making to produce appropriate sex-role behavior. When they did see differences in their own behavior—and some who had both sons and daughters did—they tended to interpret such differences as natural reactions to innate differences between boys and girls. They thought a mother had to adjust her behavior to the sex-determined temperament of her child, but did not consider that her own actions might be responsible for any such characteristics. Thus, if a mother reported that she would spank a boy more often than she would a girl, she might add that this was because boys get into trouble more often and hence "need" spanking.

In spite of the difficulty of securing accurate reports of attitudes and practices with respect to sex-role differentiation, our raters were able to make reasonably reliable estimates of almost all the interviews. There was no difference between the mothers of boys and those of girls in the degree of differentiation they made.

Our next step, in evaluating the influence of direct training for sex-typing, is to examine the ways in which boys' and girls' mothers differed in their child rearing. So far, we have been considering only their verbalized values and attitudes about this matter, their own conclusions as to whether they should or should not give differential treatment to the sexes. Did they actually treat boys and girls the same? Or were there differences in treatment that might possibly contribute to some of the sex-typed personality characteristics of children?

DIFFERENCES IN REARING OF BOYS AND GIRLS

To answer these questions, we have compared the ratings assigned to the 202 mothers of boys and the 177 mothers of girls on all the scales listed in Appendix B. As may be seen from Table XI:2, there were surprisingly few dimensions on

TABLE XI:2

COMPARISON OF CHILD TRAINING IN RELATION TO SEX OF CHILD *

Scales	Boys	Girls	p
Percentage of mothers rated *high* on:			
Time for completion of weaning	16%	26%	.01
Warmth toward infant	49%	60%	.02
Permissiveness for aggression toward neighborhood children	43%	23%	.01
Non-permissiveness for aggression toward parents	25%	39%	< .01
Encouraging child to fight back if attacked	34%	14%	< .01
Use of withdrawal of love	13%	28%	< .01
Use of praise	35%	45%	< .05
Percentage of mothers rated *low* on physical punishment	8%	23%	< .01
Percentage of mothers who used maids or sitters as caretakers	27%	19%	< .05
Percentage of children disciplined primarily by (when both parents were home):			
Father	33%	27%	.11
Both	34%	25%	< .05
Mother	33%	48%	< .01
Percentage of mothers assigning tasks and chores:			
Making beds	6%	14%	< .01
Setting table	8%	12%	.12
Emptying trash, ash trays, wastebaskets	43%	16%	< .01
Doing dishes	19%	28%	.02
Percentage who expected child to go to college	61%	34%	< .01

* All relevant scales in Appendix B were tested for significance of sex differences between means (*t*-test). The *p*'s given in this table are based on the percentage differences as shown here.

which the sexes were differently treated. Even with such large groups as these, one would expect that a few comparisons out of so many would show a difference just by chance, and it may well be that at least some of the differences listed here would not be found in a wider sample of mothers. There are a few of the scales, however, that deserve further comment.

Feeding and warmth. The only way in which girls seem to have had different experiences from boys with respect to infant feeding was that their weaning took a little longer—three months as compared with two, on the average. As we saw in Chapter Three, long weaning was somewhat more likely to upset the child than weaning that was carried out with a certain dispatch, so this treatment cannot be regarded as gentler in its effects. However, slow weaning may imply a more indulgent attitude toward the child. This is a plausible interpretation in this instance, for girls were somewhat more *warmly* treated in infancy than were boys. Indeed, when we use a statistical device for holding constant the amount of warmth expressed to the infant, the sex difference in the length of weaning disappears. The more basic finding, then, is that a mother was likely to be warmer toward her infant if it was a girl.

We can only speculate as to why such a difference may occur. Do mothers think girls are more fragile, requiring more tender treatment? Are girls easier to take care of as infants? Do mothers feel boys ought not to be "coddled" for fear they will not be independent and manly enough as they grow older? Are mothers less sure of themselves with boys? We can only guess.

Toilet training. We found no significant differences in the way boys and girls were toilet trained, although there was a slight tendency for the training of boys to be more severe and to be completed later. Since boys were no more likely than girls to be enuretic at age five, this can probably be disregarded.

Sex training. Surprisingly, boys and girls were treated much the same with respect to sex training. We rather expected that girls would be more restricted, as far as immodesty and sex play were concerned, since we share the common notion that there is greater control exercised over girls at adolescence. But any differences in treatment of the two sexes evidently did not begin as early as kindergarten age. There was a slight tendency for mothers to be more permissive about masturbation with boys, but for the group as a whole the difference was too slight to be of significance.

Aggression. Our discussion of the treatment of the sexes in Chapter Seven needs only a summary here. Aggression was the area of child behavior in which the greatest sex distinctions were made by parents. Boys were allowed more aggression in their dealings with other children in the neighborhood, and were more frequently encouraged to fight back if another child started a fight. Boys were *not* allowed more freedom to fight with their brothers and sisters, however. So far as aggression toward the parents was concerned, a significantly larger proportion of girls were treated *very* non-permissively; at the other extreme, a slightly larger proportion of boys (16 per cent) than girls (11 per cent) were given high freedom of expression. We were unable to find any differences, however, with respect to the severity of punishment for aggression toward parents.

While the parents evidently thought that quarreling and fighting were more natural, and even desirable, in a boy under some circumstances, they expected this boyish behavior to manifest itself outside the home; they did not encourage its being directed toward members of the immediate family, although strongly non-permissive attitudes were more frequently applied to girls. These parental attitudes seem to have been reflected directly in the behavior of the children. It will be recalled that the mothers reported that boys were no more likely than girls to quarrel frequently with their brothers and sisters, and were only slightly (not significantly) more inclined to show outbursts of temper toward their parents. Other studies have shown, however, that boys *are* more likely to be aggressive at school and in the play yard. Perhaps this is why they long ago got the reputation of being made of "snips and snails, and puppy-dogs' tails."

It is evident that, for a number of mothers, being "boylike" implied being aggressive with one's playmates, especially in self-defense. An example of indulgence of aggression (and even its encouragement) in boys was provided by the mother who said:

I. *How important do you think it is for a boy of Ted's age to act like a real boy?*

M. *Very important, very important—I will repeat that. By a real boy, I mean not being a sissy; it is very important. I wouldn't want him otherwise—I would give him boxing lessons if I had to.*
I. *Have you ever encouraged him to fight back?*
M. *Oh, yes. I have told him if he can't fight back and take care of his own battle, I am not going out there. You see, that is another thing that he is going to have to learn: to give as well as take; and that is going to make him get away from these other feminine l:kes of his. But, you see, he runs away from it, which isn't good. This summer will be the test, because then he'll be six, and he'll be meeting up with the gang around here, and unless he establishes himself as being a good kid and a good boy in their eyes, he might feel it from that point on, you see. That is why I am playing up this big, strong angle. All the boy needs is confidence. I mean, if he can stop this youngster once and hurt him, that, I think, gives him so much confidence that he can do it again without being hurt himself too much. I am not one that goes out and just hits for the sake of hitting, but I think around here if a child hits you, you can't run home and cry to your mother; you've got to hit him back and learn to take it and give it too.*

Whether or not there are constitutional differences between boys and girls in the amount of aggressive impulse they have, it is clear that many mothers have provided ample learning experiences for the development of aggressive behavior by the time the child is five years old.

Tasks and chores. Other instances of training in appropriate sex-role behavior occurred in the kinds of tasks and chores that the mothers assigned their five-year-olds. In the over-all amount of tasks and chores assigned, there were no sex differences, but there were clear evidences of sex-typing in the nature of the chores that were assigned. Doing the dishes and making the beds were more often "girls' work," and there was a slight tendency for girls to set the table more commonly. The tasks of emptying the trash, cleaning ash trays, and emptying wastebaskets were male-typed, however.

School achievement. It is no surprise that boys were expected to go farther in school than girls. Their mothers usually had planned to send them to college, while the girls' mothers were more likely to expect that their girls would finish high school: college was a possibility, of course, if a girl showed unusual promise. Despite the great liberalizing of attitudes toward education for women in the last half century, a college education appears still to have been regarded as something of a luxury for women. For men, it was viewed as an essential avenue to high occupational status.

Techniques of training. There were three rather interesting differences in the use of techniques for training and disciplining: (1) Boys received somewhat more physical punishment than girls. Or, putting it more accurately, there were more girls who practically never received physical punishment. This sex

difference in the amount of spanking occurred only among the relatively non-aggressive children: among aggressive children, girls were spanked as often as boys. The girls, in contrast, were more often disciplined by love-oriented techniques. (2) They received somewhat more praise for "good" behavior than boys did; and (3) they were more often subjected to withdrawal of love for "bad" behavior.

These three differences may offer a clue to the reasons why girls showed more signs of conscience at this age, and were more likely than boys to assume adult roles in doll play. We saw in

Chapter Ten that physical punishment seemed to have inhibited the development of conscience, while love-oriented techniques had the opposite effect. We suggested that girls had an easier time taking on their appropriately sex-typed adult role because they did not have to shift from an initial identification with the mother, while boys have to shift to the father. Now we see that mothers more often used, with girls, the particular techniques of training which promoted this development.

One other point may be relevant here. The task of disciplining girls of kindergarten age was primarily in the hands of their mothers (Table XI:2). For boys, the father took a larger role in discipline when both parents were at home. According to our theory of identification, the development of conscience should be facilitated if discipline is administered by the same-sexed parent. Both nurturance and discipline appear to aid identification. On the assumption that the mother is generally a more nurturant figure than the father during the child's early years, her discipline should be more effective than his in ensuring the growth of self-control and conscience. The findings suggest, then, that this disciplining of girls by the parent who is the initial identificand would offer an additional factor favoring conscience development in girls, just as it favors more adequate sex-typing. Fathers are nurturant, too, however, and their greater participation in the disciplining of their sons may promote the boys' identification with the father. This would increase not only the boys' sex-typing, but should produce a more rapid development of conscience as well. But since the father is the second identificand for a boy, his influence on his son should be less than the mother's on a daughter. The evidence supports this conclusion.

Restrictions and demands. In this comparison of the total groups of boys' and girls' mothers, we found no evidence that the demands for ordinary mannerly behavior were more strongly pressed on one sex than on the other. We had anticipated that the seemingly greater mannerliness of little girls, as it is often noted in nursery schools and kindergartens, would be reflected in greater attention to these matters by the girls' mothers. On the other hand, as we noted earlier in this chapter, a good many mothers did not have very strong attitudes about differentiating the roles of boys and girls. It then occurred to us that perhaps our nursery school impressions of little girls (who are traditionally said to be made of "sugar and spice, and everything nice") were based on a few rather obtrusive examples rather than the generality of girls. If this were the case, possibly the strong training for niceness was occurring mainly among those mothers who did make a definite differentiation of sex roles.

To test this possibility, we compared all the child-rearing dimensions again, this time between the 91 mothers of boys and the 83 mothers of girls who were most strongly inclined to differentiate sex roles. We found only one new area of difference in the handling of the two sexes, and it fulfilled our anticipations. Between these two groups of mothers, there were definitely higher demands placed upon girls for table manners ($p<.05$), for being neat and orderly ($p<.05$), and for instant obedience ($p<.07$). Perhaps these mothers were the kind who produced the more ladylike little girls we have sometimes seen. Unfortunately, we made no observations of the children's manners, so we cannot be sure.

One other finding, of minor interest, resulted from this comparison of the more sex-role differentiating mothers. In the comparison of the total groups, boys' mothers were only slightly more permissive about masturbation. In the more restricted groups, this difference became large enough to be significant ($p<.05$).

ORDINAL POSITION

Parents often express amazement at the great differences they see among children in the same family. One child may be quiet and serious, more interested in reading and day-dreaming; another may be a happy-go-lucky youngster with a great enthusiasm for social play, full of fun, and interested in sports. Parental surprise about these differences stems from the supposition that the children have the same biological parents and the same family environment. But do they? In fact, siblings conceived at different times do not receive the same genetic input from their parents. There is some overlap, but it is far from complete. Neither is the family environment identical. A first-born child, for example, always has relatively inexperienced parents. He is an only child for a while. Later he has a younger sibling, or perhaps several. A second-born child never has the experience of being an only child; he always has an older sibling. One could multiply the differences almost endlessly.

In the last section we indicated what stable differences we found in the rearing of boys and girls. Are there similar consistencies in the rearing of children who arrive in different birth-order positions? There is a certain amount of folklore that suggests an affirmative answer. One mother stated her views quite succinctly:

> **M.** *Of course, I think the middle child takes an awful beating—they are just sort of pushed in between. They don't get as much attention as the first one got, and, of course, the last one gets all the loving, they're the baby. The middle one is sort of the lost one, I think.*

We can find a provisional indication of such patterns by comparing the average of the practices of mothers whose children were in one of the four ordinal positions which we used for classification: *only child, oldest* of two or more, *middle* of three or more, and *youngest* of two or more. The list of differences we find (see Table XI:3) is only provisional, however, for when the families are divided into groups in this fashion, there are other aspects of family life that vary with ordinal position. In other words, this division does not give a pure measure of the effects of birth order. For example, these four groups obviously differ in family size: "only" children live in a three-person family; a good many "oldest" and "youngest" children live in four-person families; and all "middle" children live in families that include five or more persons. Thus, the differences noted in Table XI:3 reflect not only the influence of the child's birth order but also the effect of family size.

We can—and will, below—make some corrections for this particular source of confusion, but there are many other variables that we cannot eliminate. For instance, there is the problem of age-gap between each child and his next-older or next-younger sibling. We saw in Chapter Two that the closer together her children came, the less frequently "delighted" about her pregnancies a mother was likely to be. If the size of the average age-gap varies with ordinal position (it does), then this becomes a contaminating influence. Likewise, there is the matter of the mother's age. In our present study, all the children whose child rearing we were examining were five years old. On the average,

TABLE XI:3

COMPARISON OF CHILD TRAINING IN RELATION TO THE ORDINAL POSITION OF THE CHILD

Scales	Only	Oldest	Middle	Youngest	F	p
Percentage breast-fed	42%	47%	42%	30%		
Median duration of breast feeding for those breast-fed (in months)	1.4	2.8	2.3	2.2	3.10	< .05
Median age at beginning of bowel training (in months)	9.6	9.0	11.0	9.9	3.40	< .05
Percentage rated *high* on:						
Severity of weaning	42%	26%	30%	43%	3.88	.01
Permissiveness for aggression toward siblings	—	27%	18%	15%	4.08	< .01
Restrictions of physical mobility	24%	18%	14%	15%	2.24	< .10
Giving child regular jobs	12%	12%	24%	5%	6.64	< .01
Keeping track of child	39%	32%	23%	32%	4.45	< .01
Praise if children play well together for a time	—	41%	36%	52%	3.23	< .05
Use of deprivation of privileges	41%	44%	39%	28%	3.85	.01
Mother finding time to play with child	78%	74%	57%	71%	3.93	.01
Percentage delighted when mother found she was pregnant	74%	68%	49%	40%	9.80	< .01
Percentage delighted when father learned wife was pregnant	72%	72%	58%	57%	3.95	.01
Who is the disciplinarian (when both parents present)?						
Primarily father	24%	37%	29%	29%		
Shared equally	27%	33%	29%	26%	3.76	.01
Primarily mother	49%	30%	42%	45%		
Who is stricter with child?						
Mother	38%	20%	30%	23%		
Equally strict	28%	39%	28%	34%	3.25	< .05
Father	34%	50%	42%	43%		

then, a mother whose *youngest* child was five was older than a mother whose *oldest* child was five. Not only were the mothers' ages different at the time of the interview, but their child rearing was begun at different times in the history of our child-rearing culture. Some of the older mothers, for example, had had little or no contact with such notions as self-demand feeding at the time they began their families.

We cannot hope to untangle this complex web of influences and thus discover a "pure" pattern of child-rearing practices that were consistently related to ordinal position alone. From a practical standpoint, however, we can compare the four positions and see what appear to have been the differences among them, whatever the reasons, even though we may remain skeptical that it was birth order *per se* that determined the mothers' different practices. It is important to remember that any such variable as sex of child or ordinal position can be only an *index* of common cultural factors that lead—possibly—to somewhat consistent child-rearing behavior by the mother.

Our method of comparison is to examine the four groups of mothers' rated practices to determine on what scales there were differences between the groups. All the relevant scales listed in Appendix B were examined, and those which were found (by *F*-test) to show significant differences among the ordinal positions are listed in Table XI:3. The reader who is interested in teasing out the extraneous influence of family size can examine the comparable findings for two-child families and for three- and four-child families in Appendix Tables D:24 and D:25. We will indicate some of the major influences of family size in our discussion below of the separate training areas and ordinal positions.

It is likely that one could secure a more exact impression of the differences in child rearing that depend on ordinal position alone by comparing the methods used with successive children in the same family. For reasons of research design, we could not do this in the present study. We did not directly question the mothers who had had several children concerning any changes they may have made from one child to the next. Many discussed this problem spontaneously, however, and we gained a general impression that both feeding and toilet-training methods were likely to be modified for later children as a result of experience with the first.

A

I. *Now we'd like to consider toilet training. When did you start bowel training with Jackie?*
M. *Much later than I did with his sister. I fussed over that terrifically with her, and I felt that it wasn't worth while, and I just waited, and*

he took care of himself very quickly. It just came naturally without any trouble at all.

B

M. [*Same question*] *There, again, you'll have to realize that I had two children before her. I did everything wrong with them so when it came to her, I didn't train her at all. When she was about twenty months old, I started showing her the bathroom and tried to get her interested, but she would have nothing to do with it. Then finally one day she decided she would, and she climbed up herself on the toilet seat, walked around and sat down, and from then on she went to the bathroom. In a short time she would wake up dry at night and there was no problem there. So she was the ideally trained one, and to this day, of the three oldest, she's the best trained. I have her sleeping in the guest room, because she's the one I can trust not to wet the bed. Her oldest sister wets the bed every other night.*

C

I. *There has been a lot of talk about whether it is better to have a regular feeding schedule for a baby, or to feed him whenever he is hungry. How do you feel about this?*
M. *Well, I do know I can compare the first and last most vividly, and with the first child, he was completely a schedule. It didn't make any difference if he cried an hour before, he waited for the time to come; but with Douglas, as I say, he was a child that—he would sleep through until ten o'clock in the morning sometimes, and he would get his bottle then—whenever he woke up.*

These quotations suggest changes mainly in the direction of greater indulgence of the younger children. As will be seen below, this principle did not hold true generally. In some areas of training and control, one ordinal position seems to have been treated more indulgently, and in other areas, other positions were. There does not appear to have been any "general indulgence" that was given consistently in greater degree to one position than another.

Feeding. There was an interesting difference between the ordinal positions with respect to breast feeding. Fewer *youngest* children were breast-fed. The difference was not very great in two-child families, but in the larger families, more than twice as many *oldest* children were put on the breast—the later the child in birth order, the less likely he was to be breast-fed. And even if he was, the length of time (number of months) he was kept on that kind of feeding was less than for the older children. The *middle* or *younger* children were weaned earlier and more severely. This tendency to avoid or to abbreviate breast feeding may have resulted, in some instances, from the mother's desire for modesty in the presence of other family members, including the children. In other instances, doubtless bottle feeding was dictated by the amount of personal time involved in breast feeding. The father or an older child could give the baby a bottle, leaving the mother free for the heavy housework entailed by three or more children in the family.

Toilet training. There was a slight tendency for mothers to begin the first child's bowel training earlier than the second child's. This was true regardless of family size. Then, in the larger families, the mothers tended to start a little earlier again when the youngest child came along. These differences are not large enough to have much significance, however, and there is no evidence of any consistent variation in the severity of toilet training.

Aggression. There were no differences among the various ordinal positions with respect to either permissiveness for aggression toward parents or the severity with which such aggression was punished. There was a fairly substantial difference, however, with respect to permissiveness for quarreling among the siblings. *Older* children were given more freedom than younger ones. In the two-child families, the older was also permitted more leeway in fighting with neighborhood children.

Restrictions and demands. There was little difference in the restrictions placed on children in the various positions. There was some tendency for second or later children to be held "under wraps" more with respect to making noise or interrupting adults at the table, and likely this was a function of family size. The more people there are, in a room or at a table, the more control is required to maintain a reasonable degree of peace and quiet. One other difference in restrictions that seems understandable was the greater limitation on physical mobility in the neighborhood, the stronger tendency to keep close track of the child, among mothers of *only* children.

On the demand side of the matter, there was a definite tendency for the *older* and *middle* children to be assigned more tasks and chores than were the *younger* children. This trend, not surprisingly, occurred mostly in the larger families, where the help of the older children represented a real saving in time and energy for the mother. The mothers of *youngest* children already had two or more older children, of course, and were probably less in need of what help the five-year-old could give. Spending time training the child to help was less essential than it would be if there were a still younger brood on the way.

The four positions

There were certain other differences in the treatment of children in the four birth-order positions, especially in connection with discipline and the role of the father in child care. These can best be described if we summarize the differentiating characteristics of each of the positions.

The only child. Actually, the only child differed from the others primarily in the extent to which his movements were restricted. The mother checked on his whereabouts more frequently and was inclined to confine him to his own yard at kindergarten age when other children were allowed to roam the block more freely. This is the only finding we have that suggests an element of "overprotection" in the mother's dealing with an only child, and even this was of a controlling rather than an indulgent kind.

One other aspect of the only child's experience is worth mentioning. This is the disciplinary role of his parents. There was a clear tendency for the mothers of only-girls to assume the chief disciplinary control of their daughters, and for the fathers of only-boys to do the same for their sons. Perhaps the chief emphasis should be placed on the former fact (mother-daughter), for in general there was a definite tendency for fathers to be more strongly participant in the rearing of first children than later ones, regardless of the children's sex. But this was not the case with those first children (*only*) who were not followed by later ones. The mothers, who were stricter than the fathers in this case, retained control over their daughters.

The oldest child. There was no indication that mothers placed higher demands on their first-born children than on later ones. In fact, in one important respect, they placed *fewer* demands: the oldest child was allowed to show more aggression toward his brothers and sisters than were the middle and youngest children. This fact has surprised us somewhat, for one would think that the oldest child, who is strongest and most skillful in hurting, would have to be the most carefully restrained if the younger children were to be protected. Perhaps the explanation lies in the age of these children. Our *oldest* children were five years old, on the average, and their younger brothers and sisters were therefore quite young. Our *youngest* and *middle* children were also five years old, which means that they were members of families where the age-range was greater and the average age of the children older. Mothers may have felt that the oldest children should be allowed a good deal of self-defense, since in many cases they were dealing with brothers and sisters who were too young to reason and who were given to unrestrained grabbing, pushing, and screaming. A five-year-old who is the youngest in a family, on the other hand, is dealing with brothers and sisters who have already attained a measure of self-control, and he must learn to match them in this respect. Possibly mothers directed their greatest efforts at aggression-control to the point where it was needed most: toward the youngest child, whose aggression may have appeared the most frequent and violent by comparison with that of the rest of the family.

An interesting facet of the life of an oldest child is the greater role played in his upbringing by his father. When the oldest child reached kindergarten age, the father was more likely to assume the disciplinary function (when he was home) than he was with the other children.

As we saw in Chapter Two, parents were more apt to be "delighted" over the advent of their first-born child, a situation which favored the only and oldest children to the very slight extent to which these feelings persisted after the child was born.

The middle child. Does the middle child really occupy the most difficult position? So far as demands for help with household tasks were concerned, these middle children did. Even when family size is held constant (see Appendix Table D:25), the middle child was most often expected to help with dishes, empty wastebaskets, etc. He also was praised less often for good behavior, if we may judge by what the mothers said they did when the children played nicely together for a while. For the middle child this virtuous behavior was likely to pass without comment, while for the youngest child it was cause for commendation. And the middle child, as might be expected, had less of his mother's time for fun and games: she said she less often had time to play with him. But the middle child was not being neglected in this sense *because* he was a middle child. As we pointed out earlier, the middle children were growing up in larger families, on the average, than were the oldest and youngest children. Mothers of large families had less time to play with *any* of their children, and when we make our comparisons within a group of three- and four-child families, we find that the mother did not play with her oldest or youngest child any more frequently than with her middle child.

In one respect the middle child was subject to *less* pressure than other children. His bowel training was begun later. In some cases, at least, this practice was followed because the mother had learned from experience with her first child that it was futile to begin very early. Curiously enough, however, in three- and four-child families the bowel training of the youngest child was begun earliest of all! Whether the later beginning for middle children operated as an advantage for them, implying an easier socialization experience, is a moot point. We saw in Chapter Four that the later-trained children tended to be more emotionally upset over their training, so perhaps middle children did not escape lightly in the matter of bowel training after all.

The youngest child. Was the youngest child—"the baby of the family"—more indulged than other children? With respect to feeding experiences in infancy, the answer is clearly "no." Regardless of the number of children in the family, the youngest was less often breast-fed. Weaning was more severe and also his feeding was just as rigidly scheduled as that of the older children in the family.

As we suggested earlier, a possible explanation for these facts is that the mothers of youngest children, having older children to care for, too, could not take on the personal restrictions of lengthy breast feeding. Possibly, too, experience with the older children made these mothers less anxious about the youngest child's vulnerability; they felt free to wean more abruptly. In any case, these findings contradict the widely held notion that youngest children are especially indulged in infancy.

But what about later, when they have reached kindergarten age? The answer depends on how many children there were in the family: in two-child families, the younger was *not* especially indulged; in three- and four-child families, he did tend to be (see Appendix Tables D:24 and D:25). In these latter families, there was quite a contrast between the treatment of the oldest and the youngest children. The oldest ones received more physical punishment, and affection was less openly shown toward them. The youngest, on the other hand, received little physical punishment; they were expected to do very little in the way of helping with household tasks; and their mothers were warmer toward them than toward middle or oldest children. There was a cloudy horizon for these youngest children in relatively large families, however: their mothers more often used withdrawal of love as a technique of discipline.

In two-child families, the situation of the younger child was seemingly quite different. These children were not shown greater warmth than were the older children, nor were they freer from physical punishment. Their parents were more strict with them about noise and about fighting with neighborhood children than they were with the older children.

The only thing that appears to have been a constant feature of being a youngest child, regardless of family size, was the greater role the mother played in caretaking and discipline. The father had less to do with the youngest child than he did with other children, regardless of their sexes. We saw earlier that he participated most with the oldest child, but *not*—be it noted —with an only child. When later children were born, and the mother required help from her husband, it was the oldest child, rather than the baby, whom she was most likely to turn over to him for brief periods. His relationship to the oldest child was not an unusually nurturant one, however, for he was stricter than the mother with this child.

Effects of ordinal position on child behavior. Of all these rather complex differences between the treatments given to children in the four ordinal positions, there are only three that we would expect to have an influence on the measures we obtained of the children's behavior.

1. In Chapter Three we described the effects of prolonged feeding at breast or bottle; the later the child was weaned, the greater was his emotional upset. Now we note that when oldest children were breast-fed, this mode of feeding continued longer with them than it did with children of any of the other birth-order positions. We would therefore expect that the oldest children had shown the greatest emotional upset at weaning. This proved to be the case.

2. In Chapter Seven we described the effect of permissiveness for aggression toward parents, and noted that high permissiveness was associated with high aggression toward parents. There was no difference among the four ordinal positions with respect to such permissiveness, and we therefore would expect no significant difference in amount of aggression. However, the fact is that *only* and *oldest* children were a little more aggressive ($p = .04$) than middle and youngest children.

Another unexpected finding is that the mothers reported *more* quarreling with siblings by middle and youngest children ($p < .05$), although mothers of oldest children tended to be more permissive of such behavior.

These reversals of the general principles described in Chapter Seven suggest an additional factor that may influence aggression. One could look at the children's aggression in this light: the unpredicted aggression was directed toward the next-highest available persons in the power hierarchy in the family. That is, *only* and *oldest* children were more aggressive toward the parents than would be predicted from the amount of permissiveness and punitiveness they received; *middle* and *youngest* were more aggressive toward their oldest siblings than would be predicted from the *lesser* amount of permissiveness allowed them for such quarreling. We may suggest, as a possible hypothesis for further research consideration, the following principle: relatively greater amounts of frustration and discomforting control in a family come from the persons who are immediately above the child in the power hierarchy than from other family members, and regardless of the parents' permissiveness and punitiveness, the younger child tends to be more aggressive toward those persons.

3. In Chapter Ten we noted the influence of love-oriented methods of discipline as sources of the "confession" reaction that we used to measure the development of conscience. Here, among the ordinal positions, we find a disturbing reversal. The *only* and *oldest* children had more strongly developed consciences, but they also suffered significantly more physical punishment and deprivation of privileges. This is just the opposite of the general finding. However, the *only* boys, and the *oldest* children of both sexes, were more commonly disciplined by the fathers, and this may have accounted for some of the more rapid conscience development in the boys.

We are more inclined to suspect that another principle is required to explain these differences, however. As in our discussion of aggression above, we look to the social structure of the family as a possible source. As we suggested in Chapter Ten, the development of conscience is a part of the larger process of learning through role practice. Within the family, the oldest child is often placed in the position of having more knowledge, power, and authority—and more responsibility for tasks and chores. These are adult-like role qualities. We suggest this further hypothesis: the direct training for adult role practice is greater in *oldest* children, and serves to increase the rate of development of conscience.

COMMENT

The patterns of child rearing associated with the two sexes are not greatly different, but what differences we found in this present group of mothers were pretty much what might be expected from our knowledge of sex differences in children's behavior. The findings with respect to ordinal position were limited and equivocal in this latter respect. They serve to point up the nature of such demographic concepts as sex and birth order, and at once suggest a caution concerning their use and a possible value to be gained from them.

The sex of her child provides an important stimulus to a mother. It places the child in a social category that has enormous implications for training. She knows the many differences in role that apply to the two sexes; she has expectancies that are congruent with these roles. Even by the age of five, the child elicits some kinds of behavior from the mother that are direct responses to the fact of the child's being a boy or a girl.

The mothers' discussions of this role differentiation made clear, however, that there are wide differences among mothers in the extent to which sex of the child influences her in the child's earliest years. Furthermore, there were not inconsiderable differences among the mothers in just what was to be expected in terms of sex role. Sex of the child, in other words, *is* a stimulus to the mother that instigates a whole set of patterned child-rearing practices, but the patterns are by no means perfectly uniform for all mothers.

This suggests a caution. The study of patterns related to sex of child may have some descriptive interest, providing one kind of ethnographic data, but it is an inferior way to study the relations between child rearing and personality development. There are so many differences among mothers of girls (or boys) that a crude comparison between the two groups is an inefficient way of discovering cause-and-effect relationships. The more useful approach, we believe, is the direct comparison of mother dimensions with child personality dimensions.

At the same time, we cannot ignore the fact that the child's sex, and especially his ordinal position in the family, place him in a particular social role. He lives in a social organization that has discoverable *group* characteristics. The analysis of ordinal position in this chapter has led us to two hypotheses that would not likely have suggested themselves had we limited our examination of the data to the kinds of mother-child dimensional correlations that characterized most of our reporting in Chapters Three through Ten. Indeed, such comparisons actually hide the social structure variables that we see dimly through the ordinal-position analysis. We suggest, then, that the study of demographic variables as determinants of differences in child rearing may have only descriptive value in itself, but that it may provide a tool by which new hypotheses involving *group* or *social structure* variables can be obtained.

CHAPTER TWELVE

Socio-economic Level, Education, and Age of Mother

In discussing the background for parenthood, in Chapter Two, we pointed out that a mother's child-rearing practices are one aspect of her personality. She was a child herself once, and was subjected to the child-rearing practices of her own parents. What she is and what she does are, in part, products of those experiences. For want of information, we have not been able to examine in detail the sources of each mother's practices; it would have been a most difficult investigative task to attempt a measure of the grandparental generation's practices, too!

There are two closely related aspects of a mother's experience, however, that can be measured with ease and reasonable accuracy. These are the amount of education she has had and the socio-economic level of society in which she has been living. Because of the way in which the latter variable is measured, the two aspects are almost one and the same. Whether we focus on occupation and income level, or on number of years of schooling, the experiences implied by the measures are very complex. Differences among people in these respects involve not only differ-

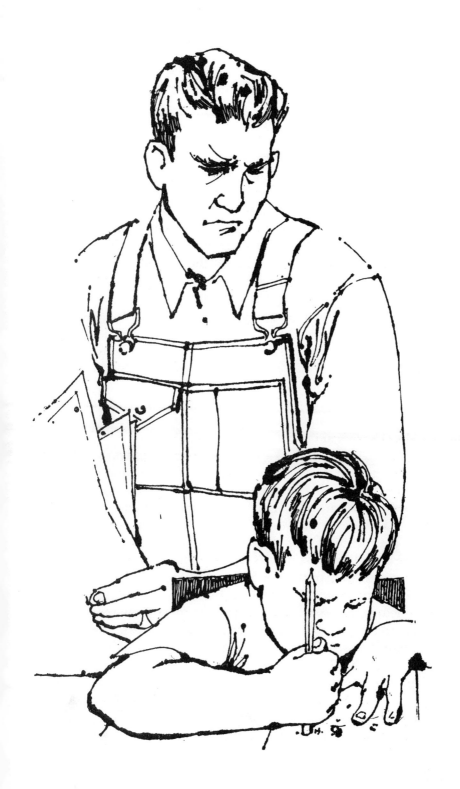

ences in original training but also in the manifold influences that are associated with specialized group membership. The child who stops his education with high school has not only the specific learning implied by that amount of education; he also enters adult life with skills that determine his occupational level and hence the income he can secure and the associates he will have. These associates, in turn, provide a constant stimulation of certain attitudes, values, and interests. He becomes a member of their group, and to the extent that the group members have a feeling of identity—a self-consciousness of status in relation to other groups—to that extent he continues to be influenced by contemporary experiences that are quite independent of those earlier ones specifically induced by the schooling he had. The same may be said for his level of income; the comfort of his life and the qualities of experience he can have are determined in part by the amount of money he has available for purchasing such commodities.

Differences among families in respect to these variables are associated with many other differences, some of which lead us to suspect that there may be pervasive differences in child rearing as well. There appear to be differences in the types of mental disease that are most common to people of working-class and middle-class origin. Types of juvenile delinquency vary, likewise, and there are substantial differences between high school and college educated males in the kinds and amounts of sex behavior that they report. All these kinds of behavior are ones that are presumably much influenced by parental child-rearing practices.

Does this mean that there are differences in the patterns of child rearing displayed by mothers of different socio-economic statuses and different amounts of education? Common observation says yes, but to date there has been little research evidence as to precisely what these differences are. The information we have obtained from the present group of mothers provides an opportunity to compare the practices and attitudes of two groups, those of middle-class socio-economic level and those of the working class. We can also compare groups which are divided in terms of amount of education. The results of these comparisons must be viewed with some caution. Our sample of mothers can hardly be called representative of the entire American population, and certainly we cannot have any conviction that the two subgroups defined in terms of SES (socio-economic status) or education are representative of their class or educational groups throughout the country. For a really definitive conclusion on the question we are posing, many other samples of mothers from other parts of the country will have to be interviewed. Furthermore, as we have emphasized repeatedly, the dimensions we have chosen for measurement by no means exhaust the possibilities for the description and measurement of child rearing. There are many other dimensions besides those we have examined, and we have no way of knowing whether some of the unmeasured dimensions would show SES and educational differences. Nevertheless, we can make a start with the present data.

SEPARATING THE SUBGROUPS

The definition of social class is a ticklish problem. Sociological studies have found that the status a person occupies in the eyes of the community is more a function of his occupation than any other single factor; although how well educated he is, and how much income he has, are important, too. These three factors are closely linked, of course, for the amount of money a man can earn is at least partly determined by his occupation; membership in some occupations or professions is limited to people who have met certain minimum educational standards. It is not surprising, then, that what we have called the family's socio-economic status (a composite of the husband's occupation and income) proves to be correlated with the educational level of the mother ($r = .58$). In our consideration of education, we have limited our analysis to the relationship with amount of schooling the mother had, since it was her child-rearing behavior about which we had the main findings. The two members of most husband-and-wife teams had similar educational backgrounds.

The measure of socio-economic status. At the beginning of the interview, the mother was asked a number of factual questions about the family's background. These included queries about husband's occupation, family income, education of the two parents and of the grandparents, country of origin of the grandparents, and the age of the parents. To get an index of SES, we combined a measure of occupational level with one of income. The occupation was scored on a scale of occupational status,[1] a rating of "1" being given to the most prestigeful occupations (doctor, lawyer, owner or manager of large business) and a rating of "7" to the least (unskilled laborer). The score on occupational status was then given a weight of 2, and was combined with a score on income (weighted 1) to produce a score on socio-economic status. There were 7 cases in our sample for whom we did not have sufficient information to permit a scoring of SES.

In order to discover on which, if any, dimensions of child rearing there were SES differences, we divided the remaining 372 cases into two subgroups: the "middle class" (198 cases) and the "working class" (174 cases). The middle-class group included primarily business and professional occupations, together with other white-collar occupations such as salesmen and clerical workers. The working-class group was composed primarily of blue-collar workers; they ranged from unskilled laborers to self-employed plumbers and carpenters, the largest number being relatively skilled workers who were not self-employed. In addition, the working-class group included gas station attendants, policemen and firemen, ticket agents, butchers, bartenders, etc. These same two class groups were labeled "upper-middle" and "upper-lower" in our previous publication (Maccoby and Gibbs, 1954).

The measure of educational level. For comparison of child training at different educational levels, we divided the sample into two slightly different subgroups: the mothers who went beyond high school (including those who attended nursing school, business school, or college), and those who completed their education with high school graduation or less. In the first group, there were 192 mothers; in the second, 180 mothers. For this analysis we excluded the 7 cases for whom we could not secure a score on socio-economic status. The education and social-class comparisons are therefore derived from the same mothers.

[1] The scale is described by Warner, Meeker, and Eells, *Social Class in America* (1949). Our "middle-class" group was approximately the same as their Groups 1 to 3, our "working-class" group the same as their Groups 4 to 7. A more detailed description of our method of measuring SES has been published by Maccoby and Gibbs, "Methods of child rearing in two social classes," in *Readings in Child Development,* edited by W. E. Martin and C. B. Stendler, pp. 380–396.

Relation of SES to education. Since SES and mother's education are rather highly correlated (.58), there is a big overlap in the groups. Most of the mothers who were in the middle-class group were also in the upper group on education (72 per cent); most of those in the working-class group were in the lower education group (71 per cent). Whenever we compare the child-training methods of middle-class families with those of working-class families, then, we are of necessity comparing the methods of well-educated with those of less well-educated mothers at the same time. If we wish to disentangle these factors, and study the influence of class level alone upon child training, we must compare people who differed in class level but had the same education. Conversely, to study the effects of education alone, we must compare people who had similar socio-economic level but different educational backgrounds. For some segments of our sample, such comparisons are impossible: for example, we did not have a single instance of a mother with graduate training whose husband's occupation and income placed her in the working-class group. Nor did we have any case of a woman who went only through grade school but whose husband had middle-class status. Thus we cannot study social-class differences at these educational levels. In the middle part of our scales, however, there was considerable variation in class for any education level, so some evaluation of the separate contributions of education and social class will be possible at these levels.

Since there is so much overlap between the two methods of splitting the total group, we will present the comparisons for SES only in Table XII:1. In those rare instances in which educational level appears to have been the more important determinant of differences, we will so indicate in the text.

All the scales given in Appendix B were examined to see whether they showed differences between the two SES subgroups and between the two education subgroups. In Table XII:1 are shown the dimensions on which there were statistically significant differences between the ratings given middle-class and working-class mothers.

In spite of the overlap between SES and education—a fact that makes their separate influences difficult to untangle in a simple comparison like that of Table XII:1—there is evidence, in a few instances, that one was more important than the other.

TABLE XII:1

DIFFERENCES IN CHILD-TRAINING PRACTICES BETWEEN MOTHERS OF TWO SOCIAL CLASSES

Scales	Middle Class	Working Class	p
Median age at completion of bowel training	18.8 months	16.4 months	.01
Percentage rated *high* on:			
Severity of toilet training	15%	26%	.01
Permissiveness for dependency	42%	29%	.02
Punishment, irritation, for dependency	44%	56%	.02
Sex permissiveness (summary)	53%	22%	< .01
Permissiveness for aggression toward neighborhood children	38%	31%	n.s.*
Permissiveness for aggression toward parents	19%	7%	< .01
Severity of punishment for aggression toward parents	36%	51%	< .01
Amount of restriction on the use of fingers for eating	66%	81%	< .05
Pressure for conformity with table standards and restrictions	23%	39%	< .01
Restrictions on care of house and furniture	65%	78%	< .01
Pressure for neatness and orderliness	43%	57%	< .01
Strictness about bedtime	28%	38%	< .05
Strictness about noise	28%	38%	< .05
Keeping track of child (frequency of checking whereabouts)	26%	33%	n.s.*
Extent of father's demands for instant obedience	53%	67%	< .05
Importance of child's doing well at school	35%	50%	< .01
Percentage who expect child to go to college	70%	24%	< .01
Percentage rated *high* on:			
Use of praise if child gives no trouble at table	49%	63%	< .05
Use of ridicule	31%	47%	< .01
Deprivation of privileges	34%	42%	n.s.*
Use of physical punishment	17%	33%	< .01
Amount of caretaking of infant by person other than mother or father	18%	11%	n.s.*
Mother's warmth to child	51%	37%	.01
Father's warmth to child	60%	56%	n.s.*
Percentage showing some rejection of child	24%	40%	< .01
Percentage of mothers "delighted" over pregnancy	73%	65%	.05
Percentage rated *high* on:			
Mother's esteem for father	54%	37%	.01
Parents' disagreement on child-rearing policies	15%	19%	n.s.*

(*continued*)

TABLE XII:1 (*continued*)
DIFFERENCES IN CHILD-TRAINING PRACTICES BETWEEN MOTHERS OF TWO SOCIAL
CLASSES

Scales	Middle Class	Working Class	*p*
Family authority exercised primarily by:			
Father	29%	25%	n.s.*
Both equally	62%	59%	n.s.*
Mother	9%	16%	n.s.*

* The difference between percentages is *not significant*, but the difference between mean ratings, as evaluated by a *t*-test, is significant at the *p* = .05 level or better.

The appropriate partial correlations are given in Appendix Table D:26.

SES COMPARISONS

Infant feeding. There was no reliable difference between the two social classes with respect to any of our measures of infant-feeding practices. However, there was a slight tendency for the working-class mothers to schedule feedings less rigidly than the middle-class mothers, but the difference was too small to have significance. There was no difference between the two classes, either, in a mother's report on her *child's emotional reaction to weaning*.[1]

Toilet training. The working-class mothers began toilet training no earlier than the middle-class mothers, but they completed the task nearly two and a half months quicker. They were also significantly more severe in their training: there was more punishment and scolding for accidents, more "shaming," more worry by the mother when she thought the child was slow in learning sphincter control. This class difference in severity, while significant, was not very large, however, and there was almost no difference between the two groups of children in the amount of disturbance shown in connection with being toilet-trained.

[1] In the previous publication of these findings (Maccoby and Gibbs, *op. cit.*), the figures on length of breast feeding, age at beginning of weaning, and age at completion of weaning, were presented in terms of *means* (averages) rather than medians. Because of the nature of the distributions, we have concluded that the central tendency is better described by medians than by means.

Dependency. Again we find greater strictness—less permissiveness—among the mothers of the working class. Likwise, as could be inferred from the correlation between strictness and punishment, the working-class mothers were more inclined to be irritated by dependency behavior and to reject it with a punishing attitude.

Sex training. In Table XII:1, we have presented only the summary scale on sex permissiveness. It will be recalled that this measure is simply the arithmetical sum of the ratings on the three permissiveness scales for modesty training, masturbation, and social sex play. In fact, as can be inferred easily from the enormous class difference shown on the summary scale, the working-class mothers were far less permissive on all three sex permissiveness scales, and used much more pressure (all three pressure scales) to prevent sex exploration. There is no question that within these eastern metropolitan communities, sex training was much more severe among poorly educated, working-class families.

Incidents of sex play that occurred among neighborhood children were described at length in Chapter Six. Such incidents occurred in all kinds of neighborhoods, of course, but the reactions of mothers to them varied greatly. Among the working-class mothers, the chief emotions appeared to be shock and shame, and the children were punished. Better-educated, middle-class mothers discouraged the more active forms of sex behavior, to be sure, but more often by separating the children, or admonishing them, than by punishment; and these mothers seemed to react with less emotional intensity.

It is interesting to note that Professor Kinsey (1948, 1953) reported marked differences, in several relevant forms of adult sexual activity, between subgroups of different educational level. He found that masturbation, nudity during marital intercourse, and variations in sexual technique were all more frequent among men and women of the higher educational levels. So, among women, was the degree of satisfaction obtained from marital sexuality, if we may take adequacy of orgasm as a measure. These findings suggest that permissiveness may have the same influence in the realm of sex as our findings in Chapter Seven showed it to have in connection with aggression—the greater the permissiveness, the more freely the permitted behavior occurred.

But certain other findings of Kinsey's make the matter appear not so simple. Among working-class men, he found the frequency of premarital and extramarital intercourse to be much greater, and marital intercourse too was somewhat more frequent for this group than among upper-middle-class men. How can the non-permissive, punitive attitudes of lower-class parents lead their children to be more sexually active as adults? Possibly we are witnessing here some of the energizing effects of punishment, or of conflict, which we discussed near the end of Chapter Five. In any case, it is clear that the greater freedom of upper-educational groups in certain aspects of their adult sexual behavior is paralleled by the greater permissiveness of this group toward the sexual explorations and display of their children.

Aggression. Class differences in the control of aggression were fairly marked. Although aggression toward parents was generally rather restricted, the middle-class mothers were more likely to overlook such incidents; these mothers were more permissive and less punitive, on the average, than were the working-class mothers; and fewer of them were judged to be extreme in punitiveness or non-permissiveness. On the average, too, they were most permissive of aggression toward neighborhood children, although there was no class difference in the proportion who were extremely permissive. The two classes showed equal tendencies to encourage aggressive behavior, and neither was more permissive than the other about fighting and quarreling between siblings.

Restrictions and demands. The middle-class mothers, and those with higher education, seemed to impose fewer restrictions and demands upon their five-year-olds than did the working-class mothers of lesser education. Messiness at the table was somewhat less often permitted for children in the lower groups, and those children were subject to more stringent requirements about such things as hanging up their clothes, keeping their feet off the furniture, and being quiet around the house. As we saw in Chapter Eight, few mothers gave their kindergarten-age children regular jobs to do around the house; as a general thing, the children were not required to help with the dishes, make beds, set the table, or take care of younger children. The assignment of household tasks to young children was equally rare in both social-class groups. The mother's education, however, did seem to have some bearing upon this aspect of child training; the better educated she was, the more likely she was to assign regular tasks to the child.

The children of middle-class, better-educated mothers were allowed more freedom to cross streets or go several houses away to visit other children, and the mothers were less likely to check constantly on the youngsters' whereabouts. Whether this was because their neighborhoods were safer, we do not know.

Achievement pressures and standards. The middle-class, better-educated families took it for granted that their children would go to college, but they did not seem to be so concerned about current school achievement as did the working-class families. Possibly the middle-class children, with their well-educated parents from whom they had already learned a good many school-related things before the age of five, adjusted to school more easily and worried their parents less. Current school performance may have been more of a problem for the working-class families. More parental pressure may have been required to keep working-class children performing at reasonable standards. In any case, our study does not show any tendency for the working-class, or the less well-educated, parents to take school achievement lightly. On the contrary, they seemed emphatically interested in having their children do well in school, and placed much more pressure on their children than did the middle-class families. At the same time, the reports show very clearly that parental aspirations for college education were much higher in the middle class.

Historically, the middle class has supplied the largest proportion of college students in the United States. As Warner, Havighurst, and Loeb (1944) have shown in their challenging little book *Who Shall Be Educated?*, part of the reason for this social-class imbalance is financial. We may suspect that scholastic aptitude plays a role, too. But from our present data we infer that some of the reason may well lie in parental expectancies and planning. Even in 1951, we find that although more of the working-class mothers were placing high pressures on their children to do well in school, only about a third as many of them (as of the middle-class mothers) had any real expectation that their children would go to college.

Techniques of discipline. As we have noted above, the working-class mothers were more punitive toward their children with respect to toilet training, dependency, sex, and aggression training.

Their methods differed somewhat from those of middle-class mothers, too. There was little or no class difference in the ratings on *isolation* and *withdrawal of love*, although on this latter dimension there was a significantly higher average rating for the lower educational level mothers when the comparison was made on the basis of education rather than SES. The greater amount of punishment used by working-class mothers was composed mainly of *physical punishment* and *deprivation of privileges*. As Table

XII:1 shows, there was a larger proportion of working-class than of middle-class mothers who were rated high on these latter two techniques. *Ridicule* also was more frequent in the working class, although so few cases could be judged on this scale that its importance is slight. In general, these comparisons suggest that there was more punishment applied to the children of working-class families—possibly, even, more punishment of every kind—but that, relatively speaking, there was a greater difference with respect to object-oriented than love-oriented techniques.

Interestingly enough, this greater use of object-oriented than of love-oriented techniques was true of punishment only. It did not apply to the rewarding aspects of discipline. There was no class difference at all with respect to the use of tangible rewards or the over-all use of praise. Indeed, the working-class mothers tended to use more praise for good table behavior than did the middle-class mothers.

Agents of child care. Not surprisingly, the financially better off middle-class families had a slight tendency to use non-family members a little more frequently for child care. When educational levels are compared, however, this difference disappears.

Warmth and family adjustment. The middle-class mothers were slightly more demonstrative toward their five-year-olds, and seemed to have a somewhat warmer relationship with them than did mothers in the working class, although the majority of mothers in both groups were warm toward their children and displayed only minor elements of hostility toward them. There were a few cases in which a clear pattern of rejection emerged, and those which did occur were found more often among the working-class, lesser-educated families. Mothers in both groups seemed to accept the role of mother easily, and subordinated other roles to it without discomfort. Mothers in the middle-class, better-educated groups were somewhat more pleased about the advent of a new child—possibly because, on the average, they waited longer to begin their families.

The relationships between the mother and father differed somewhat along class and education lines: the working-class, less well-educated mothers were more critical of their husbands, and there was more open quarreling between the two parents over child-rearing practices than there was among the middle-class families. Regardless of SES or education, the husbands were inclined to believe that their wives were not strict enough with the children, while the wives tended to believe that their husbands were too strict.

Summary. These various comparisons seem reasonably clear in their implications. By and large, the middle-class mothers were gentler than the working-class mothers. They were more permissive in four of the five major areas of socialization that we investigated, and they were less punitive toward changeworthy behavior in their children. They were relatively less object-oriented in their punishment techniques, and they were less restrictive about vigorous activity in the home and free-ranging exploration out of it. They were warmer toward their children, more comfortable with themselves, and had a more concordant relationship with their husbands so far as child rearing was concerned. In terms of our factor analysis, the two classes differed quite significantly with respect to Factors A, B, C, and E.

These are fairly radical differences. It must be kept in mind that we are comparing here not two fully discriminable groups, such as men and women, but two halves of what some observers would consider a homogeneous population—a sample of the American people. Evidently the sample is not as homogeneous as that nationalistic label implies. But are the differences really related to class (occupational and income) position, or are they the accidental result of some possible hidden correlation between our measure of class and some other determinant? We have already considered level of education as a contaminant. More about that later. There are three other ways in which our social-class groups conceivably could differ. One is family size—historically, families of lower socio-economic status have had more children than those of the middle class have had. The second is age of mother—middle-class girls commonly marry later than working-class girls. The third is the ethnic and religious backgrounds of the families.

In the following sections, we will examine these four influences —mother's education, the family size, mother's age, and ethnic background—to discover what each contributes, if anything, to the differences we have described above as the correlates of socio-economic status.

EDUCATION OF MOTHER

By and large, the same trends emerged whether we compared mothers on the basis of their education or on the basis of their socio-economic status. This fact is not surprising, in view of the close correlation between these two measures. It is interesting to inquire, nevertheless, about the effects of the mother's education (apart from her social-class level) on her child-training methods, and the effects of social class alone when education is held constant. For this analysis, we have singled out those child-training practices which differed either between class or between education groups. With partial correlations, we have determined how much correlation remains between socio-economic status and each of these child-training variables when the mother's education is "partialed out," and how much correlation remains between education and the child-training practice when SES is partialed out. The full table of correlations and partial correlations is given in Appendix D, Table D:26.

There were a number of child-training practices for which the variation appeared to be a function of socio-economic class rather than of education. When mothers of the same educational level but of different socio-economic class are compared, we find that the *middle-class mothers:*

1. More often left their children with a maid or sitter.

2. Were more affectionately warm toward their children and less likely to display whatever signs of rejection we could detect in an interview.

3. Admired their husbands more, and quarreled with them less over the way children should be raised.

4. Used ridicule less as a technique of discipline.

5. Used isolation more as a technique of discipline.

Better-educated mothers did not differ from mothers of lesser education with respect to these aspects of child training, once social-class level was held constant.

On the other hand, there were a number of aspects of child training for which the mother's education appeared to be the more critical factor. When we compare people of the same socio-economic level but of different educational achievement, we find that the *better-educated mothers:*

1. Toilet-trained their children later.

2. Gave them more regular household tasks to perform.

3. Used reasoning more, and tangible reward less, as techniques of training.

4. Were less restrictive on the child's use of fingers for eating, less restrictive about his treatment of the house and furniture, and applied less pressure for neatness and orderliness.

5. Were less inclined to insist that a boy must be masculine and a girl feminine.

6. Were more permissive of the child's dependency.

The social-class groups did not differ with respect to these matters, once the mother's education was held constant.

Beyond these differences, there were a number of instances in which both education *and* social class, each taken separately, seemed to be important as correlates of child-training practices. Better-educated mothers regardless of socio-economic level, and middle-class mothers regardless of education level, differed from their lesser-educated, working-class counterparts in the following ways:

1. They were somewhat less severe in toilet training.
2. They expected the child to go farther in school.
3. They permitted their children to express aggression somewhat more freely toward their parents, and punished such aggressive outbursts less severely.
4. They were more permissive about sex behavior in their children.
5. They less often punished their children physically or by depriving them of privileges.
6. They praised less when the child behaved well at table.

It should be pointed out that while both the mother's education and the socio-economic level of the family contributed independently to the differences in permissiveness for aggression, education contributed more than SES. And surprisingly, the family's feeling about whether the child should be expected to go to college was more strongly related to socio-economic level than to the mother's education, although both did make a difference.

FAMILY SIZE

Although the working-class mothers were somewhat more severe with their children than were middle-class mothers, this difference may have had nothing to do with social-class level *per se*. Perhaps the problem was that the working-class mothers had larger families and less help in caring for them so that they did not have the time to give much individual attention to their children, and had to be stricter in order to cope with the many demands the children made. In other words, it is possible that if we compared working-class families who had a certain number of children with middle-class families having the same number, there would be little or no difference between them in their child-training methods.

In our sample, surprisingly enough, there was no appreciable difference between working-class and middle-class families in the number of children they had. The average was 2.7 children for the middle-class families, 2.5 for the working class. This does not mean that no such differences could have been found in the neighborhoods in which we worked. But we made a special effort to see to it that our sample included an adequate number of *only* children, *oldest* children, *youngest* children, and *middle* children. In the process of balancing our sample for this factor, we discarded a number of children because they had family-compositions which were already adequately (or overly) represented. Instead, we went in search of the rarer families (those with *only* children, for example). Our procedure seems to have erased any class differences in family size which might otherwise have appeared. Thus the class differences in child-rearing methods which have been described above could not have been due to differences in the number of children with whom the mothers had to cope.

Mother's Age

Another factor which must be examined is the mother's age. The middle-class women had tended to marry later than the working-class women, and hence the average middle-class mother was somewhat older than the average working-class mother at the time she had her children and at the time of our interview. Similarly, the better-educated mothers were older than the less well-educated mothers. This means that the class or educational differences in child-training methods that have emerged in our analysis may have been a function of the mother's age rather than of her social or educational background. As may be seen from Table XII:2, in which older and younger mothers are compared with respect to those child-training practices on which they differed, the younger mothers did in fact tend to be somewhat more severe in their treatment of young children.

This comparison of older and younger mothers is particularly interesting in view of the widely held belief that younger mothers are more relaxed, more spontaneously warm, and more able

to cope with the demands of child care. There is a common belief that it is best for parents to be "young with their children,"
and that older mothers tire more easily and are consequently
more irritable. Our findings suggest a quite different state of
affairs; *younger* mothers appeared to be more irritable, in that
they were quick to punish, more likely to quarrel with their
husbands, and somewhat more likely to express an underlying
feeling of hostility toward their children.

We can only speculate about why this should have been the
case. We saw earlier that one source of dissatisfaction for some
young mothers was having to settle down to child rearing in

TABLE XII:2

CHILD TRAINING IN RELATION TO THE AGE OF THE MOTHER

Scales	Younger Mothers	Older Mothers	p
Percentage rate *high* on:			
Severity of toilet training	24%	16%	.05
Sex permissiveness	34%	42%	.05
Encouraging child to fight back if attacked	35%	17%	< .01
Use of physical punishment	30%	21%	.05
Use of deprivation of privileges	43%	33%	.05
Use of ridicule	33%	22%	< .05
Warmth to child	41%	48%	n.s. *
Mother's esteem for father	42%	49%	n.s. *
Parents' disagreement on child-rearing policies	21%	12%	< .05

* The difference between percentages is *not significant,* but the difference between mean
ratings, as evaluated by a *t*-test, is significant at the $p = .05$ level or better.

relative social isolation. The difficulty was not so much that the
mother had a yearning after a career but that she regretted that
the glamorous days of courtship were over. Possibly younger
mothers would feel this loss more keenly. We have no direct
evidence. In any case, whether their severity with their children
stemmed from a general sense of frustration with their life situation or simply from a lack of experience and maturity in interpersonal relations, the fact remains that the average young
mother in our sample was more severe than the average older
one.

It should be noted here that the aspects of child training listed
in Table XII:2 are *not* (with one exception) matters concern-

ing which the ordinal position of the child made any difference (see Chapter Eleven). This means that the younger mothers' greater severity was not due to the fact that they were dealing with their first child; nor was the greater gentleness of the older mothers due to the experience of having dealt with previous children.

Since the working-class mothers, on the average, were both younger and more severe in their child training than middle-class mothers, our next question must be as to whether it was the mother's age *per se* or her social class which had a greater bearing upon the differences in child training. The general answer to this question is that social class carried more weight than the mother's age. Appendix Table D:27 presents the relevant partial correlations. There it may be seen that social class *alone* was important with respect to:

1. Severity of toilet training
2. Sex permissiveness
3. The mother's esteem for her husband
4. The mother's warmth toward her kindergarten-age child

This means that with respect to the above aspects of child training, the age of the mother did not make any difference when the influence of her social-class level was held constant. Social class did make a difference in these matters, however, even when the mother's age was held constant. On the other hand, the younger mother's tendency to urge the child to fight back when attacked, and her tendency to use withdrawal of privileges as a technique of controlling the child, seemed to be a function of the mother's age alone. Social class, as such, had no relation.

There were several aspects of child training for which both the mother's age and her social class made a difference, each when the other was held constant. These aspects included:

1. The extent of agreement between the husband and wife about how the children should be reared
2. The use of physical punishment
3. The use of ridicule

Social class had a *greater* bearing on the mother's use of physical punishment and ridicule than did her age, although each was important in its own right.

Ethnic and Religious Background

A final query must be made concerning the social-class differences in child training which have been described in this chapter. The families we studied came from a variety of nationality and religious backgrounds. While we did not ask about religion in our interviews, some of the mothers mentioned their religious affiliation spontaneously. Furthermore, we asked about the birthplace of the child's grandparents. From this information, to-

TABLE XII:3

ETHNIC BACKGROUND OF MOTHERS OF TWO SOCIAL CLASSES

Ethnic Group	Middle Class	Working Class
Italian	7	36
Irish	40	30
Jewish	64	15
Old American *	33	19
Contemporary British †	22	32
Mixed	6	10
Not ascertained	26	32
Number of cases	198	174

* Old American means a family in which neither husband's nor wife's parents were foreign born, and in which the family name was of English origin.
† Contemporary British included some Canadians, Nova Scotians, and a few Scotch; the majority were English.

gether with what we could deduce from a close study of family names, we were able to identify several "ethnic" groups within our sample—that is, several groups with distinguishably different cultural backgrounds which might have influenced their child training practices.

As one might expect, the middle-class families had a different distribution of ethnic backgrounds than the working-class families (Table XII:3). There were 74 families who were not included in this analysis, either because our information about their ethnic background was too meagre to permit our classifying them into the above groups, or because they belonged to a group that was too small, in our sample, for separate analysis (e.g., French or Armenian), or because the grandparents were from mixed backgrounds.

Several questions arise with respect to the different ethnic composition of our two class groups: (1) To what extent were the class differences which we have described a function of the different ethnic backgrounds of the two class groups? (2) Were there any social-class differences to be found only within certain ethnic groups? (3) Were there instances in which the social classes differed in one direction in one ethnic group, and in the other direction in another ethnic group, so that when all ethnic groups were combined, no class differences would be detected?

The answer to our first question is that, with one partial exception, the *major* class differences presented earlier in this chapter were found within each ethnic group taken separately. The tendency for the working-class group to be more severe in child training is not traceable to the fact that our working-class group contained more Italian and British families, and fewer Jewish, Irish and Old American families than our middle-class group.

The ethnic group which was least like the rest of the sample in terms of class differences was the Contemporary British. These families were *not* clearly more permissive at the higher levels of the socio-economic scale. The two class groups differed very little in permissiveness for sex behavior in their children, and the middle-class British families were somewhat less inclined to allow children to show aggression toward their parents than were working-class British families. Furthermore, the middle-class British families were more inclined to impose restrictions on the children with respect to neatness in the house, being quiet, going to bed promptly, etc., than were the working-class families of British origin.

Another interesting variation appears with respect to the mother's emotional warmth to her child. We saw earlier that, taking all ethnic groups together, the middle-class mothers tended to be warmer. A good deal of this class difference is contributed by the Jewish families, for among the working class, the Jewish mothers were slightly colder than other mothers of that class, while among the middle class, they were considerably warmer. Among the Irish families, on the other hand, there were no class differences; the working-class Irish mothers showed the same amount of emotional warmth toward their children as did the middle-class Irish mothers.

There was one curious instance in which a significant class difference appeared *in opposite directions* within two ethnic groups. Among British families, the working-class mothers were more likely to use isolation as a technique of controlling the child, while among Jewish mothers the reverse was true, isolation being a favored technique of the middle-class mothers. These opposite tendencies served to erase any difference between the total class subgroups.

Perhaps the best way to summarize the importance of ethnicity in relation to class differences is this: the major differences between middle-class and working-class mothers which were revealed when we compared these two groups for our whole sample were still in evidence when we studied class differences in each ethnic group separately. There were, of course, a number of instances in which the conclusions seemed to apply to all ethnic groups save one, but there were no instances in which class differences disappeared once ethnicity was held constant. Our earlier statement of class differences may be regarded as a *minimum* statement, for we did find a number of instances in which a given aspect of child training was handled differently by the working-class mothers than by the middle-class mothers in a given ethnic group, while no difference could be detected when the sample was considered as a whole.

COMMENT

To untangle fully the influences on child rearing of as many as five demographic factors would require many more cases than we have had available. The analysis we have given in this chapter leads to the conclusion that at least four of those we examined—social class, education, mother's age, and ethnicity—are related in one way or another to mothers' choices of methods. Some of the findings presented in Chapters Two and Seven indicated that the fifth—family size—also has some influence. Our main purpose in the present chapter, however, has been to determine what relation there may have been between social class and child rearing, and where such relations have appeared, to discover whether any of the other four factors were contaminating the social-class results.

Our special concern for social class has a curious history. Western man apparently always has had a penchant for distinguishing among different groups of people in terms of such categories as sex, age, class, race, and religion. Along with this labeling has gone the development of stereotypes as to what each group is like. Women are emotional; men are logical; the old are tolerant and wise; Jews are avaricious; the Scotch are dour; college professors are impractical; and so on. Whatever may have been the sources, historically, of these stereotypes, there is no question that in contemporary society they lack sufficient validity to make them useful predictors of the behavior of the individual persons who belong to such labeled groups.

One of the most venerable stereotypes has been that applied by middle-class people to lower-class people. The qualities have from time to time included lack of thrift, intellectual inferiority, habitual dirtiness, licentiousness, and many others that have derogatory implications. Some of these stereotypical notions, being essentially false, have created discord in our society and have militated against the improvement of the status of the people so described. This is not to say that there are no average group differences in the behavior and personalities of people who are members of different social-class groups. There is ample evidence of such variation, and our present data add substantially to previous knowledge. The significant points are: (1) that some of the existing stereotypes do not correspond with the group differences which actually exist, and (2) that many stereotypes are highly oversimplified and do not reflect the great individual variation among the persons composing class groups.

One stereotype about the working-class child began to create a major problem at the time of the growth of the American policy of free and universal education. Early educators recognized that there were some children who were insufficiently intelligent to profit from more than a minimal schooling. They could point to the village idiot and to the obviously feeble-minded. But how many others were there? The stereotypic notion that children of the working class were not very bright suggested to some policymakers that perhaps we needed very few educational facilities at the secondary and collegiate levels because most of the working-class children would not need so much schooling.

The development and wide-scale use of intelligence tests during the first quarter of this century made clear that a vast majority of children could benefit from much more education than many nineteenth-century laymen had supposed. Likewise, it was discovered that children of topmost intellectual caliber were almost as often found in working-class homes as in middle-class ones. As the economic prosperity of the post-World War I decade rolled on, vast numbers of working-class children were able to continue their education into secondary and collegiate levels. By the time of the Great Depression of the 1930's, educators knew full well that whatever seeming intellectual inadequacy there may have been among the working-class children of earlier generations, much of it was a product of limited education, not of lacks in native endowment.

It was nonetheless true that the class structure of America continued to exist, and that many working-class children had little motivation to secure the education which would assist them to rise in occupational status. Studies made during the Depression showed clearly that some of this immobility stemmed from economic inability of lower-income families to continue their children's education. But economics was not the only inhibitor, as we have noted in the present investigation. Only a third as many of our working-class mothers expected their children to go to college as did the middle-class mothers. Doubtless some of this difference rested on reasonably correct appraisals of children's intellectual potentialities, and some probably had an economic basis. But there were enough casual comments about occupational expectancies to make clear that some of the class difference was a reflection of differences in attitudes, motivation, and levels of aspiration. Whence *these* differences?

During the last two decades, educators and sociologists have been seeking the answer in two related places. One is the educational curriculum itself. There is good indication that until recently the schools have been rather heavily influenced by middle-class values and interests, and have provided curricula that were more suitable to middle-class career planning than to working-class expectancies. This situation has changed radically in recent years, and doubtless will change much more in the future. American society will gradually obtain the most effective types of training for the lives its many kinds of youth may expect to lead. The presumption is that, as the curriculum more fully fits the needs of working-class youth, the greater the proportion of these youth who will be motivated to continue their education to an optimum level.

The other place in which an answer to the problem of motivation has been sought is in the child-rearing practices of working-class parents. Many educators have speculated that if these parents expressed more interest in schooling, to the children, and placed more stress on academic success, the children would react more positively toward educational experience. The problem goes far beyond the academic, of course. There are other ways in which working-class and middle-class people differ, and in some of these (e.g., crime rate) there would be considerable advantage in the discovery of what, if any, child-rearing practices are responsible. The presumption is that once the origins of such differences are known, the undesirable characteristics of the behavior of *either* class (or both) could be eliminated by modification of child-rearing methods.

The first major publication to describe social-class differences in child rearing was that of Davis and Havighurst (1946). They obtained interviews with 48 middle-class and 52 lower-class mothers in Chicago. The interviews covered several of the same topics our later ones did. The class differences were similar to ours in several respects, as Havighurst and Davis (1955) have shown in a careful comparison of the two sets of data.

In contrast to our findings, however, they discovered that their middle-class mothers completed weaning earlier, scheduled infant feeding more rigidly, and toilet-trained earlier than did the lower-class mothers. They found also that middle-class children masturbated more often (a finding later clearly substantiated by Kinsey's researches). They also noted that while middle-class mothers allowed their children to go downtown alone at an earlier age than did the lower-class mothers, the middle-class mothers placed greater restrictions on going to the movies alone.

These findings led Davis and Havighurst to conclude—and quite reasonably, in terms of the knowledge about child development that was available a decade ago—that middle-class children were being more restrictively reared than lower-class children. It was not known at that time that earlier weaning creates *less* upset rather than more, and that early toilet training is by no means uniformly related to greater difficulty for the child. They interpreted masturbation as an indicator of tension and anxiety, an interpretation which undoubtedly has some validity. But frequency of mothers' observation of masturbation is probably a highly contaminated measure of a child's anxiety in this instance, since, as was shown in the present study, middle-class mothers were much more tolerant of such behavior. If permissiveness has the same effect on masturbation as it has on aggression, we would expect more masturbation by middle-class children for that reason rather than because they were necessarily more tense.

How shall we interpret these findings? There are two sets of data to compare with those of Davis and Havighurst. One is our own, which is comprised of the reports from 372 mothers. The other is a study reported by Dr. E. H. Klatskin (1952) of Yale University. Those data were secured from 223 mothers at the New Haven Hospital Rooming-In project. Neither Dr. Klatskin nor we found any class difference in age of weaning or rigidity of scheduling feedings. We are inclined to suspect, therefore, that these are not very stable or customary class differences. With respect to age at beginning of toilet training, Klatskin reported a later average age for middle-class mothers, and we found no class difference. We did find, however, that working-class mothers pressed the training through to completion earlier and were more severe in their methods. We doubt that the differences in age of toilet training are of any great consequence or stability, but the greater severity in the working class is in accord with all our other measures; and indeed, Davis and Havighurst noted the greater use of punishment by lower-class mothers. Dr. Klatskin's findings in other areas of training were similar to ours.

What about the practice of allowing children to roam the neighborhood freely or go to the movies alone? Davis and Havighurst interpreted this to mean greater permissiveness in the lower class. We found, on the other hand, that lower-class mothers were *less* likely to allow their young children to go away from the confines of their own yards without supervision. Of course it might happen that later on our working-class mothers would allow their children to go to the movies alone more willingly than a middle-class mother would. If so, our interpretation of this fact, based on the attitudes working-class mothers expressed to us, would be that the "freedom" they were allowing their children in this respect actually might be a reflection of rejection, a pushing of the child out of the way. Such freedom was associated, in our study, with a higher restriction on the child's household activities. Davis and Havighurst reported also that middle-class children were given more chores, implying that lower-class children were allowed a more carefree existence. In our own study, we found a similar difference, but it was too small to be statistically significant.

This re-examination of the Chicago findings suggests quite clearly the same conclusion that must be reached from Klatskin's study and from our own: the middle-class mothers were generally more permissive and less punitive toward their young children than were working-class mothers. Unfortunately, the opposite interpretation, as presented by Davis and Havighurst, has been widely accepted in education circles during the past decade. This notion of working-class permissiveness has been attractive for various reasons. It has provided an easy explanation of why working-class children have lower academic achievement motivation than do middle-class children—their mothers place less restrictive pressure on them. It has also provided a kind of compensatory comfort for those educators who have been working hard toward the goal of improving educational experiences for the non-college–oriented part of the school population. In effect, one could say, lower-class children may lack the so highly desirable academic motivation, but the lack stems from a "good" reason—the children were permissively reared.

Attractive or not, however, this new stereotype of the working-class mother is unsupported by the facts. False stereotypes, even idealistic ones, have no place in a society that believes in working out its social problems on a rational basis. The working-class mother needs no apologists. The last thirty years of American education have removed once and for all any notion that all intellectual talent is to be found in the middle class. Perhaps the next thirty will provide sufficient information about the effects of different child-rearing practices that *all* mothers—regardless of the conventional categories of class, color, and creed—will be able to choose the best from among them. As of mid-century, somewhat more of the working-class than of the middle-class mothers in our sample were using rather punitive and restrictive methods. With our present limited knowledge of the effects of punitiveness, we may think their children were therefore somewhat disadvantaged. But when these mothers can know the effects of what they do, will there still be the same class differences?

CHAPTER THIRTEEN

The Sum and Substance

By the very nature of research, a report of the findings must seem fragmentary. No one investigation can examine everything there is to be examined about whatever part of nature is the subject of study. Asking questions about a natural phenomenon —whether it be child rearing or igneous rocks or mold—implies the separating out of specific aspects of the phenomenon and describing them as precisely as possible. What precision is obtained depends on what instruments are available. A low-power monocular microscope limits the number and kinds of "invisible objects" that can be studied by the biologist. An electron microscope reveals a very different world. Just so, the interviewing of mothers about their child-rearing practices and attitudes provides a limited description of those phenomena. What we have learned from the present research is in large part a function of our method of study. This is inevitable, and important to keep in mind when we draw together our results.

Even within the confines of what is possible with a particular method, there are other choices that limit discovery. One's conception of the larger process of which the subject of study is a part determines the kinds of questions one asks. So does one's conception of what is important to find out first, and what can be left for later, or for someone else to study. In the present research, for example, we dwelt at length on the training methods applied to eating and toilet behavior, because we felt the great

amount of recent theoretical controversy in respect to these matters urgently demanded a few more facts. Likewise, we sought the sources of children's *actions*, rather than their *perceptions*, because our view of the process of personality development makes large use of the former but not of the latter.

These various limitations do not minimize or invalidate what results *have* come from the study, but they do remind us that there are many other knowable things about child rearing that *have not* come from it. We now know more than we did before about the ways mothers handle their children's dependency and aggression, and the effects these ways have on children. We have very substantial information about methods of controlling sex exploration, and several new facts about the influence of disciplinary methods on the development of conscience. But we know nothing new whatever about the sources of children's creativity, or their intelligence, or their achievement motivation. We did not study these aspects of nature. Hence, inevitably, our account of child rearing must seem fragmentary and our choices of topics arbitrary.

The facts we have found are important ones, however, and they will gain in importance if they are placed in the broader context of personality theory and its relation to child rearing. In the first chapter we described very briefly our view of the child's development. We did this only for the purpose of making clear why we chose to study the particular dimensions of child rearing that have been reported in the later chapters. To make these fragments of nature fall into place, so that they look a little more like nature and a little less like isolated bits and pieces, we will describe in more detail the ways in which we conceive child rearing to be related to personality.

Personality and Child Rearing

Personality, as the term is commonly used, is the cluster of *potentialities for action* that characterize the individual. These can be of many kinds and relate to a great variety of actions. Some are intellectual qualities, such as capacity for arithmetical reasoning or the imaginal manipulation of spatial concepts. Others are related to style of movement, such as quickness or tenseness or cumbersomeness. Still others describe the kinds of interpersonal action—perhaps aggressive or dependent or competitive—that will be elicited under appropriate circumstances.

It would be impossible, of course, to list all the qualities that compose a personality. Every word or phrase that specifies a way in which a person will act under a given set of circumstances is a description of one aspect of his personality. To try to describe all such potential actions, even in one individual, would be a hopeless task. The nearest approach to such an undertaking is performed by the psychological clinician, who attempts to conceptualize those aspects of an ill person that seem relevant to the illness and its sources; or by the novelist, who may describe many minutiae of character in order to gain verisimilitude.

There are certain general classes of action, however, in terms of which every human being can be described. These are the dimensions of personality that we have discussed previously. They are types of behavior that can be said either to occur or not to occur, or to occur in some degree, in everyone. Aggression is an example. So far as we know, there is no one who lacks entirely a potentiality for behaving aggressively. The varieties of action that fall under this label are uncountable, but they all have the quality we defined in detail in Chapter Seven. A person can show very little of such behavior, perhaps even a zero amount of certain varieties, but what makes aggressiveness a dimension is the fact that everyone can be scored as showing some amount between (and including) zero and an unspecified maximum.

Most of the dimensions of child rearing that we have discussed are also dimensions of the mothers' personalities. Sex permissiveness, warmth, severity of toilet training are all instances in point. One might question whether strictness of control for watching television is as universal as some of the other dimensions we have used—TV is hardly universal yet—but our factor analysis did reveal an underlying personality trait of restrictiveness. It may be that strictness about TV is just a variety of this trait, as aggression toward siblings is a variety of aggression. Some people, obviously, do not have siblings, just as some households do not have television sets. With most of our child-rearing measures, however, it is proper to say that they are dimensions of mothers' personalities. That is, they are statements of probability that a mother will perform some particular action toward her child.

To be accurate, a description of a potentiality for action must specify the external conditions under which the act will occur. Equally, there must be an indication of what other internal states of affairs (e.g., anger) must be occurring simultaneously. Some aspects of personality are exhibited only under quite limited external circumstances. For instance, a tendency to straighten pictures or mirrors on walls is likely to be detectable only when there is a crooked picture in sight. Other acts may be elicited by so many situations, or may be the result of such a continuously present internal state of affairs, that the person can be described as having a *trait*. An "ambitious man," for example, may be one who responds to so many social situations by an effort to better his status in them that we characterize him as having a trait of ambitiousness.

Some potentialities for action, i.e., some properties of a personality, may exist but briefly, while others will characterize the person for most of his lifetime. The reasons for these differences presumably lie partly in the circumstances that create the qualities and partly in the environment. A very stable environment, presenting the same situations year after year, can produce more continuity in a person's actions than an environment that changes rapidly. But likewise, the strength with which an action was endowed by the original conditions of its establishment can be a determinant of its persistence.

A major problem in the study of personality is the discovery of what conditions produce it. We have discussed the influence of mothers' child-rearing practices on the behavior of kindergarten-age children sufficiently so that we scarcely need repeat our opinion that child-rearing practices are important determinants. To say that personality is a product of child-rearing practices, however, is *not* to say that nothing else has any effect. Other influences are obvious and easily demonstrable. Not only are there constitutional differences among children, but the effect on a child of any given experience doubtless depends on what kind of personality he has developed up to that point. What he learns in his third year leads him to certain kinds of action in his fourth. And what he does in his fourth year will determine in part what he can and cannot do in his fifth.

Take, for example, the consequences of sheer physical size. A boy whose weight is in the lower fourth of the population during his preadolescent and adolescent years is unlikely to play football during his senior year in high school. Whatever may have been his father's hopes for him at birth, he will never have had the opportunity to practice the necessary skills, nor to enjoy the gratifications, of football play. He will never have learned the myriad habits, feelings, attitudes, and interests that characterize the social role of "football player." His peer group choices for friendship and recreation are affected in many ways—negatively in the sense that he cannot be a part of the ball-playing group, positively in the sense that he joins a different kind of group. If his father set great store by athletic success, the boy may have lived with a certain sense of inadequacy; and this in turn will have influenced his reactions to his peers, who in their turn will have responded to his behavior with whatever actions their personalities made possible. These peer group experiences contribute to the boy's own attitudes toward others and toward himself. So, too, do the attitudes and actions of non-family adults, such as teachers and policemen and the host of people the growing youngster comes to admire or emulate or detest. It would be nonsense to attribute his personality, at age eighteen, to any single one of the many things that had happened to him. His size was important, but so was his father's disappointment. His own reaction to his father was a factor, but so were the reactions of his peers to this reaction. Personality is a product of many things. Child-rearing experience is but one of them.

In addition, characteristically, the individual members of any species show great differences from one another even before they have had opportunity for any learning. These constitutional variations provide the substratum for the uniqueness of the developing organism. One could mention, for example, the activity level of human infants. During even the first week after birth, babies show distinctively individualized patterns of excitability as they lie in their cribs. Their activity is cyclical, apparently related to food intake, among other things. Some babies have cycles that reach a peak as rapidly as every two-and-a-half hours; others may be as slow as five hours between peaks. And quite aside from rhythm, there are differences in average amount of activity, even the wiggles that occur during sleep. Some babies are more than twice as active as others.

In sum, a person's behavior at any given time is a product of his native endowment, of his immediate situation, and of the qualities of personality he has developed up to that moment in his life. His every action, from birth, has its own consequences on his personality. Hence both the personality and the actual behavior displayed by the person must be viewed as consequences of the *interactive* effects of all the influences, both constitutional and experiential, that have impinged on the child before.

But a bit of caution is in order. In the research process of seeking antecedents for children's behavior patterns, the proper question to ask is *how much contribution* has a certain factor made. Consider the example offered by studies of intelligence. There is ample evidence that ability varies from one animal to another in the same species. At the University of California, Professor Robert Tryon has bred groups of white rats, through several generations, that show radical differences in maze-learning ability. And in man, studies of twins reared apart indicate that biological constitution contributes a considerable amount to the observed differences among people.

It is worth noting, however, that early childhood experiences, too, have been shown to influence performance on intelligence tests. Children who attend nursery schools often show a slight improvement from autumn to spring, while they are in the stimulating environment, and certain types of orphanages appear to retard intellectual development. In one such institution, barren of adult interaction with the younger children, the introduction of a nursery school produced a marked improvement in test performances.

These various findings indicate that life experiences and native differences in ability both contribute to the differences among children in their performances on intelligence tests. Similarly, in considering the relation of child rearing to personality development, we are concerned to discover those aspects of the former that contribute in some degree to measures of the latter. For example, we showed in Chapter Seven that both the mother's permissiveness and her punitiveness about aggression influenced the amount of aggression the child displayed in the home. We know well that in many lower animals there are quite stable sex differences in aggression, the males being more aggressive than the females except under certain special circumstances. Doubtless within each sex there are also individual differences of a constitutional nature. In showing that permissiveness and punitiveness influenced this behavior, we are not in any sense denying the other influences, but are simply demonstrating that child-rearing practices do account for part of the differences among the children. The importance of child rearing as an object for study does not lie in any *unique* role that it plays as a determinant of personality, but in the fact that at some stages in the child's growth it introduces *some* effect.

Perhaps this point is worth belaboring, for it is much misunderstood. The trouble lies in the fact that there are two quite distinct aims to personality study. One is to try to understand *everything* (as nearly as possible) about some one person—to know what traits he has, what stimulates him to action, what his capacities are, and just exactly what has produced all this. The professional worker with children, whether he be teacher, pediatrician, clinical psychologist, psychiatrist, or social worker, must usually take this point of view. He is engaged in working for the betterment of a whole child, and he must understand as much as he can about his subject.

The other aim of personality study is to discover relationships between specific experiences (or other kinds of antecedent events) and specific qualities in the personality. This is the job of the researcher. He must uncover the principles—physiological, psychological, sociological or what not—that account for behavior. These, in turn, are the principles the professional worker uses in his attempts to understand any one particular child.

When the researcher starts his study of personality, he must select a few variables with which to work. He can measure *accurately* only a few things at a time, and he deliberately limits his study to them. In the present study, for example, we have concerned ourselves with the impact of but one kind of experience, the child-rearing practices of mothers during their children's first five years of life. We have shown, for instance, how the use of love-oriented methods of discipline conduce toward a "confession" kind of reaction to naughty behavior, and how the punitive handling of dependency is associated with the child's high demands for nurturance and attention.

These child-rearing practices are not the only influences affecting the personalities of children, however. Indeed, the statistically trained reader will have noted long since that many of our correlations between mothers' practices and children's reported behavior are quite small. They are large enough, in several instances, to do no more than give a reasonably conclusive demonstration that the mothers' behavior did have a measurable amount of influence.

In some types of research, correlation coefficients in the neighborhood of .15 to .20 would be considered too trivial for further attention, even if, as in the present instance, they are based upon a large enough number of cases that one can have confidence that *some* correlation exists. Correlations of this size indicate that the particular antecedent variables contribute only 3 or 4 per cent of the total influences that affect the consequent measures. We feel that we have made some progress, nevertheless, when we can uncover any *real* influence, however small. If our general assumption is correct—i.e., that any given behavior is the product of many influences—it would be quite impossible to obtain high correlations between single child-rearing dimensions and the measures of child behavior. But it is to be expected that when one combines two or more of the child-rearing practices that have a little influence on the child's behavior, the size of that influence will increase. The combination of punishment and permissiveness for aggression accounts for about 20 per cent of the total influence on aggressive behavior in these five-year-old children, for example, while either factor taken alone accounts for much less. We can anticipate that eventually we will discover and be able to measure the separate effects of a fairly high proportion of the variables that influence the behavior, and by combining them we can hope to obtain much higher predictive power.

But it is wise to be cautious about the effects of child rearing on children's personalities. Mothers' practices and attitudes unquestionably have *some* importance, but with respect to many kinds of child behavior, they may not be the most important determiners. And we as yet know very little indeed about their relative importance to the adult personality. Furthermore, even within such a general set of antecedents, there must be selection. It would be impossible to measure *all* relevant aspects of child rearing. We have chosen those that have seemed most significant to us, the ones that we believe most likely to be influential in determining some of the major attributes of children's personalities.

What are the mechanics by which maternal behavior is translated into child personality? A major part of this book has been devoted to a description of the child-rearing practices of a group of American mothers, so this question has immediate importance. Unless the purely descriptive parts of our findings are to be looked on simply as entertaining curiosa, they must be placed in their proper role as descriptions of the conditions under which a large group of American children were having their personalities formed in the early 1950's. What is the process by which personalities are influenced by the experience of living?

THE CHILD-REARING PROCESS

Child rearing is not a technical term with precise significance. It refers generally to *all the interactions between parents and their children.* These interactions include the parents' expressions of attitudes, values, interests, and beliefs as well as their caretaking and training behavior. Sociologically speaking, these interactions are one separable class of events that prepare the child, intentionally or not, for continuing his life. If a society survives beyond one generation, it quite evidently has cared for some of its offspring, and has provided opportunity for them to develop the values and skills needed for living. Some of this learning comes from parent-child interaction, and much does not. Relatives, neighbors, and peers play an important role, too, as do teachers or others specifically charged with the training function. Once he is beyond infancy, a youngster's personality is always a product of more social experiences than just those offered by his parents.

Not all parent-child interactions are intended, by the parents, to train the child. Some are simply for caretaking, such as feeding and cleaning and protecting. Others are expressions of love or annoyance, of concern or pride—reactions that have no significant purposes for the child's future nor even for his control at the moment; but they are nonetheless elicited by the child and impinge on him when they occur. Child rearing includes all such interactions, for they all affect his behavior, and, whether by intention or not, change his potentialities for future action.

To understand the implications of these defining statements about child rearing, one must examine the apparent mechanisms by which parents and children influence one another. There are two ways, as we pointed out in discussing the control of aggression. One is with respect to action and the other to learning. Action is what a person is doing on any given occasion; a theory of action attempts to define the conditions under which specified kinds of action do or do not occur. Anything a parent does to or with a child that has as its aim *control,* i.e., the changing or maintaining of a particular form of behavior, is an influence on action.

Learning, on the other hand, is the changing of a person's potentialities for acting in the future; a theory of learning attempts to define the conditions under which a second presentation of a given situation will produce a different reaction from that elicited by the first presentation of the situation. Learning is the process involved in personality development. Parental behavior that is intended to *train* the child, to change his customary way of acting, is an influence via learning.

This distinction between action and learning is not always clear either to a mother or to a child. In one way this is just as well, but in another it leads to confusion. Actually, every interaction between two people has an effect both on their present actions and on their potentialities for future actions. An affectionate hug or a testy reprimand not only influences what the child is doing at the moment, but adds a small change into his expectations of what will happen on future similar occasions. This expectancy, in turn, increases or decreases the probability that he will act the same way in the future. Likewise, a mother's discipline—which she may view strictly as a method of training for the future—has some immediate impact on the child and leads to a change in his behavior at the moment.

However, when a child has developed adequate language skills, it is possible for a mother to make clear what her intentions are, whether to control for the moment or to modify permanently. This verbal understanding helps a child discriminate somewhat the difference between his "now" behavior and his "next." Better discrimination of his mother's intent leads to more efficient learning.

The most convenient way to view behavior is not simply as action, but as reaction. Every motion is a function of some immediately preceding state of affairs. Some of these antecedent conditions are internal to the person, such as thirstiness or a desire for affection. These include the various organic drives as well as a good many wishes, ideas, desires, or knowledge that can only be inferred to exist—sometimes from what the person says, sometimes from other things he does, and sometimes simply from a knowledge of what experiences he has had in the past. (It is safe enough to infer, for example, that an adolescent who has gone four hours without food, in the afternoon, has internal instigation to eat!)

Still other antecedents of behavior can be observed directly by an outsider—a smile or a request or a spank or a warning look. Not all those that affect a child are equally noticeable to a disinterested stranger, of course. When two people live closely together, they become sensitive to each other's expressions, to postures, manners of movement, and expressions of tension or mood. Even a husband may not note all the little signs of a mother's impending actions that a child does. Or at least not the same ones.

One can distinguish two functions of the conditions which precede action: to *direct* behavior and to *impel* it. Some conditions have more importance for the former purpose and others for the latter, while some do both equally (e.g., a slap). By *directing* is meant giving a signal as to what to do next. A child must move around in his world, and manipulate it to a certain extent, if he is to stay alive and get satisfaction from living. He must reach for the food in front of him, accept or refuse the glass of water for drinking, comply with his mother's "no!" or suffer uncomfortable consequences. In the life of a young child, a mother provides a great many directive signals. Her words and her gestures, even the faint and intangible expressions of mood in her gait or her posture, help him to find his way around in his world and interact with it in the most effective fashion.

But there must also be some *impulsion* to action. Even a chocolate pie has little directive effect on a child already full-fed: it does not make him reach for it. The strongest impulsions in the beginning come from bodily needs—the so-called primary drives. These are native and universal, and some of them are referable to reasonably well understood physiological processes. They initiate action with varying degrees of specificity. In the newborn infant, for example, hunger and thirst may produce no more than a general thrashing about and crying. In an older child they set off quite specific actions of asking for food or water, or of turning on a tap, or opening the bread box. The primary drives include hunger, thirst, sex tensions, fatigue, need for activity, waste elimination, optimum temperature maintenance, pain, and probably a number of metabolic ones. Also, the internal states of affairs reflected by the emotions of rage and fear probably belong in the same category. The impelling quality of primary drive states is a constitutional characteristic of the organism. The directed behavior with which the organism satisfies its needs is (in man) almost entirely learned. Furthermore, through learning, the child comes to want and need certain conditions, such as the presence of the mother. Learning is a crucial process underlying not only the child's actions in pursuing a goal, but his choice of goals themselves. A brief consideration of the learning process, that is, of the principles by which life experiences change the child's potentialities for action, appears to be in order.

For purposes of description, it is convenient to break up the continuous flow of a person's behavior into segments called *action sequences*. These are somewhat arbitrary units that have the following qualities in common. Each starts with some impelling state of affairs, such as the state of being hungry (the hunger drive), and ends with a consummatory (goal) response (e.g., eating) that reduces the drive. Between the beginning and the end, there is a series of instrumental acts which puts the person in such contact with his environment that he can make the goal response; for instance, a child runs to his mother and asks for a sandwich. Actions that lead to gratification (whether conscious or not) are learned, and may be expected to occur more quickly, more skillfully and more customarily on future occasions when the child finds himself in a same or similar situation.

It is not only the acts immediately preceding gratification that are learned, however. For most activities, especially those that involve social interaction, there are intermediate (or concurrent) events that must be produced in order that the goal may be achieved. For example, a two-year-old child who is hungry needs co-operative action by his mother in order to perform his own goal response of eating. He may cry, or gesture, or ask in words for help. Whatever instrumental techniques he uses, the necessary event must be the same—his mother's giving him food. And he must learn to perform the necessary acts to produce her response. As time goes on, the child develops a "want" for any object, person, or social situation that happened to be associated with the original satisfying experience, and he will learn to perform whatever actions are necessary to produce the desired state of affairs.

It is important to keep in mind that this learning process is, in at least one respect, a highly *mechanical* one. The child learns to want *whatever events regularly occur* in the satisfying context. He does not discriminate between those that are physically efficacious and those that are simply inadvertent accompaniments. For example, the mother must nearly always be present when a child is fed; she orients herself toward him physically, looks at him, often smiles and talks while she is giving food. To the observer trying to decide which of the mother's acts are relevant to the child's food-seeking behavior, the mere handing out of food may seem all that is essential. But the orientations and other actions of the mother nearly always occur, too, and hence the child learns to want them as much as the giving of food. To him, they are part of the whole pattern accompanying the satisfaction of his hunger, and he learns to want the entire pattern. A new item has been added to the list of things the world can do for that child to make him happy—it can be labeled as "mother looking at me and smiling and talking."

When one considers the myriad situations in which children are rewarded throughout childhood, the variety of actions their mothers perform in the process of child rearing, it does not seem surprising that there are so many subgoal systems of this sort. Or that there should be a unique set of them for each child. Every mother has her own temperament, her own attitudes, her own methods of rewarding and punishing. It is these ways of behaving that her child learns to want. If she is warm and loquacious, he will treasure demonstrativeness; if she is reserved, he will seek her normal reserved expressions toward him. It should be evident now why the term child rearing includes *all* the interactions between parents and their children, not just the ones which directly satisfy primary drives, or those that are consciously *intended* to have a training effect.

The problem of punishment must be raised in connection with both these kinds of learning. Punishment, in its broadest sense, is the inflicting of pain or anxiety. Such an act may be intentional on a mother's part, or it may not. From the standpoint of its effect on the child, any maternal act that hurts or shames or frightens the child is punishment. This is the technical, not the ordinary, use of the word.

The effects of punishment are relevant to both ongoing action and learning. Punishment motivates a child to do something which will reduce the pain created by the punishment; for example, something which will get him away from the source of pain. In the beginning, when there are only reflexes available, infants cry and thrash about. Gradually they learn to move away from external sources of discomfort, mainly sharp things and hot things. But when the source of pain is a punishing parent, the problem cannot be solved merely by avoidance, for the child is dependent upon the parent's presence for the gratification of many of his needs.

There are many kinds of behavior the child can learn in response to punishment that emanates from his mother. Those responses will be selected and retained which serve best to reduce the discomfort. What kind of behavior by him will placate the mother will depend to some extent on her personality characteristics. Sheer flight may work—if the mother has lost her temper or is irritably nagging. Passivity may help, or a counterattack may do the trick. If the mother's punishing actions are accompanied by some indication of what behavior she *does* desire from the child, then he can follow this clue. And then his reaction to the punishment likely will be effective in reducing the pain.

Once a child develops a repertory of responses to threatening or punishing situations, he will use those that are appropriate to any specific instance. This does not mean that what he does will actually work. Many of the reactions to punishment that are learned in early childhood are quite ineffectual in later years. Bursting into tears may be useful at four, but it is less likely to be so at ten or twelve. Passivity toward a mother may be established because she stops punishing under those circumstances, but passivity in a threatened adult is often quite the least useful form of response. But usefulness or "sensibleness" is not the only determiner of behavior; both actions and desires are the products of previous learning experiences, and which ones are activated at any given moment depends on what situation is present.

Whether a particular action is effective for achieving its aim depends on what may be called the *response qualities* of the environment, that is, what reaction the environment can make to the actions the person imposes on it. A child may learn, as a great joke, to pummel his father's knee when his father is reading the newspaper. He learns to do this because his father always responds affectionately, rewardingly. If the child does the same thing to a newspaper reader on a train, he may get the same friendly response or he may get a swat on his behind. It depends on the response qualities of the man who, in this instance, is the relevant "environment" of the child. The effectiveness of a given action is only as great as is the similarity of the response qualities of the environment in which the behavior was originally learned. Since it is always possible for aspects of the new situation (man on train reading a newspaper) to resemble those of many previous ones, without there being any similarity in the environment's response qualities (the man is *not* tolerant and affectionate to this child at this moment), much human social behavior inevitably is maladaptive and "senseless."

We have said little about the intentional training that is a part of child rearing. From a mother's standpoint, there is much to teach a child, or to help him learn. There are all the motor activities that will enable him to manipulate his environment and to get around in it. There are eating habits, toileting, independence, responsibility. Speaking and understanding of speech must be developed. He must learn what are desirable things to have, what to avoid. He must develop proper control of his aggressive impulses and his sex drive. He must learn what is good and what is bad. He must learn the names and functions of things, and the proper techniques of behaving toward other people. And much of this learning is not simply the adding of new responses to the collection he already has: it requires the replacing of undesired actions or attitudes or desires with ones the mother conceives as more appropriate.

Teaching is a delicate and complex process. It requires the

selection of appropriate kinds of behavior for the child to perform, the providing of sufficient opportunity for him to practice
them, the introducing of adequate motivation to induce him to
do the practicing, and the insuring that he enjoys the rewards
of his labors so that he will be inclined to repeat them. This is
all there is to teaching—in theory. In practice, there is a serious
stumbling block. A child often knows what he wants to do,
knows how to do it in some degree, and insists on doing it. If
his existing action patterns do not coincide with those his tutors
would like to teach him, the teacher must undertake an additional
task—eliminating his old actions. This is what makes the theoretically simple process so difficult. No child is ever a *tabula rasa;*
he always has a repertory of actions that need replacing. Many
of them he likes and does not want to change. Any one can teach
a person whose desire to learn comes from being dissatisfied
with what he already knows. But the socialization of children
is not so easy. Many an action a mother wants to introduce comes
in conflict with actions the child already has. She must find a
way of eliminating the old before she can establish the new.

There is one infallible way to stop a child from doing what
he is doing: start him doing something else. Like all panaceas,
however, this one has a joker in it. *How* do you start him doing
something else? Actions occur because the child wants something,
and certain situations have impinged on him—situations to which
he has learned to react with a specific kind of behavior. To change
these actions, new wants or new situations must be introduced.

Much of the maternal control and teaching in child rearing
is accomplished by manipulating the child's wants. Mothers
quickly learn that a youngster can be induced to do all manner
of things if these are a part of some pleasurable sequence of
activities. If she joins him in cleaning up the toys, he works like
a Trojan with her just to have her company and to gain the sense
of being useful in an adult fashion. He can relish the wash-up
job if she shows him how much fun it is to slop and squeeze the
fluffy soapsuds. He will attend seriously to his table manners if
she calls this "the grown-up way." To the extent that a mother
can introduce new actions into already existing motivational systems, or can construct new goals and values by associating them
with such desirable achievements as being *mature* or *big* or *strong*
or *beautiful,* to that extent is child rearing made easy, and the

inculcation of new actions made a pleasure for both teacher and learner.

But not *always,* with *every* child, can a mother think up an effective way of doing this. She has trouble during temper tantrums, some frights, some stubborn spells. When children have strong emotional reactions, they are not easy to control. But the real problem is not with the unmodifiability of the child, but with the fact that mothers are not always themselves calm or rational or profound. They get angry, frightened, tired, and

neither their wit nor their wisdom can ever be perfect. The upshot of it is that they are not infrequently driven into interaction with children on a basis that has little to do with teaching. But teaching or not, the continuing interaction has a lasting effect on the child, in the sense that it affects his potentialities for future action as well as his present behavior.

Obviously not all, or perhaps even very much, of a mother's interaction with her child is of an intentional teaching variety. But the need to ensure the child's development, to socialize him, is always present and creeps into expression whenever the mother observes a kind of action, on the child's part, that she wishes to see modified.

It is these various changeworthy actions that cause the trouble.

Some of them relate to eating habits or table manners, some to speech and language. Some involve cleanliness or neatness or orderliness or noise or play habits or interests. A large proportion, however, have to do with the child's relation to other people. After all, the word *socialization* does have a social reference. It means, in large part, the development of socially appropriate behavior, the proper (i.e., adult) kinds of interactions with others.

Child rearing is a continuous process. Every moment of a child's life that he spends in contact with his parents has some effect on both his present behavior and his potentialities for future action. Happily, the importance of many of these moments is small, but those that provide repetitions of common and consistent experiences add up, over the years, to the production of consistent ways of behaving toward the kinds of people he knows.

So much for the mechanics of interpersonal influence. Left at this, the process would seem to dictate a unique personality for each child. Every mother behaves differently, and hence even without constitutional variation every child should be different. Strictly speaking, this appears to be the case. Although the process by which learning occurs is the same for everyone, the specific environmental conditions that determine just what wants and actions will be learned are unique to each human being.

The researcher's task is not as impossible as this conclusion may suggest, however. He does not have to study every living human being, for his interest is in those aspects of personality that are common to many. As we have seen, there are quite a few dimensions of this kind. Our interest has been largely in those that describe mothers' child-rearing activities. These represent a part of mothers' personalities, just as our measures of eating problems, enuresis, aggressiveness, and other aspects of children's behavior are indicators of children's personalities.

In the above description of the way in which child rearing influences the child's personality, we have said little about the substantive aspect of the matter. We have concentrated on the *process* and left out what it is the mother does and how her child responds. This substantive matter has been the subject of our research, of course. In the context of the process, we can now return to some of our findings, not for purposes of summary but to suggest what seem to us a few of the implications of the research.

THE RANGE OF PRACTICES

In the beginning we asked three kinds of questions. The first was purely descriptive: How *do* mothers rear their children? The second was: What effects do these practices have on the children's personalities? The third was: What leads a mother to use one method rather than another? We have been able to present more complete answers to the first and third of these questions than to the second. Even so, there is a distinct limitation to the scope of our report. Clearly, we have devoted much more attention to the handling of children's changeworthy behavior than to the positive training for activities that replace it. Our comments on the range of practices must be understood to refer only to those we have measured.

The commonest phrase in this book is, "The mothers varied widely. . . ." It applied to almost every dimension of child rearing we measured. The most notable examples were sex permissiveness and permissiveness for aggression toward parents. In both these spheres of strongly motivated child behavior, there were some mothers who took a quite categorical position that such behavior must *never under any circumstances* be allowed to occur. But there were also some mothers who virtually ignored such activities, characterizing them as natural for children to do and of no real significance for the child's development. Then, of course, there were plenty of mothers whose attitudes represented every step in between.

We made no attempt to measure the strength of these convictions. It was evident from the phrasing of the mothers' comments—from the kinds of verbs and adjectives they used—that some aspects of child behavior had more importance than others. Again sex and aggression are candidates for prominence. Not every mother felt strong conviction that she knew the right way to handle these matters; indeed, some expressed a very discouraged sort of uncertainty. But by and large, there was a good deal of firmness. Similarly, the choice of disciplinary methods rested on beliefs that were often strongly held. In contrast, the majority of mothers seemed to describe their methods of feeding without much apparent feeling of certainty that their own method was the best. Many reported experimenting, or at least changing their methods, from one child to another in the family.

Although nearly every dimension showed a great range of practices, the proportions of mothers who were rated at different points on the scales varied a good deal from one dimension to another. It will be recalled that nearly 50 per cent described themselves as "delighted" at becoming pregnant; there was a heavy bunching at that end of the scale. Likewise, permissiveness for aggression toward parents was bunched. On a good many other scales, however, there was a reasonably normal distribution, with a few mothers falling at both extremes and the majority somewhere in between.

These are rather prosaic facts. No one could be surprised in this day and age by a discovery of individual differences in any aspect of human behavior. We have indicated previously some of the implications of this variability for the individual personality development of children. Here we need add only one further comment, this one relating to societal consequences.

The socialization of their young children is extremely important to most mothers. It is their chief occupation. Whatever uncertainties they may feel on some aspects of the task, there is little question that the decisions they make are important to them. Furthermore, these decisions have to do with all our most powerful motives and emotions. The changeworthy aspects of child behavior are laden with strong values. Individual differences—hence potential disagreements—among mothers are therefore of more than casual significance. One woman can forgive another's bad taste in hats or soap powder, but "wrong-headedness" about sex or aggression or the care of private property is harder to ignore.

There is bound to be conflict among the mothers of a community. Attitudes and values concerning child rearing can never be private: they have to come right out in the open. The product—the child—is always visible to the neighbors. His qualities are not only on public display; they form an integral part of the neighbors' living environment. If his behavior is not like that of the other children, or if his expressed attitudes do not correspond to those cherished by other mothers for their own children, he becomes a pest, a nuisance, a "bad example."

When there is strong conviction behind a mother's policies— particularly if her views are at the punitive and non-permissive end of a dimension—she will likely react to differences of opinion with more than casual disapproval. Vindictive gossip, efforts at ostracism, and complaints to authority are not infrequent results. In some instances, such aggressive actions may create severe strains in a neighborhood or a school. If the woman who initiates the attack has access to important power channels in the community, she may be able temporarily to impose her views and practices on other mothers.

As our measures show clearly, however, there was substantially less than a majority of the mothers who were rated at the punitive and non-permissive extreme on any dimension. The most extensive bunching, not surprisingly, occurred with respect to sex, and aggression toward parents. Even with respect to sex play among young children, only 28 per cent of the mothers were rated in the most extreme group (Table VI:5); and in respect to permissiveness for aggression toward other children, only 5 per cent were at the non-permissive extreme (Table VII:3). These figures suggest that much of the "viewing with alarm," the public vituperation, and the demands for interference with other mothers' child-rearing practices, stems from a relatively small group of anxious, aggressive women whose capacity for noisemaking is somewhat out of proportion to their numerical importance in the community.

Since they are extreme in their views, they are living in what is essentially an alien culture, of course. Their discomfort and *anxiety* lead them to take strongly punitive action toward those who disagree with them. But the majority of mothers, whose views are more relaxed, suffer less anxiety and are less combative in their attitudes. Hence, the non-permissive minority, on occasion, can not only make more noise but can drive themselves to greater exertions to manipulate and control the behavior of the community. School authorities, juvenile court agencies, and neighborhood groups of mothers who are faced with social conflicts, involving demands for punitive or restrictive controls of one kind or another, would do well to ponder the small proportions of mothers who were rated at the non-permissive extremes of most of our various scales.

Lest these comments be too hastily interpreted simply as an indictment of non-permissiveness, let us quickly consider another implication of the great range of practices we have described. On most dimensions, mothers' values do not bunch at either extreme. The majority of these are to be found in the middle. The adoption of practices that are different—to an extreme—in *any* direction represents a source of conflict with majority opinions. Furthermore, to the extent that a mother's practices influence the personality of her child, to that extent the child of a mother whose policies are extreme is likely to become something of a deviant himself. Whatever the dimension involved, the mother and child both can find themselves in a minority position in their respective groups. The child who is too aggressive can suffer as much isolation as the one who is too non-aggressive. Extreme dirtiness is as revolting to other children as is extreme cleanliness. Social living requires that each child shall be an acceptable interactor with other children, in some degree.

This can be a depressing thought to those who see variation in personality as the true lifeblood for a society. There is no great need for worry. The extraordinary range of practices we found in this one group of mothers is unquestionably much less than the range for America as a whole. Whatever correctives toward communality of practices the society may impose, there is still opportunity for as wide variation in child rearing as any society could possibly need.

PATTERNS AND DIMENSIONS

The pattern of any mother's child-rearing practices and attitudes is as individual as her fingerprints. It is unique. Our first task, as we pointed out in Chapter One, was to reduce this diversity to some common elements. These were the *dimensions* which we measured with our many rating scales. The next step was to reconstruct *patterns* from these separable elements, to discover whether there were certain dimensions that were ordinarily related to one another, and to discover whether there were combinations of dimensions that formed underlying traits. The answers to these last two questions are clearly in the affirmative, of course, and we can now bring together the results of the factor analysis with other kinds of evidence to see just what patterns did exist in this group of mothers.

Obviously, the kinds of patterns that could be revealed depended on what dimensions we used. Our selection was based on clinical observations and general child-development theory, and the criterion we had constantly in mind was whether a dimension would be likely to have a consistent influence on the personality qualities of a child. We will review the successfulness of our selections, as judged by this criterion, in the next section. But first we must note the patterns revealed by our various types of analysis.

Factors

The factor analysis, first discussed in Chapter Two, was an important technique for discovering underlying traits. It is a statistical device that permits an objective examination of the way in which a set of intercorrelations among dimensions cluster together. These clusters are indicators of the traits. One can look at a list of all the dimensions included in the analysis, with their respective loadings that show how much each dimension is correlated with each "factor," and then make a judgment of what kind of trait is represented by each factor.

We included 44 of our scales in such an analysis (Milton, 1957). We selected those which seemed to have the most theoretical significance. These 44 scales are listed in Appendix Table D:4. The seven columns of figures in that table show how large was the correlation of each of the 44 scales with each of the seven factors. The nature of the seven traits can be judged by noting which scales had a loading of .30 or more with each one. The choice of .30 is arbitrary, of course; that much loading indicates that nine per cent of the scale's variance is contributed by the underlying trait. The + or − sign indicates the direction in which the scale runs. For example, in Factor A, *sex-play permissiveness* has a negative sign, while *restrictions relating to care of house and furniture* has a positive sign. This means only that a high scale value on one scale meant the mother was permissive, and a high scale value on the other meant she was restrictive.

Permissiveness-strictness (A). Perhaps the most prominent trait that influenced mothers' child-rearing practices was the one we discussed at length in Chapter Eight. Of the 44 dimensions, or scales, we analyzed, there were 16 that were influenced by this trait to a significant degree. If we convert the descriptive titles of these scales in such a way that they all describe the strict (non-permissive) aspect of the trait, then we can say that at one extreme it is represented by the following qualities of behavior:

1. High restrictions on play in the house and with furniture.
2. High demands for good table manners.
3. High restriction on making noise.
4. High demands for being neat and orderly.
5. Severe toilet training.
6. High standards for strict obedience.
7. Strong emphasis on doing well in school.
8. Strict and rejective response to dependency.
9. High use of physical punishment.
10. Severe punishment for aggression toward parents.
11. Low permissiveness for aggression toward parents.
12. Low permissiveness for aggression among siblings.
13. Low permissiveness for aggression to other children.
14. Low permissiveness for nudity or immodesty.
15. Low permissiveness for masturbation.
16. Low permissiveness for sex play with other children.

These scales describe the qualities of child-rearing behavior which are combined to form this trait. Each mother may be presumed to possess some degree of the trait and to be ratable at some point between extreme strictness and extreme permissiveness. The various scales that contribute to the factor, or trait, are to be viewed as partial measures of it. Thus, a mother who was very permissive about noise might also be expected to be at least somewhat on the permissive side about each of the other kinds of behavior mentioned in the list. She would be characterized as a somewhat *permissive* mother.

This way of talking about the *factor* makes it seem much like what we have been calling a *dimension*. It is. That is to say, it is a quality of behavior that characterizes the mother's reactions to her child. It is measured by several scales, however, rather than by just one; and hence, to avoid confusion, we have referred to it as an *underlying trait* rather than as a *dimension*.

The fact that we can discern such a deep underlying trait does not necessarily mean that it is the most important source of the child's behavior. As we saw in connection with toilet training, the severity of this procedure was related to the development of nocturnal enuresis, but the other scales that are associated with Factor A were not. In other words, a given kind of behavior in a child may be the product of one quite isolated aspect of the mother's practices. At the same time, there seems a good possibility that some aspects of a child's behavior may be more closely related to an underlying trait of the mother than to any specific representation of it. The frequent references we have made to severity of punishment for aggression toward parents and to non-permissiveness about sex behavior are clues that suggest the desirability, in future research, of an attempt to discover possible consequences of the whole factor as well as of specific measures of it.

General family adjustment (B). In our discussion of the mother's personality qualities that provided a background for parenthood, we described another underlying trait. Factor B seems to be a dimension that involves the mother's acceptance of, and confidence in, both herself and her husband. It includes, too, several estimates of the father's attitudes and of the husband-wife relationship. For this reason, we interpret the trait as having to do with general family adjustment. The scales that contribute the most to this factor may be described, at the well-adjusted extreme, as follows:

1. Mother has high self-esteem.
2. Mother makes a high evaluation of the father.
3. Mother is very satisfied with her current life situation.
4. Mother has little anxiety about her ability for child rearing.
5. Mother felt delighted at becoming pregnant.
6. Mother reports that father was also delighted.
7. Mother reports that she has no disagreements with father about child rearing.
8. Mother enjoyed affectionate interaction with her baby.
9. Mother reports that there is a strongly affectionate bond between the father and the child.

10. Mother has no difficulty in following through on her disciplinary actions.

In respect to this factor, perhaps more than in the case of the others, we are reminded of the possibility that some of the intercorrelations among scales may be a product of what we earlier called a response set. These measures were all taken from a single unbroken interview. One can easily imagine that a happy or unhappy mood produced by relatively temporary family affections or squabbles could have produced a general set toward one kind of answer or another to an interviewer's questions. A mother who was disappointed in some recent decision by her husband, or who had recently had a vigorous disagreement about the child, could easily have been jaundiced to the point of letting her pessimism influence many of her responses. Likewise, an affectionate week end, a good night's sleep, or a sudden observation of more rapid maturing in her child, could have given her a generally optimistic view of life—and of herself and her husband. We are inclined to believe that this trait of family adjustment has much deeper roots in the personality than are implied by the term *response set,* but we have no evidence, in the present study, with which we can test our conviction.

Warmth of mother-child relationship (C). The third factor seems to describe an underlying trait that might equally well be defined as a dimension ranging from warm to cold. There were only six scales that had a significant loading with this factor. Regrettably, we did not include the scale for *warmth of mother to child* in our factor analysis, because it was, by definition, a summary scale itself, an attempt at a direct rating of what we had anticipated might prove to be one of these underlying traits. However, the size of the correlations between *warmth* and the scales below are so high that there is little doubt that, had it been included, it would have provided a seventh scale to define the quality represented by this factor.

Mothers who were high—toward the warm end—can be described as follows:

1. Much affectionate interaction with the baby.
2. High affectionate demonstrativeness toward the child.
3. Found ample time to play with the child.
4. Reacted acceptingly to child's dependency.

5. Praised the child when he showed good table manners.

6. Used reasoning as a method of training.

Responsible child-training orientation (D). Giving a name to one of these underlying traits is a risky business. It tends to crystallize the description of the trait simply because any summarizing phrase carries surplus meanings with it. This fourth factor is particularly difficult to name, and we hold no strong brief for our selection. The scales to which the factor contributes provide the only accurate definition; the positive end of the dimension can be described as follows:

1. High self-esteem on mother's part.
2. High demands for neatness and orderliness.
3. High restrictions on play in the house and with furniture.
4. High demands for good table manners.
5. High use of praise for good table manners.
6. High use of praise for playing nicely.
7. High standards for strict obedience.
8. Predominant use of deprivation of privileges for punishing.
9. High use of tangible rewards.

A mother who displays a high degree of this trait is probably very earnestly and responsibly oriented to her child-training duties. She has high regard for herself and she wants her child to develop rapidly toward mature status. She pays attention to those attributes of his behavior that are important for providing a well-mannered household, and she gives enough time and energy to her task to think up appropriate rewards and punishment for the training process. She uses praise, as well, and we get the impression that she keeps her attention rather continuously (and mainly pleasantly) directed toward the child, viewing him as a person who must be taught many things.

Aggressiveness and punitiveness (E). This factor is defined by only five scales, but its nature seems quite clear. Mothers at the high end of the distribution showed:

1. High demands for the child to be aggressive toward other children.
2. High permissiveness for such aggression.
3. High use of physical punishment.
4. Severe punishment for aggression toward parents.
5. Low permissiveness for aggression toward parents.

One other scale, which does not have a very high loading, is of interest, too—low self-esteem on the mother's part.

This factor seems to isolate a quality that involves a high level of aggressiveness in the mother. She displays it in her punishment and in her attempts to get the child to be aggressive. At the same time, she will not tolerate aggression toward herself. Her low self-esteem suggests the possibility that this trait is a rather stable form of defense against feelings of insecurity, a defense that involves a hitting-out and a demand for outward displays of aggression. The defensive quality is suggested not only by the low self-esteem but by the severity of punishment for aggression directed toward the parents.

Perception of husband (F). This is a minor factor. In fact, it may not be a true factor at all. The loadings of the three relevant scales are low. The picture they give of a father-trait, through the mother's eyes, is reasonably clear and simple. According to the mothers, these fathers varied on a dimension which can be described at one extreme as follows:

1. Displeased when wife became pregnant.
2. Had chief responsibility for child-rearing policies.
3. High permissiveness for child to be aggressive to other children.

In saying that these "father scales" provide only a minor factor, we are not implying that fathers are unimportant in child rearing. Our interview was not constructed to secure much information about his role, and hence he does not appear as frequently or intensively in our book as he obviously does in children's lives.

Orientation toward child's physical well-being (G). This final factor is relatively minor also. The scales to which it contributes seem to be related to various child-rearing practices or attitudes concerned with health and safety. A mother at the more anxious extreme can be described as follows:

1. High use of scheduled feedings in infancy.
2. High demands for good table manners (which included an insistence on eating everything).
3. Strict about bedtime.
4. High restrictions on physical mobility (not allowed away from the house much).
5. High anxiety about her ability at child rearing.

Occasionally, in factor analysis, a particular scale will turn up in two or more factors. For example, in the present analysis, ratings of severe *punishment for aggression toward parents* is shown to be influenced by both Factor A and Factor D. What this means is that either of these factors—or both of them—may be responsible for a high or low rating of a given mother. One can make a rough estimate of which factor is influencing that rating by noting which other scales are high for that mother. If several of the restrictiveness scales were high, we would conclude that Factor A was responsible, but if they were low while all the other aggression scales were rated at the non-permissive end, we might infer that Factor D was responsible.

Love-oriented vs. *object-oriented discipline*

We can consider now one other apparently patterned aspect of maternal behavior. Our notice of this does not come from the factor analysis, but from a study of the intercorrelations among methods of discipline. In the discussion of techniques of training in Chapter Nine, we suggested one basic distinction that can be made between methods of discipline. This distinction is with reference to the kind of *impelling* force used by the mother to elicit desired actions by her child. Sometimes she may offer an incentive; other times she may threaten its withholding. Either is a way of getting the child to do what she wants, i.e., to control action. For training purposes, likewise, she may offer a reward in order to reinforce what the child has already done, or she may withhold an expected reward in order to discourage his previous actions. Or she may actually take away something he values, as a punishment. The distinction we have made is between two general classes of things that mothers use for these purposes.

One class is her own love and affection. She can give love as a reward; she can hold out the expectation of affectionate inter-action as an inducement. Or she can withhold or withdraw love as a means of punishment. There are many ways in which her expression of love can be used as the environmental event, the expectancy of which provides the impelling force to the child's actions.

The other class of events are those material or physical things that the child either wants or wants to avoid. The things he wants—including specific objects, privileges, and non-interference with his own affairs—can serve as incentives and rewards in the same way the mother's love and affection serve. Equally, the deprivation of privileges or the infliction of physical pain can be what the child seeks to avoid; they can be used, after an action has occurred, as a means of punishment.

The pattern that we have concluded may be isolated in connection with these disciplinary differences is not a "factor," in the same statistical sense as are the seven factors derived from the factor analysis.

Unfortunately, we could not include in our factor analysis several of the scales measuring techniques of discipline. We have no means of knowing whether this distinction between love-oriented and object-oriented discipline would provide a factor comparable to the seven described above. However, the table of intercorrelations among the techniques discussed in Chapter Nine (Appendix Table D:22) shows that mothers who had preference for one love-oriented method had a tendency to use others also, and tended *not* to use object-oriented methods. In Chapter Ten, furthermore, we saw that there was some relationship between the mother's high use of love-oriented techniques and the occurrence of confession and guilt about misbehavior in her child. Both the intercorrelations among scales and the apparent relevance of the dimension, or trait, to conscience development have led us to conclude that the following contrasting groups of disciplinary techniques represent an important patterning of maternal behavior:

> *Love-oriented techniques*
> > Praise as a means of reward
> > Isolation as a punishment
> > Withdrawal of love as punishment
>
> *Object-oriented techniques*
> > Tangible rewards as incentives and rewards
> > Deprivation of privileges as a punishment
> > Physical punishment

It is interesting to note, as we did in Chapter Nine, that high *use of reasoning* as a form of guidance for the child tended to occur more commonly among mothers who used love-oriented techniques. There is nothing essential about this connection; a mother who relied heavily on physical punishment could perfectly well use reasoning to explain what she was punishing for. Certainly we can find no justification for calling *reasoning* a love-oriented technique in itself. However, by and large, those mothers who did have the love-orientation were more likely to use the reasoning method of guidance.

The various patterns described above have represented inter-relationships among the dimensions of child rearing. They are descriptions of what appear to be underlying traits in mothers. One could characterize a mother as "very strict" or "moderately warm," and in so doing imply what ratings she would obtain on the several scales that contribute most heavily to those factors.

What seems evident is that the actual dimensions we selected for measuring the interviews are overt but fallible indicators of other—"deeper"—dimensions. The rating that a mother received on one of our scales reflected the underlying dimension in part, but it was also influenced by other matters that were relevant only to the specific behavior rated. Thus, a mother who was quite strict about noise might have adopted this attitude mainly because of the family's living arrangements rather than because she was "a strict mother."

The evident existence of these underlying dimensions is a challenge to the researcher. He must find some way of obtaining more direct and precise measures of them. There seems a strong likelihood that they may be more closely related to the developing qualities of the child's behavior than are many of the dimensions we have defined and measured with our rating scales. Our assumption is that, since a given "factor" is reflected in a number of scales, the factor must be exhibited pervasively in many of the interactions between mother and child. It should therefore have maximum influence on the child's behavior.

Sex and ordinal position of the child

There are other sources of patterned maternal behavior besides those arising from the way in which the mother's own personality is structured. One element that can create consistent patterns is some quality of the child that differentiates him in a significant way from other children. We have examined two of these qualities: sex and ordinal position. In Chapter Eleven we saw that, although there are not a great many ways in which these two qualities have a general influence on mothers, there are some. For instance, the mothers of our sample were more tolerant of aggression toward neighborhood children by their sons than by their daughters. In two-child families, the older child was given greater freedom in this respect than the younger child.

Doubtless some of the sex and ordinal position differences are the result of pervasive, culturally determined attitudes about the nature and privileges and responsibilities of children belonging to various cultural categories. Other differences may result from increased experience as the family grows larger, or from the changes that occur in the mother's duties when she must care for more children, or for ones of different ages.

Socio-economic status and education of the mother

Still another kind of influence that can create patterns is membership in a group having a certain community of experience that differentiates it from other groups. To the extent that mothers have had the same values and attitudes trained into them, to that extent we should expect them to have similar child-training practices.

Such group identity can be based on socio-economic status, on educational background, on religion, on ethnic origins, and possibly on many other social factors. In the present study we have explored the effects of the first two of these variables. There were marked differences in the practices and attitudes reported by middle-class and working-class mothers; and because of the overlap between class and educational level, the differences were much the same between mothers with a high school education or less and those with more than a high school education.

The pattern of differences is remarkably consistent. On virtually all of the scales to which Factor A (permissiveness-strictness) contributes, the working-class mothers were more punitive and more restrictive. They were less permissive and exerted more pressure with respect to sex behavior; similarly with regard to aggression and dependency; and they placed high restrictions and demands on their children in all major respects. On the scales that contribute to Factor C (warmth), working-class mothers were "colder" than middle-class mothers on all but *praise for table manners*. With respect to disciplinary techniques, there was some tendency for the working-class mothers to be more punitive in general and also to rely more on those techniques we have labeled *object-oriented* (physical punishment, deprivation of privilege).

It is surprisingly easy to think up *ad hoc* explanations for some of these differences. For example, the disciplinary techniques characteristic of the working-class mothers are less effective for the rapid development of conscience (inner control), and hence the greater strictness about sex behavior may be necessary. The trouble is that this reasoning does not explain the class difference in *warmth*. Or again: perhaps the relatively higher economic and social status frustrations of the working class might lead to greater aggressiveness and, hence, more punitiveness about children's aggression. But this explanation does not account for sex restrictions. Or yet again: the more constricted living conditions of the working-class mothers may lead them to withdraw more into themselves and thus be less affectionately demonstrative toward their children. But how does this relate to pressure for school achievement? Perhaps they have greater motivation to see their children improve their social status through better education. But this interpretation goes counter to the difference that shows working-class mothers to have much lower educational aspirations for their children than do the middle-class mothers.

Perhaps all these explanations have some validity, but certainly we have been able to think of no single sociological or psychological attribute of social-class membership that would explain all the differences we have found associated with such status. On the other hand, it seems doubtful that social-class membership provides as much reference group affiliation as is offered by ethnic, religious, or even some geographically determined group memberships. Belonging to a reference group—that is, having the sense of being one of "our kind of people"—is an important influence on anyone's behavior. "We" eat this way, or dress that way, or believe such-and-such. It is possible that a feeling of being a working-class person or a middle-class person tends to stabilize and perpetuate the attitudes and practices which characterize those groups. Most reference groups that seem to have such an influence on the individual members are smaller and more cohesive than socio-economic status groups, however.

Pending further research on the matter, we are more inclined to conclude that the significance of these SES findings lies in what they reveal as to communality of experience within social groups. We are skeptical that there are any very fixed or immutable characteristics of social classes that make them sources of "naturally different" patterns. On the contrary, it seems probable that as there is a breaking down of the communication barriers between groups—whether the grouping be based on ethnic or occupational or religious identity—there will be an increasing similarity of child-training patterns.

EFFECTS OF CHILD REARING

Now, finally, we can consider the effects of child rearing on the children. In this present book we have reported only a portion of the findings of our main research. The project as a whole was designed to discover the child-rearing antecedents of certain kinds of fantasy behavior displayed by five-year-old children. All our *direct* measures of child behavior were tests of fantasy activity. We have mentioned a few of our findings on that problem in Chapter Ten, but the major portion of them will be presented in technical publications; they will be of interest primarily to our research colleagues. Because the main problems we were investigating did not require measurement of the overt social behavior of the children, we limited our non-fantasy child behavior measures to those which could be secured through the mothers' own reports. As we have emphasized several times earlier, we would be happier if there had been a greater independence between the mother measures and the child measures. However, within these limits, there were a few maternal qualities that stood out as having considerable significance for the kindergarten-age child's personality.

The mother's warmth

Perhaps the most pervasive quality we attempted to measure was the warmth of the mother's feelings for her child. Although our main measure of this was the single rating scale called *warmth,* the quality itself seems to have been an underlying contributor to several of the scales and, indeed, appeared as Factor C in the factor analysis.

Warmth proved equally pervasive in its effects on the child.

Maternal *coldness* was associated with the development of feeding problems and persistent bed-wetting. It contributed to high aggression. It was an important background condition for emotional upset during severe toilet training, and for the slowing of conscience development. Indeed, the only one of our measures of child behavior with which warmth was not associated was de-

pendency, and even in that instance the closely related scale for *affectionate demonstrativeness* was slightly correlated.

There is no clear evidence in our findings to explain why warmth should have such widespread influence. We can speculate, on the basis of our general theory of the learning process, about the possibility that it may play several roles. A warm mother spends more time with her child. She offers him more rewards, technically speaking, and gives him more guidance. He develops stronger expectancies of her reciprocal affection, and thus is more highly motivated to learn how to behave as she wants him to. He becomes more susceptible to control by her, for he has more to gain and more to lose. It seems likely, too, that he gets proportionately more satisfaction and less frustration from his growing desire for affection. We offer the hypothesis, for further research, that the children of warm mothers mature more rapidly, in their social behavior, than those of cold mothers.

Punishment

In our discussion of the training process we have contrasted punishment with reward. Both are techniques used for changing the child's habitual ways of acting. Do they work equally well? The answer is unequivocally "no"; but to be truly unequivocal, the answer must be understood as referring to the kind of punishment we were able to measure by our interview method. We could not, as one can with laboratory experiments on white rats or pigeons, examine the effects of punishment on isolated bits of behavior. Our measures of punishment, whether of the object-oriented or love-oriented variety, referred to *levels of punitiveness* in the mothers. That is, the amount of use of punishment that we measured was essentially a measure of a personality quality of the mothers. Punitiveness, in contrast with rewardingness, was a quite ineffectual quality for a mother to inject into her child training.

The evidence for this conclusion is overwhelming. The unhappy effects of punishment have run like a dismal thread through our findings. Mothers who punished toilet accidents severely ended up with bed-wetting children. Mothers who punished dependency to get rid of it had more dependent children than mothers who did not punish. Mothers who punished aggressive behavior severely had more aggressive children than mothers who punished lightly. They also had more dependent children. Harsh physical punishment was associated with high childhood aggressiveness and with the development of feeding problems.

Our evaluation of punishment is that *it is ineffectual over the long term as a technique for eliminating the kind of behavior toward which it is directed.* This sentence must be read carefully. We are not concerned here with whether aggressiveness and dependency are good or bad, or whether a mother should or should not want to eliminate them. A good many mothers in our group *did* want their maturing children to behave unaggressively and non-dependently toward the parents, and certainly none of the mothers liked either feeding problems or chronic bed-wetting. But these attitudes are beside the point. Having decided to eliminate certain kinds of changeworthy behavior, mothers varied in the extent to which they used punishment as the *method*. By their own reports of their children's behavior, the method did not work.

As we emphasized in our earlier discussions of this matter, our present data do not permit a sure conclusion on the question of whether punishment actually increased the kinds of behavior it was designed to reduce; there is always the possibility that children who initially showed more of a particular kind of un-desired behavior received more severe punishment. Whether this was the case or not, however, there is clear evidence that con-tinuing punishment of changeworthy behavior was associated with greater intensity of such behavior than was a non-punitive method of handling the behavior.

In addition, of course, we have seen a demonstration of the side-effects of punishment, particularly physical punishment and the severe punishment of aggression toward parents. The former was associated with feeding problems, with aggression in the home, and with flight or aggressive reactions to deviant behav-ior—what we have called the slow development of conscience.

These findings all relate to child behavior that occurred over reasonably long periods of time. That is, the aggressiveness that we measured was a *level* of such action, a day-in-and-day-out frequency and intensity. We did not—and could not with the interview—determine the effectiveness of punishment as a de-vice for eliminating single items of behavior, such as a single kind of aggressive act like biting. From the details as reported by a number of mothers, we are inclined to believe that punish-ment of specific acts not infrequently had just the effect the mother wanted. This seemed especially to be the case when she was able to explain fully what she was punishing for and what substitute behavior would be desirable. It must be remembered that punishment is not only an impelling force, but also a di-rective one. A slap on the hand will not only make a child jerk:

it will make him jerk *away* from the forbidden object. If the punishment is of a kind that produces (directs) action of a kind the mother wants, the punishment is likely to have a salutary effect—just as an offered reward would have. Some of the mothers seemed to have discovered this principle, and thought they were able to get good results from punishment. But we report this as an impression, only; a different method of research will be required to discover what, if any, is an efficient way of using punishment for the elimination of isolated bits of changeworthy behavior.

Permissiveness

We have discussed the nature of permissiveness sufficiently, in connection with the mothers' handling of sex and aggression, and restrictions and demands, so that there is little left to add except a note about its effects on children. Our findings are very limited. Permissiveness for dependent behavior had no effect that we could discover. Permissiveness for aggression, however, was an important source of continuing aggressive behavior, and was also associated with a low frequency of feeding problems. Sex permissiveness was associated with a low frequency of bed-wetting.

There seems little doubt that a permissive attitude toward aggression encourages the child to express himself in an aggressive fashion. Why the same effect was not evidenced in connection with dependency, we do not know. The fact that bed-wetting and feeding problems are associated with forms of non-permissiveness suggests that this latter end of the dimension may produce some degree of strain for the child. It is entirely possible that the otherwise desirable non-aggressiveness that is achieved by the mother's non-permissiveness, is achieved at a sufficient cost to the child's comfort that he develops these symptoms. We have no direct evidence on this point.

From a theoretical standpoint, permissiveness is a puzzling dimension. There have long been two opposing conceptions of the nature of motivation. One views the child as having within him a sort of reservoir of impelling forces that are continuously being replenished from the energic sources of life itself. This notion seems to assume that societal counterpressures prevent the uninhibited expression of these forces, and that the forces therefore build up greater and greater pressure. Eventually they must find release, either directly or through some of the so-called psychodynamic processes like projection and displacement. Permissive child rearing, according to this view, is a way of reducing the societal counterpressures, and hence may be expected to reduce both the strain and tension within and the probability of explosive or neurotic expressions outward.

The other view of motivation is that the main social motives are developed as a product of experience. Hence, the child learns to respond to certain cues or symbols with a *motivated reaction.* According to this notion, he does not have a reservoir of impelling forces, but his motives are themselves reactions to cues that have previously been associated with the satisfaction of drives. From this viewpoint, the child who is allowed to *be* aggressive (and get some satisfaction for it) will be more likely to resort to aggressive actions on future similar occasions. The impelling forces to much of his behavior, then, are not constantly being replenished, but are activated only when certain cues present themselves to him. And what acts he performs (e.g., aggressive acts) in response to these impulsions will be determined by what ones he has found by practice to be the most rewarding. Thus a mother's permissiveness for aggression toward the parents would be expected to produce a stronger tendency for the child to react to frustrations with *aggression* rather than with some other response like dependency.

The difference between these two conceptions is of much more than academic interest. If the *reservoir* notion is substantially correct, permissive child rearing should be helpful in preventing emotional tension, explosions of uncontrollable aggression, and the socially disruptive forms of indirect expression of strong motives. The apparent connection between non-permissiveness and the disturbances we have defined as feeding problems and bed-wetting suggests some support for this view. But supporting the alternative view are the facts that the one measure of indirect expression of aggression that we obtained—fantasy aggression in doll play—was not greater in non-permissively treated children; and clearly there was a greater overt aggressiveness by those children who were permitted to act in that way.

We must acknowledge that our present findings are ambiguous; they do not provide any decisive conclusion as to which of

the notions about the nature of motivation is correct. That problem, like many of the others we have encountered, awaits further investigation.

WHAT NEXT?

So, in a way, we end where we began—with many questions.
We know more than we did about how a large sample of American mothers are rearing their children at mid-century. We can
see something of how their practices and attitudes fall into patterns. We know a little more, too, about some of the effects of
various methods. But there remains so much to be discovered.
Research is endless. Every step, every answer, shows new paths
to be followed, new questions to be asked. We have pointed to
some of these in this report, and our wise colleagues will note
many others that have escaped our notice.

There can be only one answer to the question: "What next?"
Our society has turned firmly and convincedly to rational methods for the solutions to its problems. If we are correct in our
fundamental assumption that child-rearing methods contribute
much to the quality of human personality, then we must face
squarely the conclusion that many of our problems, both individual and societal, stem in some fashion from that same source.
To solve these problems rationally will require more facts, more
principles—and more research. More and more and more.

Appendixes

APPENDIX A

The Interview Schedule

1. First of all we'd like to get a picture of the family. How many children do you have?
   1a. How old are they?

[If more than one child] In this interview we want to talk mostly about X, since he's in the kindergarten group we are working with.

2. Has X been with you all his life, or have you been separated from him at any time?
   2a. [If separated] For how long? How old was he then?
3. And how about his father—has X been separated from his father at any time?
   3a. [If separated] For how long? How old was X then?
4. Now would you think back to when X was a baby. Who took care of him mostly then?
   4a. How much did your husband do in connection with taking care of X when he was a baby?
   4b. Did he ever change the baby's diapers? feed him? give him his bath?
5. All babies cry, of course. Some mothers feel that if you pick up a baby every time it cries, you will spoil it. Others think you should never let a baby cry for very long. How do you feel about this?

5a. What did you do about this with X?

5b. How about in the middle of the night?

6. Did you have time to spend with the baby besides the time that was necessary for feeding him, changing him, and just regular care like that?

    6a. [If yes] Tell me about what you did in this time. How much did you cuddle him and sing to him and that sort of thing?

7. Do you think that babies are fun to take care of when they're very little, or do you think they're more interesting when they're older?

8. Now would you tell me something about how the feeding went when he was a baby?

    8a. Was he breast-fed?

    8b. [If not] How did you happen to decide to use a bottle instead of breast feeding?

    8c. [If yes] For how long?

    8d. [If yes] Did you go directly to the cup or did you use a bottle?

    8e. And how about weaning him (from the bottle) (from the breast) to a cup? When did you start this?

    8f. How did you decide it was time to begin this?

    8g. How did you go about this?

    8h. How did he react to being taken off the bottle (breast)?

    8i. Had you been giving him liquid from a cup before?

    8j. How long did it take to get him to give up the bottle (breast) completely?

9. There has been a lot of talk about whether it is better to have a regular feeding schedule for a baby, or to feed him whenever he is hungry. How do you feel about this?

    9a. How did you handle this with X?

    9b. [If schedule] How closely did you stick to that schedule?

10. Have you had any problems about X eating enough, or eating the kinds of food he needs?

    10a. What do you do about it?

11. Does X eat at the table with the family for the evening meal?

12. What do you expect of X in the way of table manners?

    12a. Do you expect him to stay at the table through the meal or is he allowed to leave the table?

12*b*. Is he allowed to use his fingers?

12*c*. How about interrupting adult conversation—is that allowed?

12*d*. What else do you think can be expected of a five-year-old in the way of table manners?

13. How have you gone about teaching him his table manners?

14. What do you do about it if he does some of the things you don't allow?

15. And suppose for several days he eats very nicely and doesn't give you any trouble at the table. What would you do?

16. Now we'd like to consider toilet training. When did you start bowel training with X?

16*a*. How did it go?

16*b*. How did you go about it?

16*c*. How long did it take till he was pretty well trained?

16*d*. What did you do about it when he had accidents after he was mostly trained?

17. Now would you tell me what you have done with X about bed-wetting?

17*a*. How do you feel about it when he wets his bed?

17*b*. How do you handle the situation when you find his bed is wet? (Or how did you the last time it happened?)

18. Now we want to talk about sex and modesty training. How do you feel about allowing X to run about without his clothes on?

18*a*. [If opposed to it] What have you done to teach X about this?

18*b*. When did you start teaching him about it?

18*c*. [If not mentioned] How about modesty outdoors?

19. What have you done about it when you have noticed him playing with himself?

19*a*. How important do you feel it is to prevent this in a child?

20. How about sex play with other children—has this come up yet?

20*a*. What happened, and what did you do about it?

20*b*. What about the children wanting to look at each other, or go to the toilet together, or giggling together—how do you feel about it when you notice this sort of thing going on among the children?

20c. [If "never noticed it"] Would you allow this or do you think you'd step in?

21. Now we want to change the subject: the question of being neat and orderly and keeping things clean. What do you expect of X as far as neatness is concerned?

   21a. How do you go about getting him to do this?

22. How important do you think it is for him to be careful about marking on the walls and jumping on the furniture and things like that?

   22a. What do you do about it if he does these things?

   22b. And how about teaching children to respect the things that belong to other members of the family? What have you done about this with X?

23. We'd like to get some idea of the sort of rules you have for X in general—the sort of things he is allowed to do and the sort of things he isn't allowed to do. What are some of the rules?

   23a. How about bedtime?

   23b. How about making noise in the house—how much of that do you allow?

   23c. How about the amount of time he can spend listening to the radio or watching TV programs?

   23d. How far away is he allowed to go by himself?

   23e. Any other rules?

24. Do you think a child of X's age should be given any regular jobs to do around the house?

   24a. Does X have any regular jobs he is supposed to do?

   24b. [If yes] How do you go about getting him to do this?

25. How much do you have to keep after X to get him to do the things he is supposed to do?

26. Some parents expect their children to obey immediately when they tell them to be quiet or pick something up and so on. Others don't think it's terribly important for a child to obey right away. How do you feel about this?

   26a. How does your husband feel about strict obedience?

27. If you ask X to do something, and he jumps up right away and does it, how do you react? (Do you say something to him?)

28. If he doesn't do what you ask, do you ever just drop the subject, or do you always see to it that he does it?

29. Do you keep track of exactly where X is and what he is doing

most of the time, or can you let him watch out for himself quite a bit?

29a. How often do you check?

30. How much attention does X seem to want from you?

    30a. How about following you around and hanging on to your skirts?

    30b. [If not much] Did he ever go through a stage of doing this?

    30c. How do you (did you) feel about it when he hangs on to you and follows you around?

    30d. How do you generally react, if he demands attention when you're busy?

    30e. How about if X asks you to help him with something you think he could probably do by himself?

31. How does X react generally when you go out of the house and leave him with someone else?

32. Have you ever felt that X is growing up too fast in any way?

    32a. How did you feel about his starting school?

    32b. Have things been easier or pleasanter for you in any way since he's been in school?

33. I'm wondering if you could tell me more about how you and X get along together. What sort of things do you enjoy in X?

    33a. In what ways do you get on each other's nerves?

    33b. Do you show your affection toward each other quite a bit, or are you fairly reserved people, you and X?

    33c. Do you ever find time to play with X just for your own pleasure? Tell me about that.

34. Before X started kindergarten, did you teach him anything like reading words, or writing the alphabet, or drawing, or telling time—things like that?

    34a. Anything else you taught him?

    34b. How did you happen to teach him these things?

35. How important is it to you for X to do well in school?

    35a. How far would you like him to go in school?

36. Now we want to talk about whether you think there are any differences in bringing up boys and bringing up girls. How important do you think it is for a boy of X's age to act like a real boy (for a girl to be ladylike)?

    36a. [For boys] How about playing with dolls and that sort of thing?

36b. [For girls] How about playing rough games and that sort of thing?

36c. Do you feel there is any difference in the way boys and girls ought to act at X's age?

36d. What have you taught him about how you want him to treat little girls?

37. [If X has siblings] Would you tell me something about how X and his brother (sister) get along together?

37a. How do you feel about it when they quarrel?

37b. How bad does it have to get before you do something about it?

37c. How do you handle it when the children quarrel? Give me an example.

37d. Now how about when things are going smoothly among the children: do you do anything to show them that you have noticed this?

37e. [If yes] What sort of thing would you do?

38. In general, how does X get along with the neighbor children?

39. Have you ever encouraged him to go out and play with other children instead of playing by himself?

39a. [If yes] Tell me about that—how did the subject come up?

39b. How about other children coming in to play here?

39c. Does he play mostly with boys or girls? How do you feel about this?

40. Now how about when X is playing with one of the other children in the neighborhood and there is a quarrel or a fight— how do you handle this?

41. Some people feel it is very important for a child to learn not to fight with other children, and other people feel there are times when a child has to learn to fight. How do you feel about this?

41a. Have you ever encouraged your child to fight back?

42. Sometimes a child will get angry at his parents and hit them or kick them or shout angry things at them. How much of this sort of thing do you think parents ought to allow in a child of X's age?

42a. How do you handle it when X acts like this? Give me an example.

42*b*. [If this doesn't happen] How did you teach him not to do this?

42*c*. How much of a problem have you had with X about shows of temper and angry shouting and that sort of thing around the house?

43. How do you handle it if X is saucy or deliberately disobedient?

44. We'd like to get some idea of how X acts when he's naughty. (I know we've been talking about naughty behavior a lot, and we don't mean to imply that he's naughty all the time or anything, but most children do act up once in a while, and we're interested in knowing about it.) For instance, when he has deliberately done something he knows you don't want him to do, when your back is turned, how does he act?

44*a*. Does he ever come and tell you about it without your having to ask him?

44*b*. When you ask him about something he has done that he knows he's not supposed to do, does he usually admit it or deny it?

44*c*. What do you do about it if he denies something you are pretty sure he has done?

We have been talking about how you handle X in many different kinds of situations: table manners, neatness, and so on. Now we'd like to know something about how you go about correcting X and getting him to behave the way you want him to, regardless of the particular kind of behavior that is involved.

45. Do you have any system of rewarding him for good behavior?
45*a*. Do you have any ways that he can earn money?
45*b*. Can he earn points or gold stars or anything like that?

46. Some parents praise their children quite a bit when they are good, and others think that you ought to take good behavior for granted and that there's no point in praising a child for it. How do you feel about this?

47. In training X, do you ever say: "Your daddy and mother do it this way"? Do you say that? Under what circumstances?

47*a*. Who else do you hold up as an example—his older brother (sister)? grandparents? other relatives? playmates?

47*b*. Is there anyone you mention as an example of what *not*

to do? For instance—you're acting just like so-and-so—
you wouldn't want to be like him, would you?

48. How often do you spank X?

    48a. How about your husband? How often does he spank
him?

    48b. For instance, how often has X been spanked in the last
two weeks?

49. How about when he was younger—say two or three years old.
How often did you spank him then?

50. How does he act when you spank him—does it seem to hurt
his feelings, or make him angry, or what?

51. How much good do you think it does to spank X?

52. Do you ever deprive X of something he wants as a way of
disciplining him? [*Give examples, if necessary*] [If yes] How
often? (Frequently or rarely)

53. Would you imagine now that you are scolding X for something he has done that you don't want him to do. What would
you say to him?

    53a. What else might you say?

    53b. Do you warn him about what you might do if he doesn't
behave?

    53c. Do you ever tell him what else might happen if he doesn't
behave? (For instance, how about warning him that he
might get hurt? How would you say it?)

54. Is there any other kind of remark you make fairly often to X?

55. How often do you tell X that you're going to have to punish
him and then for some reason you don't follow through?

    55a. What kinds of things might keep you from following
through?

56. Now we'd like to talk for awhile about X and his father. Will
you tell me something about the way they act toward each
other?

    56a. For instance, when your husband comes home from
work, when X is there, what happens?

    56b. How about after dinner?

    56c. What other kinds of things do they do together?

57. How much does your husband do these days in connection
with taking care of X? What kinds of things does he do?

    57a. How about helping him to get dressed? getting his meals?
taking him to school?

57*b*. Does he ever stay with him when you are out?

58. What do you think your husband's attitude is toward the child?

    58*a*. Does he show affection toward him quite often (hugging him and kissing him and that sort of thing) or is he fairly reserved with him?

59. When X has to be disciplined, who usually does it, you or your husband (assuming both of you are there)?

    59*a*. How strict is your husband with X?

    59*b*. Does he ever do anything in disciplining X that you'd rather he didn't do?

60. In general, how well would you say you and your husband agree about the best way to handle X?

    60*a*. Does he ever think you are too strict or not strict enough?

    60*b*. Can you give me an example of a case where you didn't agree entirely?

61. We are wondering about who makes the main decisions about the children. In some families it is the father; in others, he leaves it all to the mother. How does that work out in your family?

    61*a*. For instance, in deciding how far away from the house he's allowed to go by himself?

    61*b*. How about health matters such as:

        1) calling the doctor

        2) or keeping him indoors for the day

    Who decides that?

    61*c*. Who decides how much X should help you or his father around the house?

62. How about in other things besides things that affect the children—who generally makes the decisions in your family?

    62*a*. How about money matters?

    62*b*. Who handles the money, pays the bills, and so on?

    62*c*. Who has most to say in deciding what you will do in your leisure time?

    62*d*. How about if you were considering moving to a different house—who would have most to say about a decision like that?

63. In some families, the work is more or less divided up between what the wife does and what the husband does. For instance,

it will be the wife's job to wash dishes and the husband's job to mow the lawn and take care of the furnace. In other families everybody helps with everything. How is this in your family?

64. Do you think X takes after you or after his father more? In what ways?

   64a. Does he imitate your speech or walk or mannerisms at all?

   64b. Does he imitate these things in his father?

65. Do you think X behaves better with you or with his father?

   65a. How do you account for that?

66. How much alike would you say you and your husband are? That is, in terms of your temperament, and the things you think are important in life, and so on?

   66a. In what ways are you different from each other? How about in little things?

   66b. [With respect to traits in which different] Would you rather have X be like you or like your husband in this respect?

   66c. [If no difference] In what ways would you like the child to be like the two of you and what ways different?

This brings us pretty much to the end of the interview. There's just one more thing we'd like to consider, and that is how you feel about being a mother.

67. I wonder if you would think back to when you first discovered you were pregnant with X. How did you feel about it?

   67a. How about your husband—how did he feel about it?

68. From the standpoint of your financial condition, and the ages of the other children, and so on, did you feel this was a good time to have a baby?

69. Looking back on it now, do you think things would have worked out better for you if you had waited longer to have X? Tell me about this.

70. Did you have any kind of job before you started having your family?

   70a. What kind of work did you do?

   70b. [If yes] How did you feel about giving up your work?

71. Some mothers feel that their main job is to stay home and take care of the children. At the same time they sometimes

feel that they owe it to themselves to do some outside work or at least have quite a few outside interests. What is your point of view about this?

71*a*. How well do you feel you've been able to solve this problem in your own case?

71*b*. Have you ever felt you'd rather be doing something else than what you're doing now?

72. Now looking back to your own childhood—how would you compare the way your mother raised you with the way you're raising your own children?

72*a*. [If difference] How do you feel about these changes?

APPENDIX B

Rating Scales for the Mother Interview

The following list contains all the main rating scales that were used for analyzing and quantifying the mother interviews. There were a number of additional codings that could not be evaluated conveniently for the reliability of the ratings, because they involved non-scalar items such as sex of child, ordinal position, number of siblings, etc.

Column 1. *Code number*. This is the IBM *card* number (Roman) and *column* number (Arabic) in the original data files. Complete sets of cards containing these data are on file at the

Laboratory of Human Development, Graduate School of Education, Harvard University, and at the Laboratory of Human Development, Stanford University.

Column 2. *Title of scale.* A brief descriptive title.*

Column 3. *Direction of scale.* The numbers indicate how many points there were on the scale, and the direction in which the scale ran. This information is required for interpreting the meaning of positive and negative correlations in the text and tables.

Column 4. *N.* Reliability data were available on 375 of the 379 cases. The correlations are computed only on the cases where both of the raters made a scalar judgment. When the number in this column differs from 375, the difference indicates the number of cases on which a non-scalar judgment was made.

Column 5. *r.* The reliability coefficient of the two independent ratings of each scale. Since the scores used in the analyses were the combination of independent ratings made by two judges, the correlations in this column may be corrected by the Spearman-Brown formula, $r_2 = \dfrac{2r}{1+r}$, where r_2 is the new estimate of reliability and r is the correlation reported in this column.

---

* Scale titles preceded by an asterisk (column 2) were included in the factor analysis shown in Appendix Table D:4.

Code Number	Title of Scale	Direction of Scale	N	r
II 6	Number of children in family	1 = one 6 = six or more	375	.991
II 9	Age difference between child and next-older sibling	1 = 15 months or less 7 = more than 67 months	207	.959
II 10	Age difference between child and next-younger sibling	1 = 15 months or less 5 = more than 43 months	206	.922
II 11	Separations from mother, first 9 months	1 = never 9 = often	369	.546
II 12	Separations from mother, 9 to 24 months	1 = never 9 = often	369	.730
II 13	Separations from mother, after 24 months	1 = never 9 = often	372	.719
II 14	Separations from father, first 9 months	1 = never 9 = often	363	.771
II 15	Separations from father, 9 to 24 months	1 = never 9 = often	364	.760
II 16	Separations from father, after 24 months	1 = never 9 = often	366	.832
II 17	Amount of caretaking in infancy by mother	1 = practically none 9 = all	375	.691
II 18	Amount of caretaking in infancy by father	1 = none 8 = more than mother	369	.745
II 19	Amount of caretaking in infancy by other agent	1 = none 8 = more than half	321	.851
II 21	* Mother's responsiveness to infant's crying	1 = unresponsive 9 = highly responsive	361	.691
II 22	How much did baby cry	1 = very little 7 = a great deal	255	.756
II 23	* Amount of mother's affectionate interaction with baby	1 = none 9 = a great deal	372	.658
II 24	* Amount of fun taking care of small baby	1 = none 9 = a great deal	368	.721
II 25	Warmth, affectional bond, mother to infant	1 = very cold 9 = very warm	374	.592
II 26	Duration of breast feeding	1 = not breast-fed 9 = more than 15 months	370	.972
II 29	Age at which change-of-mode weaning was begun	1 = under 2 months 7 = 2 years or older	342	.803

(*continued*)

Code Number	Title of Scale	Direction of Scale	N	r
II 30	Age at completion of weaning	1 = under 5 months 8 = 2½ years or older	361	.948
II 31	Time taken to complete weaning	1 = instantly 9 = 2 years or more	332	.848
II 34	Severity of reaction to weaning	1 = no reaction 9 = severe reaction	338	.805
II 35	* Severity of weaning	1 = mild 9 = severe	368	.584
II 36	* Scheduling of feeding	3 = vague attempts 6 = rigid schedule	376	.740
II 37	Severity of feeding problems	1 = mild 9 = severe	373	.696
II 38	* Severity of handling feeding problems	1 = mild 8 = severe	361	.712
II 40	Restrictions on physical mobility during meals	1 = no restrictions 8 = high restrictions	330	.597
II 41	Restrictions on use of fingers for eating	1 = no restrictions 9 = high restrictions	319	.743
II 42	Restrictions on interrupting adult conversation	1 = no restrictions 9 = high restrictions	345	.636
II 43	* Level of demands for table manners	1 = low demands 9 = high demands	369	.542
II 44	Pressure for conformity with table standards	1 = no pressure 9 = high pressure	363	.572
II 45	* Amount of praise for good behavior at the table	1 = always praises 8 = never praises	323	.853
II 46	Age at which bowel training was begun	1 = 0–4 months 9 = 40–44 months	352	.868
II 48	Age at which bowel training was completed	1 = 0–4 months 9 = 40–44 months	354	.832
II 49	Duration of bowel training	1 = 1–2 months 9 = 17 or more months	331	.823
II 50	How often child wets bed	1 = never 8 = almost every night	366	.797
II 51	* Severity of toilet training	1 = mild 9 = severe	365	.643

(continued)

Code Number	Title of Scale	Direction of Scale	N	r
II 52	Child's reaction to toilet training	1 = no reaction 9 = severe reaction	130	.659
II 53	* Permissiveness for going without clothes indoors	1 = not at all permissive 9 = completely permissive	356	.842
II 54	Amount of pressure for modesty	1 = no pressure 8 = great deal of pressure	244	.761
II 56	* Masturbation permissiveness	1 = not at all permissive 9 = completely permissive	367	.721
II 57	Severity of pressures against masturbation	1 = no pressure 9 = great deal of pressure	207	.770
II 58	* Permissiveness concerning sex play (among children)	1 = not at all permissive 9 = completely permissive	353	.678
II 59	Severity of pressures against sex play	1 = no pressure 8 = severe pressure	157	.700
II 60	Mother's sex anxiety	1 = no anxiety 9 = high anxiety	371	.608
II 61	* Standards for neatness and orderliness	1 = low standards 9 = high standards	371	.455
II 62	* Restrictions relating to care of house and furniture	1 = few restrictions 9 = many restrictions	371	.538
II 63	Pressures for neatness and orderliness	1 = no pressure 9 = high pressure	364	.516
II 64	Hour of child's bedtime	1 = 6:00 or earlier 7 = after 8:30	277	.874
II 65	* Strictness about bedtime	1 = not at all strict 9 = very strict	312	.586
II 66	* Strictness about noise	1 = not at all strict 9 = very strict	357	.659
II 67	Restrictions on radio and TV	1 = no restrictions 9 = high restrictions	326	.715
II 68	Amount of interest child expresses in TV	1 = much interest 8 = no interest	190	.706
II 69	* Restrictions on physical mobility	1 = no restrictions 9 = high restrictions	357	.589
II 70	Giving child regular jobs and chores	1 = no jobs 9 = many regular jobs	365	.691

(continued)

Code Number	Title of Scale	Direction of Scale	N	r
II 73 *	Mother's realistic standards for child's obedience	1 = does not expect obedience 9 = expects instant obedience	367	.594
II 74	Father's realistic standards for child's obedience	1 = does not expect obedience 9 = expects instant obedience	328	.790
II 75	Which parent more strict about obedience	1 = father 3 = mother	340	.853
II 76 *	Amount of praise for obedience	1 = always praises 7 = never praises	322	.724
II 77	How much problem with obedience	1 = no problem 5 = constant problem	358	.491
II 78	Does mother drop subject or follow through	1 = does not follow through 9 = always follows through	366	.776
III 5	Keeping track of child	1 = rarely checks 9 = constantly checks	361	.746
III 6	Amount attention child wants	1 = none 9 = a great deal	355	.744
III 7	Amount child clings to mother	1 = none 7 = a great deal	361	.745
III 8	Child's earlier tendency to cling	1 = none 5 = a great deal	282	.785
III 9	Amount child objects to separation from mother	1 = none 8 = a great deal	349	.751
III 10	Amount of dependency child shows	1 = none 9 = a great deal	367	.531
III 11 *	Mother's response to dependency	1 = rewards dependency 9 = punishes dependency	365	.574
III 13 *	Amount of mother's affectionate demonstrativeness	1 = none 9 = a great deal	358	.621
III 14 *	Does mother find time to play with child	1 = very often 9 = practically never	357	.671
III 15	Affectionate relationship, (warmth) mother to child	1 = predominantly hostile 9 = very warm	369	.533
III 16	Amount of teaching before child starts school	1 = no teaching 5 = considerable teaching	176	.497

(*continued*)

Code Number	Title of Scale	Direction of Scale	N	r
III 17	Child's demands for teaching	1 = none 5 = considerable	155	.532
III 18	* How important that child do well in school	1 = unimportant 9 = very important	359	.748
III 19	How far is child expected to go in school	1 = grade school 9 = graduate school	342	.833
III 20	Sex role differentiation	1 = no differentiation 9 = high differentiation	366	.667
III 21	Amount of quarreling among siblings	1 = none 8 = a great deal	306	.665
III 22	* Permissiveness for aggression toward siblings	1 = not at all permissive 9 = completely permissive	293	.596
III 23	* Praise for playing nicely with children	1 = always praises 8 = never praises	272	.854
III 25	Demands for child to be sociable	1 = high demands 7 = restricts social contacts	200	.679
III 26	* Demands for child to be aggressive	1 = none 9 = high	352	.657
III 27	Extent child encouraged to fight back	1 = never 8 = strongly encouraged	289	.791
III 28	* Permissiveness for inappropriate aggression toward children	1 = not at all permissive 9 = completely permissive	323	.537
III 29	Amount of aggression child exhibits at home	1 = none 9 = a great deal	358	.523
III 30	* Permissiveness for aggression toward parents	1 = not at all permissive 9 = completely permissive	359	.707
III 31	* Punishment for aggression toward parents	1 = no punishment 8 = severe punishment	337	.620
III 32	Does child tell about deviations	1 = seldom 7 = always	332	.334
III 33	Does child admit deviations when asked	1 = admits 5 = denies	350	.677
III 34	Evidence of conscience development	1 = weak conscience 9 = strong conscience	364	.631
III 35	Can child earn money	1 = regular earning system 9 = money not used as reward	349	.708

(continued)

Code Number	Title of Scale	Direction of Scale	N	r
III 36	* Extent of use of tangible rewards	1 = never used 9 = regularly used	357	.680
III 37	Extent of use of praise	1 = never used 9 = very often used	367	.665
III 38	Setting up positive models	1 = never 8 = often	344	.739
III 39	Setting up negative models	1 = never 7 = often	355	.874
III 40	Frequency with which mother spanks	1 = never 8 = every day	295	.866
III 41	Frequency with which father spanks	1 = never 8 = every day	245	.843
III 45	How much good it does to spank	1 = does good 8 = does no good	335	.874
III 46	* Extent of use of physical punishment	1 = never used 9 = very often used	365	.743
III 47	* Extent of use of deprivation of privileges	1 = never used 9 = very often used	366	.667
III 52	Extent of use of isolation	1 = never used 9 = very often used	294	.528
III 53	Extent of use of withdrawal of love	1 = never used 9 = very often used	118	.496
III 55	Warnings of danger from environment	1 = never warns 7 = very often warns	334	.516
III 57	* Extent of use of reasoning	1 = never used 9 = very often used	214	.421
III 60	* How often threaten to punish, then not follow through	1 = never 8 = very often	357	.883
III 62	How child and father act toward each other	1 = affectionate 9 = cold	373	.691
III 63	Does father stay with child when mother out	1 = never 8 = frequently	203	.757
III 64	Amount of caretaking father does now	1 = none 9 = quite a bit	366	.604
III 65	* Affectional bond, father to child	1 = very warm 9 = predominantly hostile	373	.710

(continued)

Code Number	Title of Scale	Direction of Scale	N	r
III 66	* Which parent disciplines	1 = father 9 = mother	363	.906
III 67	How strict is father	1 = very strict 5 = lenient	356	.712
III 68	Does mother disapprove of father's discipline	1 = no disapproval 5 = much disapproval	340	.723
III 71	Does mother think father too strict	1 = too strict 5 = not strict enough	351	.559
III 72	Does father think mother too strict	1 = too strict 5 = not strict enough	297	.770
III 73	* Parents' agreement on child-rearing policies	1 = perfect agreement 9 = complete disagreement	372	.644
III 74	* Responsibility for child-rearing policies	1 = mother entirely 9 = father entirely	371	.635
III 76	Responsibility for financial policy	1 = wife responsible 9 = husband responsible	368	.770
III 77	Responsibility for deciding how to spend leisure time	1 = wife responsible 5 = husband responsible	332	.848
III 78	Responsibility for decision to move	1 = wife responsible 5 = husband responsible	353	.882
IV 5	Division of labor between husband and wife	1 = definite division 9 = no division	353	.638
IV 6	Family authority	1 = mother complete authority 9 = father complete authority	373	.472
IV 7	Which parent child takes after	1 = takes after mother 7 = takes after father	297	.882
IV 8	How much child takes after mother	1 = not like mother 7 = like mother in many ways	337	.829
IV 9	How much child takes after father	1 = not like father 7 = like father in many ways	341	.840
IV 12	How much alike are mother and father	1 = completely different 9 = completely alike	363	.692
IV 13	* Mother's evaluation of father	1 = critical 9 = admiring	370	.636

(continued)

Code Number	Title of Scale	Direction of Scale	N	r
IV 14	* Mother's reaction to pregnancy	1 = delighted 9 = displeased	369	.884
IV 15	* Husband's reaction to wife's pregnancy	1 = delighted 9 = displeased	355	.860
IV 17	Mother's feeling about giving up job	1 = sacrifice 7 = glad to stop work	279	.815
IV 18	Mother's attitude toward mother role	1 = values it highly 9 = subordinate to other roles	372	.517
IV 19	* Mother's dissatisfaction with current situation	1 = entirely satisfied 9 = very much dissatisfied	366	.652
IV 20	Mother working during child's first two years	1 = never worked 6 = worked full time	306	.851
IV 21	Mother working after child is two years old	1 = did not work 5 = worked more than half time	341	.869
IV 22	* Mother's self-esteem	1 = low self-esteem 9 = high self-esteem	370	.493
IV 23	Which parent stricter	1 = father 9 = mother	366	.794
IV 29	Mother's rejection of child	1 = no rejection 9 = complete rejection	272	.566
IV 31	* Mother's child-rearing anxiety	1 = no anxiety 9 = high anxiety	368	.485
IV 32	Extent of child dominance	1 = none 5 = a great deal	362	.355
IV 33	Amount of caretaking by others than parents	1 = none 8 = half or more	263	.658
IV 36	Were mother's parents more strict	1 = more strict 5 = less strict	187	.821
IV 37	Does mother pattern herself after own mother	1 = tries to be same 5 = tries to be different	282	.790
XV 5	Permissiveness for dependency	1 = not at all permissive 9 = completely permissive	368	.630
XV 6	Extent of reward for dependency	1 = does not reward 9 = tries always to comply	368	.730
XV 7	Punishment for dependency, and amount of irritation mother feels	1 = no irritation; no punishment 9 = considerable irritation	316	.680

* See Appendix Table D:4 for factor analysis of these 44 child-rearing scales.

Selection and Composition of the Sample

Initially eight elementary schools in two communities were selected. The following table summarizes the reasons for the shrinkage of the final sample to 379 cases from 640 kindergarten children enrolled in the eight schools (see Chapter One).

TABLE C:1

SELECTION OF THE SAMPLE

Total number of kindergarten children in eight schools		640
Shrinkage due to sample requirements:		
1. Either or both parents foreign born	38	
2. Child not living with natural parents	13	
3. Parents separated, divorced, dead	15	
4. Twins	8	
5. Disproportionate ordinal position	41	
6. Disproportionate socio-economic status	38	
7. Other (child deaf, retarded, etc.)	6	
Total shrinkage for sample requirements		159
Total number of kindergarten children after initial selection		481
Shrinkage due to cases becoming unobtainable:		
1. Mother refused to participate	38	
2. Mother did not have time to be interviewed	24	
3. Sickness in family	7	
4. Family moved	19	
5. Child would not co-operate in doll play	7	
6. Interview recording defective	3	
7. Unknown reasons	4	
Total shrinkage for dropouts		102
Total sample		379

TABLE C:2

COMPOSITION OF SAMPLE: FREQUENCY IN TERMS OF SEX AND
ORDINAL POSITION OF CHILD AND SOCIO-ECONOMIC STATUS OF
FAMILY *

| | ORDINAL POSITION | | | |
	Only	Oldest	Middle	Youngest
Boys:				
Middle class	16	28	33	35
Working class	17	30	15	24
Girls:				
Middle class	4	23	27	32
Working class	15	25	29	19

* The total obtained sample was 379 mothers, but 7 of them have been omitted from this table because no estimate of their SES could be made. Of the omitted cases, 4 were boys' mothers, and 3 were girls'; 3 of them were mothers of oldest children, 1 was the mother of a middle child, and 3 were mothers of youngest children.

Supplementary Tables

TABLE D:1

MOTHER'S ATTITUDE TOWARD PREGNANCY: RELATIONSHIP TO COMPOSITION OF EXISTING FAMILY

Mother's Attitude toward Pregnancy	Already Had Boy or Boys, No Girls	Already Had Girl or Girls, No Boys	Already Had Children of Both Sexes
Delighted	29%	44%	24%
Generally pleased	39	29	20
Mixed feelings or displeased	32	27	56
Total	100%	100%	100%
Number of cases	87	96	34

$p = .05$ (Chi^2 = 3.81)

TABLE D:2

MOTHER'S WARMTH TOWARD INFANT AND CHILD: RELATIONSHIP TO SEXES OF PREVIOUS CHILDREN

MOTHER'S WARMTH TOWARD CHILD	FAMILY ALREADY HAS			
	Boys, No Girls	Girls, No Boys	Children of Both Sexes	No Older Children
	DURING INFANCY			
When the new child is a boy				
Very warm	17%	50%	30%	34%
Moderately warm	64	42	50	46
Relatively cold	19 *	8 *	20	20
Total	100%	100%	100%	100%
Number of cases	42	48	20	90
When the new child is a girl				
Very warm	48%	36%	43%	45%
Moderately warm	41	47	36	40
Relatively cold	11	17	21	15
Total	100%	100%	100%	100%
Number of cases	46	47	14	68
	AT KINDERGARTEN AGE			
When the new child is a boy				
Very warm	31%	43%	40%	29%
Moderately warm	21	33	50	38
Relatively cold	48 †	24 †	10	33
Total	100%	100%	100%	100%
Number of cases	42	49	20	91
When the new child is a girl				
Very warm	35%	39%	43%	31%
Moderately warm	41	28	43	44
Relatively cold	24	33	14	25
Total	100%	100%	100%	100%
Number of cases	46	46	14	68

* The difference between the mean scale values for these two columns has a t value of 2.96 ($p<.01$).

† The difference between the mean scale values for these two columns has a t value of 2.35 ($p<.05$).

TABLE D:3

INTERCORRELATIONS

Scale	Mother's Evaluation of Father	Dissatisfaction with Current Situation	How Mother Felt When Pregnant	Warmth toward Infant	Warmth toward Child
Mother's self-esteem (1 = low; 9 = high)	.16	−.33	−.17	.24	.39
Mother's evaluation of father (1 = low; 9 = high)		−.23	−.19	.12	.31
Dissatisfaction with current situation (1 = satisfied; 9 = very dissatisfied)			.18	−.19	−.27
How mother felt when pregnant (1 = delighted; 9 = unhappy)				−.23	−.13
Warmth toward infant (1 = cold; 9 = very warm)					.36
Warmth toward child (1 = cold; 9 = very warm)					

TABLE D:4

FACTOR ANALYSIS OF 44 CHILD-REARING SCALES: ROTATED FACTOR MATRIX SHOWING LOADING OF EACH SCALE ON EACH OF 7 FACTORS *

(Loadings greater than .30 are italicized)

APPENDIX B CODE NO.	SCALE †	A	B	C	D	E	F	G	h^2
II 21	Mother's responsiveness to infant's crying	−15	05	27	00	00	−07	−11	.13
II 23	Amount of mother's affectionate interaction with baby	02	30	34	−10	14	−26	09	.31
II 24	Amount of fun taking care of small baby	−06	19	26	−05	06	−04	−09	.12
II 35	Severity of weaning	11	−14	−03	−05	03	07	05	.04
II 36	Scheduling of feeding	09	−11	−18	01	−10	−02	37	.20
II 38	Severity of handling feeding problems	22	−06	01	16	17	−11	14	.14
II 43	Level of demands for table manners	37	−02	04	32	−15	10	35	.40
II 45	Amount of praise for good behavior at the table	−07	02	−38	−37	−06	00	21	.33
II 51	Severity of toilet training	34	−25	−15	24	19	06	02	.30
II 53	Permissiveness for going without clothes indoors	−66	11	10	09	00	−05	14	.49
II 56	Masturbation permissiveness	−70	04	19	05	−01	−11	11	.55
II 58	Permissiveness concerning sex play (among children)	−77	06	13	18	−08	−14	07	.59
II 61	Standards for neatness and orderliness	35	19	−05	38	−11	12	13	.35
II 62	Restrictions relating to care of house and furniture	48	−01	04	32	−13	08	19	.39
II 65	Strictness about bedtime	10	14	−08	26	−20	10	33	.26
II 66	Strictness about noise	38	−13	00	21	−12	20	00	.26

(continued)

FACTOR ANALYSIS OF 44 CHILD-REARING SCALES: ROTATED FACTOR MATRIX SHOWING LOADING OF EACH SCALE ON EACH OF 7 FACTORS *
(Loadings greater than .30 are italicized)

APPENDIX B CODE No.	SCALE †	A	B	C	D	E	F	G	h²
II 69	Restrictions on physical mobility	18	08	06	−05	−05	−02	*32*	.15
II 73	Mother's realistic standards for child's obedience (1 = low)	*32*	10	−09	*45*	−05	−05	02	.33
II 76	Amount of praise for obedience	05	−15	04	−09	00	−05	24	.10
III 11	Mother's response to dependency (1 = favorable)	*38*	−07	*−36*	−12	−06	04	03	.30
III 13	Amount of mother's affectionate demonstrativeness	−03	28	*41*	10	−04	20	21	.34
III 14	Does mother find time to play with child (1 = frequently)	−04	−24	*−50*	−14	02	22	*−23*	.43
III 18	How important that child do well in school (1 = unimportant)	*32*	−02	−01	03	05	18	−06	.14
III 22	Permissiveness for aggression toward siblings	*−31*	−12	−03	06	−04	−21	09	.17
III 23	Praise for playing nicely with children	−03	−01	−28	*−38*	−01	09	08	.24
III 26	Demands for child to be aggressive	−23	−05	−10	06	*45*	−01	19	.31
III 28	Permissiveness for inappropriate aggression toward other children	*−30*	−09	−05	−10	*42*	*35*	21	.45
III 30	Permissiveness for aggression toward parents	*−51*	−09	−20	−17	*−35*	16	00	.48
III 31	Punishment for aggression toward parents	*43*	−13	02	15	*41*	−06	−12	.41
III 36	Extent of use of tangible rewards	04	14	09	*40*	10	−04	05	.20
III 46	Extent of use of physical punishment	*37*	−15	−05	19	*44*	05	−14	.37
III 47	Extent of use of deprivation of privileges	16	08	−10	*51*	13	00	08	.32

(*continued*)

TABLE D:4 (continued)

FACTOR ANALYSIS OF 44 CHILD-REARING SCALES: ROTATED FACTOR MATRIX SHOWING LOADING OF EACH SCALE ON EACH OF 7 FACTORS *

(Loadings greater than .30 are italicized)

APPENDIX B CODE No.	SCALE †	FACTORS							h^2
		A	B	C	D	E	F	G	
III 57	Extent of use of reasoning	-04	07	*37*	-18	26	-11	05	.26
III 60	How often threaten to punish, then not follow through (1 = never)	06	*-35*	-05	-12	09	16	-17	.21
III 65	Affectional bond, father to child (1 = father warm)	-02	*-48*	-04	-18	-04	-02	07	.27
III 66	Which parent disciplines (1 = father; 9 = mother)	15	01	04	-08	11	-22	-10	.10
III 73	Parents' agreement on child-rearing policies (1 = high agreement)	-01	*-60*	09	15	-05	-23	-06	.45
III 74	Responsibility for child-rearing policies (1 = mother)	-20	00	05	00	07	*30*	18	.17
IV 13	Mother's evaluation of father (1 = low evaluation)	-06	*56*	-01	-10	09	18	23	.42
IV 14	Mother's reaction to pregnancy (1 = delighted)	-07	*-42*	-15	05	-16	28	-05	.31
IV 15	Husband's reaction to wife's pregnancy (1 = delighted)	-13	*-51*	06	07	-09	*34*	-08	.42
IV 19	Mother's dissatisfaction with current situation	-08	*-47*	-01	04	15	01	-02	.25
IV 22	Mother's self-esteem (1 = low)	-10	*59*	09	*34*	-21	13	-08	.55
IV 31	Mother's child-rearing anxiety	10	*-56*	08	-17	19	16	*33*	.53

* The factor analysis of these 44 scales isolated 7 Factors, or underlying traits:

A: Permissiveness-strictness
B: General family adjustment
C: Warmth of mother-child relationship
D: Responsible child-training orientation
E: Aggressiveness and punitiveness
F: Perception of husband
G: Orientation toward child's physical well-being

The figures in the h^2 column denote a measure of the extent to which the ratings on a scale were accounted for by all 7 Factors combined and may be interpreted as "percentage of total variance determined by Factors A to G, inclusive." A high figure means that the scale was highly affected by them; a low figure means that there were mainly other influences besides these 7 underlying traits that were determining what rating a mother obtained on the scale.

† A *low* amount of the quality described by each scale was represented by scale-point "1." Where the scale description does not make clear which was the low end of the scale, this information is given in parentheses.

TABLE D:5

PERCENTAGE OF CHILDREN SHOWING EMOTIONAL DISTURBANCE: INTERACTIVE EFFECT OF DURATION OF WEANING AND AGE AT BEGINNING OF WEANING

		CHILD WEANED AT MOTHER'S INSTIGATION		
DURATION OF WEANING	CHILD WEANED SELF	Weaning Begun Before 8 Months	Weaning Begun at 8–10.9 Months	Weaning Begun at 11 Months or Later
Under 1 month	0% (18) *	23% (27)	19% (32)	35% (33)
1–3.9 months	0% (12)	15% (31)	18% (36)	32% (23)
4 months or more	0% (20)	46% (55)	23% (31)	50% (30)
		Line 1: $r = .08$		
		Line 2: $r = .20$		
		Line 3: $r = .05$		

* Figures in parentheses are number of cases.

TABLE D:6

AMOUNT OF BABY'S CRYING: RELATION TO HIS REACTION TO WEANING AND THE ABRUPTNESS OF HIS WEANING *

	HOW MUCH DID BABY CRY?		
	Very Little	Moderate Amount	A Good Deal
Percentage of children showing some emotional upset at weaning	17%	27%	29%
Percentage weaned relatively severely	41%	34%	32%
Number of cases	109	122	59
		Line 1: $r = .12$	
		Line 2: $r = -.09$	

* These figures are obtained from the categories shown in Table III:7.

TABLE D:7

RELATIONSHIP BETWEEN CHILDREN'S FEEDING PROBLEMS AND THE TRAINING
PRACTICES OF THEIR PARENTS *

Scales	Children Having Feeding Problems	Number of Cases	
Breast feeding:			
Did not breast-feed	25%	226	
Baby breast-fed for less than 1 month	12%	48	p = N.S.
Breast-fed for 1–2.9 months	16%	45	r = .01
Breast-fed for 3 months or more	14%	56	
Scheduling of feeding:			
Self-demand	22%	100	
Vague attempts at scheduling	22%	72	p = N.S.
Rough schedule, which mother would modify by half hour or so	19%	107	r = .01
Fairly rigid schedule	19%	97	
Age at beginning of weaning:			
Under five months	19%	21	
5–7.9 months	23%	112	
8–10.9 months	20%	115	p = N.S.
11–15.9 months	20%	87	r = −.06
16 months or more	14%	21	
Time taken for completion of weaning:			
Under 1 month	19%	111	
1 month to 3.9 months	22%	102	p = N.S.
4 months or more	22%	136	r = −.02
Severity of weaning:			
Severe	18%	73	
Fairly severe	24%	54	
Moderate	22%	97	p = N.S.
Mild	16%	93	r = −.01
Very mild	26%	54	
Child's emotional upset over weaning:			
No upset	20%	219	
Slight upset	18%	57	p = N.S.
Moderate upset	28%	47	r = −.02
Considerable upset	21%	33	
Severity of toilet training:			
Severe	23%	75	
Fairly severe	27%	129	p < .05
Moderate	15%	117	r = .12
Mild	15%	54	
Permissiveness for aggression toward parents:			
Not at all permissive	29%	120	
Slightly permissive	15%	100	p < .05
Moderately permissive	20%	103	r = −.12
Quite permissive	12%	52	
Mother's response to dependency:			
Negative (punishes, discourages it)	22%	125	
Neutral or ambivalent	26%	126	p < .10
Positive (rewards, encourages it)	13%	126	r = .09

(continued)

TABLE D:7 (*continued*)

RELATIONSHIP BETWEEN CHILDREN'S FEEDING PROBLEMS AND THE TRAINING
PRACTICES OF THEIR PARENTS *

Scales	Children Having Feeding Problems	Number of Cases
Extent of use of physical punishment:		
Rarely or never used	17%	58
Occasionally used	21%	105
Used moderately often	20%	118
Fairly often used	20%	70
Regularly used	36%	25
Mother's affectional warmth toward child:		
Exceptionally warm	11%	36
Quite warm	20%	132
Warm	18%	101
Matter-of-fact	22%	63
Cold, some hostility	35%	46

For physical punishment group: $p < .01$, $r = .14$

For affectional warmth group: $p < .01$, $r = -.14$

* The series of child-training scales which are shown here are not independent of each other. For example, severity of toilet training has a correlation of between .22 and .30 with each of the scales which follow it in the table. Thus, it is difficult to say whether it is severity of toilet training *per se*, or generally severe child training, which is associated with an increase in feeding problems.

TABLE D:8

Intercorrelations of Six Ratings of Child Behavior

Boys					
Child Behavior Dimension	2	3	4	5	6
1. Severity of feeding problems	.00	.08	−.08	.03	−.12
2. Bed-wetting		.02	−.04	.02	−.21
3. Amount of dependency, age five			−.20	.02	.09
4. Sociability of child				−.07	.07
5. Amount of aggression toward parents					−.15
6. Amount of conscience					
Girls					
Child Behavior Dimension	2	3	4	5	6
1. Severity of feeding problems	−.10	.12	−.03	.04	−.05
2. Bed-wetting		.01	.01	−.04	−.05
3. Amount of dependency, age five			−.13	.14	.02
4. Sociability of child				−.11	.01
5. Amount of aggression toward parents					−.11
6. Amount of conscience					

TABLE D:9

AGE AT BEGINNING OF BOWEL TRAINING: RELATIONSHIP TO AMOUNT OF EMOTIONAL UPSET

	AGE AT BEGINNING OF BOWEL TRAINING				
	Under 5 Months	5–9 Months	10–14 Months	15–19 Months	20 Months or More
Child showed emotional disturbance *	67%	41%	60%	71%	35%
Number of cases	12	66	55	24	17

* These percentages are based upon the group of mothers who volunteered information about the child's emotional reactions to toilet training. The figures mean, for example, that among the 55 mothers who began bowel training during the ten-fourteen months age range, and who discussed their children's emotional reactions to the process, 60 per cent reported that their children were upset, and 40 per cent said they were *not* upset.

TABLE D:10

PERCENTAGE OF CHILDREN WHO TOOK LESS THAN FIVE MONTHS TO COMPLETE BOWEL TRAINING

AGE AT BEGINNING OF TOILET TRAINING	SEVERITY OF TOILET TRAINING			
	Not at All Severe	Slight Pressure	Moderate Pressure	Very Severe
Under 10 months	33% (20) *	20% (53)	28% (66)	25% (37)
10–14 months	55% (12)	35% (38)	22% (41)	19% (22)
15–44 months	41% (17)	41% (23)	29% (15)	46% (14)

Where, 1 = duration of toilet training
2 = severity of toilet training
3 = age at beginning of toilet training

$$r12 = .10$$
$$r13 = -.21$$
$$r23 = -.08$$
$$r_{12 \cdot 3} = .09$$
$$r_{13 \cdot 2} = -.20$$

* Figures in parentheses are number of cases.

TABLE D:11

SEVERITY OF TOILET TRAINING: RELATIONSHIP TO AMOUNT OF EMOTIONAL UPSET

	SEVERITY OF TOILET TRAINING			
	Not at All Severe	Slight Pressure	Moderate Pressure	Very Severe
Child showed emotional disturbance *	32%	26%	60%	84%
Number of cases	28	49	55	49

* These percentages are based upon the group of mothers who volunteered information about the child's emotional reactions to toilet training.

TABLE D:12

INTERCORRELATIONS AMONG CHILD DEPENDENCY MEASURES

Scale	2	3	4	5
1. How much attention wanted	.50	.21	.20	.71
2. Wanting to be near; clinging		.27	.17	.63
3. Earlier tendency to cling			.16	.29
4. Objection to separation				.43
5. Over-all rating of dependency				

TABLE D:13

AMOUNT OF DEPENDENCY EXHIBITED BY THE CHILD AT PRESENT

1. None. Wants little or no attention from mother; doesn't follow around; doesn't object when she leaves; asks for little unnecessary help	3%
2. A little. Occasionally does some of the above things	39
3. Some. Does most of these things once in a while, or one or two of them quite often	35
4. Quite a bit. Often exhibits several items of dependency behavior	18
5. A great deal. Wants much attention; follows frequently; constantly asks for help; doesn't want mother to go out	4
Not ascertained	1
Total	100%

TABLE D:14

INTERCORRELATIONS AMONG THE THREE SCALES
MEASURING THE MOTHER'S HANDLING OF DEPENDENCY

Scale	2	3
1. Permissiveness	.57	−.52
2. Reward		−.45
3. Punishment		

TABLE D:15

RELATIONSHIP OF CHILD'S CURRENT DEPENDENCY TO
MATERNAL BEHAVIOR THREATENING THE LOVE RELATIONSHIP
BETWEEN MOTHER AND CHILD

Scales	Percentage Showing Considerable Dependency at Kindergarten Age	Number of Cases
Use of withdrawal of love as a technique of discipline:		
Seldom or never uses	20%	88
Occasionally uses	24%	62
Fairly often uses	46%	39
	$(r = .19, p < .01)$	
Severity of punishment for aggression toward parents:		
Little punishment	14%	44
Moderate punishment	24%	158
Severe punishment	30%	154
	$(r = .15, p < .01)$	
Amount of rejection:		
No rejection	20%	220
Some rejection	35%	101
	(biserial $r = .12, p < .05$)	

TABLE D:16

RELATIONSHIP OF CHILD'S CURRENT DEPENDENCY TO COMBINED RE-
WARD AND PUNISHMENT FOR DEPENDENCY

	Percentage Showing Considerable Dependency at Kindergarten Age	Number of Cases
High reward for dependency:		
Low punishment for dependency	9%	68
Medium punishment	25%	59
High punishment	42%	31
Low reward for dependency:		
Low punishment for dependency	21%	28
Medium punishment	38%	45
High punishment	33%	85

TABLE D:17

INTERCORRELATIONS AMONG SEX SCALES

Scale	2	3	4	5	6
1. Permissiveness for immodesty	−.85	.57	−.28	.59	−.40
2. Pressure for modesty		−.51	.36	−.50	.31
3. Permissiveness for masturbation			−.67	.63	−.41
4. Pressure against masturbation				−.35	.47
5. Permissiveness for sex play					−.72
6. Pressure against sex play					

TABLE D:18

INTERCORRELATIONS AMONG SCALES RELATED TO AGGRESSION

Scale	2	3	4	5	6
1. Permissiveness: aggression toward siblings	.11	.34	.09	.15	−.11
2. Demand: show aggression toward other children		.39	.04	.03	.10
3. Permissiveness: inappropriate aggression toward other children			.06	.05	−.06
4. Amount of aggression X shows at home				.23	.16
5. Permissiveness: aggression toward parents					−.46
6. Punishment: aggression toward parents					

TABLE D:19

AGGRESSION: INTERCORRELATIONS AND PARTIAL CORRELATIONS OF AGGRESSIVE BE-
HAVIOR IN CHILD AND FOUR MATERNAL DIMENSIONS

Scale	2	3	4	5
1. Amount of aggression X shows at home	.23	.16	.22	−.20
2. Permissiveness: aggression toward parents		−.46	−.21	.10
3. Punishment: aggression toward parents			.44	−.22
4. Physical punishment				−.26
5. Mother's warmth toward child (cold = low)				

$$r_{12\cdot345} = .35$$
$$r_{13\cdot245} = .20$$
$$r_{14\cdot235} = .14$$
$$r_{15\cdot234} = -.14$$

TABLE D:20

INTERCORRELATIONS AMONG SCALES MEASURING MOTHER'S DEMANDS AND RESTRICTIONS

Scales	2	3	4	5	6	7
1. Table manners	.34	.44	.24	.19	.22	.26
2. Neatness and orderliness		.33	.26	.24	.12	.29
3. Care of house and furniture			.18	.35	.16	.32
4. Bedtime rules				.20	.06	.19
5. Noise					.06	.22
6. Physical mobility						.10
7. Standards of obedience						

TABLE D:21

CORRELATIONS BETWEEN TWO MEASURES OF TOILET TRAINING AND FOUR MEASURES OF RESTRICTIVENESS

Restrictiveness Scales	Age at Beginning of Toilet Training	Rated Severity of Toilet Training
Use of fingers at table	−.15	.16
Neatness and orderliness	−.06	.21
Care of house and furniture	−.16	.18
Summary: household restrictions	−.17	.27

TABLE D:22

INTERCORRELATIONS AMONG SCALES THAT MEASURED THE EXTENT TO WHICH
MOTHERS USED TEN TECHNIQUES OF DISCIPLINE, AND CORRELATIONS WITH
MOTHERS' ESTIMATES OF THE USEFULNESS OF SPANKING

Technique	2	3	4	5	6	7	8	9	10	11
1. Tangible rewards	.06	.08	−.01	.11	.22	−.03	.00	.07	.00	−.19
2. Praise		.11	−.03	−.10	.02	.13	.22	.05	−.03	−.05
3. Good models			.16	.07	.15	.04	.02	−.03	.08	.05
4. Bad models				.14	−.04	−.10	−.33	.00	.06	−.03
5. Physical punishment					.17	.02	−.34	.03	.08	−.18
6. Deprivation of privileges						.01	.01	.08	.05	−.03
7. Isolation							−.03	.07	−.08	.07
8. Reasoning								−.05	−.18	.02
9. Withdrawal of love									.02	.00
10. Following through on threats										.05
11. "Does good" to spank										

TABLE D:23

THE EFFECTIVENESS OF PHYSICAL PUNISHMENT, IN RELATION TO THE AFFECTIONAL
WARMTH OF THE CHILD'S MOTHER AND FATHER AND THE IDENTITY OF THE DIS-
CIPLINARIAN

	PERCENTAGE OF CHILDREN FOR WHOM THEIR MOTHERS REPORTED THAT SPANKING "DOES GOOD"			
PARENTS' AFFECTIONAL WARMTH	Mother Disciplines		Father Disciplines	
Both mother and father warm	39%	(34) *	58%	(37)
Both mother and father relatively cold	47%	(44)	45%	(40)
Mother warmer than father	62%	(30)	53%	(15)
Father warmer than mother	38%	(40)	68%	(19)

* Figures in parentheses are number of cases.

TABLE D:24

COMPARISON OF CHILD TRAINING OF OLDER AND YOUNGER CHILDREN IN TWO-
CHILD FAMILIES

Scales	Older	Younger	p *
Percentage breast-fed	43%	33%	.12
Median age at beginning of bowel training (in months)	8.8	10.8	< .05
Percentage of families rated high on:			
Proportion of caretaking by mother in child's infancy	35%	50%	< .05
Severity of weaning	26%	49%	< .01
Strictness about noise	24%	47%	< .01
Permissiveness for aggression toward neighborhood children	42%	27%	< .05
Use of deprivation of privileges	44%	28%	.02
Mother having primary responsibility for child-rearing policy	25%	41%	.02
Mother being delighted over pregnancy	63%	46%	.02
Number of cases	77	70	

* These p values are based on the significance of the difference between the two percentages.

TABLE D:25

COMPARISON OF CHILD TRAINING OF OLDEST, MIDDLE, AND YOUNGEST CHILDREN
IN THREE- AND FOUR-CHILD FAMILIES

Scales	Oldest	Middle	Youngest	p *
Percentage breast-fed	55%	43%	26%	< .05
Median duration of breast feeding for those breast-fed (in months)	4.0	2.1	1.7	N.S.†
Median age at beginning of weaning (in months)	10.2	9.3	8.9	N.S.†
Median age at beginning of bowel training (in months)	10.1	11.3	9.0	N.S.†
Percentage rated high on:				
Strictness about interrupting adults at table	50%	73%	53%	< .05
Assigning jobs and chores	19%	26%	5%	.02
Affectionate demonstrativeness: mother to child	32%	54%	59%	.05
Frequency of spanking by mother	52%	30%	29%	.10
Frequency of spanking by father	48%	6%	10%	< .01
Total physical punishment	52%	22%	32%	.02
Extent of mother-father disagreement	58%	30%	35%	< .05
Mother's esteem for her husband	48%	81%	58%	.01
Mother delighted when pregnant	58%	40%	10%	< .01
Father delighted when mother pregnant	55%	49%	15%	< .01
Number of cases	31	75	39	

* These p values are based on χ^2 analysis of the proportions, as given, for the three groups.
† Significant near, but not at, the $p = .05$ level by F-test between the three distributions.

TABLE D:26

CORRELATIONS AND PARTIAL CORRELATIONS OF CHILD-TRAINING PRACTICES WITH
THE MOTHER'S EDUCATION AND FAMILY'S SOCIO-ECONOMIC STATUS

Scales	Correlation with Mother's Education *	Correlation with Socioeconomic Status *	Correlation with Mother's Education, SES Held Constant	Correlation with SES, Mother's Education Held Constant
Scheduling of feeding	−.10	−.12	−.04	−.07
Age at beginning of toilet training	−.17	−.07	−.16	.04
Age at completion of toilet training	−.18	−.13	−.13	−.03
Severity of toilet training	.18	.17	.10	.09
Amount of caretaking by other agents	−.10	−.19	.01	−.16
Sex permissiveness (summary)	−.39	−.42	−.21	−.25
Permissiveness: aggression toward other children	−.12	−.12	−.06	−.06
Permissiveness: aggression toward parents	−.29	−.23	−.20	−.10
Punishment: aggression toward parents	.25	.23	.15	.11
What mother does when child eats well at table (1 = always praise)	−.15	−.15	−.07	−.07
Extent of use of praise	−.01	.01	−.02	.02
Extent of use of tangible reward	.11	.03	.11	−.04
Withdrawal of love (rating)	.21	.20	.11	.10
Extent of use of reasoning	−.17	−.11	−.14	−.01
Extent of use of deprivation of privileges	.03	.11	−.04	.11
Extent of use of physical punishment	.27	.26	.15	.13
Use of isolation as a technique of training	.03	−.06	.07	−.10
Use of ridicule	.14	.24	.00	.20
How far is child expected to go in school	−.41	−.50	−.17	−.35
How important is it for child to do well in school	.14	.13	.07	.06
Strictness about noise	.12	.14	.05	.09
Pressure for conformity to demands for table manners	.13	.16	.05	.10
Restrictions on use of fingers at table	.19	.16	.12	.06
Restrictions relating to use of house and furniture	.14	.11	.10	.03
Pressure for neatness and orderliness	.20	.16	.14	.05
Household restrictions (summary)	.10	.07	.07	.01

(continued)

TABLE D:26 *(continued)*

CORRELATIONS AND PARTIAL CORRELATIONS OF CHILD-TRAINING PRACTICES WITH
THE MOTHER'S EDUCATION AND FAMILY'S SOCIO-ECONOMIC STATUS

Scales	Correlation with Mother's Education *	Correlation with Socioeconomic Status *	Correlation with Mother's Education, SES Held Constant	Correlation with SES, Mother's Education Held Constant
Giving child regular jobs	−.15	−.04	−.16	.06
Keeping track of child	.13	.13	.06	.06
How mother felt when pregnant	.11	.12	.05	.07
Mother's warmth to child	−.11	−.19	.00	−.16
Affectional demonstrativeness	−.11	−.16	−.03	−.12
Rejection of child by mother	.12	.16	.04	.11
Sex-role differentiation	.19	.09	.17	−.03
Extent of parents' disagreement on child-rearing policies	.10	.21	−.03	.19
Mother's evaluation of father	−.17	−.24	−.04	−.17
Family authority	.12	.13	.05	.07

* Mother's education is scaled from 1 (graduate work) to 7 (grade school or less). Socioeconomic status is scaled from 1 (high-income professional or business family) to 9 (low-income laborer). Thus, a negative correlation means that high education is associated with a high degree of the child-training practice being considered. For example, the correlation of − .29 between education and permissiveness for aggression toward parents means that better-educated parents tend to be characterized by high permissiveness in this area of behavior.

TABLE D:27

CORRELATIONS AND PARTIAL CORRELATIONS OF CHILD-TRAINING PRACTICES WITH
THE MOTHER'S AGE AND THE FAMILY'S SOCIO-ECONOMIC STATUS

Scales	Age of the Mother	Socioeconomic Status	Age, with SES Held Constant	SES, with Age of Mother Held Constant
Severity of toilet training	−.09	.17	−.05	.16
Sex permissiveness (summary)	.11	−.42	.01	−.40
Extent to which mother encourages child to fight back when attacked	−.21	.09	−.20	.04
Use of deprivation of privileges	−.19	.11	−.17	.06
Use of physical punishment	−.15	.26	−.10	.23
Use of ridicule	−.17	.24	−.12	.21
Mother's warmth to child	.11	−.19	.06	−.17
Extent of parents' disagreement on child-rearing policies	−.21	.21	−.17	.17
Mother's evaluation of father	.11	−.24	.05	−.22

References

References

[* References marked by an asterisk contain descriptions of child rearing in America.]

Aldrich, C. A., Sung, C., and Knop, C. (1945) The crying of newly born babies. II. The individual phase. *J. Pediatrics,* **27,** 89–96.

* Anderson, J. E. (1936) *The Young Child in the Home.* New York: Appleton-Century.

* Baldwin, A. L. (1946) Differences in parent behavior toward three- and nine-year-old children. *J. Personality,* **15,** 143–165.

* Baldwin, A. L. (1948) Socialization and the parent-child relationship. *Child Development,* **19,** 127–136.

* Baldwin, A. L., Kalhorn, J., and Breese, F. H. (1945) Patterns of parent behavior. *Psychological Monographs,* **58** (No. 3), pp. iii and 1–75.

* Brody, S. (1956) *Patterns of Mothering.* New York: International Universities Press.

* Davis, W. A., and Havighurst, R. J. (1946) Social class and color differences in child rearing. *American Sociological Review,* **11,** 698–710.

* Davis, W. A., and Havighurst, R. J. (1947) *Father of the Man.* Boston: Houghton Mifflin.

* Duval, E. M. (1946) Conceptions of parenthood. *American J. Sociology,* **52,** 193–203.

* Escalona, S. (1949) A commentary upon some recent changes in child-rearing practices. *Child Development,* **20,** 157–163.

Ford, C. S., and Beach, F. A. (1951) *Patterns of Sexual Behavior.* New York: Harper & Bros.

Freud, A. (1937) *The Ego and Mechanisms of Defense.* London: Hogarth Press.

Freud, S. (1905) Three contributions to the theory of sex. In *The Basic Writings of Sigmund Freud.* New York: Random House, 1938. Pp. 553–629.

Freud, S. (1908) Character and anal erotism. In *Collected Papers,* Vol. II. London: Hogarth Press, 1924. Pp. 45–50.

Glueck, S., and Glueck, E. T. (1950) *Unravelling Juvenile Delinquency.* New York: Commonwealth Fund.

Goodenough, F. L. (1931) *Anger in Young Children.* Minneapolis: University of Minnesota Press.

* Grant, E. I. (1939) The effect of certain factors in the home environment upon child behavior. *University of Iowa Studies in Child Welfare,* **17,** 61–97.

* Haeflin, R. (1954) Child-rearing practices and child care resources used by Ohio farm families with preschool children. *J. Genetic Psychology,* **84,** 271–297.

Havighurst, R. J., and Davis, A. (1955) A comparison of the Chicago and Harvard studies of social class differences in child rearing. *American Sociological Review,* **20,** 438–442.

Heinicke, C., and Whiting, B. B. (1953) *Bibliographies on Personality and Social Development of the Child.* New York: Social Science Research Council Pamphlet No. 10.

Infant Care (1955) Children's Bureau Publication No. 8. U. S. Department of Health, Education, and Welfare.

* Jersild, A. T., Woodyard, E. S., and del Solar, C. (1949) *Joys and Problems of Child Rearing.* New York: Bureau of Publications, Teachers College, Columbia University.

Johnson, E. Z. (1951) Attitudes of children toward authority as projected in their doll play at two age levels. Unpublished doctor's dissertation, Harvard University.

Kinsey, A. C., Pomeroy, W. B., and Martin, C. E. (1948) *Sexual Behavior in the Human Male.* Philadelphia: Saunders.

Kinsey, A. C., Pomeroy, W. B., and Gebhard, P. H. (1953) *Sexual Behavior in the Human Female.* Philadelphia: Saunders.

* Klatskin, E. H. (1952) Shifts in child-care practices in three social classes under an infant care program of flexible methodology. *American J. Orthopsychiatry,* **22,** 52–61.

* Lasko, J. K. (1954) Parent behavior toward first and second children. *Genetic Psychology Monographs,* **49,** 97–137.

Levin, H., and Sears, R. R. (1956) Identification with parents as a determinant of doll play aggression. *Child Development,* **27,** 135–153.

Levy, D. M. (1928) Fingersucking and accessory movements in early infancy. *American J. Psychiatry,* **7,** 881–918.

Levy, D. M. (1934) Experiments on the sucking reflex and social behavior of dogs. *American J. Orthopsychiatry,* **4,** 203–224.

* Maccoby, E. E., and Gibbs, P. K. (1954) Methods of child rearing in two social classes. In W. E. Martin and C. B. Stendler (Eds.), *Readings in Child Development.* New York: Harcourt, Brace & Co.

Milton, G. A. (1957) A factor-analytic study of child-rearing behaviors. (In press)

Murdock, G. P. (1949) *Social Structure.* New York: Macmillan Co.

* Newton, N. R. (1951) The relationship between infant feeding experience and later behavior. *J. Pediatrics,* **38,** 28–40.

Piaget, J. (1932) *The Moral Judgment of the Child.* New York: Harcourt, Brace & Co.

* Radke, M. J. (1946) The relation of parental authority to children's behavior and attitudes. *University of Minnesota Child Welfare Monographs,* No. 22, pp. x and 1–123.

Sears, P. S. (1953) Child-rearing factors as related to playing of sex-typed roles. *American Psychologist,* **8,** 431 (Abstract).

Sears, R. R., and Wise, G. W. (1950) Relation of cup feeding in infancy to thumb-sucking and the oral drive. *American J. Orthopsychiatry,* **20,** 123–138.

* Sears, R. R., Whiting, J. W. M., Nowlis, V., and Sears, P. S. (1953) Some child-rearing antecedents of aggression and dependency in young children. *Genetic Psychology Monographs,* **47,** 135–234.

* Sewell, W. H. (1952) Infant training and the personality of the child. *American J. Sociology,* **58,** 150–159.

* Sewell, W. H., and Mussen, P. H. (1952) The effects of feeding, weaning, and scheduling procedures on childhood adjustment and the formation of oral symptoms. *Child Development,* **23,** 185–191.

* Sewell, W. H., Mussen, P. H., and Harris, C. W. (1955) Relationships among child-training practices. *American Sociological Review,* **20,** 137–148.

* Stendler, C. B. (1950) Sixty years of child-training practices. *J. Pediatrics,* **36,** 122–136.

Terman, L. M. (1938) *Psychological Factors in Marital Happiness.* New York: McGraw-Hill.

* Vincent, C. E. (1951) Trends in infant care ideas. *Child Development,* **22,** 199–209.

Warner, W. L., Havighurst, R. J., and Loeb, M. B. (1944) *Who Shall Be Educated?* New York: Harper & Bros.

Warner, W. L., Meeker, M., and Eells, K. (1949) *Social Class in America.* Chicago: Science Research Associates.

* White, M. S. (1955) Effects of social class position on child-rearing practices and child behavior. *American Psychologist,* **10,** 440 (Abstract).

Whiting, J. W. M. (1954) The cross-cultural method. In G. Lindzey (Ed.), *Handbook of Social Psychology,* Vol. I. Cambridge, Mass.: Addison-Wesley. Pp. 523–531.

Whiting, J. W. M., and Child, I. L. (1953) *Child Training and Per-*

sonality: *A Cross-Cultural Study.* New Haven: Yale University Press.

* Wolfenstein, M. (1953) Trends in infant care. *American J. Orthopsychiatry,* **33,** 120–130.

Wright, G. O. (1954) Projection and displacement: a cross-cultural study of folktale aggression. *J. Abnormal and Social Psychology,* **49,** 523–528.

Index

Italicized items refer to scales listed in Appendix B, pages 501–510. Additional references to many of these scales will be found in Tables XI:2, XI:3, XII:1, XII:2, and the Supplementary Tables of Appendix D.